The Hanoverian Dimension in British History, 1714–1837

For more than 120 years (1714–1837) Great Britain was linked to the German Electorate, later Kingdom, of Hanover through Personal Union. This made Britain a continental European state in many respects, and diluted her sense of insular apartness. The geopolitical focus of Britain was now as much on Germany, on the Elbe and the Weser, as it was on the Channel or overseas. At the same time, the Hanoverian connection was a major and highly controversial factor in British high politics and popular political debate. This volume is the first to explore the subject systematically by employing a team of experts drawn from the UK, USA and Germany. They integrate the burgeoning specialist literature on aspects of the Personal Union into the broader history of eighteenth- and early nineteenth-century Britain. Never before has the impact of the Hanoverian connection on British politics, monarchy and the public sphere been so thoroughly investigated.

BRENDAN SIMMS is Reader in the History of International Relations at the University of Cambridge, and a Fellow of Peterhouse. His previous publications include *The impact of Napoleon: Prussian high politics, foreign policy and the crisis of the executive, 1797–1806* (1997) and *The struggle for mastery in Germany, 1779–1850* (1998).

TORSTEN RIOTTE is a Research Fellow at the German Historical Institute London. His PhD thesis on Hanover in British policy, 1792–1815, has been published in German translation (2005). He has produced a number of articles on the topic and is currently preparing a study of George III and the Old Reich, 1760–1815.

The Hanoverian Dimension in British History, 1714–1837

Edited by
Brendan Simms
and
Torsten Riotte

CAMBRIDGE UNIVERSITY PRESS
Cambridge, New York, Melbourne, Madrid, Cape Town, Singapore,
São Paulo, Delhi, Dubai, Tokyo, Mexico City

Cambridge University Press
The Edinburgh Building, Cambridge CB2 8RU, UK

Published in the United States of America by Cambridge University Press, New York

www.cambridge.org
Information on this title: www.cambridge.org/9780521154628

© Cambridge University Press 2007

This publication is in copyright. Subject to statutory exception
and to the provisions of relevant collective licensing agreements,
no reproduction of any part may take place without the written
permission of Cambridge University Press.

First published 2007
First paperback printing 2010

A catalogue record for this publication is available from the British Library

ISBN 978-0-521-84222-8 Hardback
ISBN 978-0-521-15462-8 Paperback

Cambridge University Press has no responsibility for the persistence or
accuracy of URLs for external or third-party Internet Web sites referred to in
this publication, and does not guarantee that any content on such Web sites is,
or will remain, accurate or appropriate.

Contents

	List of genealogical tables	*page* vii
	List of tables	viii
	Notes on contributors	ix
	Acknowledgements	xi
1	Introduction. Hanover: the missing dimension BRENDAN SIMMS	1
2	Hanoverian nexus: Walpole and the Electorate JEREMY BLACK	10
3	Pitt and Hanover BRENDAN SIMMS	28
4	George III and Hanover TORSTEN RIOTTE	58
5	The Hanoverian dimension in early nineteenth-century British politics CHRISTOPHER D. THOMPSON	86
6	The end of the dynastic union, 1815–1837 MIJNDERT BERTRAM	111
7	The university of Göttingen and the Personal Union, 1737–1837 THOMAS BISKUP	128
8	The confessional dimension ANDREW C. THOMPSON	161
9	Hanover and the public sphere BOB HARRIS	183
10	Dynastic perspectives CLARISSA CAMPBELL ORR	213

11	British maritime strategy and Hanover 1714–1763	
	RICHARD HARDING	252
12	Hanover in mid-eighteenth-century Franco-British geopolitics	
	H. M. SCOTT	275
13	Hanover and British republicanism	
	NICHOLAS B. HARDING	301
	Index	324

Genealogical tables

10.1 The House of Hohenzollern and its links to
 the House of Brunswick   *page* 222
10.2 Saxon claims to Bavaria   239
10.3 Zweibrücken claims to Bavaria   240
10.4 Sulzbach and Palatinate links to Zweibrücken,
 and claims to Bavaria   240
10.5 Hesse-Darmstadt links to Hohnzollern
 (Prussia), Zweibrücken and Mecklenburg-Strelitz   241

Tables

11.1 Disposition of ships, 1739–1741   *page* 262
11.2 Comparative fleet sizes, 1745, 1750, 1755   268

Notes on contributors

MIJNDERT BERTRAM is an independent author. The former Director of the Boman Museum in Celle completed his PhD thesis on the Hanoverian Diet in 1986. Since then he has published widely on Hanoverian history including a biography of George II (2004) and a history of the kingdom of Hanover, 1814–66.

THOMAS BISKUP is currently a Fellow of the Herzog August Bibliothek Wolfenbüttel. His main fields of interest are political communication in eighteenth-century Germany and transnational networks of scholarship. His publications include 'The transformation of ceremonial in eighteenth-century Germany: ducal weddings in Brunswick', in Karin Friedrich (ed.), *Festive culture in Germany and Europe* (2000) and 'The hidden queen. Elisabeth Christine of Prussia and Hohenzollern Queenship in the eighteenth century', in Clarissa Campbell Orr (ed.), *Queenship in Europe* (2004).

JEREMY BLACK is Professor of History at the University of Exeter and author of *British foreign policy in the age of Walpole* (1985). His most recent publications on Hanoverian Britain include *Parliament and foreign policy in the 18th century* (2004) and *Continental commitment. Britain, Hanover and interventionism, 1714–1793* (2005). He is currently completing a biography of George III.

CLARISSA CAMPBELL ORR is a Senior Lecturer in History at Anglia Ruskin University, Cambridge Campus. She has edited and contributed to *Queenship in Britain 1660–1837: royal patronage, dynastic politics, and court culture* (2002), and *Queenship in Europe 1660–1815: the role of the consort* (2004).

NICHOLAS B. HARDING received his doctorate from Columbia University with a thesis on 'Dynastic union in British and Hanoverian ideology'. His most recent publication is a major study on *Hanover and the British Empire, 1700–1837* (2006).

Notes on contributors

RICHARD HARDING is Professor of Organisational History at the University of Westminster. He is author of *Amphibious warfare in the eighteenth century: the British expedition to the West Indies, 1740–1742* (1991); *The evolution of the sailing navy* (1995); and *Seapower and naval warfare* (1991). He is a Fellow of the Royal Historical Society and Chairman of the Society for Nautical Research.

BOB HARRIS is Professor of History at the University of Dundee. His *A patriot press: national politics and the London press of the 1740s* (1993) is one of the most influential books on the public sphere in Hanoverian Britain. He has also published amongst others *Politics and the rise of the press: Britain and France 1620–1800* (1996) and *Politics and the nation: Britain in the mid-eighteenth century* (2002).

TORSTEN RIOTTE is a research fellow at the German Historical Institute, London. His PhD on 'Hanover in British policies, 1792–1815' has been published in German translation (2003). He is currently working on a monograph on 'George III and the Holy Roman Empire'.

HAMISH SCOTT is Professor of International History at the University of St Andrews. He is the author of *British foreign policy in the age of the American Revolution* (1990); *The emergence of the eastern powers 1756–1775* (2001); and *The birth of a great power system 1740–1815* (Harlow, 2006). He is currently writing a study of aristocracy in Europe c. 1400–1750.

BRENDAN SIMMS is Reader in the History of International Relations at the Centre for International Studies, University of Cambridge, and a Fellow of Peterhouse. His publications include the article ' "An odd question enough". Charles James Fox, the crown and British policy during the Hanoverian crisis of 1806' (1995), and *The impact of Napoleon: Prussian high politics, foreign policy and the crisis of the executive, 1797–1806* (1997). He is currently writing a study of British foreign policy in the eighteenth century.

ANDREW C. THOMPSON is a College Lecturer in History at Queens' College, Cambridge. He is the author of several articles on British and European history and a revised version of his PhD thesis recently appeared as *Britain, Hanover and the protestant interest* (2006). He is currently writing a biography of George II for Yale University Press.

CHRISTOPHER D. THOMPSON is currently completing his PhD at Christ's College Cambridge on 'Politics and state-building in Vormärz Hanover: the role of King Ernst August, c. 1837–51'. His research interests are conservatism in nineteenth-century Britain and Germany and the role of history in identity formation.

Acknowledgements

The volume contains the revised and expanded papers given at a colloquium organised by the German Historical Institute London and the Centre for International Studies at the University of Cambridge, held at Peterhouse, in September 2004. The editors wish to express their profound thanks to the Director of the Institute, Professor Hagen Schulze, for providing the funding which made the colloquium and thus this publication possible.

1 Introduction. Hanover: the missing dimension

Brendan Simms

When Queen Victoria ascended the throne in 1837, the resulting end of the Personal Union with Hanover occasioned little comment. The fact that Britain had been linked to a continental European state for over 120 years was easily forgotten in a nineteenth-century world whose horizons were now very much global, imperial and naval. If the centenary of the Personal Union in August 1814 had been marked by royal celebrations, by the time of the bicentenary, the mid-Victorian fascination with German culture had been replaced by industrial and commercial competition. In August 1914, in any case, Britain's leaders had other things on their minds. An era during which the royal family felt obliged to change its name from 'Saxe-Coburg-Gotha' to the anodyne confection of 'House of Windsor' was perhaps not best suited to an understanding of Britain's German heritage and continental links. The British story was, after all, an 'island story'.[1]

It has remained one, more or less, ever since. The importance, and sometimes the centrality, of the Hanoverian context to British history is still not fully recognised. For example, J. C. D Clark, himself an exponent of viewing eighteenth-century Britain in the framework of the European 'ancien régime', wrote nearly 600 pages on the 1750s without giving due attention to the fact that one of his major protagonists, the duke of Newcastle, was both a defender of the Hanoverian preoccupations of the crown and the most prominent exponent of engagement in Europe.[2] Similarly, Kathleen Wilson and Linda Colley, despite their

---

[1] Thus the title of H. E. Marshall's hugely influential *Our island story* (1905), which was reprinted by the think-tank Civitas in 2005.
[2] J. C. D. Clark, *The dynamics of change. The crisis of the 1750s and English party systems* (Cambridge, 1982). For the *ancien régime* debate see J. C. D. Clark, *English society 1688–1832. Ideology, social structure and political practice during the ancien régime* (Cambridge, 1985); and Joanna Innes, 'Jonathan Clark, social history and England's "ancien régime"', *Past and Present*, 115 (1987), 165–200. Later Clark – reflecting the early work of Jeremy Black – did address the Hanoverian dimension briefly in *Revolution and rebellion. State and society in England in the seventeenth and eighteenth centuries* (Cambridge, 1986), pp. 77–82.

interest in Toryism and Whig radicalism critiques, and in colonial and popular issues, make virtually no reference to Europe, in Wilson's case, or Hanover, in both instances.[3] Likewise, John Brooke's as yet unsurpassed biography of George III passes over the fact that his subject was also the ruler of a German state, and at times a very committed one.[4] On the other side of the Atlantic, both Theodore Draper and Fred Anderson tend to caricature the Hanoverian connection and its role in British grand strategy.[5] None of David Armitage's various discussions of the British problem and composite monarchies, which stress the need to consider Scottish, Irish and imperial contexts, take the Hanoverian dimension into account.[6]

There are exceptions. Foreign policy was not his forte, but J. H. Plumb's unfinished study of Walpole was seized of the importance of the international and particularly the Hanoverian dimension to early eighteenth-century British politics.[7] More recently, both Julian Hoppit and Paul Langford – who wrote an excellent though now inevitably dated textbook on eighteenth-century British foreign policy – give some prominence to the Hanoverian dimension.[8] There are also the general syntheses of Jeremy Black, who has contributed so much to our understanding of foreign policy and the role of Hanover in British politics before 1760.[9]

*

There is, of course, a considerable and growing specialist literature on British foreign policy and the role of the Hanoverian Electorate. Ragnhild Hatton's biography of George I – revealingly subtitled 'Elector and king' – remains the standard work. Graham Gibbs has explored the role

---

[3] Kathleen Wilson, *Politics, culture and imperialism in England, 1715–1785* (Cambridge, 1995); Wilson, *The island race. Englishness, empire and gender in the eighteenth century* (London, 2002); and Linda Colley, *In defiance of oligarchy. The Tory party 1714–1760* (Cambridge, 1982). See also, most recently, Kathleen Wilson, ed., *A new imperial history: culture, identity and modernity in Britain and the empire, 1660–1840* (Cambridge, 2004).
[4] J. B. Brooke, *George III* (London, 1972).
[5] Theodore Draper, *A struggle for power. The American Revolution* (New York, 1996); Fred Anderson, *Crucible of war: the Seven Years War and the fate of empire in British North America, 1754–1766* (New York, 2000).
[6] E.g. David Armitage, 'Greater Britain: a useful category of historical analysis?', *American Historical Review*, 104, 2, (April 1999), 427–45.
[7] See for example J. H. Plumb, *Sir Robert Walpole. The king's minister* (London, 1960), pp. 116–54 *et passim*.
[8] See Julian Hoppit, *A land of liberty? England 1689–1727* (Oxford, 2000); Paul Langford, *A polite and commercial people, England 1727–1783* (Oxford, 1989); Paul Langford, *Modern British foreign policy: the eighteenth century, 1688–1815* (London, 1976).
[9] E.g. Jeremy Black, *The politics of Britain, 1688–1800* (Manchester, 1993); and Black, *Walpole in power* (Sutton, 2001).

of the Hanoverian connection in parliament for the first decade after 1714. Uriel Dann has looked closely at the Personal Union during the wars of the Austrian Succession and the Seven Years War (1740–60). The implications of the Hanoverian connection for British 'high politics' have been explored for the early eighteenth century by J. M Beattie, J. J. Murray and – rather obscurely – H. J. Finke. More generally, the period before 1760 has been covered in numerous articles and books by Jeremy Black, while British foreign policy in the era of the American Revolution has received masterful treatment from Hamish Scott. Finally, T. C. W. Blanning has highlighted the importance of Hanover during the *Fürstenbund* and Regency crises of the 1780s.[10]

More recently, there has been a modest increase of interest in the Hanoverian connection led by younger scholars such Andrew Thompson, Nick Harding, and the editors, all of whom have contributed to this volume.[11] Andrew Thompson's work on the early eighteenth

---

[10] See J. M. Beattie, *The English court in the reign of George I* (Cambridge, 1967); J. J. Murray, *George I, the Baltic and the Whig Split of 1717. A study in diplomacy and propaganda* (London, 1969); Hans-Joachim Finke, 'The Hanoverian Junta, 1714–1719', (DPhil dissertation, University of Michigan, Ann Arbor, 1970); Ragnhild Hatton, *George I. Elector and king* (London, 1978); Ragnhild Hatton, *The Anglo-Hanoverian connection, 1714–1760* (London, 1982); G. C. Gibbs, 'English attitudes towards Hanover and the Hanoverian succession in the first half of the eighteenth century', in Adolf Birke and Kurt Kluxen, eds., *England und Hannover. England and Hanover* (Munich, 1986), pp. 33–50; Uta Richter-Uhlig, *Hof und Politik unter den Bedingungen der Personalunion zwischen Hannover und England* (Hanover, 1992); Walther Mediger, *Mecklenburg, Russland und England-Hannover* (2 vols., Hildesheim, 1967); Uriel Dann, *Hanover and Great Britain, 1740–1760* (Leicester, 1991); Jeremy Black, 'British foreign policy in the eighteenth century: a survey', *Journal of British Studies* 26 (1987), 26–53; Jeremy Black, 'The British state and foreign policy in the eighteenth century', *Trivium* 23 (1988), 127–48; and the relevant sections on Hanover in Jeremy Black, *British foreign policy in the age of Walpole* (Edinburgh, 1985); and Black, *A system of ambition? British foreign policy, 1660–1793* (London and New York, 1991), pp. 31–42; Black, 'The crown, Hanover and the shift in British foreign policy in the 1760s', in: Jeremy Black, ed., *Knights Errant and true Englishmen. British foreign policy, 1600–1800* (Edinburgh, 1989), pp. 113–34; H. M. Scott, *British foreign policy in the age of the American Revolution* (Oxford, 1990); T. C. W. Blanning, ' "That horrid Electorate" or "Ma patrie Germanique"? George III, Hanover and the Fürstenbund of 1785', *Historical Journal*, 20 (1977), 311–44; and T. C. W. Blanning and Carl Haase, 'Kurhannover, der Kaiser und die Regency Crisis von 1788/89', *Blätter für Landesgeschichte* 113 (1979), 432–49.

[11] Andrew Thompson, *Britain, Hanover and the protestant interest, 1688–1756* (Woodbridge, Suffolk, 2006); Nicholas B. Harding, 'North African piracy, the Hanoverian carrying trade, and the British state, 1728–1828', *Historical Journal*, 43, (2002), 25–47; and Harding, 'Dynastic union in British and Hanoverian ideology' (unpublished PhD dissertation, Columbia, 2001); Brendan Simms, ' "An odd question enough." Charles James Fox, the crown and British policy during the Hanoverian crisis of 1806', *Historical Journal*, 38 (1995), 567–96 and Fox, *The impact of Napoleon. Prussian high politics, foreign policy, and the crisis of the executive, 1797–1806* (Cambridge, 1997), especially pp. 201–18; and Torsten Riotte, *Hannover in der britischen Politik*

century shows just how central the confessional argument was, not just in British domestic politics, but also in the diplomatic posture which Britain-Hanover adopted in Europe, particularly the Holy Roman Empire. Nicholas Harding has written a systematic study of the role which the Personal Union played in eighteenth-century British political thought and discourse. Brendan Simms drew attention to the periodic centrality of Hanover in British strategy, and the importance of a Hanoverian faction in British high politics, during the crisis of 1806. Torsten Riotte has just published the first comprehensive study of the role of Hanover in British policy throughout the Revolutionary and Napoleonic period.

The Hanoverian dimension brings together the work of these and other scholars working on the Personal Union or related fields and integrates their findings into the history of eighteenth-century Britain as a whole. It draws upon material – much of it never before used in this context – from both British and German archives. The volume is structured in such a way as to allow both chronological and thematic access. Chapters 2 to 5 will cover the entire period from 1714 to 1837, but they are also intended to allow authors to organise the narrative around a particular individual or theme, such as Walpole, the elder Pitt, the French Revolutionary Wars and Napoleon, and the final stages of the Personal Union. The more thematic chapters are designed to cover the full length of the Personal Union, but generally contain a specific narrative 'spine'.

In putting the Hanoverian dimension back into British history, this collection attempts two things. First of all, by filling in many gaps in our knowledge of the Personal Union, it makes an 'additive' contribution to the secondary literature. For example, the chapter by Torsten Riotte on George III and Hanover after 1760; Hamish Scott's systematic analysis of the role of Hanover in French strategy; Thomas Biskup's discussion of the intellectual legacy; Nicholas Harding's dissection of the role of Hanover in the development of British republicanism; Clarissa Campbell Orr's investigation of the dynastic ramifications; and Christopher Thompson on the Personal Union after 1815, all put the spotlight on neglected areas. Secondly, this volume is the first step in a collective 'substitutive' project to persuade eighteenth-century British

---

(1792–1815). Dynastische Verbindung als Element außenpolitischer Entscheidungsprozesse (Münster, 2005). Jeremy Black has also kept up his interest in the area. Recent publications include: 'International relations in the eighteenth century: Britain and Poland compared', *Diplomacy and Statecraft*, 13 (2002), 83–112; Black, 'Hanover and British foreign policy 1714–1760', *English Historical Review*, 120 (2005), 303–39; and Black, ' "George II and all that stuff." On the value of the neglected', *Albion*, 4 (2004), 581–607.

historiography to take more account of the Hanoverian dimension in general.

In the first chapter, Jeremy Black highlights the controversial nature of the Hanoverian succession in 1714. He reminds us that although Britain's links to the continent long predated the Personal Union, the Hanoverian connection was a major high-political and foreign-political bone of contention during the twenty-year ascendancy of Robert Walpole. It was, moreover, an issue 'in the context not of an established constitution with clear conventions but of the testing out of new arrangements'. Hanover became a focal point around which the 'national interest' could be articulated. As Bob Harris shows, this had profound impact on the development of the British 'public sphere', particularly in the absence of other issues around which opinion could polarise. There was a huge outpouring of anti-Hanoverian pamphlets, prints, ballads centred on but not confined to London. The quality of the material varied, but some of it was very sophisticated. Harris notes that 'Europe and European power politics [were] at the very centre of public attention' in the period before 1760, and in this context the question of Hanover gained particular popular salience. Indeed, Harris writes that at times 'the issue of Hanover and its influence dominated press and political debate, for long periods completely overshadowing consideration of other political issues'. Attacks on the Hanoverian connection not only served to highlight the corrupt and foreign nature of the Walpolean oligarchy, but also enabled opposition writers to burnish their own patriotic credentials.

Alongside, this 'low' debate, there was also a vibrant and no less impassioned 'high' debate in the sphere of political thought. Nicholas Harding's chapter documents how attacks on the Personal Union were driven by a British republicanism of both ancient and recent provenance. Here the Hanoverian link was seen as a continental absolutist Trojan Horse, designed to smother English liberties with the help of a standing army and German mercenaries. In some cases, such as that of Bolingbroke, this camp shaded into that of Jacobitism; but it also embraced many radical Whigs.

In the republican critique, the Lutheranism of the Hanoverians was akin to popery and thus of no comfort. Yet as Andrew Thompson stresses in his chapter on confessional dimensions, the Protestantism of the Hanoverians was what made them attractive to the political nation: contemporaries, after all, spoke of the 'protestant' not the Hanoverian succession. Religious solidarity with the victims of popish aggression was also an important part of British foreign policy, particularly in the 1720s; Thompson sees this as an example of British 'soft power' in the eighteenth century. The Hanoverian link was thus a central plank in the defence both of British domestic liberties and the European balance of power against attempts to erect a universal monarchy. Here Thompson adds a new spin to the debate on the British 'confessional state', initiated by Jonathan Clark some twenty years ago.

The eighteenth century also saw the emergence of strong intellectual ties. Hanover, as Thomas Biskup shows in his chapter, played a central role in the growth of British involvement in the 'international republic of letters', by producing a 'unique framework for scholarly curiosity' focused on the new electoral university of Göttingen. This compensated for the weaknesses of British academic institutions particularly in the fields of natural sciences, oriental studies and philology. Interestingly, it was the British who were the mere 'collectors' and 'gatherers' while the Hanoverians concentrated on analysis. In this way, as Biskup puts it, 'Göttingen ... helped England to make sense of her own imperial experiences'. Here the Hanoverian connection and the imperial project were not contradictory but complementary.

This theme is picked up by Brendan Simms. He shows that the Elder Pitt's relationship to Hanover provides a valuable prism through which to view his political career and strategic vision. A complex, sometimes paradoxical and yet essentially coherent picture emerges. Pitt undoubtedly used the Hanoverian stick to beat his political rivals and to massage his 'popular' constituency; this stance earned him the hatred of George II and nearly cost him high office. And yet it was the very fact that Pitt – as Newcastle so starkly put it – could 'do the King's business' over Hanover that finally speeded his rise. At the same time, Pitt's commitment to the defence of Hanover in the Seven Years War should not be seen as an opportunistic sop to George, but as part of an integrated 'continental' strategy against France, which was intended to secure British colonial and naval dominance through the diversion of French resources.

For, as the naval historian Richard Harding explains, the European and maritime theatres of war should not – *pace* much of the anti-Hanoverian critique – be seen as distinct and separate, but rather as two sides of the same coin. 'Flanders and Hanover', he writes, 'could not be divorced from a maritime policy. They were parts of the same policy.' It is true that in the early years of George I's reign, the Royal Navy was used to further Hanoverian interests in the Baltic. But by the mid-eighteenth century, Harding identifies 'an essential link' between the defence of Hanover, which tied down French forces, and 'aggressive action in the Americas'. 'Britain's essential European interests, including Hanover', he reminds us, came first; the shift to maritime and colonial priorities only came after 1760.

Throughout the first fifty years or so of the Personal Union, therefore, British strategy was obsessed with the protection of Hanover against first Russian, then Austrian, periodically Prussian and then French attack. The fear was that the king would be made, as George II put it, as 'Hanoverian Elector ... [to] pay for the King of England'. British ministries, in turn, feared that Britain would have to pay for the elector of Hanover at the peace agreement. It is certainly true that at key moments in the War of the Austrian Succession and the Seven Years War, French strategists regarded the Electorate as a hostage to be traded for losses overseas.

Yet as Hamish Scott shows in a highly original analysis, 'the direct military threat which France posed was consistently exaggerated by British statesmen'. Large French formations had never before operated so far from their bases and the logistical obstacles were considerable. If one also takes into account the political costs of violating the constitution of the Holy Roman Empire, French willingness to countenance the neutralisation of Hanover rather than its straightforward occupation becomes more understandable. Scott concludes that practical considerations prevented the French from applying more than temporary military pressure for most of the eighteenth century. It was only the revolutionary transformation in warfare after 1792 which changed this calculus and cleared the way for longer-term occupations under Napoleon.

The accession of George III in 1760 is often taken to mark the beginning of a completely new phase in which the importance of the Personal Union was played down by a monarch who 'gloried in the name of Britain [sic]'. It is certainly true that George III broke with the tradition of royal visits to Germany; and the Hanoverian issue lost much of the political currency it had enjoyed for more than four decades since 1714. Yet, as Torsten Riotte shows, George III took a keen interest in the welfare of the Electorate. In some ways, George was more of a German prince than his grandfather: he sought to protect Hanover not so much by British-sponsored great-power alliances as through the institutions of the Holy Roman Empire. Riotte's George III is therefore much more 'German' than the conventional picture allows.

The German interests and identity of the royal family are the theme of Clarissa Campbell Orr's chapter on the dynastic context. She adopts a broad – 'polycentric' – approach which looks not just at the ruler but also at the consort, siblings, offspring, their respective marriage partners and the sometimes competing strategies of the elder branch of the Guelph family. This enables her not only to stress the very contingent nature of dynastic permutations, but also to bring out the existence of a coherent Hanoverian dynastic strategy designed to promote British interests and enhance the security of the Electorate. Yet if George II – who married his daughters off to actual or prospective British allies – was relatively successful in this regard, Campbell Orr shows George III to have been a dynastic failure. He proved unable to marry off his thirteen unruly offspring in any systematic way. All the same, George retained a keen interest in the German dynastic scene. This was reinforced by the activities of his own consort, Charlotte of Mecklenburg-Strelitz, whom Campbell Orr shows to have been a quietly determined 'lobbyist' during the War of the Bavarian Succession.

Nor did royal interest in the Personal Union die with George III in 1820. The Prince Regent and later King George IV was in close physical and political touch with the Hanoverian envoy in London, Count Münster, as the chapter by Mijndert Bertram shows. Both shared a firmly conservative outlook. At the same time, with the dispatch of the duke of Cambridge as governor general, the monarchy was represented in person in Hanover for the first time since the recall of the Prince of Wales in 1728, albeit by a cipher since Münster continued to pull all the strings from London. The links were more than just political: Bertram reminds us that Hanover functioned as a 'bridgehead for British trade in Germany', which received preferential, though unreciprocated, tariff treatment.

Moreover, as Christopher Thompson shows, Hanover 'remained a significant foreign policy factor' in Britain after the Napoleonic War, and thus also played a major role in high politics. George IV was able to use his Hanoverian diplomatic and intelligence service – which by all accounts was far superior to the British one – to support British strategy and to bypass the hated Canning. Moreover, as Christopher Thompson adds as a parting shot, the Personal Union enjoyed a controversial afterlife in nineteenth-century Britain: so long as Queen Victoria remained childless, there was every prospect that her sybaritic and (allegedly) despotic uncle, the king of Hanover, would renew the Personal Union on her death.

The emerging picture is of an eighteenth-century Britain which was very much a European state, strategically, dynastically, confessionally, intellectually linked to the continent. The German connection also profoundly influenced many spheres of what one might otherwise regard as purely domestic politics. Hanoverians were powerful players in British high politics not just in the early eighteenth century but, periodically, during the Revolutionary and Napoleonic period and, as the case of Münster shows, well into the second decade of the nineteenth century as well. We are also left with a strong sense of the contingency of British history. As Jeremy Black points out, it was the dynastic accident of a regular supply of legitimate protestant male heirs from the Hanoverians, which spared Britain a return to the travails of the seventeenth century, and indeed the eighteenth-century wars of succession. The Personal Union, Clarissa Campbell Orr reminds us, 'began partly and ended solely for dynastic purposes'. Had it not so concluded, Mijndert Bertram muses, the history of nineteenth-century Germany would have looked very different. For in 1866, Bismarck would have come up not only against the king of Hanover, who proved intractable enough, but also against the king of Great Britain (as he would have been).

Of course, this volume can only be a first step and it is by no means comprehensive. Ideally, it should have included a systematic discussion of the Hanoverian faction at court; of the role of Hanover in the formation of British identity; and the ramifications of the Personal Union within the framework of composite statehood. These themes could only be hinted at: they require further investigation and elaboration. All this volume can hope to do is to remind historians of the importance of the Hanoverian dimension and to suggest an agenda for further research.

2 Hanoverian nexus: Walpole and the Electorate

Jeremy Black

Much of the problem in assessing the implications of the Hanoverian relationship comes from the tension between considering short periods and, on the other hand, assessing the relationship over the longer term. The former appears the most desirable approach, because it restricts coverage to a period for which it is simpler to carry out the necessary archival research. It is also flawed, however, both because it limits the experience of contemporaries and because it removes the comparative element, which is valuable for scholarly analysis, just as it was useful for contemporary debate about foreign policy. 'Walpole and Hanover' as a topic provides a good instance of this. While it focuses attention on the failure in existing treatments of Walpole to devote much attention to Hanover, this approach underrates the importance of considering Walpole at least in part in the light of developments after his fall from office in 1742. Not only did Walpole, from then 1st earl of Orford, maintain links with George II and also continue to influence the Pelham brothers until his death in 1745, but, in order to assess Walpole it is necessary to consider his policies in the light of the events of subsequent years as they provide a way of probing the alternatives. Hence this chapter closes in 1760. The accession of George III led, at least in the short term, to a different degree of royal commitment to the Electorate, and, certainly, to the cause of its aggrandisement, while the political parameters within which Walpole had operated – the relatively assured ascendancy of the Old Corps Whigs – came to a close. The period can therefore be seen as a unity, but it is one in which the role of Hanover has not received systematic treatment, a task that this volume valuably sets out to attempt.[1]

---

[1] For earlier discussion, G.C. Gibbs, 'English attitudes towards Hanover and the Hanoverian succession in the first half of the eighteenth century', in: A.M. Birke and K. Kluxen, eds., *England und Hannover* (Munich, 1986), pp. 33–51; J.M. Black, 'Hanover and British foreign policy 1714–60', *English Historical Review*, 120 (2005), 303–39; and Black, *Continental commitment. Britain, Hanover and interventionism 1714–1793* (London, 2005).

Politicians and the political nation in Britain alike faced in the early eighteenth century a situation of great volatility, and this conditioned the debate over the Hanoverian connection, and, indeed, over foreign policy more generally.[2] The benchmarks that had helped define policy and debate in the late seventeenth century – at home, the issue of Stuart intentions and, abroad, the response to the growing power of Bourbon France under Louis XIV – no longer served as an appropriate response, although both still played an important role in the debate over policy. Instead, there were different issues: at home the workings out of the Revolution Settlement stemming from the Glorious Revolution of 1688–9 but not in any linear or inevitable fashion, and, abroad, the consequences of major developments in the European system, in particular (but not only) a shift of relative power east from Western Europe as Austria, Russia and Prussia became more powerful, a situation that was readily apparent in the 1710s. The controversy that followed the accession of the Hanoverian dynasty to the British throne in 1714 was set in these contexts, and much of the problem that faces discussion about the Hanoverian dimension stems from the difficulty in distinguishing the subject from the issues arising from these changes in the domestic and international circumstances. This also helps explain why scholars have disagreed in their views, because there is no clear methodology available to address this difficulty, a point that needs to be outlined at the outset. As a consequence, it is understandable that scholars come to clashing conclusions as a result of contrasting cause-and-effect models of the relationship between Hanoverianism and the wider domestic and international contexts. My own approach differs from that of Brendan Simms. It is not that one of us is correct and the other not, but rather that differing analyses are possible, both from the evidence and from the assessment of the domestic and international contexts.

To turn first to these contexts is not to ignore the role of the individual, the particular, and the contingent, but, rather, to be reminded of the complexity of the issues at stake, as well as the extent to which history did not begin in 1714, in either Britain or in Hanover, and thus the memory of earlier years had an important impact. In terms of domestic politics, the legacy was a difficult one, and there was no clear, acceptable standard of royal behaviour on which George I could model himself, nor by which he

---

[2] On this see, in particular, G. C. Gibbs, 'Parliament and foreign policy in the age of Stanhope and Walpole', *English Historical Review*, 77 (1962), 18–37; and Gibbs, 'Newspapers, parliament and foreign policy in the age of Stanhope and Walpole', *Mélanges offerts à G. Jacquemyns* (Brussels, 1968). There is no equivalent for this period to the work of Bob Harris on the 1740s.

could be judged. The last exemplary monarch in public memory was Elizabeth I (r. 1558–1603), and, aside from the seriously distorting perspective of mythmaking, she did not face the problems of dealing with a composite state spanning the North Sea, although opposition in Ireland during her reign had served as a pointed reminder of the difficulties of composite statehood. These were underlined in the shape of a broader 'British Question' under her four Stuart successors, with the additional problem of serious suspicion about their domestic intentions.

William III had 'solved', or at least shelved, the British question through force in 1689–92, but, aside from the controversial character of his linkage of Britain to his interests in the United Provinces, William's attitude towards his position as king aroused both concern and opposition in Britain. This led to a serious political storm in 1700 and, in the Act of Settlement of 1701, to what were intended as constitutional limitations on his eventual successors, the Hanoverians. In the meanwhile, Queen Anne (r. 1702–14) was personally more popular than William, particularly because political anxiety and anger were focused on her ministers; while she lacked the 'foreignness' associated with William, for all his Stuart connections by parentage and marriage, not least as a result of his foreign position and his distance from the Church of England.

Nevertheless many of the political issues that had faced William in the working out of the 'Glorious Revolution' remained acute. This was especially true of the collective responsibility of ministers, and also of the relationships between party cohesion, policy formulation, and the choice of ministers. These issues were to erupt anew under George I, with the Whig Split of 1717.[3] Although this ministerial and party division owed much to contention about George I's Baltic policy, the constitutional problems posed, especially the relationship between monarch and minister, did not stem from this issue. Of course, looked at differently, political skill involves management within existing constraints, or shifting the parameters of the latter, however difficult, and George was unable to do either in the late 1710s.

The long-term shift in the international system was the rise of Russia, Austria and Prussia. This receives most attention from mid-century, in particular with the diplomacy surrounding the Seven Years War (1756–63), and the First Partition of Poland (1772),[4] but should more

---

[3] J.J. Murray, *George I, the Baltic and the Whig Split of 1717* (London, 1969); D. McKay, 'The struggle for control of George I's Northern policy 1718–19', *Journal of Modern History*, 45 (1973), 377–83; J.M. Black, 'Parliament and the political and diplomatic crisis of 1717–1718', *Parliamentary History*, 3 (1984), 77–101.

[4] H.M. Scott, *The emergence of the Eastern powers, 1756–1775* (Cambridge, 2001).

accurately be dated earlier. For Austria, the defeat of the Ottomans outside Vienna in 1683, and the subsequent conquest of Hungary were crucial, as were the major gains made from the Spanish Habsburg inheritance as a consequence of the War of the Spanish Succession (1701–14), while Russia benefited from the extent to which it, and not Saxony-Poland, Sweden or Denmark, gained from the Great Northern War (1700–21).

The shift in the international system created serious and unexpected problems for Hanover, and helped ensure that, alongside the theme of Hanoverian expansionism, came that of Hanoverian security. Although interrelated, these were also different themes, and this had important implications for British foreign policy, and for the debate within Britain about the impact of the Hanoverian connection. The role of Hanover in British public debate owed much to the original character and impact of the connection. A focus on expansionism was initially part of the Hanoverian optimum that began in 1714. That was the period of bright prospects. Despite initial problems, the new dynasty in Britain rapidly overcame the attempt at a Stuart *revanche* in the '15: there was certainly no equivalent to the long civil war over the Spanish succession. Britain's ministers established, in 1716, an effective alliance with France that, while pushed hard for Hanoverian reasons, greatly lessened British vulnerability.[5] They also formulated a peace plan for the Mediterranean that led to a short war that helped establish a settlement there, with a spectacular naval victory over Spain (off Cape Passaro in Sicily in 1718), which eventually helped in 1720 to give force to this plan. Hanover itself looked set to benefit territorially from the partition of Sweden's trans-Baltic empire, a benefit seen not only in the gain of territory, but also in denying territories to other powers, especially Denmark, a rival in north Germany.

Royal opportunism, however, helped to divide the, admittedly already very divided, Whigs, with ministers separating over George I's expectation of support for his Baltic policy; differences over power in Britain and between George and his heir also contributed greatly to the Whig Split, the first foreign policy issue in which Walpole played a major role. This split did not stop George and his advisors from continuing with their policies, but the Hanoverian optimum ended in 1719–21, as the Stanhope–Sunderland ministry proved unable to retain or regain control of parliament. Furthermore, the bursting of the South Sea Bubble in 1720 caused a political as well as a fiscal crisis, and the attempt to

---

[5] E. Bourgeois, *La diplomatie secrète au XVIII siècle. Le secret du Régent et la politique de l'Abbé Dubois* (Paris, 1907).

intimate Peter the Great of Russia into accepting the British peace plan for northern Europe failed miserably.[6] There were parallel problems within the Hanoverian ministry.

Once Russian troops had advanced into Mecklenburg in 1716 there was the repeated, and reasonable, fear that they would return. Thus, the possibilities that had opened up for Hanover in 1716, when George encouraged a Russian invasion of Scania (southern Sweden) as a knockout blow against Charles XII of Sweden that would secure Hanover's gains from Sweden in north Germany (the duchies of Bremen and Verden), were rudely replaced by fears that increased George's need for British assistance. At the same time, the dangerous prospect emerged of hostile cooperation between Peter the Great and Frederick William I of Prussia, who was fearful of Russian strength. Rumours about this circulated widely in the late 1710s. Furthermore, the acquisition of Bremen and Verden from Sweden had proved to be not a speedy and clearly successful move but, rather, one that had led to lasting international commitments that proved difficult to limit, prefiguring the situation when Frederick the Great of Prussia conquered Silesia in 1740–1. From the late 1710s, in response, first, to Russia's Baltic policy in the early 1720s, which threatened to exploit continued disputes over Mecklenburg, and the unsettled nature of the Schleswig question,[7] and then to the Austro-Spanish alliance negotiated in 1725, there was a switch from expansionism to defence, setting a new agenda for the Hanoverian dimension of British foreign policy and for public debate.

Concern about Hanover and the commitments stemming from the Electorate's gain of Bremen and Verden led to an anxiety about Baltic developments that certainly seemed rash to Walpole, although Baltic issues were also of direct importance to Britain, not least because the Baltic was the key source of the naval stores vital for British maritime and naval strength. In response, in 1723, to pressure from George I for a promise of assistance for Sweden if it was attacked by Peter the Great, Walpole expressed his concern that competition among the ministers for royal favour 'should transport us into very rash engagements'. He was able to offer cogent reasons which indicated his concern to frame foreign policy in terms of domestic practicality, and his sense that the latter included fiscal exigencies and the management of Parliament and public opinion,

The £150,000 may certainly be had ... I cannot but wish from my heart that this money may not be demanded ... nor do I see how it can be employed at all by way

---

[6] J. F. Chance, *George I and the Great Northern War* (London, 1909).
[7] W. Mediger, *Moskaus Weg nach Europa* (Brunswick, 1952); and Mediger, *Mecklenburg, Russland und England-Hannover 1706–21* (Hildesheim, 1967).

of prevention, for if the Czar's fleet was ready to sail, any agreement for this subsidy will come too late, and the blow be struck before a force can be got ready to repel it ... I am mightily inclined to be cautious ... if we enter into any engagements upon this occasion, we shall not carry the nation, nor perhaps the Parliament along with us, but if we wait and are driven into it, it will be seen and thought to be the interest of Great Britain alone that made us engage ... I wish to God we may at least for a little time remain neuters, and look on, if all the rest of Europe do the same thing.

Aside from also warning about the danger of Russian support for the Jacobites, who, indeed, were looking widely for assistance, Walpole was concerned that the Russian threat to Sweden would affect credit 'as all our money matters here depend entirely upon credit'.[8]

However slanted, a sense of Hanover as an incubus stemmed directly from the persistent crisis of Britain and Hanover's Baltic policy from 1716 until 1731. The resulting problem of Hanoverian security tended to arouse more ministerial concern than the French alliance. In domestic political terms, the latter was an embarrassment that in fact owed much to the wish to secure the Hanoverian succession. Nevertheless, until the parliamentary storm in 1730 over illicit and illegal repairs to the harbour at Dunkirk, the French alliance did not challenge the ministry's conduct of foreign policy as Baltic policy was to do.

If during the Whig Split (as well as at a time of later Whig divisions) the dynamic tension of interests that can be simplified in terms of Britain and Hanover became the focus of crown–ministerial relations, it was in the context not of an established constitution with clear conventions, but of the testing out of new arrangements. When, for example, MPs debated whether Hessian subsidies were a breach of the constitution, it was far from clear how assertions were to be disproved. Aside from the issue of relations with Hanover, there was also the question of what the monarch could do with other aspects of British foreign policy, especially the legality and/or acceptability of peacetime subsidies for foreign powers, whether or not these were intended for the benefit of Hanover. The unfixed nature of the Revolution Settlement had been clear from the outset, and indeed the changes in 1694–1707, especially, but not only, the Triennial Act, the establishment of the Bank of England, the lapsing of the Licensing Act, and the passage of the Acts of Settlement and Union, were in some respects more significant than the constitutional changes in 1689. This situation did not cease in 1707, nor 1714, and relations with Hanover in

---

[8] Walpole to Thomas, duke of Newcastle, 25 July 1723, London, British Library, Add. Mss. vol. 32686, fol. 285; Walpole to Charles, 2nd Viscount Townshend, secretary of state for the Northern Department, 23 July 1723, London, National Archives, State Papers 43/4 fols. 116–17, 43/66.

part should be considered in this context. The changes introduced, or attempted, in 1716–19, including the replacement of the Triennial by the Septennial Act, the repeal of legislation against nonconformists passed by Queen Anne's Tory ministers, and the Peerage Bill, indicated, however, the willingness of Whig ministers to make substantial revisions. Furthermore, the restrictions on royal journeys were removed, so that George I and George II were able to make frequent visits to their native Electorate, although their duration led to criticism in Britain.[9]

From the perspective of George I (which is difficult to demonstrate conclusively because of the sparse nature of the sources), it was reasonable to expect the same men to provide support for his Baltic policy. This issue, which split the ministry in 1717, indicated, however, the problems of defining acceptable parameters. It was particularly difficult, in a period of rapid constitutional change, for ministers to argue that a given policy was unacceptable on constitutional grounds, not least when doing so risked serious royal displeasure. Instead, it was more appropriate to fall back on the arguments of political acceptability and prudent policymaking.

This indeed was Walpole's position: he promised the monarch parliamentary management (and thus money for foreign policy commitments such as subsidies or increases in the armed forces), but, at the same time, used the exigencies of such management to urge restraint in governmental initiatives and demands. This was a far from easy process, but Walpole's defeat of his major political rivals in 1720–2 rested on the crucial governmental need for parliamentary support and, in turn, made his position easier. This, in turn, led to a shift in the position of Hanover in British politics. The opportunities George I had sought, with the support of Stanhope and Sunderland, were replaced, in his later years, by caution. This owed much to George's age, and to the lesser opportunities for expansion stemming from the international situation, especially, the end of the Great Northern War in 1721, but Walpolean politics also played a role; although it would be foolish to pretend that these factors can be readily measured or assessed in an hierarchy of importance.

More generally, British ministers and commentators who sought, indeed depended on, a conception of international relations, national interests and foreign policy as fixed and predictable were all challenged by the extent, pace and unpredictability of change. Culprits were sought for both the resulting uncertainty and for the problems arising from international developments, and in Britain, as it was easy to attribute

---

[9] U. Richter-Uhlig, *Hof und Politik unter den Bedingungen der Personalunion zwischen Hannover und England* (Hanover, 1992).

difficulties to what was new, so there was a temptation to attribute blame to the Hanoverian connection. In part, this was justified, as, at the very least, the connection created serious difficulties for British foreign policy, but, at this point, that is not the topic at issue. Instead, in order to understand the contours of the public debate and how it changed, there is the question of the construction of blame. In many respects, Hanover acted as the equivalent opposite to another geographical locator of blame, Utrecht.

The latter, a reference to the peace settlement of 1713, was used, from the Hanoverian accession in 1714, by pro-government spokesmen in order to query the loyalty and probity of the Tories and to suggest that Whig critics who cooperated with the Tories from 1717, such as Walpole in 1717–20, had abandoned crucial principles. Similar to Utrecht, in that its legacy for British foreign policy seemed longstanding,[10] Hanover also served as a mirror image, enabling opposition spokesmen to berate the ministry for failing to understand and/or defend national interests, and thus for being unfit to govern. However artificially, Britishness could therefore be constructed as an alternative to Hanoverianism. This offered a valuable *leitmotif* of political debate, and a more 'modern' alternative to the notion of dynastic legitimacy as the key issue in that debate. Instead of the opposition focusing on the rights to the British throne of the Hanoverians, an issue that left little space for political debate, other than of a treasonable character, it was possible to ask whether the ministry was legitimate in the sense of sustaining the national interest, or to embarrass the ministry on this head by pushing it to defend foreign policy in the light of discussion of this interest.

This was an aspect of a more widespread European political development during the eighteenth century: the separation of ruler from nation, not least in terms of an automatic assumption that the identity and interest of the latter were submerged in the former. The causes of this across Europe were varied, but included a lesser stress on the themes and idioms of sacral monarchy, seen in Britain in the way in which the Hanoverians followed William III, but not Anne, in not touching for scrofula, 'the King's Evil'. In the case of Britain, the legacy of seventeenth-century constitutional struggles was a distinctive degree of dissociation of ruler from nation that was expressed in particular in the position and rights of parliament.

To shift the focus, and provide an additional level of complexity, that the Georges had important and difficult responsibilities as electors did not

---

[10] G. H. Jones, *Great Britain and the Tuscan Succession question, 1710–1737* (New York, 1998).

mean that their espousal of Hanoverian interests was free from criticism within the Electorate. This was an aspect of a more general question about the extent to which the dynasty, both as electors and as kings, were following goals that posed problems for their German subjects. In particular, the territorial expansionism they pursued as electors, and the power politics they were involved in as kings, as well as the implications for Hanover of the link to Britain, led to disquiet among the Hanoverian ministers, and was part of a more general tension between elector and ministers that matched those of crown and ministers, and that was neglected by British writers. At the same time, it is important to note tensions within the Hanoverian ministry. While some aspects of this have been ably studied,[11] much still requires attention, especially for the late 1720s and the 1730s. In short, the Hanoverian context of Walpole's period in office, and even more, the details of policy and policy discussion, are obscure.

To note a distinction between Electorate and elector, and, also to explain the need for the electors to consider the Electorate, does not, however, diminish the issue created by the Hanoverian link for British politics and politicians. Although a parallel was offered by the disquiet among the Hanoverian ministers, this disquiet was far more pronounced in the case of Britain, not least because of the prominent role of parliament and the press there. The problem for the ruler of the balancing act among commitments required from the key figure in a Personal Union, affected George I and George II as both king and elector, and, in both capacities, it strained political assumptions. At the same time, European rulers did not always make a distinction between Britain and Hanover. Instead, they could think of George I and George II as acting in one capacity, rather than two; and thus of Britain-Hanover as a new entity, albeit not a state.[12]

Indeed, a dynamic for the Personal Union was provided by the repeated difficulties confronted by the electors: Britain-Hanover becoming a reality in response to problems. The affirmation or negotiation of peace, as in 1721, 1727, 1731, 1748 and 1763, brought relief from these difficulties, but, for much of the period, Hanover was under threat, acute or potential, and there was a dangerous 'structural' factor in the international system: the rise of Russia and Prussia. These, especially the latter, posed greater challenges to Hanover than the earlier 'great powers' that had intervened in north Germany: Austria, France, Denmark and Sweden. The rise of Prussia more than anything else defined Hanover's international situation; and that is why attempts to blame the Electorate's

---

[11] U. Dann, *Hannover und England, 1740–1760* (Hildesheim, 1986).
[12] J. M. Black, *The Hanoverians* (London, 2004), pp. 28–30.

difficulties on the dynastic link with Britain, and therefore to argue that Britain owed support, are unconvincing. Tension was accentuated by George II's poor relations with his uncle by marriage, Frederick William I of Prussia (r. 1713–40), and also with the latter's son, Frederick II, the Great (r. 1740–86). He made scant effort to manage either of them, and this could anger British ministers keen to improve relations with Prussia. In turn, both Frederick William and his son were regarded as personally hostile to George II. This was greater than the animus shown George I by Frederick William I or George III by Frederick II.

Threats to Hanover tested the acumen of the British ministers as they struggled to confront the diplomatic and political consequences. Thus, Walpole had to restrain George I over Baltic politics in 1723, and, more seriously, had in 1725–7, to defend in Britain the consequences of the Alliance of Hanover, and to seek to present the confrontation with the Alliance of Hanover as arising from British interests. The particular parliamentary problem was the voting, from 1726, of a subsidy to pay the Landgrave Karl of Hesse-Cassel, in order to acquire Hessian troops for the defence of Hanover. The first crisis of Hanoverian vulnerability during George II's reign, that in 1729, owed nothing to Anglo-Prussian differences, but stemmed directly from electoral differences with Prussia;[13] and these were to be repeated. In July 1740, Lord Harrington, secretary of state for the Northern Department, sent a private letter in his own hand to his fellow secretary of state Newcastle, from Hanover, whither he had accompanied George II, noting the impact of electoral disputes, such as the succession to East Friesland,

I will venture in great confidence to acquaint you there are certain disputes and pretensions subsisting betwixt the Houses of Hanover and Prussia, which though they may appear to the rest of the world not to deserve so immediate an attention as other matters of a more genial nature, I fear however that till those are adjusted, in which I foresee great difficulties likely to arise, the general matters will go on but lamely.[14]

The two crises with France – in 1741 when invasion threatened, and in 1757 when it occurred – were responses to George II's policies as a German prince, rather than blows against Britain: in 1741 he was backing Maria Theresa, although this also reflected the views of his British ministers, and in 1756, in pursuit of Hanoverian security, had allied with Frederick II. When, in 1756, the French, in response to British policies in

---

[13] H. Schilling, *Der Zwist Preussens und Hannovers 1729–30* (Halle, 1912). For earlier differences, J. M. Hartley, *Charles Whitworth. Diplomat in the age of Peter the Great* (Aldershot, 2002).
[14] Harrington to Newcastle, 13 July 1740, BL Add. 32693 fol. 436.

North America, wished to attack Britain in Europe, they invaded Minorca, not Hanover.

In both 1741 and 1756–7, in the difficult circumstances of European power politics, George found it impossible to control the consequences for Hanover of his policies in Germany, and in 1741 in the political crisis leading to and following his last general election this caused serious political problems for Walpole. The latter's fall, however, did not end the problem. George's ability to push Maria Theresa toward compromise helped end the First Silesian War between Austria and Prussia, but he lacked the power and intent to settle Maria Theresa's differences with Charles Albert of Bavaria. Allied to Frederick in 1756, George found that he could not prevent Prussia from precipitating war in Europe, and thus exposing Hanover to attack.

Alongside the public sphere in debate over foreign policy was a private sphere of discussion, one indeed that is generally neglected. This private sphere was the world of ministers and diplomats, and except for public breaches, as with the Whig Split of 1717–20, or William Pitt the Elder's movement into opposition in 1754–5, this debate left little trace in the public world. Its focus was also different. Instead of an emphasis on obvious differences of interest and a language of clarity and outrage, came a stress on detail and a concern about the content of policy. Although these strategies and spheres of debate can be segregated for purposes of analysis they, in reality, overlapped and part of their political importance rested on this overlap. For example, the consequences of the public debate could serve to accentuate divisions within the ministry, while an awareness of the latter could play a role in this debate.

In office, in opposition, and, returned to office, the career of Walpole, the most important member of the ministry from 1720 to 1742, illustrated these tensions within the government. As so often in the period, however, it is important to note the character of, and lacunae in, the sources.[15] Much Walpole correspondence survives, but most of it is on patronage matters, and we only glimpse his views on foreign policy episodically and, frequently, at second hand, although the sources for George II are far worse. The comments of foreign envoys keen to chart and explain British policy[16] are an important source for Walpole, as for

---

[15] Despite these lacunae, it is still unfortunate that N. Harding's interesting 'Sir Robert Walpole and Hanover', *Historical Research*, 76 (2003), 164–88 does not rest on archival research and the perspectives it can offer.

[16] Most are unprinted, but see R. A. Marini, *La politica sabauda alla corte Inglese dopo il trattato d'Hannover 1725–1730 nella Relazione dell'ambasciatore piemonte a Londra* (Chambéry, 1918).

George II, but one that needs to be handled with care. The particular episode that commands attention because it bulks large in the surviving sources, is Walpole's role in preserving British neutrality in the War of the Polish Succession (1733–5), but, aside from the one-sided nature of the sources (we know very little directly of George II's views),[17] it is unclear how far we can use this episode to provide a comprehensive account of the issue. Walpole's leading biographers, William Coxe and J. H. Plumb, were not particularly interested in foreign policy and also threw little light on his response to Hanoverian commitments in the 1720s and 1730s. As a result, their account of relations between monarch and first minister lacked depth.[18]

Allowing for these caveats, it appears clear that Walpole had a clear-cut assessment of national interest in which the Hanoverian commitment appeared as an add-on. This was an add-on made necessary by the monarch and by the protestant succession, but, nevertheless, something that could be judged in terms of prudential considerations of benefit and cost. Walpole lacked any emotional commitment to the Electorate. He never went there and did not have any close links with Hanoverian ministers. Unlike his brother who, while acting as secretary of state, went to Hanover in 1736, Walpole did not do so when he acted in this capacity in 1723 and 1729. Nor did he have any correspondence prefiguring that of Newcastle with Münchhausen. Walpole's conception of the interests involved in the connection separated it from any general discussion of the virtues and disadvantages of continental interventionism and, indeed, they were different to Walpole. The latter, general discussion attracts more interest from those concerned with the public sphere, but Walpole's more narrow conception is one that needs to be recovered in order to appreciate the range of responses possible to the Hanoverian connection.[19]

Such a recovery challenges the somewhat Manichean presentation of the debate over the pernicious, or other, implications of the Hanoverian connection. This is in terms of an apparent dichotomy between Whig ministries committed to the connection pursuing a foreign policy that benefited from it, and retrograde Tory xenophobes apparently unable to understand wider national interests or to respond sensibly to international developments. Such a presentation, however, is a travesty of the

---

[17] J. M. Black, 'British neutrality in the War of the Polish Succession', *International History Review* 8 (1986), 345–66.

[18] W. Coxe, *Memoirs of the life and administration of Sir Robert Walpole* (3 vols., London, 1798); J. H. Plumb, *Sir Robert Walpole* (2 vols., London, 1956, 1960).

[19] J. M. Black, ' "An ignoramus in European affairs"?', *British Journal for Eighteenth-Century Studies* 6 (1983), 55–65.

Tory view, not least because it crudely simplifies the latter and underrates the degree of Tory knowledge, but it also fails to appreciate the extent of critical Whig views. The travesty of Tory views is serious, as it reflects and sustains an inability to understand the character of the public debate. More seriously, treating critics of the Hanoverian impact as Tories, and therefore *ipso facto* foolish, and assessing modern scholars who present this view in the same light, is seriously distorting.[20] It is adopting the perspective of a particular Whig tradition of interventionism and failing to understand the degree to which Stanhope, Townshend, Carteret and Newcastle saw the support of Hanover as an integral aspect of this interventionism, largely because they regarded threats to the Electorate as a challenge to the policy. As a consequence of failing to appreciate the debate, it is difficult to grasp the context within which British ministers responded to options.

Adopting another approach, it is possible to probe the archives in both Britain and Germany in order to throw extensive light on contemporary criticism of the impact of the connection by British and Hanoverian ministers. This is valuable at a functional level, but fails to address adequately the ideological character of the link. The Hanoverian succession was a direct consequence of the application of political anti-Catholicism to dynastic ends in a monarchical society. From that perspective, functional problems that arose as a consequence were very much secondary. However, political anti-Catholicism was far more acceptable (and definable) in the defensive context of preventing a Stuart revanche, the theme of much propaganda and of some discussion about foreign policy, for example in 1725–7, rather than in providing a rationale for proactive policies. This was overridden to an extent during the reign of George I, when the unattractive public implications of the alliance with France from 1716 were, to an extent, made less significant by the continued rhetoric of anti-Catholicism. This was particularly seen in the early 1720s, for example in response to the treatment of protestants in the Palatinate and in Poland, and, even more, during the confrontation between the alliances of Hanover and Vienna from 1725, in which Britain allied to France was opposed to Austria and Spain.[21]

Yet, on the whole the Hanoverian connection was not followed by a protestant foreign policy.[22] Far from it: Hanover's major rival was

---

[20] J. M. Black, 'The Tory view of eighteenth-century British foreign policy', *Historical Journal* 31 (1988), 409–27.

[21] H. Naumann, *Österreich, England und das Reich, 1719–32* (Berlin, 1936).

[22] Although see A. C. Thompson, *Britain, Hanover and the protestant interest, 1688–1756* (Woodbridge, Suffolk, 2006).

Prussia, a protestant power that made much of its animosity to Austria, and Prussia was seen as a threat in a way that Saxony was not, despite the latter being a Lutheran state ruled by a catholic. Instead, Hanover and Saxony were allied for much of the 1730s–mid-1750s. Furthermore, Hanover depended for its security on the support of France until 1731,[23] and thereafter, albeit to a very varied extent, George II, as king and elector, sought to protect Austrian interests, or at least his conception of these interests, until 1756, and Walpole, perforce, supported this policy, although it is unclear that he felt much support for it.

Alliance with first France, and then Austria, could be defended as prudent, but it scarcely conformed to a confessional ideology. In its absence, there were few available defences for foreign policy. The most common, that of the balance of power, joined an ideological justification of policy to that of prudence, but the latter itself invited criticism on a prudential basis with reference to the application of the theory in policy terms, while the relationship between the Hanoverian connection and the balance was sufficiently vague to invite the rejoinder that it was not relevant.[24]

It is important to address the role of subjective considerations in contemporary and modern judgements. These are related, because it is unclear how sensible it is to abstract the process of assessing the response that 'should' have been made from the political context. If, for example, criticism of the consequences of the Hanoverian commitment is presented as xenophobic, even paranoid, and as arising from a failure to understand the major developments in Europe, then many speakers and writers, and much of the ambience and ethos of public (and private) discussion of foreign policy will be seen as unsatisfactory.

Restoring attention to contemporary debates[25] entails considering attitudes as well as interests and goals, as these attitudes were directly relevant to issues of best policy and practice. In simple terms, and again allowing for a failure to conform to party political alignments (which reflected multiple factors, not least religious views), there was a tension between 'Whig' and 'Tory' attitudes towards the international system, with the latter enjoying considerable sway, including among many who were not Tory in party politics. The Whig attitude lent itself much more readily to the pragmatic, functional defence of the Hanoverian alignment. Assuming that, through human action, it was possible to create a more

---

[23] J. M. Black, 'The Anglo-French Alliance 1716–31: a study in eighteenth-century international relations', *Francia* 13 (1986), 295–310.

[24] J. M. Black, 'The theory of the balance of power in the first half of the eighteenth century: a note on sources', *Review of International Studies* 9 (1983), 855–61.

[25] For parliamentary debates, J. M. Black, *Parliament and foreign policy in the eighteenth century* (Cambridge, 2004).

benign international system, this attitude was a mechanistic viewpoint, in many respects in thrall to Newtonian physics. In this view, there were clear-cut national interests that could be readily assessed and balanced, and it was therefore possible to devise collective security systems that encompassed Hanover, as with the Imperial Election Scheme of the early 1750s. These views made sense of, and demanded, interventionism. This was the approach of many, but by no means all, British diplomats, of some secretaries of state, most obviously Stanhope, Carteret and Newcastle, and of several influential scholars of the last half-century.

This approach required criticism of the opposite viewpoint, but the 'Tory' attitude in fact drew on a coherent intellectual and moral philosophy, as well as an informed assessment of international relations and of British options. The 'Tory' option was inherently pessimistic about the possibilities of creating trust and workable collective systems, and inclined to assume that any settlement of differences would be precarious, if not short term. This attitude was lapsarian, rather than Newtonian, and with a stress on the human volition of rulers and ministers, not the mechanics of the balance of power. In appreciating the limitations of the schematic understanding of national interests and international relations, this approach offered a powerful critique of interventionism, and thus challenged the value of collective systems of guarantee, and of commitments stemming from the Hanoverian connection.

Paradoxically, the uncertainty of parliamentary responses to foreign policy helped ensure that the clarity of diplomatic conception, and the schematic model-building of the language of the balance of power, did not describe adequately the nature of the British domestic context for foreign policy. The potential political challenge posed by the latter indeed overlapped with the tension between 'Whig' and 'Tory' attitudes already referred to. In both, the Hanoverian connection was troublesome, but the potential problems posed by royal demands on behalf of the Electorate were restrained during the 1720s and 1730s, not only by Walpole's skill, but also because repeated, but varied, threats to Hanover, for example by Russia in the early 1720s, Austria and her allies in 1726–7,[26] Prussia in 1729, or a French advance east of the Rhine in 1734 or 1735, were not realised. Crucially, there was no war involving Hanover in 1725–7, while in 1733–5, in the War of the Polish Succession, Hanover, although a combatant, was not endangered. Although Belle-Isle's advance down the Moselle Valley in 1734 briefly caused concern on this head, it was not the basis of an advance across the Rhine. Indeed, the French followed a much

---

[26] J. F. Chance, *The alliance of Hanover* (London, 1923).

more cautious policy north of the Alps than in Italy, and this included observing a neutrality for the Austrian Netherlands, an arresting instance of limited war.

George as elector sent troops to the Imperial army in 1734, but Hanover did not need to be rescued from attack by British diplomatic or, even more problematic, military action. This was important because, whatever the cause of the conflict, and however defended in public debate, the dynamic of events in such a conflict might have cruelly exposed differences over Hanover. In the 1740s, however, the situation seriously deteriorated on both heads, and this led to the major agitation over Hanoverian interests that caused such political problems in Parliament in 1742-4. These problems indicated the wisdom of Walpole's earlier caution.

From this perspective, Newcastle's post-War-of-the-Austrian-Succession attempt to arrange a strong collective security system designed to prevent war, however misguided in diplomatic terms, rested on the political insight he shared with Walpole that, in terms of relations with the king, it would not be easy for a ministry to refuse Hanover support in a conflict, but that the provision of such support might cause serious political problems in Britain.[27] In the event, even William Pitt the Elder, a scourge of Hanoverian measures (as, initially, of Walpole and George II), had to accept the dispatch of British troops and money to Germany in 1758, although he was able to present it both in terms of assistance to Prussia, a reasonable claim, at least in so far as keeping Frederick II in the war was concerned, and also, far more problematically, as a means to conquer America (i.e. New France or Canada) in Germany.

Like Newcastle's approach, this policy was riskier, because more exposed to the uncertainties of international developments, than that of Walpole; whose attitudes had, instead, been carried forward by his protégé Henry Pelham, First Lord of the Treasury from 1743 until his unexpected death in 1754. Indeed, Pelham's views provide an important way of gauging the Walpolean legacy, and indicate that the minister's influence did not cease in 1745. In contrast, while Newcastle and Pitt were very different to each other in their political methods and resonance, they shared a commitment in office to action that was not that of Walpole or Pelham, and, indeed, as a minor ministerial figure, Pitt had supported Newcastle in the late 1740s and early 1750s, defending the subsidy to Maximilian Joseph, elector of Bavaria in the Commons debate on

---

[27] J. M. Black, 'The British attempt to preserve the peace in Europe 1748-1755', in: H. Duchhardt (ed.), *Zwischenstaatliche Friedenswahrung in Mittelalter und Früher Neuzeit* (Cologne, 1991), pp. 227-43.

22 February (o.s.) 1751, although, the following year, he did not support the Saxon subsidy treaty.

Newcastle was particularly associated with the 'Old System' – an active alignment with Austria and the Dutch that clashed with Walpole's priorities, and indeed with his experience of the difficulties of acting with either power. This alignment served royal and Hanoverian ends in the 1740s and early 1750s by essentially acting as a military deterrent to Prussia, while appearing also as an anti-French step, and thus matching the assumptions of British politicians. The clash between hostility to France and opposition to Prussia had led to significant political and diplomatic difficulties during the War of the Austrian Succession, but the coming of peace in 1748 permitted the shelving of the apparent differences between the two goals.

However, securing the peace by restraining France and Prussia through a collective security system, underlined the value of Walpole's earlier caution as it made Britain dependent on her partners, left it unclear whether France or Prussia were the major challenge, and made it uncertain whether, in the event of war, intervention could surmount the problems both of Hanoverian vulnerability and of British political ambivalence toward the Electorate, and win success. As a consequence, British ministers, such as Holdernesse and Newcastle, were to be very free in their criticism of their Hanoverian counterparts in 1757.

The commitment to action carried with it serious international and diplomatic risks: in both peace and war, Newcastle's diplomatic schemes fell foul of the difficulties posed by obdurate allies, and of the duke's failure to appreciate the direction of international relations; while, in 1758, Pitt had to commit British resources to the weaker of the two alliance systems in Europe. The joy that greeted Frederick II's victories was, in part, relief that the consequences of this could be avoided.

Both Newcastle and Pitt felt constrained by George II and his Hanoverian concerns. Newcastle was greatly influenced by his visit to Hanover in 1748, not least by meeting the leading Hanoverian minister, Gerlach Adolf von Münchhausen; and his ministerial allies in Britain drew attention to the duke's new-found clarity. Newcastle's concern to rout his ministerial rival, John, 4th duke of Bedford, secretary of state for the Southern Department, as indeed happened in 1751, was also important, as he needed royal support to this end. In contrast, Walpole thwarted Townshend and Carteret in 1730 and Chesterfield, Stair and others in 1733, without having to back George's electoral views. Unlike Walpole after 1730, a sense of dependence, indeed anxiety about George's opinions, continued to characterise Newcastle's views after 1748. In his turn, Pitt was obliged to back help to Hanover if George II was to be persuaded to disavow the Hanoverian neutrality of 1757, which threatened the coherence of a foreign policy that then rested on alliance with Prussia alone. Again, Walpole had avoided any such necessity.

Ironically, it was the future George III, at least prior to the 1780s, who most powerfully represented this ambivalence toward Hanover in the late 1750s, as well as once he came to the throne in 1760. He took up the critical attitudes of Walpole towards an active foreign policy, and, in doing so, linked royal authority to non-interventionism. As Prince of Wales, and influenced by the problems of the Seven Years War, George criticised the partiality of his grandfather, George II, for Hanover, and, as king, he was determined to disengage from the 'German war', the German part of the Seven Years War, and to avoid loading Britain with subsidies.

To discuss the attitudes and policies of George III is to look far ahead from the opportunities and problems that became so rapidly apparent from the Hanoverian accession. While comparisons over such a period are instructive they also risk neglecting the specificities of debate and discussion in particular contexts. In considering the latter, it is important to reiterate that the differences of contemporaries should not be slighted or misrepresented by reference to factious opposition. Given modern scholarly disagreements over theories of international relations, as well as the clarity with which in modern democracies politicians and publics contest definitions of national interest, and disagree vigorously over how best to pursue them, it is surprising that debate over foreign policy in the past is not taken more seriously.

3 Pitt and Hanover

Brendan Simms

> The weight of his popularity, and his universally acknowledged abilitys, obtruded him upon King George the Second, to whom he was personally obnoxious. He was made Secretary of State. In this difficult and delicate situation, which one would have thought must have reduced either the patriot, or the minister to a decisive option, he managed with such ability, that while he served the King more effectually in his most unwarrantable Electoral views, than any former Minister however willing, had dared to do, He still preserved all his credit, and popularity with the Publick, whom he assured and convinced that the protection and defence of Hannover with an army of 75 000 men in British pay, was the only possible means of securing our possessions or acquisitions in North America. So much easier it is to deceive than to undeceive Mankind.
>
> Lord Chesterfield on William Pitt, 1762.[1]

Consistency and inconsistency are familiar themes in the political history of eighteenth-century Britain.[2] No one has been more investigated in this regard than William Pitt the Elder, earl of Chatham, and in no respect more so than in his relationship to the Electorate of Hanover. Uriel Dann speaks of his 'apparent inconsistency', Adolphus William Ward of 'something of inconsistency', and O. A. Sherrard of 'seeming inconsistencies' in his Hanoverian policy. Pitt's policy towards Hanover also features prominently in the two recent scholarly biographies by Marie Peters and Jeremy Black.[3] This chapter takes a fresh look at this well-studied subject. It will show that the study of Pitt and Hanover serves as a prism through

---

[1] 'A character of Mr Pitt [1762]', in Colin Franklin, ed., *Lord Chesterfield. His character and characters* (Aldershot, 1993), p. 127.

[2] E.g. Herbert Butterfield, *Sincerity and insincerity in Charles James Fox* (London, 1972).

[3] For Pitt and inconsistency generally see: Bob Harris, *Politics and the nation. Britain in the mid-eighteenth century* (Oxford, 2002), p. 80. On Pitt and Hanover in particular see: Adolphus William Ward, *Great Britain and Hanover: some aspects of the Personal Union* (Oxford, 1899) p. 171; Harris, *Politics and the nation*, p. 6; Jeremy Black, *Pitt the Elder* (Cambridge, 1992), p. 143 *et passim*; and Marie Peters, *The Elder Pitt* (London and New York, 1998), p. 73 *et passim*; O. A. Sherrard, *Lord Chatham. A war minister in the making* (London, 1952), pp. 126–31; and Uriel Dann, *Hanover and Great Britain, 1740–1760* (Leicester and London, 1991) speaks of 'apparent inconsistency', p. 109.

which central aspects of his career and contemporary British politics can be viewed: opportunism and principle; high politics and the role of the monarch; the public sphere; the nature of popularity; and grand strategy.

The Elder Pitt is famously an elusive subject. Unlike many other eighteenth-century political figures, such as the earl of Chesterfield or the Elder Horace Walpole, he was not a pamphleteer. In contrast to his colleague and rival, the duke of Newcastle, Pitt was an infrequent and brief correspondent.[4] A great deal of what we know about his political and strategic thinking, and still more his high-political machinations, comes from the accounts of others, especially the correspondence of the duke of Newcastle, the earl of Hardwicke and the duke of Bedford.[5] If we want to establish what Pitt himself thought, or wanted us to think he thought, we generally have to turn to his parliamentary speeches, which are unreliably and incompletely documented.[6] The surviving record is particularly disappointing for the crucial period of the Seven Years War, much better for the early stages of the War of the Austrian Succession. 'New' speeches, or fuller and alternative accounts of known speeches, are still cropping up. A particularly striking example would be Pitt's speech of December 1761 on the German war, which Karl Schweizer unearthed just over a decade ago.[7]

The study of Pitt and Hanover is further complicated by the fact that Pitt never served in a capacity which brought him formally into contact with the management of the German war and British-Hanoverian relations at the highest level. He was secretary of state for the South during his celebrated wartime ministry; the relevant secretary of state for the

---

[4] On this see Richard Middleton, *The bells of victory. The Pitt–Newcastle ministry and the conduct of the Seven Years War, 1757–1762* (Cambridge, 1985), p. 8.

[5] Lord John Russell, ed., *Correspondence of John, fourth duke of Bedford* (3 vols., London, 1842–1846); P. C. Yorke, ed., *The life and correspondence of Philip Yorke, earl of Hardwicke* (3 vols., Cambridge, 1913). The duke of Newcastle's papers are to be found in the Add. Mss. of the British Library. Some of the letters have been printed in Yorke, ed., *Hardwicke*; the originals have been used where extracts relating to Pitt have been missed. Pitt's own surviving correspondence is sparse: W. S. Taylor and J. H. Pringle, eds., *The correspondence of William Pitt, earl of Chatham* (4 vols., London, 1838–1840). The printed version does not always seem to be entirely reliable. For example, liberties are taken with the text of the letter from Pitt to the duke of Brunswick, 28 October 1760, though the sense is retained: Taylor and Pringle, eds., *Chatham*, II, p. 76 and Niedersächsisches Hauptstaatsarchiv Hannover (NHStH), Hann 9e Nr. 109, fol. 101. The author has not knowingly used an archival source where a satisfactory printed version was available.

[6] On this problem generally see Jeremy Black, *Parliament and foreign policy in the eighteenth century* (Cambridge, 2004), pp. 137–63. For Pitt in particular see Peter D. G. Thomas, '"The great Commoner". The Elder Pitt as parliamentarian', *Parliamentary History* 22 (2003), 148.

[7] Karl Schweizer, ed., 'An unpublished parliamentary speech by the Elder Pitt, 9 December 1761', *Historical Research* 64 (1991), 98–105.

Northern Department was the earl of Holdernesse.[8] For this reason the material in the National Archives tells us relatively little.[9] Likewise, the British envoy to Prussia, Andrew Mitchell, dealt principally with Holdernesse and the printed version of his papers and journal is singularly unenlightening about Pitt and Hanover.[10] The few contacts that are recorded with the Hanoverian chief minister, Gerlach Adolf von Münchhausen, and the commander of the army in Germany, the duke of Brunswick, in the Hanoverian archives, do not add much.[11] If it has been noted that Münchhausen chose to deal with Pitt rather than Holdernesse or even Newcastle,[12] this willingness to communicate was not much reciprocated.[13]

This chapter is by no means the first study of Pitt and Hanover.[14] It is, however, the first systematic exploration of Pitt's complex relationship with the king's German dominions. It investigates whether Pitt was simply a classic eighteenth-century opportunist, who castigated Hanover in opposition, but deferred to the king's German sensibilities when in office. It assesses, more generally, whether there was a coherence to Pitt's strategy at all. It also examines whether, as the heroic narrative suggested, Pitt so skilfully interwove continental and colonial measures

---

[8] E.g. see duke of Brunswick to Pitt, 7 January 1759, Münster fol. 20, PRO 30/8/90, which makes clear that the regular channel of communication was through Holdernesse and not Pitt: 'L'absence de Mylord Comte Holdernesse me fournit d'occasion d'écrire a votre excellence en suite des affaires, qui regardit l'armée sous mes ordres,' (The absence of Lord Holdernesse gives me the opportunity to write to your Excellency about the matters regarding the army I am commanding).

[9] There is some material in PRO 30/8/89–90 (Chatham Papers). PRO 30/8/91 contains chiefly copies of translations of various treaties of alliance and subsidy with German powers, principally Prussia.

[10] Andrew Bisset, ed., *Memoirs and papers of Sir Andrew Mitchell* (2 vols., London, 1850).

[11] See for example NHStH Hann 9e Nr. 1098, fols. 9, 39–40, 49, which includes detailed military reports from the duke of Brunswick to Pitt.

[12] See Dann, *Hanover and Great Britain*, p. 110. An example of this would be Münchhausen to Pitt, 27 October 1759, PRO 30/8/89, fol. 223, in which he sends – at the request of George II – a translation of a dispatch of the Hanoverian envoy to Copenhagen, Steinberg.

[13] As noted by Mitchell Dale Allen, 'The Anglo-Hanoverian connection, 1727–1760', (PhD dissertation, Boston University, 2000), p. 285.

[14] See for example the section 'Pitt and Hanover' in Karl W. Schweizer's *William Pitt, earl of Chatham 1708–1778. A bibliography* (Westport/Conn. and London, 1993), pp. 115–16. For recent work see: Robert Harris, *A patriot press. National politics and the London press in the 1740s* (Oxford, 1993); Nicholas Harding, 'Dynastic union in British and Hanoverian ideology 1701–1803' (PhD dissertation, Columbia University, 2001), pp. 191, 293–6 *et passim*; Black, *Pitt the Elder, passim* but especially pp. 43–5, 169–70, 195–6; and Peters, *The elder Pitt, passim* but especially, 31–2, 89–90. Thomas, ' "The great Commoner"', pp. 151, 163, has relatively little to say about the role of Hanover in Pitt's parliamentary career.

that, in the famous phrase, 'America was conquered in Germany'.[15] Or was Pitt's strategy, as Richard Middleton argued in an arresting revisionist account nearly twenty years ago, a collective effort, to which he made only a piecemeal and subsequently over-rationalised contribution?[16] More recently, Marie Peters has shown that Pitt was not the great imperialist of myth either.[17] Indeed, we now know rather more about what Pitt was not, than what he was.

I

Whatever his public rhetoric, Pitt was throughout his career never a pure 'blue-water' colonialist but an opposition Whig supporter of engagement in Europe. His foreign-political horizon was shaped by the attacks launched by opposition Whigs, under the loose leadership of the earl of Chesterfield on the ministry of Sir Robert Walpole in the decade before 1740. To be sure, these Whigs scourged Walpole's reluctance first to declare war on Spain in the late 1730s, and then to prosecute that war with sufficient vigour. But the core of the Chesterfieldian critique of British foreign policy was not colonial or naval. Its principal charge was that the turn away from the traditional alliance with Austria in the mid-1720s – epitomised by the Treaty of Hanover in 1725 – had allowed French power to grow unchecked, to threaten the European balance of power and thus British liberties; the Treaty of Hanover between Britain, France and Prussia had marked the nadir of relations with Vienna. Far from being opposed to all continental entanglements, these Whigs rebuked Walpole for failing to support the Habsburgs during the War of the Polish Succession. To the best of my knowledge, Pitt's views on these subjects in the 1730s have not been recorded, but as we shall see his retrospective assessments of British policy of that period in the early

---

[15] Richard Pares, 'American versus continental warfare, 1739–1763', *English Historical Review* 51 (1936), 460, on how Pitt 'learned the lesson' that Europe mattered.

[16] Richard Middleton, *The bells of victory. The Pitt–Newcastle ministry and the conduct of the Seven Years War 1757–1762* (Cambridge, 1985). Peters, *Elder Pitt*, pp. 105–6, largely accepts this view. For an interesting contribution to the Pitt legend and 'combined operations' see Richard Harding, 'Sailors and gentlemen of parade: some professional and technical problems concerning the conduct of combined operations in the eighteenth century', *Historical Journal* 23 (1989), 33–55, especially 37–40. For a recent view of Pitt as a navalist see N. A. M. Rodger, *The command of the ocean. A naval history of Britain, 1649–1815* (London, 2004), p. 290.

[17] Marie Peters, 'The myth of William Pitt, earl of Chatham, great imperialist. Part I: Pitt and imperial expansion 1738–1763', *Journal of Imperial and Commonwealth History* 21, 1 (1993), 31–74. A good example of the view of Pitt as a great colonialist is Kate Hotblack, *Chatham's colonial policy. A study in the fiscal and economic implications of the colonial policy of the Elder Pitt* (London, 1917, reprinted Philadelphia, 1980), especially pp. xii–xiv.

1740s all stressed the failure to bolster Austria against France, far more than colonial differences with Spain.

Pitt was first confronted with the Hanoverian connection in this context. 'The Treaty of Hanover', he told the House of Commons in mid-February 1741, 'was calculated only for the advancement of the house of Bourbon' and had 'disunite[d] us from the only power [Austria], with which it is our interest to cultivate an inseparable friendship. This disunion therefore may justly be charged upon the minister, who has weakened the interest of this country, and endangered the liberties of Europe.'[18] Just over a year later, he elaborated that 'The treaty of Hanover deserves indeed to be first mentioned, because from thence springs the danger which Europe is now exposed to; and it is impossible to assign a reason for our entering into that treaty, without supposing that we then resolved to be revenged upon the emperor for refusing to grant us some favour in Germany [i.e. for Hanover].'[19] It is a striking feature of this, and most other contemporaneous parliamentary attacks on Walpole, that concerns about European policy far outweighed those relating to colonial and naval matters.

The first substantial evidence of Pitt's thinking on Hanover can be found in his parliamentary speeches of 1742–4, which were delivered against the background of the War of the Austrian Succession. This pitted Prussia, France and Bavaria against British-backed Austria. In late 1741, a French army had moved into northern Germany and compelled George II to conclude a neutrality convention in his capacity as elector. Not long after, Walpole had resigned, largely because of the collapse of his European policy, and been replaced by Carteret, who had renounced the neutrality convention and invested large sums of British money in hiring Hanoverian troops to engage the French in Germany and Flanders. These payments provoked an extraordinary outburst of parliamentary and public outrage.

It was in this context that Pitt delivered his famous diatribe against the Hanoverian connection, which did so much to colour contemporary and subsequent perceptions of him as a diehard critic of the Personal Union. 'It does not yet appear', he said, 'that either justice or policy required us to engage in the quarrels of the continent'. And yet now Britain was being asked to pay for the upkeep of Hanoverian forces. 'It is now too apparent', he pronounced at the climax of his speech, 'that this great, this powerful,

---

[18] Pitt speech in Commons, 13 February 1741, in William Cobbett, ed., *The parliamentary history of England from the earliest period to the year 1803* (36 vols., London, 1806–20) [Cobbett], XI, cols. 1360–1.

[19] Cobbett XII, 9 March 1742, col. 493.

this formidable kingdom, is considered only as a province to a despicable Electorate; and that in consequence of a scheme formed long ago, and invariably pursued, these troops are hired only to drain this unhappy nation of its money.' He concluded by saying that 'however the interest of Hanover has been preferred by the ministers, the parliament pays no regard but to that of Great Britain'.[20] All this was a transparent pitch for popularity: the contemptuous dismissal of the 'quarrels of the continent', the slighting reference to the Electorate, the suggestion of Hanoverian corruption, and the critique of ministerial toadying to Hanover and the crown.

But Pitt was really making an argument against Hanover opting out of full involvement in the war, rather than a case against the war in general or Hanover in particular. His point was that Hanover was equally if not more threatened than Britain and should therefore pull her financial and military weight. 'Can we imagine', Pitt asked, 'that the power of France is less, or that her designs are less formidable to Hanover than to Great Britain? Nor is it less necessary for the security of Hanover that the House of Austria should be re-established in its former grandeur, and enabled to support the liberties of Europe against the bold attempts for universal monarchy.' In short, 'why should the elector of Hanover exert his liberality at the expense of Great Britain?'. He returned to these themes a year later when he argued that British support for Maria Theresa had been put on hold in late 1741 because the French had threatened Hanover. 'As soon as France began to appear', he said, 'our schemes were all dropt, and our promises forgot; because then it began to be unsafe for Hanover to engage in the affair, and England surely is never to mind any promises, or engage in any schemes, that may possibly bring Hanover into any danger or distress.'[21]

In fact, Pitt was making a case for more extensive British involvement on the continent, perhaps even looking forward to the time when Prussia rather than Austria would lead the containment of France. 'What ought our ministers to have done?' he asked. 'Since it was impossible', Pitt answered, 'to re-establish the balance of power in Europe, upon the single power of the House of Austria ... it was our business to think of restoring the peace of Germany as soon as possible by our good offices in order thereby to establish a confederacy sufficient for opposing France.'[22] There is no trace of patriot navalism here: the thinking entirely reflects the traditional Whig continentalist framework within which Pitt had spent his politically formative years in the 1730s.

[20] Pitt speech, 10 December 1742, Cobbett, XII, cols. 1033–6.
[21] Pitt speech, 1 December 1743, Cobbett, XIII, col. 158.   [22] *Ibid.*, col. 161.

Pitt, in short, was critical of the Electorate, but not of the European commitment as such. He condemned Hanover for 'the great acquisitions it has made, and the many expensive broils England has been involved in upon the sole account of that Electorate'.[23] Again in January 1744 Pitt did not dispute that one should 'support the queen of Hungary, or [that] we shall keep up a sufficient strength on the continent to oppose France'. At issue, he argued, was whether one should pay for the Hanoverians, when others might do a job better and more cheaply, which Hanover should really be doing at its own expense. Hanover could also be blamed for the failures of continental operations: 'Hanover councils and Hanover troops have lamed all our operations from the beginning.'[24]

For Pitt, playing the Hanoverian card was also a way of undermining Carteret's ministry and burnishing his own patriotic credentials. Carteret, wrote one observer, 'was severely reflected upon, and styled ... an execrable, a sole minister, who had renounced the British nation'. Pitt further claimed that at the battle of Dettingen in 1743, the king had been 'hemmed in by German officers, and one English minister without an English heart'.[25] Carteret was described as 'the most enormous minister ever heard of ... one who had deserted his native country and turned German'.[26] Carteret was, in short, a 'Hanover troop minister'.[27] Pitt by contrast, championed the cause of British officers supposedly passed over in favour of Hanoverians.[28] By implication, Pitt was portraying himself as an Englishman who was fearlessly prepared to oppose royal corruption. As one hagiographical pamphleteer was to put it:

> You pleaded Liberty's, and Britain's cause
> Foremost in ardent Patriot-Bands you stood
> A firm opposer for the public good.[29]

By the mid-1740s, therefore, Pitt enjoyed a considerable reputation as an anti-Hanoverian firebrand.[30] But once Carteret had fallen by the end of 1744, Pitt radically toned down his rhetoric. To be sure, the capture of the French Canadian fortress of Louisburg in the summer of 1745 prompted him, as Newcastle put it, to promote his 'favourite notion of

---

[23] *Ibid.*, col. 157.
[24] Parliamentary Journal of Philip Yorke, 18–19 January 1744, in Cobbett, XIII, col. 470. On this see also Black, *Pitt the Elder*, pp. 55–6.
[25] Cited in Peters, *The Elder Pitt*, pp. 30–1.   [26] Cited in Black, *Pitt*, p. 52.
[27] Parliamentary Journal of Philip Yorke, 19 January 1744, in Cobbett, XIII, col. 465.
[28] *Ibid.*   [29] [Anon.], *An epistle to William Pitt Esq.* (London, 1746), p. 4.
[30] Marie Peters, *Pitt and popularity. The patriot minister and London opinion during the Seven Years War* (Oxford, 1980), pp. 1 and 32; Dann, *Hanover and Great Britain*, p. 107; Black, *Pitt the Elder*, p. 45.

a maritime war'.³¹ The navalist theme came across strongly when he told the parliamentary 'Committee of Supply' in the same year that 'our naval power is what we must expect peace with France from', and when he stated to the House of Commons that he 'always thought it the policy of this nation to be as strong at sea as possible ... I wish the navy was greater'.³² In the negotiations with Henry Pelham in October 1745 he made a concentration on the naval war against the Bourbons a condition of joining the ministry.³³ But Pitt did not use the renewed popular surge for colonial expansion, comparable only to the response to Admiral Vernon's capture of Porto Bello in 1739, as a pretext to launch a renewed attack on Hanover and continental entanglements.

On the contrary, in February 1745, Pitt supported the scheme for paying Hanoverian troops through Maria Theresa, which he described as 'a meritorious and popular measure'.³⁴ In April 1746 he was among those defending the continued employment of Hanoverian troops.³⁵ Indeed, once he became paymaster general in the revised Pelham administration of May 1746, Pitt was in charge of the payments to Hanoverians.³⁶ His earlier phillipics now came back to haunt him. Could this be the same man, one ballad asked satirically, 'who could talk and could prate ... and bellowed and roared at the troops of Hanover'.³⁷ 'Such was your case', an anonymous broadside mocked,

> Scarce warm in place
> Defil'd all o'er
> An errant Whore
> You changed your stile
> Like Turn-coat vile.³⁸

One pamphleteer dubbed him 'orator Hanover Pitt' and another critic was so appalled at Pitt's apostasy that he announced that 'My patience is worn out, in seeing Patriots swallow down ministerial puddings piping hot without so much as blistering their tongues.'³⁹

Pitt's commitment to a continental policy was sustained throughout the late 1740s and early 1750s. As paymaster general he had to execute

---

³¹ Cited in Black, *Pitt*, p. 65.   ³² *Ibid.*, p. 76.   ³³ Black, *Pitt*, p. 62.
³⁴ Cobbett, XIII, 18 February 1745, col. 1176.   ³⁵ Peters, *The elder Pitt*, p. 47.
³⁶ See Peregrine Furse [secretary and accountant of paymaster's Office] to Pitt, paymaster general's Office, 31 July 1746, in Taylor and Pringle, eds., *Chatham correspondence*, I, p. 5.
³⁷ Cited in Black, *Pitt*, p. 74.
³⁸ *Short verses in imitation of long verses in an epistle to William Pitt* (London, 1746), pp. 4–5.
³⁹ See *A duchess's ghost to orator Hanover Pitt* (London, 1746); and the words of Edward Turner, cited in Harris, *Politics and the nation*, p. 6. For continued rancour over this 'apostasy' ten years later see the anti-Pittite journal *The Test*, 6 November 1756, p. 4 and 5 February 1757, pp. 68–9.

and justify Newcastle's expensive proposed subsidies for the imperial election scheme, a British initiative to secure the Habsburg succession in the German empire and thus its preservation as a bulwark against France.[40] This should have been a red rag to Pitt, but unlike Newcastle's brother Henry Pelham at the Treasury, for whom peacetime subsidies were an anathema, Pitt does not seem to have reacted against the costs involved. Quite the reverse: when Newcastle triumphantly announced that he had won – or rather bought – the Bavarian electoral vote, Pitt replied that 'I rejoice on the public account at the success of a most wise and salutary measure'.[41] He even took up Newcastle's invitation to correspond with him when he went to Hanover in 1750. Pitt had certainly come around to the view that involvement in the affairs of the Holy Roman Empire was useful to British policy. In January 1751, one observer characterised his defence of a resulting subsidy treaty as 'a great panegyric on the Duke of Newcastle's German negotiations'.[42]

Significantly, Pitt's support for the abortive imperial election scheme was justified by a very clear sense of British interests in Europe in general, and Germany in particular. In a speech which seems to have been largely ignored by earlier scholars, Pitt noted that Britain could not uphold the 'balance of power' on its own, but only by uniting with 'our most proper, our most natural allies', the Dutch, and the states of the German Empire.[43] He then embarked on a detailed and reasonably accurate exposition of the 'laws of the empire', and their implications for the British interest, which was to 'restore the vigour of the Germanic body'.[44] In short, as Marie Peters argues, by the late 1740s, Pitt had become a 'continentalist by conviction'.[45]

II

Against this background, Pitt's dramatic shift back to an anti-Hanoverian and anti-continental rhetoric in the mid-1750s came as something of a surprise. As war with France over North America loomed, the ministry under Newcastle scrambled to construct a protective carapace of subsidy treaties around Hanover. A repeat of the French invasion of 1741 was feared, and the ministry did not want to find itself accused, as it had been

---

[40] Black, *Pitt*, p. 85.
[41] Pitt to Newcastle, Pay Office, 24 August 1750, in Taylor and Pringle, eds., *Chatham correspondence*, I, p. 45. For Pitt's support for the imperial election scheme in parliament see his speech of 17 January 1751, in Cobbett, XIV, col. 802.
[42] Cited in Black, *America or Europe*, p. 147.
[43] Cobbett XIV, 22 February 1751, col. 965.   [44] *Ibid.*, cols. 966–7.
[45] Peters, *Pitt*, p. 56. See also Black, *Pitt the Elder*, p. 55.

in 1748 at the peace treaty of Aix la Chapelle, of surrendering colonial gains for European purposes, especially not Hanoverian ones. Newcastle therefore aimed not to draw off French resources through a European coalition against her, but simply to neutralise the continent – or at least screen off Hanover with a shield of local mercenaries – and concentrate on the war overseas. To that end, treaties were concluded with various smaller German princes, in late 1755, with Russia, and in 1756 with Prussia. In early 1756, Hanoverian and Hessian troops were deployed in Britain itself to guard against a threatened French invasion.

In 1755–6, Pitt subjected these arrangements to withering attack. He dismissed the subsidy treaties as a 'chain and a connection, [which] would end in a general plan for the continent which this country would not support'.[46] Some three weeks later Pitt reiterated his view that 'both Russian and Hessian treaties [were] singly entered into on account of Hanover, and what disservice must it do to the King and his Royal family, when the people of England saw that they could not enter into a war for the support of their own rights [overseas] without exposing themselves to such consequences'.[47] That same month, the younger Horace Walpole observed that Pitt was 'scouring his old Hanoverian trumpet', to refresh his patriot credentials and embarrass Newcastle.[48] In mid-November, Pitt launched a ninety-minute assault on the Hessian and Russian treaties on the grounds of their partiality to Hanover, and predicted that 'that measure would hang like a millstone about the neck of the minister who supported it and sink him into disrepute amongst the people'.[49] A week later, Newcastle finally dismissed Pitt as paymaster general for his attacks on the government's continental policy.

Out of office, Pitt intensified his attacks. In December, he claimed that the treaties were 'advised, framed, and executed, not with a view to the defence of Great Britain ... but purely and entirely for the preservation of Hanover'. The tail, in other words, was wagging the dog. Britain, as Pitt lamented in what was surely not a coincidental allusion to military compulsion, was being 'pressed into the service of an Electorate'.[50] In May 1756, he condemned the convention of Westminster with Prussia, designed to defend Hanover, as another example of electoral manipulation and 'ardently wished to break these fetters which chained us, like

[46] Pitt's remarks cited in Hardwicke to Newcastle, 9 August 1755, Powis House in Hardwicke, *Yorke*, II, p. 231.
[47] Pitt's remarks as cited in P. S. to Newcastle to Hardwicke, 3 September 1755, Powis House, in Yorke, ed., *Hardwicke*, II, p. 243.
[48] Cited in Cardwell, *Arts and arms*, p. 23.
[49] Cited in Black, *Parliament and foreign policy*, p. 93.
[50] Cobbett XV, 15 December 1755, col. 664.

Prometheus, to that barren rock', that was Hanover.[51] In the same speech, Pitt told the House of Commons that Hanover was 'a place of such inconsiderable note that its name was not to be found in the map'.[52] At the same time, Pitt used the presence of the Hanoverians on British soil to highlight the failure of government policy and press for a popular militia instead. 'What an inglorious picture for this country', he remarked in May 1756, to see 'gentlemen driven by an invasion like a flock of sheep'.[53] In so doing, Pitt was able to borrow from a venerable anti-absolutist rhetoric in which the Hanoverian connection figured as a Trojan Horse for continental militarism and absolutism. Responding to Pitt's transparent bid for popularity, his great rival Henry Fox, secretary of state for the Southern Department, accused him of trying to make 'the fatal distinction ... of Englishman and Hanoverian'.[54]

Behind the rhetoric, however, lay a more-thoughtful and better-informed Pitt. He had already shown during the controversy over the imperial election scheme, that he was well aware of the constitution of the Holy Roman Empire.[55] Even as he expectorated in parliament on the Hanoverian connection, Pitt was corresponding civilly with his nephew Thomas Pitt in Cambridge on the subject of the Imperial Constitution. 'The book relating to the Empire of Germany', he wrote, 'is *Vitrarius's Jus Publicum* [*Institutiones Juris Publici selectissimae*] an admirable book in its kind, and esteemed of the best authority in matters much controverted.'[56] He also seems to have recommended the classic works by Pufendorf on the Holy Roman Empire.

In any case, Pitt's attempts to revive the anti-Hanoverian fervour of the mid-1740s and turn it to his immediate advantage, failed. As was to be expected in a House of Commons dominated by royal and governmental patronage, the treaties were passed by massive majorities. More remarkable was Pitt's inability to reignite public opinion.[57] According to Uriel Dann, his speeches of December 1755 were 'far beneath his inflammatory best'.[58] His dramatic reversal on the issue of Hanoverian troops had not been forgotten. In 1754, one satirist reminded Pitt of his earlier rhetoric and had him say 'Must I not expect to have the *name of*

---

[51] Cobbett XV, 11 May 1756, col. 704.
[52] Pitt speech of 17 May 1756, Cobbett, XV, col. 704.
[53] Cited in Yorke, ed., *Hardwicke*, II, p. 261.   [54] Cited in Black, *America or Europe*, p. 124.
[55] See Cobbett, XV, cols. 965–7.
[56] Pitt to Thomas Pitt, 13 January 1756, Horse Guards, in Taylor and Pringle, eds., *Chatham correspondence*, I, p. 152; and the reply: Thomas Pitt to Pitt, 12 October 1756. Clare Hall, in Taylor and Pringle, eds., *Chatham correspondence*, I, pp. 176–7, which mentions Pufendorf.
[57] See Cardwell, *Arts and arms*, p. 35.   [58] Dann, *Hanover and Great Britain*, p. 91.

Hanover resounded in my ears, as I once wished it might be branded on my forehead if ever I voted for the hire of the troops of the Electorate?'[59] Pitt's appeal was also blunted by the fact that the strategic case for the subsidy treaties and the deployment of the Hanoverians was compelling. His associate Thomas Potter reported gloomily in June 1756 that 'Hanover treaties and Hanover troops are popular throughout every county. The almost universal language is, opposition must be wrong, when we are ready to be eat up by the French.'[60]

In late 1756, Pitt made a last attempt to blow on the embers. One of the Hanoverian soldiers deployed in southern England was accused of the theft of a handkerchief and thrown into prison. He was released on the intercession of his Hanoverian commanding officer and that of the secretary of state for the North, Holdernesse. This incident, which seemed to imply some sort of legal extraterritoriality for the Hanoverians, caused public outrage. Pitt condemned the decision as 'the most atrocious act of power and the grossest attempt to dispense with the laws of England since the days of Lord Strafford'.[61] In this way, he was once again able to appeal to the enduring contemporary stereotype of the pilfering and absolutist Hanoverian. Indeed, one of Pitt's stated conditions for joining the administration in October 1756 was that Hessian and Hanoverian troops be placed under English law for civil offences.[62] In short, the whole incident allowed Pitt, as Middleton has pointed out, 'to exploit the intense chauvinism of eighteenth-century English society'.[63] When the Hanoverians were finally sent home at the close of the year, Pitt was quick to claim the credit.[64]

What Pitt's Hanoverian rhetoric could not do was return him to power. For this reason he was privately concerned not to burn all his boats with the ministry and the crown. The duke of Newcastle reported that Pitt 'talked with the greatest respect of Hanover; said he would take care, whatever he might do, not to let drop an unguarded expression with regard to Hanover', though he remained adamant that defending Hanover militarily was not practical.[65] He seems to have hinted that, as the younger

---

[59] See *The orator's political meditation* [1754], p. 20, cited in Cardwell, *Arts and arms*, p. 20.
[60] Thomas Potter to Pitt, 4 June 1756, Bath, in Taylor and Pringle, eds., *Chatham correspondence*, I, p. 161.
[61] Cited in J. C. D. Clark, *The dynamics of power*, p. 271.
[62] For Pitt's preoccupation with the affair of the Hanoverian soldier see Hardwicke's 'Relation of my conference with Mr Pitt', 24 October 1756, in Yorke, ed., *Hardwicke*, II, p. 278; Hardwicke to Newcastle, 6 December 1756, Powis House, in *ibid.*, pp. 376–7; Peters, *Pitt and popularity*, p. 61.
[63] Middleton, *Bells of victory*, p. 6.
[64] On this see Peters, *Pitt and popularity*, p. 66 and Cardwell, *Arts and arms*, pp. 167–8; 157.
[65] See Newcastle to Hardwicke, 3 September 1755, in Yorke, ed., *Hardwicke*, II, p. 240. See also the entry for 'September [1755]', in John Carswell and Lewis Arnold Dralle, eds., *The political journal of George Bubb Dodington* (Oxford, 1965), p. 322.

Horace Walpole recalled, 'Hanover might not lose all its friends' after he came to power.[66] Moreover, he was a confidant of the countess of Yarmouth, a naturalised Hanoverian who was the king's mistress.[67] The Pittite press now began to prepare the ground for a reversal on Hanover. As the *Con-Test* wrote in November 1756:

> An *accidental* and *immediate* exigency may render a regard for a *foreign* interest a probable security for the preservation of our own ... So that an alteration of principles, is so far from being a conclusive argument of inconsistency, that, on the contrary, it may be evidence of a steady attention to national benefit. A member of the legislative, therefore, ought not to be condemned for standing in opposition to the same measures, which he once earnestly patronized.[68]

Pitt now pulled off a delicate but highly successful balancing act. He would need to render himself privately less obnoxious on Hanover, while at the same time trading on his 'popularity' with the king and the ministry. His value to them lay in the patriotic credentials they lacked. As Earl Waldegrave told George, 'being thought an enemy to Hanover, was the solid foundation of Pitt's popularity'.[69] Paradoxically, therefore, Pitt was the only man who was able to satisfy royal concerns about the Electorate. This comes across in a remarkable exchange between the duke of Newcastle and the king, who resisted including Pitt in a new ministry, in October 1756. 'But Mr Pitt won't do my German business', objected George II. 'If he comes into your service Sir', Newcastle responded, 'he must be told he must do your Majesty's business.' The king remained sceptical: 'But I don't like Pitt: he won't do my business.' Newcastle simply repeated that 'But unfortunately, Sir, he is the only one [in the opposition] who has the ability to do the business.' He subsequently reflected that 'if the King could be assured that Pitt would do his business, I think he might be brought to take him in ... I think Pitt must come ... He will come as a *conqueror*. I always dreaded it. But I had rather be conquered by an enemy who can do our business.'[70]

The underlying dynamics here were not only complex but sometimes contradictory. In September 1755, for example, Pitt prevaricated on the question of the Hessian and Russian treaties, saying that 'he must know the sentiments of his friends; that if his own inclination should be to support the defence of Hanover this way (which he was far from saying

---

[66] Cited in Harding, 'Dynastic union in British and Hanoverian ideology', p. 261.
[67] Black, *Pitt*, p. 124.
[68] Cited in Harding, 'Dynastic union in British and Hanoverian ideology', p. 262.
[69] Clark, ed., *Memoirs and speeches of Earl Waldegrave*, p. 206.
[70] Newcastle to Hardwicke, 14 October 1756, Newcastle House, in Yorke, ed., *Hardwicke*, II, p. 323.

it would), yet he must have the concurrence of his friends'. Hardwicke's response was that 'I could not suffer myself to doubt but his opinion would have the deciding influence with his friends.'[71] Pitt, in other words, should act as a persuader on Hanover. A year later, Pitt said of opposition demands for an enquiry into the affair of the Hanoverian soldier 'That he would neither move nor instigate it, but somebody or other would do it: and if it was brought in, he could not help going along with it to a certain degree.'[72] Both exchanges are illustrative of Pitt's fabled 'popularity' on matters Hanoverian: he was at the same time in command of it, in thrall to it, and hiding behind it.

So when Pitt took office again in late 1756, he was committed not only to the continental policy against France, but also to the defence of Hanover. Almost the very first thing he had to do was to go before the Commons in February 1757 to ask for £200,000 to pay for an army of some 60,000 men in Germany.[73] This was couched in terms of the need to confront French designs 'against His Majesty's Electoral dominions and those of his good ally the King of Prussia'.[74] Crucially, however, Britain was committed to paying for the Hessians and some Prussians, but not for the Hanoverians, who were to be funded by the King out of his electoral revenues. The distinction was by no means a 'semantic' one:[75] Pitt had made good his promise to turn Hanover from a liability into a net contributor to the allied cause on the continent. Picking up his earlier rhetoric, he claimed to have transformed Hanover from a 'millstone' around Britain's neck to one around that of France.[76] Here Pitt was being perfectly sincere: his concern to mobilise Hanoverian resources to relieve the burden on Britain and put maximum pressure on France comes across very clearly in his correspondence with the commander of the army in Germany.[77]

To many at the time and since, however, Pitt's volte-face on Hanover in 1756–7 smacked of the most cynical opportunism. His new colleague Holdernesse observed in late November 1756 that Pitt's 'opinions upon foreign affairs now he is in office [were] exactly the same with mine, however different they were some time ago'.[78] One of Pitt's principal

---

[71] Hardwicke to Newcastle, 9 August 1755, Powis House, in Yorke, ed., *Hardwicke*, II, p. 232.
[72] As reported in Hardwicke to Newcastle, 6 December 1756, Powis House, in Yorke, ed., *Hardwicke*, II, pp. 376–7.
[73] See 'The king's message concerning an Army of Observation and the treaty with the king of Prussia', 17 February 1757, Cobbett, XV, cols. 782–3.
[74] *Ibid.*   [75] Pace Middleton, *Bells of victory*, p. 11.   [76] *Ibid.*
[77] See for example his draft of 'October 1759' to the Duke of Brunswick, PRO 30/8/90, fols. 81–5.
[78] Cited in Middleton, *Bells of victory*, p. 11.

scourges, *The Test*, wheeled on a 'baronet' to lampoon him: 'Zookers', he says, 'that won't look well from one, who proposed last year that a single shilling of money should never be sent to *Germany*.'[79] The *Monitor*, which had been, and would once again become, a staunch defender of Pitt, wondered whether 'he, who was adored for his upright professions, had veered about; deserted the cause of his country; adopted the German measures, was never sincere ... and only attentive to serve some private passion or interest in preference to his country'.[80] Henry Fox jeered that 'He had been told indeed that the German measures of last year would be a millstone about the neck of the minister. He hoped that this German measure would be an ornament about the minister's neck!'; this image resonated in contemporary pamphlets and prints.[81] Most crushingly of all, Earl Waldegrave remarked in June 1757 that Pitt's 'former violence against Hanover' would not be 'any kind of obstacle, as he had given frequent proofs that he could change sides whenever he found it necessary, and could deny his own words with an unembarras'd countenance'.[82]

In fact, Pitt had an acknowledged history of retractions, which did not start or end in 1756. Having been a scourge of Spain in the late 1730s Pitt, as the younger Horace Walpole observed in January 1751, 'recanted his having seconded the famous question for the *no* search ... said it was a mad and foolish notion, and that he was since grown ten years older and wiser'.[83] Eight years later he announced in another context that he had 'unlearned his juvenile errors, and thought no longer that England could do it all by herself'.[84] In any case, Pitt never denied his earlier anti-Hanoverian rhetoric, or that he had modified his policy. He replied to his critics in February 1757 'that he did not insist upon being literally and nominally consistent as long as he thought he was substantially so; that he never was against granting moderate sums of money to the support of a continent war as long as we did not squander it away by millions'.[85] Likewise his mouthpiece, *The Con-Test*, argued in defence of Pitt's 'consistency' that 'there is a wide difference, between our moral and political conduct. In the one, we may preserve uniformity in the means, as well as the end; in the other, the means will often appear to be inconsistent, though the end is uniform.'[86]

---

[79] *The Test*, 19 February 1757, p. 81. In the same vein see also 26 March 1757, pp. 112–13.
[80] Cited in Peters, *Popularity*, p. 85.
[81] See Cardwell, *Arts and arms*, p. 172 for quotation and further examples.
[82] See J. C. D. Clark, ed., *The memoirs and speeches of James, 2nd earl Waldegrave, 1742–1763* (Cambridge, 1988), p. 206.
[83] Cited in Black, *Pitt*, p. 84.   [84] Cited in Peters, *Pitt*, p. 105.
[85] Cited in Black, *Pitt*, p. 135.   [86] *Con-Test*, 2 July 1757, p. 195.

Moreover, whatever the rhetorical packaging, there was a coherence to Pitt's strategic thinking on Hanover. His real objection had always been to the subordination of British to Hanoverian interests, rather than the defence of the Electorate as such. Pitt even initially demanded the Northern secretaryship for himself; hardly the actions of a man determined to prosecute a colonial war, which fell within the purview of the Southern Secretary.[87] Since this would have involved Pitt in the day-to-day relations with Hanover, it was rejected by George II out of hand.

All the same, the issue of Hanover did put Pitt on the back foot politically and rhetorically at the beginning. His dilemma was summed up with a certain *Schadenfreude* by the younger Horace Walpole in November 1756: 'If he Hanoverizes, or checks any inquiries, he loses popularity, and falls that way: if he humours the present rage of the people, he provokes two powerful factions [Fox and Newcastle].'[88] But near the start of his administration Pitt was rescued by a stroke of good luck. His difficult relationship with the Commander of the Army of Observation, the duke of Cumberland, led to Pitt's brief sacking by George II in April 1757. He immediately turned this to his advantage by resuming his anti-Hanoverian rhetoric in parliament, and insinuating that he had been dropped because of his adherence to patriot principles on Hanover and the maritime policy.[89] George paid a price for this. The Sardinian envoy remarked in May 1757 that 'the anger of the people on the recent change of government has lessened the eagerness that some people had shown at the beginning of the season to help Hanover'.[90]

In the medium term, however, Pitt needed to devise various rhetorical, political and military strategies in order to vindicate his support for Hanover. One of his tactics was to blame Newcastle for pro-Hanoverian measures. As Stephen Cardwell has recently shown, popular prints and ballads largely accepted the argument that Pitt was the patriotic opponent of Hanover in cabinet against the courtly machinations of rival ministers.[91] Another strategem was Pitt's enthusiastic support for amphibious assaults against the French coast, which could not simply be dismissed as measures in support of Hanover.[92] If their true strategic rationale was to draw off French troops from Germany, and thus relieve Frederick the Great, these operations also appealed to a public opinion susceptible to displays of British naval virtue. The problem was that in the perfervid, Germanophobe atmosphere which Pitt had done so much to create, the

---

[87] Middleton, *Bells of victory*, p. 7.   [88] Cited in Peters, *Popularity*, p. 66.
[89] Ibid., pp. 75–6; Cardwell, *Arts and arms*, pp. 184–5.
[90] Cited in Black, *Pitt*, p. 140.   [91] See Cardwell, *Arts and arms*, p. 217, also p. 228.
[92] On this see Middleton, *Bells of victory*, p. 26.

failure of some of the attacks was attributed to Hanoverian machinations. Thus the failure to land troops at Rochefort was attributed to a nefarious ministerial scheme to secure better terms for the Hanoverian army at Kloster-Zeven.[93] His associate Thomas Potter reported in October 1757, that 'at Bristol, and all this country, the discontent at the sudden return of the fleet rises to a degree, and points to a place which makes me tremble ... The people ... will not be persuaded that this pacific disposition [the failure to attack Rochefort] was not a preliminary for the Convention of Stade'.[94] It is no coincidence that at around this time – October–November 1757 – the *Monitor* resumed its attacks on the Hanoverian connection.[95]

Yet another device was to distinguish between financial aid for the Hanoverian army and the dispatch of British ground troops, which Pitt opposed with contrived venom. One observer recalls him saying that 'He had never been against continental measures when practicable; but would not now send a drop of our blood to the Elbe, to be lost in that ocean of gore.'[96] He affected great outrage when the British envoy to Prussia passed on Frederick the Great's request for British troops. 'I find to my extreme concern', he wrote in January 1758, 'Mr Mitchell's letters so constantly in the same strain, with regard to sending British troops to reinforce the army in the Electorate.'[97] Two months later he rejected further demands for British troops on the grounds that 'he shall lose his credit, having promised the nation, that not a man should go out of the Kingdom on account of the connections of the Electorate'.[98] At the same time, Pitt was not above trading Tory support for Hanoverian subsidies in return for a commitment against the dispatch of British ground troops.[99]

But perhaps the most effective way of 'laundering' help for Hanover was by subsuming it into the prosecution of the continental war against France. As one of Pitt's correspondents observed, 'The bitter part of the pill is Hanover troops, the Sugar Plumb, the King of Prussia'.[100] This has been argued by Patrick Doran in his study of Anglo-Prussian relations during the Seven Years War.[101] Marie Peters takes much the same

---

[93] See Horace Walpole's remarks of 13 October 1757, cited in Taylor and Pringle, eds., *Chatham correspondence*, I, p. 281.
[94] Thomas Potter to Pitt, 11 October 1757, Bath, in Taylor and Pringle, eds., *Pitt correspondence*, I, p. 277.
[95] See Peters, *Pitt and popularity*, pp. 94–5.
[96] Cited in Peters, *Pitt and popularity*, p. 104.   [97] Cited in Black, *Pitt*, p. 158.
[98] As reported in d'Abreu to Wall, 3 March 1758, London, in Taylor and Pringle, eds, *Chatham correspondence*, I, p. 296.
[99] On this see Cardwell, *Arts and arms*, p. 222.   [100] Cited in Peters, *Popularity*, p. 109.
[101] See Patrick Francis Doran, *Andrew Mitchell and Anglo-Prussian diplomatic relations during the Seven Years War* (New York and London, 1986), especially pp. 126–7.

view: she stresses an extremely uneasy relationship between Pitt and his Tory mercantile supporters in the city for whom continental measures were bad enough, and Hanoverian ones complete anathema.[102] On this reading, to quote Jeremy Black, 'the Prussian alliance provided the possibility for bridging the traditional antithesis of pro-Hanoverian ministerial continental interventionism and "patriot" isolationism, a bridging that Pitt represented and helped to popularize'.[103]

This is certainly a very important part of the picture, but it does not quite capture the essence of Pitt's position. First of all, Pitt was never in any meaningful sense of the word, an 'isolationist'; he never occupied a middle or bridging position in much more than the rhetorical sense. Secondly, protecting Hanover and keeping her in the war was central to Pitt's strategy and not simply a sop to the king, which had to be concealed from a suspicious public. It is true that Pitt used the Prussian alliance to emulsify the Hanoverian commitment for public consumption, but that does not make the Electorate any less central to his strategy. This is demonstrated by Pitt's reaction to the convention of Kloster-Zeven in mid- to late 1757. A mixed British-funded Hanoverian force had been sent to the Electorate under the duke of Cumberland to defend it against the French. This heavily outnumbered 'Army of Observation' had been defeated at the battle of Hastenbeck. Shortly afterwards, Cumberland had concluded the convention of Kloster-Zeven with the French which stipulated the neutrality of Hanover.

If Pitt just wanted to be shot of Hanover, with the king's blessing, he had simply to acquiesce in the convention, concentrate on America and let things take their course between Frederick the Great and his enemies in central Europe.[104] He would not even have had to pay a monetary or territorial indemnity for its return at a peace agreement. Instead, as we shall see, Pitt insisted that neutrality was incompatible with British interests, and pledged increased help both for Frederick and the defence of the Electorate. Likewise, Pitt strongly disapproved of Hanoverian approaches to the Austrians in 1757 to work out some sort of neutrality arrangement, possibly including the transit of French troops to attack Prussia from the west; he condemned these as 'black machinations' of the

---

[102] Peters, *Pitt and popularity*, *passim*.
[103] Black, *America or Europe*, p. 153. See also the same phrase in Jeremy Black, 'The crown, Hanover and the shift in British foreign policy in the 1760s', in: Jeremy Black, ed., *Knights Errant and true Englishmen: British foreign policy, 1660–1800* (Edinburgh, 1989), p. 123. The same point is also made in Black, *Pitt*, p. 174; Black, *Parliament and foreign policy*, p. 94; and in Peters, *The elder Pitt*, p. 114.
[104] This point is made *en passant* in Black, *America or Europe*, p. 151, and in Doran, *Andrew Mitchell*, p. 112, though it is not developed.

Hanoverian ministers.[105] In other words, Pitt turned down two perfect opportunities to neutralise Hanover, wind up the continental commitment and confine himself to a maritime war.

To understand why this was so, why – as Henry Fox predicted with such bitter accuracy in September 1757 – 'those who were most against assisting the Electorate will be most angry at this neutrality',[106] one has to look back to the autumn of 1741. It will be remembered that George II had then concluded a similar agreement under French duress and had been forced to renounce it by Carteret. The reason then had been that George could not head a coalition against France as king, and call upon the powers of Europe to join him, while opting out of the struggle himself as elector. So it was also in 1757. The neutrality of the elector would cast doubt on the commitment of Britain itself. Terrified of being associated with the convention, Pitt insisted 'that the British ministers must, for the sake of their honour, disculpate themselves' and instruct their diplomats in Germany accordingly.[107] Coming to a separate arrangement with Vienna only added insult to injury. For Pitt argued that 'the application to the Court of Vienna was worse than to France. For that implied a *change of system*, by flinging off the King of Prussia and returning to the Queen of Hungary.'[108]

But there was another factor this time: the neutralisation of Hanover would immediately expose Prussia's western flank. As Newcastle reported in early August 1757, Pitt's response to Kloster-Zeven was largely couched in terms of its effect on Frederick, who might be given the impression that he was about to be abandoned by Britain.[109] 'Mr Pitt', Newcastle reported, 'was much alarmed at the effect this would have upon the King of Prussia and declared his opinion that we should forthwith send him most large offers of money in order to engage him to continue in his present system, and not to make peace, or at least not to give him a pretence to say that he abandoned by England.' Pitt feared that 'when the King has made his peace as Elector ... it will be impossible for the King of Prussia, attacked on all sides, to stand out alone. The army of observation, which will now be dissolved, was the only

---

[105] Cited in Peters, *Pitt*, pp. 89. On this see also Yorke, ed., *Hardwicke*, III, pp. 172–3; Allen, 'The Anglo-Hanoverian connection', pp. 234, 251, 256.
[106] Cited in Black, *Pitt*, p. 169.
[107] As reported in Newcastle to Hardwicke, 10 September 1757, in Yorke, ed., *Hardwicke*, III, p. 173.
[108] As reported in Newcastle to Hardwicke, 10 September 1757, Claremont, in Yorke, ed., *Hardwicke*, III, p. 174.
[109] As reported in Newcastle to Hardwicke, Newcastle House, 3 August 1757, in Yorke, ed., *Hardwicke*, III, p. 161.

Pitt and Hanover

barrier for the King of Prussia's country on that side.' If Prussia was to be kept in the war, so must Hanover.

Here Pitt was absolutely right. The British envoy to Prussia, Andrew Mitchell, repeatedly noted Frederick's suspicion of the clandestine overtures to Austria, and his fury at the convention of Kloster-Zeven.[110] Even more worrying, Frederick's wrath began to extend beyond the king's Hanoverian servants to the British ministry itself, and by mid-October Mitchell noted that 'I cannot help suspecting that the King of Prussia is treating.' So at a meeting in early October 1757, at which Münchhausen was in attendance, the ministry agreed to encourage the King – tactfully – to break the treaty, by offering to pay for Hanoverian troops 'from the day that they shall recommence the operations of war, against the forces of France, in concert with the King of Prussia'.[111] This would add to the total number of troops fighting France without, in the first instance, committing British forces. Indeed, Pitt told Frederick that he should content himself with the Hanoverians, Hessians and Brunswickers 'which would not be on foot but for the sake of assisting that Prince, since the Elector would otherwise have made a neutrality from the beginning with France'.[112]

The logical upshot of Pitt's Hanoverian policy was a huge and politically unpopular increase in expenditure. As the head of the German Chancery in London, Philipp von Münchhausen pointed out in a paper of early August 1757, 'if England wishes that the King – as Elector – continues the struggle it will be necessary for her to find the means'.[113] Britain would now have to support a force of 38,000 men from Hanover, Hesse-Kassel, Saxony-Gotha, Brunswick and Wolfenbüttel.[114] Pitt was perfectly prepared to pay[115] – he spoke of the need to 'depart from the rigidness of our [previous] declarations'[116] – but

---

[110] See Bisset, ed., *Memoirs and papers of Sir Andrew Mitchell*, I, 'Journal' entries for 30 August 1757 (p. 366), 19 September 1757 (pp. 371–2), 11 October 1757 (p. 377), 20 October 1757 (p. 378).

[111] 'Minute of meeting at Sir Conyers d'Arcy's lodgings, 7 October 1757', attended by the Lord President, duke of Newcastle, earl of Holdernese, Lord Anson, Lord Mansfield, Mr Secretary Pitt, Sir John Ligonier, and Baron Münchhausen, PRO 30/8/89, fol. 52.

[112] See his reported remarks in the intercepted dispatch of d'Abreu to Wall, 3 March 1758, in Taylor and Pringle, eds., *Chatham correspondence*, I, p. 296.

[113] 'Papier donnée par Mo. De Munchhausen, 5 August 1757' in BL Add. Mss. 35417, fol. 21.

[114] On this see Tony Hayter, 'England, Hannover, Preussen. Gesellschaftliche und wirtschaftliche Grundlagen der britischen Beteiligung an Operationen auf dem Kontinent während des Siebenjährigen Krieges', in: Bernhard R. Kroener, ed., *Europa im Zeitalter Friedrichs des Grossen. Wirtschaft, Gesellschaft, Krieg* (Munich, 1989), p. 178.

[115] See Middleton, *Bells of victory*, p. 31.   [116] Cited in Peters, *The elder Pitt*, p. 89.

only if the Hanoverians actually pulled their weight.[117] As Newcastle reported in early October 1757, 'Mr Pitt is strongly for ... sending an order' to the Hanoverian commander 'to fall upon the French immediately ... Mr Pitt declares against giving ... [a] single farthing from hence till the troops are in activity.'[118] Pitt's sense of relief once the Hanoverian army was back in action was palpable. On the first day of December 1757, he wrote to his wife that 'The army of observation was before Harburg, on the Elbe, and operations actually begun'.[119]

At the same time, Pitt knew that if the protection of Hanover would be domestically difficult for him, it would cause nothing like the storm of the Electorate dropping out of the war. He therefore spent the final months of 1757 trying to ensure that some mention would be made of breaking the convention in the king's speech to Parliament.[120] The king's mistress, Lady Yarmouth, found that 'Mr Pitt puts the whole upon it [breaking the convention], and lays it down for certain that the convention will be talked of in parliament, and that what are the King's ministers to say if it is not broke? Are they to sit quiet and say nothing? He wants to have the merit of breaking it.' Newcastle himself found Pitt similarly preoccupied. 'I find He [Pitt] thinks the convention will be a matter of Debate. I am afraid it will; and there will be our sore place.'[121] In the event, the message of the speech came across clearly enough: it was now Britain, not Hanover which was firmly in charge of the continental war. The Bavarian envoy immediately picked up the implications of George's assurance that he would, henceforth, never undertake anything on behalf of his German dominions, which would harm the common cause. 'The system', he concluded, 'is now completely changed. It has today become that of England.'[122]

In short, throughout the middle stages of the Seven Years War, the Hanoverian connection was not something which disrupted his continental policy or which that policy helped to disguise. It was in fact central to Pitt's whole war strategy. For this reason Pitt passed up several opportunities to make political capital out of Hanover. He did toy with blaming

---

[117] See Middleton, *Bells of victory*, p. 38.
[118] Newcastle to Hardwicke, Kensington, 3 October 1757, in Yorke, ed., *Hardwicke*, III, p. 185 and Add. Mss. 35417, fols. 82–3. The last clause is not in the printed version.
[119] Pitt to Lady Hester Pitt, 1 December, in Taylor and Pringle, eds., *Chatham correspondence*, II, p. 2.
[120] See (copy) Newcastle to Hardwicke, Claremont, 5 November 1757, BL Add. Mss. 32875, fols. 391–2 (not in printed version).
[121] Newcastle to Hardwicke, Claremont, 5 November 1757, in Yorke, ed., *Hardwicke*, III, p. 194.
[122] See the intercepted dispatch from Haslang to Comte Preysing, 2 December 1757, London, PRO 30/8/89, fol. 58.

the Electorate for the fiasco at Rochefort: Chesterfield reported that 'Mr Pitt is convinced that the principal wheel, or if you will, *spoke* in the wheel, came from Stade [i.e. Hanover].'[123] But he very soon decided to 'clear the King and his ministers of having any Hand in preventing the expedition on account of apprehension of Hanover'.[124] Pitt did not indulge British generals who felt slighted by the Hanoverians. One of these was the duke of Marlborough, to whom the appointment of a General Sporcken over his head was evidence 'of the English being thought fit for nothing, but to be cleavers of wood and drawers of water to the Hanoverians'.[125] Perhaps even more remarkably, Pitt did not take up the cause of Lord George Sackville, the most senior British officer at the battle of Minden in 1759, whom the duke of Brunswick had all but accused of cowardice.[126] Both men belonged to the oppositional Leicester House nexus and had been on good terms;[127] it would have been natural for Pitt to champion Sackville against the 'German interest', as some of the press did, and his failure to do so certainly cost him some popular support.[128] Finally, Pitt ignored the allegations of the British envoy to Prussia, with whom his relationship was in any case rather strained, that the Hanoverian representative in London, Münchhausen, was trying to undermine him there.[129] In short, Pitt dealt far more effectively with the same minefield of personal ambition and national sensitivities, which had so bedevilled the deployment of the 'Pragmatic Army' in the 1740s.

The dispatch of British regular infantry to Northern Germany in 1758 – in violation of earlier promises – broke the final taboo. The *Gazetteer* remarked that most people had no objection to subsidising the Prussians, but would 'repine at the sending of forces to Germany, because they imagine it is done for the sake of Hanover, and fancy they perceive something unconstitutional in it'.[130] Tory critics in parliament, such as

---

[123] See Peters, *Pitt and popularity*, pp. 96–7; and Chesterfield's comments of 4 November 1757 in Taylor and Pringle, eds., *Chatham correspondence*, I, p. 279.
[124] As reported in (copy) Newcastle to Hardwicke, 5 November 1757, Claremont, Add. Mss. 32875, fol. 391.
[125] Duke of Marlborough to Pitt, 18 August 1758, Coesveldt, in Taylor and Pringle, eds., *Chatham correspondence*, I, p. 338.
[126] For evidence of Pitt's disdain for Sackville after Minden see Pitt to Lady Hester Pitt, 19 November 1759, in Taylor and Pringle, eds., *Chatham correspondence*, I, p. 458.
[127] See Middleton, *Bells of victory*, p. 131.   [128] See Peters, *Popularity*, p. 149.
[129] See Dann, *Hanover and Great Britain*, p. 106. For Pitt's stance towards Mitchell see Yorke, ed., *Hardwicke*, III, p. 198, where he accuses the envoy of being pro-Hanoverian, Taylor and Pringle, eds., *Chatham correspondence*, I, p. 375; and Doran, *Andrew Mitchell*, *passim*. For the Mitchellite view see Bisset, ed., I, pp. 162, 164–5.
[130] Cited in Peters, *Popularity*, p. 119.

Sir John Philipps, accused Pitt of 'Hanoverizing'.[131] Journals close to Pitt, such as the previously anti-Hanoverian *Monitor*, solved the problem by criticising the deployment, but simply denying that Pitt was responsible for the decision to send troops to Germany.[132] As Newcastle warned one correspondent in July 1758, 'If you hear that Mr Pitt was against sending these troops abroad, it is entirely false. Nobody was more forward than himself and three regiments were added whilst I was at Cambridge, without my knowledge, tho' greatly with my approbation.'[133]

At the same time, Pitt was not above leveraging the Hanoverian connection to his domestic advantage. Once again Pitt pulled off a complex balancing act. On the one hand, he vigorously supported the agitation for a Habeas Corpus and a Militia Bill in April–May 1758 in order to reconcile oppositional Tories to the Prussian subsidies he was putting before parliament.[134] On the other hand, Pitt let it be known to the king – via Lady Yarmouth – that if Habeas Corpus were passed he would show his gratitude with respect to Hanover. Newcastle remarked that 'it is not a pleasant thing to have the King told that every measure, that his Majesty can wish (and it will certainly go to further offers for the support of Prince Ferdinand's army and perhaps future *dedommagement* [i.e. territorial gains for Hanover]), shall be granted, if a bill, disliked and opposed by particular persons in the King's service, could be *let* pass'.[135] It is therefore far from clear whether Pitt supported Habeas Corpus in order to distract from his continental policy, or whether he supported Hanover measures in order to win concessions from the crown over Habeas Corpus.

For most of 1758–9, however, Hanover receded as an issue. From late 1758, London was electrified by the news of victories across the globe: in Europe, India and, particularly, North America. Pitt's strategy was comprehensively vindicated. Throughout this period, Pitt enjoyed a popular and parliamentary honeymoon. Horace Walpole noted that 'Parliament is all harmony: Pitt provoked, called for, defied objections: promised enormous expence, demanded never to be judged by events. Universal silence left him arbiter of his own terms. In short, at present he is absolute master, and if he can coin twenty millions, may command them.'[136] When the House approved the once-contentious Prussian and Hessian subsidies in January 1759, the earl of Chesterfield observed that 'This is Mr Pitt's doing, and it is marvellous in our eyes. He declares only what he

---

[131] Cited in Cardwell, *Arts and arms*, p. 241.
[132] See Peters, *Popularity*, p. 118 and p. 123.
[133] (Copy) Newcastle to Henry Campion, 15 July 1758, in BL Add. Mss. 32881, fol. 335.
[134] See Peters, *Popularity*, pp. 106–7, 109.
[135] Newcastle to Hardwicke, 21 May 1758, Claremont, in Yorke, ed., *Hardwicke*, III, p. 50.
[136] Cited in Taylor and Pringle, eds., *Chatham correspondence*, I, p. 375.

would have them do, and they do it.'[137] By the end of the year, observers were noting that even the King seemed reconciled to Pitt on account of his support for 'German measures'.[138]

This truce did not last. Hanover returned to the agenda from late 1759, when the question of a negotiated peace was being discussed. Here again, Pitt's stance should be seen in classic Whig 'continentalist' terms. He was concerned, of course, to hold on to as much of Britain's colonial gains as possible. But he was adamant that Britain should not abandon her continental ally, Prussia, and thus risk another 'Utrecht', or simply cut Hanover adrift. Indeed, he believed that Hanover, whether it fell back into French hands or not, would have to be restored in full. In December 1758 he insisted that 'he would not give up an iota of our allies for any British consideration';[139] to that extent, the press voices which suspected him of being prepared to trade Louisburg for Hanover or some other consideration, were not entirely wide of the mark.[140]

What Pitt was determined to prevent was George's demand, that Hanover be enlarged in order to compensate her for sacrifices made during the war.[141] The request was not in itself unreasonable. After all, as Münchhausen pointed out in late November 1758, the monies voted by parliament were not sufficient to pay for Hanoverian troops and the continental effort generally and had to be supplemented from George's electoral funds. The king, he said, would be happy to agree to the proposed increases 'in the hope that this would be a further argument for exploring at the appropriate point and place, the possibility of compensating him in one way or the other in his capacity as Elector'.[142] Indeed, Hanoverian demands for territorial gains went back at least to late June 1758, almost as soon as the military tide on the continent had begun to turn.[143]

Pitt, however, as one observer remarked, 'talked *against all dedommagements* [underlined in the original]'.[144] To aggrandise Hanover would

---

[137] *Ibid.*, p. 401.   [138] See Peters, *Popularity*, p. 153.
[139] Cited in Harding, 'Dynastic union in British and Hanoverian ideology', p. 292.
[140] See *Examination of a letter* [November 1758] cited in Peters, *Popularity*, p. 128; and Harding, 'Dynastic union in British and Hanoverian ideology', pp. 292–3.
[141] On George's demand for the enlargement of Hanover see Newcastle to Hardwicke, 5 October 1758, Kensington, in Yorke, ed., *Hardwicke*, III, p. 230; Newcastle to Hardwicke, 16 November 1759, in Yorke, ed., *Hardwicke*, III, p. 91.
[142] Memorandum by Münchhausen, 21 November 1758, London, PRO 30/8/89, fol. 325.
[143] On this see Mitchell's journals, and Frederick's acerbic comments: Bisset, ed., *Memoirs and papers of Sir Andrew Mitchell*: journal entries for 25 June 1757 (I, p. 31) and 2 July 1757 (p. 35).
[144] (Copy) Newcastle to Hardwicke, 15 October 1759, Newcastle House, Add. Mss. 32897, fol. 90 (not in Yorke, ed., *Hardwicke*, III, p. 238).

reduce the chances of a peace with France and pose political problems for Pitt with patriot opinion.[145] In this context Pitt remarked that

> he knew very well he was thought to be governed by popularity, that he knew where to stop that to a degree, it was true, but only to a degree; that he hazarded, he might lose his popularity to a degree by the immense sums given for the support of the war upon the continent and the King's Hanover dominions; that he thought it right, and so far he risked his popularity, but then he had the comfort to think that people would see that that was done for the sake of the whole, and not to aggrandize or promote any acquisition for Hanover.[146]

This exchange sums up the complex balance between strategic thinking and sensitivity to public opinion in Pitt's policy towards Hanover.

As a result old tensions with the king quickly resurfaced. The earl of Kinnoull, chancellor of the duchy of Lancaster and confidant of Hardwicke, reported in October 1759 that 'I cannot help thinking that the King wants to get rid of Mr Pitt. His attention is now fixed upon one object in the *dedommagement*. He knows Pitt's sentiments, which he has fairly &, as your Grace truly says, honestly declared. His Majesty knows too his firmness & despairs of shaking him.'[147] Once again, Pitt tried to use the king's Hanoverian preoccupations to secure domestic concessions, in this case the conferral of the Order of the Garter on his crony, Lord Temple. 'The view', Hardwicke observed, 'is to make a *querrelle d'Allemagne*, in order to help towards gaining the main point', of the Garter.[148]

By 1760, Pitt was back on the defensive over Hanover. The appearance of Israel Mauduit's pamphlet *Considerations on the present German war* [1760] crystallised a long-simmering unease with the continental commitment.[149] Mauduit advanced no new argument, or evidence, but his case had never before been so persuasively argued.[150] The bitter debates of 1757 now blazed with renewed heat. In early 1761, one critic, surely mimicking Pitt's own attack on Carteret, condemned 'the German War and the German minister Mr Pitt'.[151] Once again Pitt was harried by those who accused him of toadying to the crown over Hanover, and some

---

[145] Middleton, *Bells of victory*, p. 142.
[146] As reported in Newcastle to Hardwicke, 31 October 1759, Claremont, in Yorke, ed., *Hardwicke*, III, pp. 241–2.
[147] Earl of Kinnoull to Hardwicke, Brodsworth, 30 October 1759, in Add. Mss. 32897, fol. 500.
[148] See Hardwicke to Newcastle, 28 October 1759, in Yorke, ed., *Hardwicke*, III, p. 75.
[149] [Israel Mauduit], *Considerations on the present German war* (London, 1760).
[150] See Karl Schweizer, 'Israel Mauduit: pamphleteering and foreign policy in the age of the Elder Pitt', in: Stephen Taylor, Richard Connors and Clyve Jones, eds., *Hanoverian Britain and empire. Essays in memory of Philip Lawson* (Woodbridge, 1998), pp. 198–209.
[151] Cited in Peters, *Popularity*, p. 191.

Pitt and Hanover

even accused him of supporting the creation of a militia in order to release regulars for service in Hanover.[152] Pitt made some concessions to the new mood. He told the duke of Newcastle in April 1761 that 'he would make war to save or regain Hanover, or rather continue, but he would never consent to give up the acquisitions that he thought necessary for this country to keep for the sake of Hanover'.[153]

By and large, however, Pitt stood by his commitment to the Electorate and the continental policy. In 1760 he supported the dispatch of still more troops to Hanover, to repel another French attack, ostensibly in order to avoid having to exchange it for colonial possessions at the peace negotiations.[154] He remained a staunch supporter of the duke of Brunswick, whom he congratulated '*comme Anglois*' and in the name of all England, on his victories.[155] At the same time, Pitt sought to limit the resulting domestic political clamour by pinning the responsibility for British troop deployments on Hardwicke and Newcastle. As Hardwicke observed of Pitt's machinations in April 1760, 'it is amazing to me that, considering how much depends upon the events of this campaign in Germany, he should not even propose the sending of some British infantry to that country. Perhaps he wants to be ravished to it.'[156]

In other ways, Pitt was quite open in his concern for Hanover. During the negotiations of 1761, for example, Pitt wanted clarified whether the French offer of *Uti possedetis* – that is of making peace on the basis of existing territorial control – included Hanover.[157] He also offered the French Guadeloupe and Martinique in return for the evacuation of the Hanoverian university city of Göttingen. This was a particularly significant gesture, as the sugar islands were regarded as highly lucrative. Indeed, there was a public controversy in Britain during the peace negotiations over whether Guadeloupe or Canada should be retained, which was only narrowly decided in favour of the latter.

Pitt's solicitude for Hanover after 1760 is the more remarkable for the fact that it was in the face of the new king's initial hostility, or at least indifference towards the Electorate.[158] Thus when the French envoy

---

[152] *Ibid.*, pp. 223, 225.
[153] Cited in Harding, 'Dynastic union in British and Hanoverian ideology', p. 306.
[154] Black, *Pitt*, p. 197.
[155] Pitt to Brunswick, 19 February 1760, Whitehall, NHStH, Hann 9e Nr. 1098, fol. 49.
[156] See Hardwicke to Newcastle, 10 April 1760, Moor Park, in Yorke, ed., *Hardwicke*, III, p. 245.
[157] Middleton, *Bells of victory*, p. 185.
[158] See Jeremy Black's seminal article 'The crown, Hanover and the shift in British foreign policy in the 1760s', in: Jeremy Black, ed., *Knights Errant and true Englishmen. British foreign policy, 1660–1800* (Edinburgh, 1989), pp. 113–34; and Middleton, *Bells of victory*, p. 183.

Bussy demanded compensation for recent French gains in Hanover, Pitt informed him that while this might have made a difference under George II, it cut no ice with his successor.[159] Indeed, during the first two years of George III's reign one can fairly say that Pitt had become more electoral than the elector himself. His perceived partiality to the Electorate and the German war was now – in an ironic reversal – held against him by the monarch.[160] It was the dynasty which had changed, not Pitt. The simultaneous withdrawal of public and royal support undermined the German war and thus Pitt's own position. As Stephen Cardwell has pointed out, it wrecked the old strategy of blaming the court or the ministry for pro-Hanoverian measures.[161] It was typical that Pitt should have resigned in 1761 over the failure to launch a pre-emptive strike on Spain. This allowed him to advertise his patriot credentials, even as his real quarrel was about Germany.

III

After his resignation, Pitt defended his German and Hanoverian policy at some length in his speech of 9 December 1761.[162] At the beginning of the speech, he reminded his listeners of the 'original cause of our present connections in Germany' in 1755–6. At that time, Newcastle, fearing a French attempt to indemnify themselves in Hanover for losses in America, had sought to protect Hanover through subsidy treaties. 'I remember that I opposed this measure', he claimed, 'and I did upon this principle: that the forwardness of this house to engage itself to defend the electoral dominions would bring on the invasion of them as a certain consequence', by 'making them appear of importance'. The problem with ministerial thinking, he argued, was that 'their whole thoughts seemed to be turned to the preservation of the electorate'. In other words, the strategy was back to front: it put Hanoverian interests – narrowly conceived – before British ones, and was counter-productive to boot. For good measure Pitt added that 'whoever preferred Hanover to England, he would pursue that gentleman to the last'.[163]

Pitt then went on to argue, implausibly, that he had simply inherited the commitment to Hanover and a continental war. 'When I had the

---

[159] Black, *Pitt*, pp. 209–10.
[160] On this see Harding, 'Dynastic union in British and Hanoverian ideology', p. 286.
[161] Cardwell, *Arts and arms*, p. 258.
[162] Schweizer, 'An unpublished parliamentary speech', pp. 98–105. There is also a brief account of the speech in Newcastle to Devonshire, 9 December 1761, Newcastle House, BL Add. Mss. 32923, fol. 81, which contains some details not in the Schweizer version.
[163] As reported in Newcastle to Devonshire, 9 December 1761, Newcastle House, BL Add. Mss. 32932, fol. 81.

honor to be called upon by the highest authority to bear a share in His Majesty's councils, it was my opinion that we being once engaged in the German war, there was nothing to be done but to make the best of it after the principal objects of this country should be provided for.' To do otherwise would have required George II to break his word. Hence

> It was impossible to get clear of the embarrassment we were in from our continental engagements and nothing remained in common prudence but to try to turn an evil as much as possible into a good: the point there was to consider whether it was not possible to make the German war useful to the interests of this country as a subordinate measure, while our marine and colonies should be the principal object.

This oddly apologetic attempt to dissociate himself from the German war should be seen as a gesture towards his popular anti-Hanoverian constituency; it need not be taken too seriously. After all, Pitt had flatly refused to allow Hanover to withdraw from the war after the convention of Kloster-Zeven in 1757.

Moreover, Pitt then immediately proceeded to have it both ways. From being the unwilling executor of an inherited policy, he portrayed himself as the advocate of a continental diversion against France. It was then that he elaborated his famous claim of the previous month that 'Had the armies of France not been employed in Germany, they would have been transported to America ... America had been conquered in Germany.'[164] 'However inconvenient and expensive the German war is for England', he now argued, 'it is more inconvenient and more expensive for France.' Pitt, in fact, portrayed himself very much in the traditional mould of Whig continentalism. 'I always thought and shall always think, that England is not a match for France singlehanded in Europe.' Pitt then went on to say that

> Whenever you leave France to do whatever she pleases upon the continent, you will leave her hands at liberty and then an invasion of this country may be no chimerical project. All the world knows how soon France established a very formidable marine in the time of Louis XIV. She may as readily re-establish that which she has now lost when she shall be at liberty to employ all her measures and men for that purpose.

This is, of course, merely a variant on Newcastle's famous 1749 dictum that France would overawe Britain at sea if she were not distracted by Britain's allies on the continent.[165]

---

[164] Cited in Middleton, *Bells of victory*, p. 148.
[165] See Paul Langford, *The eighteenth century, 1688–1815* (London, 1976), p. 141.

Crucial here is the central role played by Hanover in a continental strategy. It functioned as a bait to draw off French power on the continent, and a breakwater for Britain's principal ally Prussia. Pitt noted that

> France has beat herself in vain against the rock of Germany; she has found a resistance there that has exhausted her strength and she has been more shocked at the patience and magnanimity of His late Majesty than by the victories of his fleets and armies in the Asiatic and American world. Too much cannot be said of that greatness of soul and generosity towards this country which induced his late Majesty to expose his native land and patrimony and his unhappy Hanoverian subjects to the fury of a vengeful enemy for this country. How natural would be thought the desire to preserve them were any of us to put ourselves in the same situation.[166]

The truth, of course, is that George tried twice 1741 and 1757 to do just that, but British ministers would not let him.

Wrapped up in more navalist rhetoric – 'our marine and colonies should be the principal object' – are further pointers to Pitt's German and Hanoverian policy. He noted George III's indifference towards the Electorate and 'truly British' dispositions and suggested that 'he would, for the sake of England, intirely relinquish his Hanoverians dominions, were it the opinion of those who have the honour to advise him that it would be for the real and lasting interests of Great Britain to cease to have any power in the [German] Empire, any influence upon the continent'. In other words, Pitt was affirming the importance of Hanover as a British outpost on the continent and a strategic asset.

Pitt – by then Earl of Chatham – returned to the subject of Hanover in the entirely different context of the American War after 1775.[167] Reverting to his earlier rhetoric Pitt made a number of anti-German and anti-Hanoverian comments in the House of Lords. These were intended to contrast the patriotic virtue of the colonist with the un-British absolutist pretensions of Lord North and George III who had had to resort to foreign mercenaries in order to pursue the war against the American colonists. In late May 1777 he accused the government of 'ransack[ing] every corner of Lower Saxony; but 40,000 German boors never can conquer ten times that number of British freemen'.[168] Pitt then went on to ridicule the government for being 'at the mercy of every little German chancery'.[169] He returned to this theme when he spoke of 'traffic and barter with every little pitiful German prince', adding that 'Our

---

[166] Cited in Schweizer, 'An unpublished parliamentary speech', p. 101.
[167] The Hanoverian dimension to his speeches on America is not discussed in Thomas, ' "The Great Commoner" ', pp. 161–2.
[168] Cobbett, XIX, 30 May 1777, cols. 316–17. [169] Ibid., col. 318.

ministers have made alliances at the German shambles.'[170] The immediate target were the Hessians, but the Hanoverians did not escape. 'Gibraltar is garrisoned by Hanoverians', Pitt observed. 'I am told, if any accident should happen to the present commanding officer there, that the care of the fortress, and the command of the troops would devolve on a foreigner',[171] whose name he affected to forget.

A few months later, Pitt returned to these themes with even greater vigour: 'We had', he said, 'swept every corner of Germany for men: we had searched the darkest wilds of America for the scalping knife. [but] ... peace ... would never be effected, as long as the German bayonet and Indian scalping-knife were threatened to be buried in the bowels of our American brethren.'[172] Soon after he demanded that government should 'conciliate to gain the confidence of those who have survived the Indian tomahawk, and the German bayonet'.[173] None of this would have been out of place in one of Pitt's diatribes from the early 1740s. It is worth remembering, however, that the context in which this reversion to populism took place, was Pitt's overriding concern to conciliate the American colonists in order to concentrate on the increasing threat from Bourbon France.

*

To sum up. The study of Pitt and Hanover shows how attacks on the Hanoverian connection could be used to burnish patriotic credentials and court 'popularity'. It shows how Pitt used Hanover to torment George when in opposition, and to build bridges to him when about to enter government or in office itself. It shows how Hanover could be used to undermine political rivals, especially Carteret. But most of all, the study of Pitt and Hanover casts new light on his foreign policy, which was even more continentalist and less colonial than recent reassessments have allowed. At the same time, there was a coherence to his strategic thinking which recent revisionists have tended to downplay. Pitt was, in short, and to quote his own words, perhaps not 'literally and nominally consistent' but certainly 'substantially so'.

---

[170] Cobbett, XIX, 18 November 1777, cols. 363, 371.
[171] Cobbett, XIX, 2 December 1777, col. 476.
[172] Cobbett, XIX, 5 December 1777, col. 489.
[173] Cobbett, XIX, 11 December 1777, col. 601.

4   George III and Hanover

Torsten Riotte

Every historian dealing with George III's relationship with Hanover will sooner or later address the letter George, as a young prince, wrote to his mentor and 'dearest friend' John Stuart, Earl Bute on 5 August 1759. In a short note to Bute the future monarch commented on the policies of his grandfather, the reigning King George II, and the latter's conduct of what would become the Seven Years War. The young prince showed little understanding for what he thought to be his grandfather's favouritism towards Hanover. Writing on the military affairs in the North of Germany he referred to the king's German dominions as 'that horrid Electorate that has always lived upon the very vitals of our poor country'.[1] In the light of this emotional statement it appears a convincing argument that with the accession of George III in 1760 the relationship between the monarch and the Electorate of Hanover changed fundamentally.

A radical change in the importance of the dynastic union after 1760 seemed even more convincing due to George III's emphasis on his British origins. As the monarch stated when opening the first parliamentary session of his reign in 1761 he saw himself as genuinely British: 'Born and educated in this country I glory in the name of Britain.'[2] The majority of historians have accepted this statement as the core of George III's political beliefs and as an argument against the importance of the dynastic union under the third Hanoverian. Peter D. G. Thomas writes: 'With the accession of George III the Hanover factor disappeared.'[3] Very similarly, Uriel Dann comments about the new king: 'Whatever George III's obligation to Hanover, he was English, and the relations between the two countries would never be the same thereafter.'[4] Dann continues:

---

[1] George III to Lord Bute, 5 August 1759, in Romney Sedgwick, ed., *Letters from George III to Lord Bute, 1756–1766* (London, 1939), No. 36 (from now on quoted as: Bute).
[2] Quoted in John Brooke, *George III* (London, 1972), pp. 88, 301–2 and Christopher Hibbert, *George III – a personal history* (London, 1999), p. 77.
[3] Peter D. G. Thomas, *George III: king and politicians 1760–1770* (Manchester, 2002), p. 33.
[4] Uriel Dann, *Hanover and Great Britain 1740–1760* (Leicester, 1991), p. 146.

'George III could no longer be regarded as "Hanoverian" in a politically significant sense.'[5] Likewise, Jeremy Black sees George III as 'hostile to Electoral considerations'.[6] British historians almost unequivocally agree on George III's lack of interest towards, not to say dislike of, Hanover. Only a very small number of historians, amongst them Tim Blanning, Hamish Scott, Brendan Simms, and most recently Grayson Ditchfield, have questioned whether George III's attitude towards Germany is adequately described in historiography and have pointed towards the monarch's interest in German affairs.[7] However, even the latter group remains somewhat obscure in its conclusions. Brendan Simms writes about George III's political role in 1806: 'It was only at a moment of external crisis and domestic instability that the king could briefly come into his own.'[8] Focusing on the Hanoverian minister in London, Simms sees George III as part of a Hanoverian faction but not as an active player. He concludes: 'This is a far cry certainly from the emasculated monarch of a long-dead Whig historiography, but it is not the same as the powerful George III of an ancien régime Britain either.'[9] Hamish Scott makes some very important observations on George III's concerns for Hanover during the War of the Bavarian Succession but he does not discuss the issue extensively, simply stating that more research was needed on the Hanoverian influence on British foreign policy.[10] No British historian, perhaps with the exception of Tim Blanning in his analysis of the *Fürstenbund*, has attempted to put George III and his interest in the German Electorate back into the political narrative of British history.

Like most of their British colleagues German historians emphasised the changes under the third Hanoverian. For example, Hermann Wellenreuther writes that for Hanover the dynastic union became, 'a purely formal connection' after 1760, and, in Wellenreuther's interpretation, George III was little more to Hanover than a representative who was never present in the Electorate during his entire reign.[11] Karl Otmar von Aretin describes George III as indifferent towards the

---

[5] Dann, *Britain and Hanover*, p. 55.
[6] Jeremy Black, *America or Europe? British foreign policy 1739–63* (London, 1998), p. 101.
[7] Grayson Ditchfield, *George III: an essay in monarchy* (Basingstoke, 2002), p. 23.
[8] Brendan Simms, ' "An odd question enough". Charles James Fox, the crown and British policy during the Hanoverian crisis of 1806', *Historical Journal* 38, 3 (1995), 596.
[9] *Ibid.*
[10] Hamish M. Scott, *British foreign policy in the age of the American revolution* (Oxford, 1990), p. 270.
[11] Hermann Wellenreuther, 'Die Bedeutung des Siebenjährigen Krieges für die englisch-hannoveranischen Beziehungen', in Adolf M. Birke and Kurt Kluxen, eds., *Britain and Hanover* (Munich, 1991), p. 172.

constitution of the Holy Roman Empire while pursuing a 'destructive Reich policy'.[12] In German historiography, the analysis of George III and Hanover does not go far beyond the attempts of Sigisbert Conrady and Carl Haase who attribute to George III some, though mainly private, interests in the Electorate.[13]

Why have historians failed to perceive the importance of Hanover to George III? It is certainly true that George III's conscious efforts to represent himself as British during the early years of his reign, epitomised in his first speech to parliament, brought a new debate into the public foreground. While George II had often been accused of championing German interests, the British attitude of George III included an obvious favouritism towards the Scot Bute. The very close relationship between the monarch and the Scottish earl had a major impact on the image of the former. This is not the place to examine the debate about George's presumed Scottish preferences.[14] However, the monarch's emphasis on his Britishness included a Hanoverian dimension. The domestic opposition in Britain would no longer attack the monarch openly for his German connection, something that had been common during the reign of George II, but for the protection of his Scottish confidant.[15] This became most obvious in visual representations of the monarchy. Vincent Carretta describes the changes in his discussion of Georgian satire. He states: 'Scotland became for George III what Hanover had been for his grandfather – a target for the xenophobes who accused the king of slighting his own country in favor of another.'[16] While satirists had represented George II with German attributes, the German connection of British monarchy became less visible after 1760. Under George III the kilt and bagpipes replaced German soldiers and the white Hanoverian horse in oppositional satire of the monarch.[17]

Despite this change in visual representation (and, as one should add, in oppositional language) this chapter challenges the assumption that a

---

[12] Karl Otmar v. Aretin, *Das Alte Reich 1648–1806*, vol III: *Das Reich und der österreichisch-preußische Dualismus (1745–1806)* (Stuttgart 1997), pp. 108, 114.
[13] Sigisbert Conrady, 'Die Wirksamkeit König Georgs III. für die Hannoverschen Kurlande', *Niedersächsisches Jahrbuch für Landesgeschichte* 39 (1967), 150–91; T. C. W. Blanning and Carl Haase, 'George III and the Regency Crisis', in: Jeremy Black, ed., *Knights Errant and true Englishmen. British foreign policy 1660–1800* (Edinburgh, 1989), pp. 135–50.
[14] K. W. Schweizer, ed., *Lord Bute. Essays in re-interpretation* (Leicester, 1988).
[15] Vincent Carretta, *George III and the satirists from Hogarth to Byron* (Athens, GA, 1990), p. 18. See also Grayson Ditchfield, *George III*, p. 48.
[16] Carretta, *George III and the satirists*, p. 59.
[17] In this context see also Michael Duffy, *The Englishman and the foreigner. English satirical print, 1600–1832* (Cambridge, 1986), p. 16.

policy in support of the Electorate of Hanover was replaced, after the accession of George III, by the monarch's preferences for British or particularly Scottish interests. Although important changes occurred, historians have been misled by understanding the accession of George III as the end of the dynastic union in a political sense. Instead, this chapter intends to show that the changes after 1760 transformed the relationship between the monarch and Hanover in a way that would ultimately have a major impact on British politics, and British foreign policies in particular. Moreover, it is intended to discuss George III's impact on foreign policy with regard to the Electorate of Hanover in a more detailed narrative. By examining specific events the author aims to contribute to the important research by Ditchfield, Simms, Scott and Blanning who have started to put Hanover back into the interpretation of monarchical power during the late eighteenth century.

The hypothesis of Hanover as the monarch's exclusively private and dynastic interest is at the core of the chapter. The early stages of George III's reign up to 1780 will be examined in the first part in order to illustrate that the changes that occurred from George II to George III were not as clear-cut as they have been described by historians. The consciously made separation between George III's role as monarch and his responsibilities as elector of Hanover was intended by him to simplify the life of his British ministers. However, such separation led to a number of embarrassing incidents between British politicians and foreign diplomats, and, more importantly, to some politically significant crises. This became particularly apparent in the period that lasted from the alliance of German princes in 1785, the *Fürstenbund*, up to the end of the eighteenth century and will be discussed in the second part. The third part deals with George III's active interference in British policies in support of Hanover during the period of the Napoleonic Wars. With an emphasis on the change of government in Britain and the consequences of George III's physical crisis in 1807, the conflation of British and Hanoverian interests will be demonstrated. After these three sections the role of the monarchy as part of British politics and foreign policy is discussed in a final part.

Two aspects will become clear. First, George III was not only interested in the fate of the Electorate of Hanover but also politically and dynastically so involved in the politics of the Holy Roman Empire that it ultimately had an impact on British policies. Secondly, the discussion of George III and Hanover can also contribute to the larger debate on the transformation of monarchical power at the end of the eighteenth century. Considering George III's involvement in European politics, the political role of the British monarch is not adequately described by the paradigm of declining political influence. The changes in monarchical power during the two decades around 1800 were due much more to individual ambition and personal fate than to structural changes.

I

It is generally understood that the reign of George II was a period in which the monarch's concerns for his German dominions were dominant in the conduct of monarchical policies while under George III British considerations predominated.[18] The death of the former during the Seven Years War is thus understood as particularly tragic for Hanover which suffered under the decision of George III to withdraw his troops from the 'German War'.[19] From a contemporary Hanoverian angle, however, the accession of George III did not look like a misfortune. Gerlach Adolph von Münchhausen, the most influential Hanoverian minister of the period 1740–60, kept up a lively correspondence with his brother Philipp who was the Hanoverian minister in London. In one of the many letters between Hanover and the British capital dating to the time just after the accession of George III, Gerlach Adolph commented on the political situation of the Electorate. During the war in Europe, Hanover had suffered severely. A large number of foreign troops had been marching through the territory of the Electorate since 1757, not least the French troops who had occupied Hanover for a number of months. As the minister vividly described, the military leadership had enormous difficulties in recruiting a sufficient number of privates. Hanover's finances lay in ruins. All this made the burden of war almost unbearable and a peace based on a European concert appeared to Münchhausen as the best solution to all Hanoverian problems.[20]

In this context Münchhausen commented on the policy of George II who had died only a few days earlier. Rather critically he stated to his brother that the former king could have been a great monarch had he not insisted on an ambitious policy. However, by renewing the war effort in 1757 and following an aggressive line of conduct he had placed his personal ambition first. In order 'to gain some miserable parishes and villages'[21] George II had ruined the welfare of his German dominions.

---

[18] Aretin, *Das alte Reich*, III, p. 32.
[19] Jeremy Black, 'The crown, Hanover and the shift in British foreign policy in the 1760s', in: Black, ed., *Knights Errant and true Englishmen*, p. 120.
[20] Gerlach Adolph von Münchhausen to his brother Philipp, 25 October 1760, Niedersächsisches Hauptstaatsarchiv Hannover (NHStA), Hann 91, von Münchhausen I, No. 73, fols. 3–8. Parts of the quotation in Dann, *England and Hanover*, p. 119, and Aretin, *Das alte Reich*, III, p. 554.
[21] *Ibid*: 'Einige elende Ämter und Dörfer vor seine Teutschen Lande abzubekommen'.

As Münchhausen concluded: 'He did not secure them [the parishes and villages] but failed to achieve an even greater glory, much larger than anything else, viz. the proof that the common welfare had been his sole motivation.'[22] To the elder Münchhausen the policies of George II were not entirely positive. Instead, in the statement to his brother the accession of George III appeared as an opportunity for gaining the long-wished-for peace.

As Jeremy Black has pointed out, it is important to consider the extent 'to which dynastic interests were often different from those of the Electorate, as understood by Hanoverian ministers'.[23] Walter Mediger in his examination of European foreign policies in 1757 and 1758 has already demonstrated that George II's conceptions of Hanoverian interests were different to his ministers' points of view.[24] As Mediger shows, the ministry in Hanover had been very critical about George II's policy after the negotiations at Kloster-Zeven, the treaty that had settled an arrangement between the Hanoverians and the French, and which had inevitably led to the occupation of Hanoverian territory. Rather than following the monarch's strategy for an aggressive policy in renewing the war effort, Hanoverian politicians had hoped that the Electorate would remain neutral and thus avoid the continuing hardship of war. In Hanoverian eyes, George II was not the ideal promoter of Electoral interests.

However, it was in no way clear whether things would change for the better under George III. The Hanoverian minister in London, Philipp von Münchhausen, stated very positive expectations in a letter to Hanover. Convinced of George III's concerns for his German dominions he wrote on 30 October 1760: 'Once more I need to add that the monarch gives many proofs of his obliging and friendly heart almost every hour in a good-natured way, particularly with regard to his attachment to his German dominions.'[25] But no one really knew what to expect from the new monarch. Despite the minister's hope, the Seven Years War continued and with it the concerns for the Electorate.

---

[22] *Ibid*: 'Er [George II] hat sie [die Ämter und Dörfer] doch nicht erhalten, sich aber einem Ruhm entzogen, der größer als alle Dinge gewesen seyn würde, nämlich dass das allgemeine Wohl sein einziger Grund gewesen wäre.'
[23] Black, *America or Europe?*, p. 86.
[24] Walter Mediger, 'Hastenbeck und Zeven. Der Eintritt Hannovers in den Siebenjährigen Krieg', *Niedersächsisches Jahrbuch für Landesgeschichte* 56 (1984), 137–66.
[25] Philipp von Münchhausen to his Brother Gerlach Adolph, 31 October 1760, NHStA Hann 91, von Münchhausen I, No. 72: 'Wieder muß ich nun beyfügen, daß der König treu und stündlich mehrere Proben von seinem gütig und großen Herzen, auch besonders von seiner Liebe gegen seine Teutschen Lande gibt.'

It was at the end of 1761 that George III decided on a policy that had important consequences for Hanover. Under the influence of his advisor Bute, George III opted for peace negotiations with France, a step which, as he himself wrote to Bute, would lead to the suffering of his German subjects. However, as George III stated, 'so superior is my love to this my native country over any private interest of my own that I cannot help wishing that an end was put to that enormous expence by ordering our troops home'.[26] At this stage and with regard to European politics, George III considered his role as British monarch to be more important than his responsibilities as elector of Hanover which he understood to be of private interest. It was to be a feature recurring during all major international crises. George III valued a European peace higher than the welfare of his Electorate. As will be shown later, this included his willingness to allow the Electorate to suffer politically and economically. However, as will be equally demonstrated, George III would never give up his paternal duties as elector of Hanover and thought it his responsibility to defend Hanoverian integrity as part of the Holy Roman Empire.

This separation of monarchical duties and private interests is central to the discussion of George III and Hanover. The ambivalence of the monarch's attitude is well illustrated by an incident during the summer of 1762. Due to George III's decision to withdraw his British troops from the continent, it was rumoured that the British monarch intended to give away Hanover to the prince of Wolfenbüttel and to install the latter as stadholder for Hanover. The Hanoverian ministry showed a large degree of uncertainty about the new elector. To find out whether the rumours carried any truth, the ministry finally decided to write to George III in June 1762. As the ministers in Hanover phrased it, they hoped that the king's future political design would include not only the welfare but the integrity of the Electorate.[27] George III replied instantly to the ministry's enquiry. Rather surprised, he stated that there was no reason to worry that such a thought had ever existed, or could ever exist in the future.[28] It is true that George III saw the big picture first and intended to end the European war as soon as possible. However, he was in no way inclined to neglect or give up his responsibilities as elector of Hanover. In short, George III understood Hanoverian concerns, as he had stated to Bute, as his 'private interest', much more than George II had done. Such thinking showed in many ways, not only in his conduct of foreign policy. The German historian Sigisbert Conrady has listed a number of aspects

---

[26] George III to Lord Bute, 6 January 1762, in Bute, No. 108.
[27] Ministry in Hanover to George III, 17 June 1762, NHStA Hann 92, No. 82.
[28] George III to Ministry in Hanover, 29 June 1762, NHStA Hann 92, No. 82.

ranging from the establishment of an agricultural academy in the Electorate's city of Celle to the education of the monarch's sons to illustrate George's concerns for Hanover.[29]

Moreover, George III did not show any of the territorial ambitions his predecessor George II had shown, nor did he intend to use his foreign political influence as British monarch in order to enlarge Hanover territorially. The example most often referred to in this context is the comment by the Bavarian envoy to London, Count Joseph Haslang, who observed in 1761 that George III would not take advantage of British forces being stationed in the vacant bishopric of Hildesheim. As Haslang famously concluded: 'These are no longer the times of George II.'[30] The lack of territorial ambition, however, did not go back to the monarch's attitude alone. The geopolitical changes that occurred during the Seven Years War made it very difficult for Hanover to sensibly consider an ambitious territorial policy in Germany. Hanover's political influence in the Holy Roman Empire had suffered severely during the Seven Years War while Prussia established itself as the most prominent power in the north of Germany. As von Aretin points out, the peace of Hubertusburg in 1763, three years after the accession of George III, marked a very important turning point. 'Prussia had finally established itself as a major political power in Europe.'[31] Although this process had already started in the 1740s, it was only after Hubertusburg that Prussian political power had risen to such an extent that it could, like Austria, pursue an independent policy outside the Holy Roman Empire.[32] For the Electorate of Hanover this meant that it was not territorial enlargement within the *Reich* which became a political option but the restoration of the Electorate to the rank of an economically and politically strong middle state. George III, and with him his Hanoverian ministers, had to pay tribute to the political changes which were caused by the Seven Years War. This is an important difference between the reigns of George II and George III and is easily overlooked. Due to Prussia's overpowering position in the north of Germany, the Electorate of Hanover needed to secure its political and economic position instead of enlarging its territory.[33]

The monarch responded to the decline in influence of Hanover within the Holy Roman Empire by supporting and enforcing the institutional bonds amongst the German principalities. The reinforcement of the

---

[29] Sigisbert Conrady, 'Die Wirksamkeit König Georgs III. für die Hannoverschen Kurlande', *Niedersächsisches Jahrbuch für Landesgeschichte* 39 (1967), 150–91.
[30] Quoted in Black, *Europe or America?*, p. 102.
[31] Aretin, *Das alte Reich*, pp. 107–8. [32] Ibid.
[33] Volker Press, 'Kurhannover im System des Alten Reiches 1692–1803', in: Birke and Kluxen, eds., *England and Hanover*, pp. 53–79.

status quo by securing the political construction of the *Reich* became a central feature of George III's policy towards Hanover and his tool to protect the Electorate from the ambitious policies of the two great German powers. Already apparent during the early years of his reign, George III would approach all the major crises that concerned the Electorate of Hanover during the forty-seven years following his accession by supporting the institutions of the Holy Roman Empire and by emphatically combating every attempt to change the existing order. This has been described as a 'policy of obstruction', a failure to support the efforts of the Emperor Joseph for reform.[34] Instead, George III's policy should be understood as the effort to secure the position of the Electorate of Hanover as an influential middle state. Conservative in essence, most of the German and particularly Hanoverian crises would only arise if one of the great European powers, Prussia or Austria included, questioned the integrity of the empire and that of the Electorate in particular. In the light of this conservatism, George III's attitude to the empire and his lack of territorial ambition for Hanover acquires a very different connotation. An ambitious policy in Germany would have threatened to undermine Hanover's position as had happened during the Seven Years War.

There is further evidence that George III intended the dynastic union to continue in a way that was not so different from the praxis of his grandfather. George III corresponded very closely with his Hanoverian minister in London, Philipp von Münchhausen, discussing politics as well as possible dynastic candidates for his marriage.[35] Politically, the role of the Hanoverian minister in London remains somewhat unclear.[36] Philipp von Münchhausen, as head of the office in London from 1749 to 1762, was by no means the most powerful Hanoverian politician. However, he had two major assets, presence in the British capital and direct access to the king. Since the times of George I, one minister from Hanover had stayed with the monarch conducting the correspondence between London and the capital of the Electorate. His office based in two small rooms in St James's Palace was known as the German Chancery. The Hanoverian minister in London, therefore, occupied a post that a skilful and ambitious person could easily use for the Electorate's interests, and for his own personal career. The ministers in Hanover, however, were eager to control the London position as far as possible. They would suggest a possible candidate for the post. As the example of 1762 shows, Philipp von Münchhausen was informed by his elder brother

---

[34] Aretin, *Das alte Reich*, p. 315.
[35] George III to Lord Bute, Bute, Nos. 66–9, 79. Also Hibbert, *George III*, p. 36.
[36] Dann, *Britain and Hanover*, p. 77.

that Burckhard Heinrich von Behr was the Hanoverian ministry's candidate for the post of Head of the German Chancery. Philipp von Münchhausen then approached George III to find out whether the monarch was prepared to invite von Behr to London in order to meet him and to judge whether he was fit for the position.[37] Von Behr was invited to London in March 1762 and took up the position as head of the German Chancery soon afterwards.[38]

Two aspects need to be considered when looking at the position of Hanoverian minister in London. First of all, the minister's ability to liaise with the monarch and within British political circles was very important for a successful policy as head of the German Chancery. Most Hanoverians in the capital would have a good knowledge of the political system and party political business in Britain. Unlike the earlier period of the dynastic union when competing Hanoverian factions had struggled for the monarch's support in London, the head of the German Chancery during the second half of the century would understand his position more as that of a foreign diplomat or courtier at Windsor. This leads to the second observation. The post of head of the German Chancery during the reign of George III cannot be understood without evaluating the strength and weaknesses of the ministry in the Electorate of Hanover and the control the ministry on the continent could execute over their colleague in London. Unlike the younger Münchhausen, von Behr and the latter's successor, von Alvensleben, carried out their duties without causing controversy between Hanover and London. Decisions concerning the Electorate would be taken in Hanover and then forwarded to the capital where the minister informed and consulted the British monarch. As Alvensleben's successor Ernst Ludwig von Lenthe commented, the head of the Chancery would do little more than forward the orders from Hanover.[39] From 1762 to 1795, the potential of the post was not fully fulfilled. Thus von Lenthe attempted to reform the powers and responsibilities of the minister in London after he succeeded Alvensleben in the middle of the 1790s.[40] It was not under Lenthe but under his successor, Ernst Herbert Count Münster that the post at the head of the German Chancery became crucial for Hanoverian and British policies.[41] As we will see later, Münster was also the first minister who established links

---

[37] Philipp von Münchhausen to his brother Gerlach Adolph, March 1762, NHStA, Hann 91, von Münchhausen I, No. 78.
[38] Philipp von Münchhausen to Burckhard Heinrich von Behr, 16 March 1762, NHStA, Hann 91, von Münchhausen I, No. 78.
[39] Ernst Ludwig von Lenthe, Familientagebuch, Private Papers, Family Archives, Gut Lenthe, FA 106.
[40] Ibid.   [41] Brendan Simms, ' "An odd question enough" ', p. 595.

beyond the formal correspondence with the British foreign secretary. He actively approached British politicians and the British press.

Before Münster's accession as the head of the Chancery, British and Hanoverian policies were clearly separated. As we have seen, the monarch himself had intended this separation. George III's focus during the first twenty years of his reign was the economic restoration of Hanover. So far little is known about his interests because the evidence is stored in an unusual way. The files of the German Chancery in the state archives in Hanover contain a bundle of documents found in the private rooms of George III after his death in 1820 and simply filed as 'additions' (*sonstiges*), which is one of the reasons why they have been overlooked. These letters comprise the correspondence between George III and von Behr, as well as General Wilhelm von Freytag, George III's aide de camp and close confidant, for the years 1763 right into the 1790s. They illustrate the monarch's keen interest in financial and agricultural reform in Hanover. They also illustrate his increasing involvement in German affairs.[42] George III's sister Augusta had equally kept him informed about German politics ever since her marriage to the duke of Brunswick in the early 1760s.[43] General Freytag travelled back and forth to Hanover to keep the monarch updated about his German dominions. Only a year after his accession, George III supported the election of his son, Frederick, duke of York, though still an infant, to the position of Prince Bishop of Osnabrück.[44] Frederick took up his post in 1781 when he came of age and from then onwards George III received more detailed and more regular information about the situation in Germany.[45] During the period from the accession of George III up to the early 1780s the monarch thus grew more familiar with the political events in Germany and, as it appears, he grew fonder of his German dominions. After Frederick's arrival in Germany three of George III's other sons would be educated at the University of Göttingen. The number of letters he received from the Electorate grew steadily.[46]

The more turbulent events in British domestic policies during the first two decades of George III's reign have made historians focus on the

---

[42] 'Briefe an Georg III., welche sich nach dem Absterben des Königs 1821 vorgefunden haben', NHStA, Hann 92, No. 2100.

[43] Parts of her correspondence with George III are stored at the Royal Archives, Windsor Castle, RA Geo/51957–52288.

[44] Christine van den Heuvel, 'Justus Möser und die englisch-hannoversche Reichspolitik zwischen Siebenjährigem Krieg und Fürstenbund', *Zeitschrift für Historische Forschung* 29, 3 (2002), 383–423.

[45] Ibid., 418–22.

[46] Arthur Aspinall, ed., *The later correspondence of George III* (5 vols., Cambridge, 1962–1970), *passim*.

monarch's position as king of Great Britain. George III went through various stages struggling with parliament and public, politicians and polemics, first over the premiership of his confidant Bute, then over a number of ministries that included candidates the monarch would not, or only reluctantly and unwillingly, accept. His attack on the Fox–North coalition that led to the installation of Pitt the Younger as first minister, is the most famous example.[47] The historiographical focus on his monarchical role was reinforced by the fact that George III kept what he decided as British sovereign separate from his role as elector of Hanover. Up to 1778, British politics were not directly affected by George III's private interests in the Electorate of Hanover. However, this would change with the danger of a European war approaching.

II

Keeping his responsibilities as British sovereign separate from his dynastic duties in the German empire gave George III more flexibility in German politics. This was initially intended by the monarch to avoid criticism from the British opposition and proved successful during the first eighteen years of his reign, mainly because this period passed without a major European war. However, the military conflicts between the great powers at the end of the 1770s illustrated that a total separation between the two spheres was impossible. As Hamish Scott has shown, the first evidence of the conflation of British and Hanoverian policies appeared during the War of the Bavarian Succession. Austria's ambitions to exchange its Dutch provinces for the Electorate of Bavaria led to opposition from George III who feared an increase in Habsburg influence in the Holy Roman Empire. The secretary of the Northern Department, the earl of Suffolk, offered the Prussian government an alliance thus following 'the insistent demands of George III as Elector rather than king' to secure the position of Hanover.[48] Though nothing came out of this offer (and as a consequence the war in the American colonies was fought in Northern America alone), George III's concerns for Hanover are an indication that during this major conflict the monarch's attention was not exclusively on the struggle overseas but equally on the situation of Hanover. It also illustrates that any effort by Austria to change the balance of power within the *Reich* would be counterbalanced by George III. This became particularly clear during the events of 1785.

---

[47] George Ayling, *George III* (New York, 1972); Thomas, *George III and the politicians*.
[48] Scott, *British foreign policy*, pp. 269–70.

George III joined the *Fürstenbund* as elector of Hanover in June along with the governments of Prussia and Saxony. Like George III's intentions in 1778, the *Fürstenbund* aimed similarly at opposing Joseph II's renewed attempts on the Electorate of Bavaria. The monarch's and elector's policy again adopted a pro-Prussian, and ultimately anti-Austrian position. This time, however, this was in clear opposition to British diplomatic endeavours for an alliance with Austria. Tim Blanning writes: 'At the very same time that George III was taking the closest possible interest in the expansion of a League which was explicitly anti-Austrian, his foreign secretary was telling the Austrian ambassador that he wished "with his whole heart" for a revival of the old alliance between their two countries.'[49] Such policy by George as elector was embarrassing to the British government. Although the first minister refused to comment to foreign diplomats on the king's policy, Pitt did not hesitate to write that: 'The which your Majesty's engagements respecting your Electoral dominions may have on the general state of the continent and on your Majesty's relative situation with Foreign Powers must also eventually affect the interest of this country.'[50] George III, however, did not withdraw from his line of conduct. As he replied to Pitt, it was the dangerously ambitious policies of the Austrian emperor that made him interfere in German politics. George III wrote to Pitt that he intended 'to prevent all measures contrary to the Germanick Constitution' in order to ensure 'the future stability of the Empire'.[51] As the events of 1778 and 1785 illustrate, the *leitmotif* of stability in the Holy Roman Empire comes up in George III's German policies time and again. While Suffolk's efforts had been short-lived, the *Fürstenbund* represents an exceptional and unprecedented conflict between George III and his British government over Hanover.[52] This was in fact the first time that the 'private interests' of George III clashed with the policy of his British government.

After the struggle over the war in America and the defeat of George III's policies with regard to the former colonies the monarch was less involved in British foreign policy. This was not least due to the establishment of the ministry of Pitt the Younger. Though still in its earlier stages, Pitt's government would deprive the monarch of many of his former prerogatives and ensure that the monarch's decision would consider the

---

[49] Blanning, ' "That horrid Electorate" ', p. 334.
[50] Arthur Aspinall, *The later correspondence*, No. 235.
[51] George III to Pitt, 6 August 1785, Aspinall, *The later correspondence*, No. 235.
[52] Tim Blanning, ' "That horrid Electorate" ', pp. 311–44.

majorities in the two houses.[53] George III's disappointment at this development has, however, been misinterpreted. Tim Blanning writes: 'It is an attractive hypothesis: shackled in Great Britain by parliament, which only recently had inflicted on him a deeply felt humiliation over America, George turned to his Electorate, where his control of foreign policy was absolute.'[54] While Blanning states this as a hypothesis and leaves it open whether this was actually the case it is worth pointing out that George III did not intend to rule as an absolutist ruler, either in Britain nor in Hanover. After, as he saw it, government and parliament had undermined the right order regarding his American colonies, he undertook every effort to ensure that in the other parts of his empire, and that included Hanover and Germany, a secure and stable system would be supported. It is in this context that the *Fürstenbund* episode should be understood. Hanover's accession to the *Fürstenbund* was part of George III's broader strategy to secure the order of the *Reich* and, ultimately, of Europe. Thus the events in 1785 should not so much be seen as an attempt by the British monarch to escape constitutional bonds in Britain, or as royal ambitions to engage in German style absolutism (neither the enlightened, nor the unenlightened type) but as George III's fear that, after the loss of the American colonies, other parts of his sovereignties would be drawn into trouble.

If we follow the line of argument as developed above the monarch's conduct implies that George III saw no need to balance between his British and Hanoverian interests because the latter were understood to be exclusively private. As elector of Hanover he intended to counteract Austrian attempts to change the order of the empire. That this affected his British ministers' political negotiations was of less concern to him as there was no political or military crisis that caused him to interfere in British foreign policy. George III saw no direct threat to British power as such. In his eyes, the *Fürstenbund* ensured the status quo in the empire.

The monarch's priorities for a stable and secure political system were reinforced during his physical crisis of 1788-9. George III's decisions regarding Austrian ambitions had not helped to encourage a good relationship with the Austrian Emperor Joseph II. When George III was incapacitated for several months it was almost inevitable that Joseph II would dispute the decision of George III's eldest son to establish a Regency. The former, as the head of the Holy Roman Empire, refused to accept the Prince of Wales as the regent for Hanover and demanded

---

[53] Michael Duffy, 'Pitt, Grenville and the control of British foreign policy in the 1790s', in: Jeremy Black, ed., *Knights Errant and true Englishmen*, pp. 151-77.
[54] Blanning, ' "That horrid Electorate" ', p. 340.

Austrian control over the Electorate. It was due to George III's recovery at the beginning of 1789 that a major legal battle at the Imperial Diet in Regensburg was avoided but the events clearly illustrate the potential for political crisis.[55]

With the onset of the French revolutionary wars in 1792 the stability of continental Europe, and the Holy Roman Empire in particular, came under a severe threat. After the victories of the French revolutionary troops in the Netherlands and on the western border of the Holy Roman Empire, the former German territory at the west bank of the Rhine was lost to the French. After this defeat, little doubt existed amongst the German princes about the necessity for territorial indemnification. During the following years the German states, headed by Austria and Prussia and under the tutelage of France and Russia, would negotiate a new territorial order for the Holy Roman Empire. George III was highly critical of such a proceeding and showed no signs of engaging in the negotiations for territorial indemnification. Hanoverian politicians were highly disappointed about the lack of support they received from the British monarch in their negotiations for the territories of Hildesheim and Osnabrück. George III had different plans. Right from the beginning of 1793 he thought a war against France with the restoration of the status quo ante to be the most sensible solution to the present situation.[56] Hanoverian and British troops were mobilised to fight the French. It is hardly surprising that during this period prints appeared in the British public that showed George III as a medieval knight 'Arming in Defence of the French Princes', and fighting against the French revolutionary troops.[57]

For the first three years of the war against revolutionary France, George III hoped for a united front against the common enemy. In 1795, however, Prussia started peace negotiations with France. Financially drained and strategically more interested in the eastern battlefields, the Berlin government sued for peace with Paris. The Prussian minister Hardenberg negotiated a neutrality zone which included most of north Germany and, as part of it, the Electorate of Hanover.[58]

---

[55] Blanning and Haase, 'George III and the Regency crisis', *passim*.
[56] Christof Römer, 'Niedersachsen im 18. Jahrhundert', in Christine van den Heuvel and M. von Boetticher, eds., *Geschichte Niedersachsens* (Hanover, 1998).
[57] Dorothy M. George, *Catalogue of political and personal satires in the department of Prints and drawings in the British Museum* (vols. 5–9, London, 1870–1914), No. 8084.
[58] Guy Stanton Ford, *Hanover and Prussia. A study in neutrality, 1795–1800* (New York, 1903); Willy Real, 'Der Frieden von Basel', *Baseler Zeitschrift für Geschichte und Altertumskunde* 50 (1950), 27–112; Real, 'Die preußischen Staatsfinanzen und die Anbahnung des Sonderfriedens von Basel 1795', *Forschungen zur Brandenburgischen und Preußischen Geschichte* NF 1 (1991), pp. 53–100.

George III was unhappy about such a solution. A separate peace between Berlin and Paris would mean a serious threat to the Empire's integrity. He firmly opposed such policies. The British monarch appealed to Austria and hoped that the combined military efforts would drive the French back from Dutch and German territory.[59] In the end, however, George III could not prevent the Franco-Prussian peace. He finally, though reluctantly, agreed to the accession of Hanover to the zone of neutrality.[60]

Historiography (including my own work) has tended to emphasise that Hanover thus left the allied coalition as part of a neutral North Germany while Britain still fought France in 1795.[61] However, the ministers in the Electorate agreed to the Prussian proposal of a neutral zone much more reluctantly than is generally assumed[62] and George III was much more critical of the policies of Berlin and Vienna than of the decisions taken in his own Electorate. Additionally, the monarch thought that his British ministry's strategy of focusing on maritime warfare an important part of the continental disaster. As he wrote to the foreign secretary Lord Grenville: 'This country means to leave the German Empire to shift for itself.'[63] In George III's view Hanover was not to blame for what had happened. It was down to the great powers to save and restore continental Europe.

Similarly to the events ten years earlier, George III decided in 1795 that his policy as elector must be clearly separated from his responsibilities as British monarch. Hanover acceded to the neutral zone while Britain fought on. Extremely irritated by this royal decision anti-Hanover feelings appeared in the British political public. A feast for the opposition, the question of peace with France was raised in parliament. As the marquess of Lansdowne put it in the debate in the House of Lords on 30 October 1795: 'If ministers wished ever so much to negociate for peace, they said, they could not, and asked with whom are we to treat? Let them ask the Elector of Hanover. He had found parties to treat with, and so might they, if they chose it.'[64] The discussion in the Commons the day before had been equally aggressive. Sheridan said on 29 October that 'Jealousies were commonly entertained of the introduction of Hanoverian troops

---

[59] Torsten Riotte, *Hannover in der britischen Politik (1792–1815). Dynastische Beziehung als Element außenpolitischer Entscheidungsfindung* (Münster, 2005), pp. 73–5.
[60] Ford, *Hanover and Prussia*, pp. 97–8.
[61] Riotte, *Hannover in der britischen Politik*, pp. 77–82.
[62] Ford, *Hanover and Prussia*, pp. 97–8.
[63] George III to Lord Grenville, 10 September 1795, in: *The manuscripts of J. B. Fortescue, preserved at Dropmore*, (Dropmore) Historical Manuscript Commission, 14th report (London, 1894–1927), III, p. 134.
[64] *Parliamentary History*, XXXII (1795–1797), col. 197.

into this country, but he declared he should have no objection to import the whole Hanoverian council, and install them in the office of his majesty's present ministers.'[65]

George III, however, did not change his mind about his electoral decisions. Quite the opposite, the separation between British and Hanoverian policies became even more apparent in 1797. After the British cabinet decided to negotiate a possible peace with France the monarch showed his disagreement with such negotiations. As it was clear from the beginning that any peace offer to Prussia would include the discussion of territorial indemnifications, such policies would find no support with George III. When the cabinet decided to push through such a policy against the opposition of the monarch, foreign secretary Grenville received an angry reply from George III. He wrote on 30 July: 'what right England has to give away the rights and interests of other Princes, who have either by England or Austria been brought forward into a business their own inclinations did not covet, I cannot either see a shadow of justice or the pretence of interference'. A serious argument ensued between monarch and ministry and the debate climaxed over the following days. George III insisted that this was all 'highly blameworthy towards the whole German Empire'. He asked to see both first minister and foreign secretary personally at Windsor. Pitt and Grenville, however, backed by secretary for war, Henry Dundas, stuck to their policies. With combined efforts they forced the cabinet's will on the monarch.[66]

This clash between the monarch and his British government is generally understood as a clear indication of 'the real decline of royal influence on foreign policy'.[67] The events certainly showed that George III could not force his policies on the British government in 1797. However, the more important aspect is that he opposed the British plans because they included territorial changes in Germany as consequences of a peace with France. George III decided to accept the decision of his British ministry while he behaved quite differently as elector of Hanover. He wrote to his Hanoverian ministers that he had informed his British government that 'our German interests can, and must, of necessity, be different from our interests here'.[68] As we will see below, George III's position was not generally opposed to that of his British ministers. As long as a final peace in Europe would restore and secure the old order there was little

---

[65] Ibid., cols. 159–60. [66] The correspondence in: *Dropmore* III, pp. 227–30.
[67] Duffy, 'Pitt, Grenville and the control of British foreign policy', p. 163.
[68] George III to the ministry in Hanover, 21 April 1797, NHStA, Hann 92, 1595, fols. 30–2: 'unser Teutsches Interesse von dem hiesigen in einzelnen Fällen nothwendig leicht verschieden sein könne und müßte'.

disagreement about how to fight the war. This is not to say that George III was indifferent to the strong opposition from his cabinet ministers. After Pitt struggled and lost his colleagues' support, finally resigning from office in 1801, George III's comment reveals his anger stating that he would finally address the question he had 'long wished to bring to an issue', and had 'not admired the constant attempts for over twenty years to avoid it'.[69] In a very similar tone he wrote to the new first minister Addington.[70]

In 1801 a Northern alliance was formed in order to combat British control of the Baltic. Under the name of a 'League of Neutrality' Russia, Prussia, Denmark and Sweden combined their efforts to counterbalance the enormous damage cause by British warships. While Russia and the Scandinavian powers commanded naval forces themselves, Prussia's contribution to the league would be the occupation of Hanover. Hohenzollern troops marched into the Electorate at the beginning of the year. George III fiercely opposed to this move. However, as during the incidents before, he made a clear distinction between his British and private/Hanoverian interests. Empowering his Hanoverian ministers to negotiate an arrangement with Prussia, he instructed the ministry to negotiate with Berlin the possibility of a neutral north Germany which would prevent war for his German dominions. He enclosed a letter to the Prussian king to be submitted only if Hanoverian negotiations proved successful, 'in the opposite case, however, if the reply to the transmitted note should be negative, an autographic letter might not be appropriate'.[71] In the attached letter, George III described the neutrality of northern Germany as most important, 'especially at a time when sad incidents on behalf of my crown of a sea power extort instructions and means which execution can endanger the fortune of northern Germany'.[72] Very similar to the events in 1795 the monarch authorised a Hanoverian policy that was in no way related, not to say opposed, to the British strategy of war. To assume, however, that George III intended to pursue a policy in favour of Hanover and in opposition to British interests is inaccurate. George III's main efforts were directed towards a renewal of the allied coalition against France and towards breaking up the Armed Neutrality against Britain. When, in June 1801, the Hanoverian minister to London,

---

[69] George III to Dundas, 15 January 1801, British Library, Add. Mss. 38736, Liverpool Papers.
[70] George III to Addington, 15 January 1801, Devon Record Office, Exeter, Addington Papers, 152M C1801, OR4.
[71] George III to the ministry in Hanover, 17 February 1801, NHStA, Hann 92, No. 1635, fols. 44–7.
[72] *Ibid.*

Ernst Ludwig von Lenthe, threatened his Prussian colleague with British intervention if Prussia would not withdraw its troops from Hanover, George III did not hesitate to criticise the head of the German Chancery and apply strict censorship to his correspondence.[73] It was the peace of Europe and the return to a stable order that was George III's first priority.

III

From the accession of George III up to the turn of the century, British and Hanoverian policies had been clearly separated. Both ministries followed individual policies with the consent of George III. This had led to minor clashes, as, for example, during the *Fürstenbund* negotiations in 1785, and a rather peculiar separation of the two qualities of monarch and elector on the accession to the neutral zone negotiated at the Peace of Basle in 1795. The development of separate policies climaxed in spring 1801, when the Hanoverian envoy von der Decken went so far as to propose the inclusion of Hanover in Russia's Armed Neutrality, in effect suggesting that Hanover join an alliance against Britain.[74] This Hanoverian move for an independent policy in 1801 has so far gone unnoticed by historians. The failure of the Hanoverian strategy, however, is essential to our understanding of the events of that year. It seems highly unlikely that George III knew about Decken's offer but it remains unknown whether the king would have been prepared to consider such a political constellation. Berlin refused Decken's offer without hesitation. The peace of Basle was peculiar enough for most foreign officials. George III joining an alliance against himself was pushing things too far, not only for Berlin, but for St Petersburg and Vienna too. Therefore, instead of a neutral policy, Prussian troops marched into the Electorate.[75] This first occupation marks an important turning point. Hanover could no longer hope to rely on Prussia's policy of neutrality and to dissociate itself from the British conduct of war. Instead, the Electorate had little alternative but to turn to George III and ask for British support. As the Hanoverian

---

[73] Riotte, *Hannover in der britischen Politik*, 109–10, based on the Jacobi-Kloest correspondence in Geheimes Staatsarchiv Preußischer Kulturbesitz, 1. Hauptabteilung, Repertorium 11, No. 140c1 Faszikel 1.

[74] Decken to Lenthe, 2 March 1801, NHStA, Hann 92, No. 1635, fol. 122.

[75] For two very different accounts see Philip Dwyer, 'Prussia and the Armed Neutrality. The invasion of Hanover in 1801', *International Historical Review* 15/4 (November, 1993), 661–87; H. Ulmann, 'Preußen und die bewaffnete Meeresneutralität und die Besitznahme Hannovers im Jahre 1801', *Deutsche Zeitschrift für Geschichtswissenschaft* 2 (1897/8), 254–68.

minister Kielmansegge wrote to his colleague in London, Ernst Ludwig von Lenthe: 'Far more we are anticipating that everything will depend completely on His Majesty's British ministers.'[76] The developments in 1801 made it impossible for the monarch to continue with his clear separation of British and Hanoverian interests.

At this point, however, Great Britain showed no inclination to fight for Hanover militarily. After Russian support was secured in April and Anglo-French negotiations were under way in autumn 1801, it was not British armies but British diplomats, particularly Lords Carysfort in Berlin and St Helens in St Petersburg, who supported the interests of Hanover as part of their diplomatic missions.[77] Carysfort was to point out that no arrangement with Prussia could be agreed upon until the full restoration of Hanover was guaranteed. Efforts were made to make it clear to Berlin that Britain would not accept anything less than the evacuation of Hanover. As the foreign office put it in the instructions for Carysfort: 'no steps can be taken toward adjusting the differences which have arisen between Great Britian and Prussia, so long as His Prussian Majesty continues to menace the king's German dominions'.[78] The clear separation between British and Hanoverian policy had disappeared. For Britain and British politicians it became clear that the interests of the Electorate were too closely connected with Prussian ambitions in the north of Germany. They equally realised that their monarch was in no way prepared to agree to any attempts by Berlin to lay its hands on the German Electorate. George III would not accept a peace without a definitive guarantee of security of Hanover. So while Prussia was too important a member of any potential coalition to exclude it from future negotiation, Prussian support could not be traded for territorial indemnifications in north Germany. In short, the relationship between Britain and Hanover was ultimately defined by the relationship between Prussia and George III's German dominions.

Despite the insistence on his sovereign rights in the Electorate, the monarch was prepared for Hanover to suffer under a combined effort to defeat the French. This became clear in 1803. After the short interval from the peace preliminaries in October 1801 and the following peace of Amiens in spring 1802, the early months of 1803 saw rising tensions

---

[76] Kielmansegge to Lenthe, 19 February 1801, NHStA, Hann 92, No. 1635, fols. 88–92: 'Vielmehr sehen wir nichts anders ab, als daβ nunmehr es ganz auf Sr. Majestät britisches Ministerium ankommt.'

[77] Lenthe to Münster, 30 March 1802, NHStA, Münster's Private Papers, Hann. Dept. 110, A60.

[78] Instructions to Carysfort No. 10, 18 July 1801, Public Record Office – The National Archives (PRO), FO 64/61.

between Paris and London. George III was not unhappy about this development. As the marquess of Buckingham wrote to his brother Lord Grenville: 'The king has from the first moments of this alarm been extremely eager for the war.' Buckingham was quite surprised about George III's determination: 'with the certain loss of Hanover, I cannot explain his eagerness'.[79] Despite Buckingham's reservations, the monarch supported his ministry's decision for war. After a severe diplomatic rupture, French troops occupied the Electorate in early summer 1803. At this point, George III did not intend to give up Hanover but his first priority was the defeat of the French.[80]

While the Electorate of Hanover suffered economically first under the French occupation and subsequently under the loss of political autonomy, British diplomats were, again, negotiating behind the scenes in Berlin and St Petersburg about Hanover's future. They knew that the British monarch did not expect Britain to fight a war for the German Electorate or to risk the break up of a European coalition against France. At the same time they were aware that George III would not move one iota in his determination to restore the integrity and independence of Hanover. In a nutshell, the monarch's attitude can be described as: 'No war for Hanover, no peace without the Electorate'. Both aspects were crucial for George III's relationship with his German dominions.

Both for the British diplomats and for George III, Prussia proved to be the most difficult partner regarding the Electorate of Hanover. While this was not so clear in 1803, it became much more apparent in 1805. After Napoleon directed his military efforts southwards to fight an Austrian army, the French forces left the Electorate of Hanover and most of the north of Germany. As the British diplomat in St Petersburg wrote, Russia indicated its readiness for a new coalition. With Swedish and British troops already arriving in the north of Germany, 1805 would be the most dramatic year before the final downfall of Napoleon.[81] It appeared as if Europe was finally ready to stand up to the French emperor. London, and with it the rest of Europe, waited impatiently for a decision from Berlin. Would Prussia fight the French, remain neutral, or even subscribe to the French offer of a coalition?

Prussian aid would certainly come at a price. Lord Harrowby was sent to Berlin to find out what it would take to make the Hohenzollern state

---

[79] Buckingham to Grenvillle, 24 March 1803, *Dropmore*, VII, pp. 150–1.
[80] The hypothesis is based on George III's later comment as reported in Herbert Taylor to Castlereagh, 12 January 1806, in: Aspinall, *The later correspondence*, No. 3168.
[81] John Ehrman, *The Younger Pitt*, vol. III: *The consuming struggle* (London, 1996), p. 726.

join the alliance.[82] When the British envoy arrived in the Prussian capital he was shocked to learn that King Frederick William III, in agreement with the Russian Tsar Alexander, had decided to incorporate the Electorate of Hanover into Prussian territory. The British envoy reported back to London, and, as the historian John M. Sherwig writes, Pitt could not comprehend the news. While the latter had accepted territorial rewards for Prussia as an inducement he had not considered the monarch's German dominions as an option: 'Belgium yes, Hanover never.'[83] Thus the conflation of British and Hanoverian interests became an important aspect of the failure of the negotiations in 1805. Though Britain desperately longed for Prussian military assistance, Hanover was not to be traded, not even for a victory over Napoleon.

It needs to be said that to a British contemporary, the loss of Hanover as the price to pay for a coalition with Prussia was not an unthinkable solution. The British diplomatist Henry Beeke had asked in a letter to the first minister Addington whether it would not be sensible 'to do that with a good grace which probably Great Britain has no adequate means of preventing'. Beeke had made clear that his ultimate aim was 'a union of interest' with the northern powers, Prussia in particular.[84] However, the British ministers knew that George III would never surrender his Electoral rights. This hypothesis is undermined by the events of 1805. Foreign secretary Mulgrave decided not to inform the monarch about the Prussio-Russian agreement because, so runs the hypothesis, Berlin's conduct would ruin any chance that the monarch might, in future, reapproach Berlin for a coalition.[85] At this point, British limitations in negotiating a European coalition due to the dynastic link with Hanover were clearly visible. Rather than negotiating further, Prussia joined Napoleon's side and occupied Hanover once more.

The events since the first Prussian occupation of Hanover depended on two developments. First, the monarch, who had struggled against the unified front of Pitt, Grenville and Dundas during the 1790s had a much greater say in foreign policies dealing with politically more unstable governments of the decade after the turn of the century. Not only did George III's opposition to catholic emancipation play an important role

---

[82] See Brendan Simms, *Impact of Napoleon. Prussian high politics, foreign policy and the crisis of the executive, 1797–1806* (Cambridge, 1997) pp. 191–200, for a detailed discussion of Harrowby's mission.
[83] J. M. Sherwig, *Guineas and gunpowder. British foreign aid in the wars with France 1793–1815* (Cambridge, MA, 1969), p. 169.
[84] Henry Beeke to Addington, 28 February 1801, Devon Record Office, Exeter, Addington Papers, 152M, C1801, OF 38.
[85] Mulgrave to Harrowby, No. 4, 23 November 1805, PRO, FO 64/70.

in the downfall of the Pitt government in 1801, the monarch also forced his policies of continental commitment onto all subsequent cabinets. During all the negotiations first minister and foreign secretary were aware that they had to consider the monarch's wishes.[86] Secondly, George III's efforts were supported by a new figure in the political theatre. Ernst Herbert Count Münster had succeeded Ernst Ludwig von Lenthe as head of the German Chancery in 1805. Münster eagerly established contacts with many British politicians. The official correspondence between the Chancery and the foreign office more than tripled. Likewise, Münster wrote to his British colleagues in an extensive private correspondence and met those closest to George III during his weekly stays at Windsor. He also managed to control the Hanoverian ministry by persuading George III to dissolve the government in Hanover and assisted the monarch in filling the newly vacant positions. Münster's efforts soon showed results. Even the British press responded to the many declarations Münster drafted, whereas reports about Hanover had been the exception during the decades before.[87]

Thus it is hardly surprising that the climax of Britain's involvement in Hanoverian policies dates to the year 1806. In April 1806, the Prussian king, Frederick William III, decided to officially incorporate Hanover into his Prussian dominions. This caused strong opposition from Britain. The Prussian envoy to London, Baron Jacobi-Kloest, was hugely surprised by the severity of the response. Jacobi's interviews with foreign secretary Fox as a prime defender of the Electorate proved extremely mortifying and as Jacobi reported to Berlin about his *terrible conseil* with Fox, the situation was completely different from any negotiation before.[88] As the Prussian envoy wrote, the foreign secretary had insisted on the seizure of the blockade of the north German coast as well as on the withdrawal of Prussian troops from Hanover. Prussia's disbelief in British sincerity about its support for Hanover finally led to a declaration of war on Berlin in June 1806. The general assumption that Britain never declared war in favour of the Electorate was proven wrong.[89]

---

[86] Riotte, *Hannover in der britischen Politik*, pp. 154–8.
[87] Mijndert Bertram, *Staatseinheit und Landesvertretung. Die erste oder provisorische Allgemeine Ständeversammlung des Königreiches Hannover und ihre definitive Organisation, 1814–1819* (Hanover, 1986), pp. 37–40.
[88] Jacobi to Hardenberg, 25 April 1806, Geheimes Staatsarchiv Preuβischer Kulturbesitz, I HA, Rep. 11, No. 180c, fol. 144.
[89] Simms, ' "Odd question enough" ', p. 586, questioning the traditional assumption as in Georg Schnath, 'Die Personalunion zwischen England und Hannover', *Lüneburger Blätter* 19/20 (1968), 5–19, here p. 12.

The declaration of war was not an executive decision taken secretly without public knowledge. Parliament had discussed the options for a foreign political response to Prussia in April. Based on a declaration drafted by Count Münster and signed by George III, the two houses debated what future policy should be. In his declaration George III stated that his dignity had been undermined by the events in Hanover: 'Thus actually dispossessed of the ancient inheritance of my family, and insulted in my rights as a Sovereign, I have ordered those measures to be taken which the honour of my Crown requests.'[90] This was the first time that George III as king of Great Britain acted in support of Hanover. Had the clear separation between his monarchical duties and private interests finally disappeared? Was Britain finally prepared to fight for the monarch's German dominions?

The success of Hanoverian policies in summer 1806, and Münster's policy in particular, was based on a diplomatically and rhetorically cunning strategy. With George III's insistence that he only very reluctantly involved his British subjects in a Hanoverian conflict, he left British politicians enough room to dissociate themselves from Hanoverian interests. As Lord Grenville would say in the parliamentary session the Prussian insult affected George III 'more in his private than in his public capacity'.[91] However, Münster, in the declaration of April 1806 and his policy in general, linked the danger to the Electorate of Hanover to the dignity of the person of George III. And Grenville agreed in the parliamentary session that debated George's statement 'his majesty could feel nothing but attacked on his honour' and that British politicians thus had to act in defence of their sovereign's rights.[92] The personal dignity of the monarch, so effectively, the person of the monarch, bridged between Hanoverian and British interests. While the separate policies of the earlier period had led to an independent line of conduct in the past, Count Münster, with the support of George III, managed to combine the dignity of the British monarch with the policies of the Electorate while still keeping the British and Hanoverian spheres separate where necessary.

Count Münster was responsible for much of the excitement about Hanover in British political circles in 1806. The head of the German Chancery had not only written to leading politicians, he had also approached the press. *The Times* reported of 'a most important State Paper, the Proclamation of Count Munster, the Hanoverian Minister' and printed an extensive commentary about the events around the

---

[90] *The Times*, 24 April 1806.
[91] *Hansard*, Parliamentary Debates, 1st Series, iv, cols. 881–4.   [92] *Ibid.*

Electorate.[93] The *Morning Chronicle* followed suit.[94] We find Münster at Windsor, but also at Carlton House. Due to his encouragement, the Prince of Wales had a lengthy interview with the Prussian envoy Jacobi-Kloest, in which the former reiterated to the Prussian representative the importance of the Electorate of Hanover to the royal family.[95] Without a shadow of a doubt Münster's efforts represent an important part of the events of 1806. However, despite Münster's successes, the events after the turn of the year 1806 illustrate that the Hanoverian minister still depended on royal support.

IV

Much of the success of Münster's Hanoverian initiative in Britain was only possible because the public image of George III had changed and the monarch had risen to an unknown degree of popularity in Britain during the 1790s.[96] While the French Emperor Napoleon represented greed and ambition to his British critics, the British monarch stood for order, moderation and honesty. Therefore, George III's dignity was well worth defending. During the years of war George III acquired almost iconic status in Britain as a patriotic father figure fighting Napoleon. Historians have followed such interpretation. The apotheosis of monarchy during the 1790s and 1800s as identified by Colley, Morris and Wienfort saw the monarch as a political institution that gained enormous popularity.[97]

The problem with such interpretation is that it sees George III as nothing but iconic, and the British monarchy not as a political force but purely as a political institution. Morris sees the period 1790 onwards as a time of de-politicisation of George III, the transformation from the king as an active political player to a representative father figure. She writes: 'Indeed, during the 1790s, the crown became a powerful metaphor.'[98] In her interpretation, George III was left with very little to decide in the political arena of late eighteenth- and early nineteenth-century Britain.

---

[93] *The Times*, 20 February 1806.   [94] *The Morning Chronicle*, 20 February 1806.
[95] Jacobi to Hardenberg, 30 May 1806, Geheimes Staatsarchiv Preußischer Kulturbesitz, I. HA, Rep. 11, convolut 180c, fol. 239.
[96] H. T. Dickinson, 'Popular conservatism and militant loyalism 1789–1815', in: Dickinson, ed., *Britain and the French Revolution 1789–1815* (London, 1989), pp. 103–25.
[97] Linda Colley, 'The apotheosis of George III: loyalty, royalty and the British nation 1760–1820', *Past and Present* 102 (1984), pp. 94–129; Marilyn Morris, *The British monarchy and the French Revolution* (London/Yale, 1998); Monika Wienfort, *Monarchie in der bürgerlichen Gesellschaft. Deutschland und England von 1640 bis 1848* (Göttingen, 1993).
[98] Marilyn Morris, *The British monarchy and the French Revolution*, p. 11.

Instead, she argues: 'the king's attention to royal ritual and patronage finally paid off: the cult of monarchy became a vehicle for the development of a national identity.'[99]

Although there is much to be said in favour of such an interpretation, a closer look at the events around the Electorate of Hanover calls into question whether George III really understood himself as stripped of political power and transformed into a national icon. From a British and Hanoverian angle, George III was central to British policy towards Prussia in autumn 1806 when his interference in the events preceding Jena and Auerstedt had severely delayed a British mission to Berlin.[100] He also engaged in lively correspondence with the foreign secretary a few months later. To Canning he wrote five letters in little more than a week from 9 to 17 May to ensure that a Prussian guarantee for the restoration of Hanover would be included in the stipulations of the Treaty of Memel.[101]

The correspondence with Canning is particularly enlightening in the context of George III's physical frailty. His first severe attack of what has been identified as porphyria dates back to 1788–9. There were subsequent bouts of illness in 1795, 1801 and 1804 and the monarch was not only unable to rule during many of the severe political crises of the Napoleonic Wars, he also lost much of his physical strength.[102] Some of the monarch's incapacity was attributed to his Hanoverian concerns. As the *Saint James's Chronicle* wrote about the king's state of health in April 1801 George III's exhaustion was due to 'too violent exercise on horseback', and 'having had on the preceding evening a conversation of three hours with the Hanoverian Minister, which had caused too much exertion of mind, and produced a slight degree of spasm'.[103] Despite his physical difficulties, however, George III did interfere in support of Hanover (much encouraged by Count Münster) until the summer of 1807, and expected his foreign secretary to respond to his demands. More than 200 letters concerning Hanover are listed in Arthur Aspinall's edition of the later correspondence of George III.[104] It is enlightening to see that all except one are dated pre-1807. There is only one single entry for the period after 1807 concerned with the political

---

[99] *Ibid.*, p. 35.   [100] Riotte, *Hannover in der britischen Politik*, pp. 156–62.
[101] Letters from George Canning to the King, and the replies in Aspinall, *The later correspondence*, No. 3459, pp. 578–80.
[102] Ida Macalpine and Richard Hunter, *George III and the mad business* (London, 1969). Ernst Ludwig von Lenthe also comments on the reduced physical strength of the monarch in Familientagebuch, Private Papers, Family Archives, Gut Lenthe, FA 106.
[103] *St James's Chronicle*, 30 April 1801.
[104] Canning to George III, 4 July 1809, in Aspinall, *The later correspondence*, No. 3915.

events in Hanover. In this letter Canning informed the monarch about the insurrection in the Electorate against the French in July 1809. In an accompanying note Canning makes it clear that he leaves it to the discretion of Herbert Taylor, the king's private secretary, whether Taylor would inform the monarch immediately: Canning wrote: 'it is unnecessary to give his Majesty any trouble upon the subject'.[105] The reason for this lack of correspondence is not the transformation of monarchical power, or a lack of interest in foreign policy. In 1807 George III turned completely blind and could no longer read correspondence himself. Not structural changes of any kind but the personal fate of George III stopped the monarch from actively interfering in foreign policy.

With the disappearance of George III from the political foreground, the influence of the Hanoverian minister vanished. The absence of the monarch made the position of Count Münster in London particularly difficult. His memoranda to his British ministers were hardly replied to. The first minister and foreign secretary kept 'a mere dignified silence', as Münster himself phrased it.[106] Münster still wrote numerous memoranda. He asked for a British declaration in 1807 to protest against the French occupation, he promoted an expedition to Hanover in 1809, wrote further memoranda on the French policies in Hanover, most notably to Marquis Wellesley on 31 May 1810 and 6 February 1811. The Hanoverian minister constantly reminded the British government of 'the measures which might in his [Münster's] opinion be resorted to', but without further result. In a memorandum of December 1812, Münster wrote disillusioned: 'the name of Hanover has no more been mentioned in any public act by the British Government notwithstanding the subsequent events which induced His Majesty and afterwards the Prince Regent to order the undersigned Minister to apply to his Majesty's ministers for some public declaration to show to the world his rights'.[107] Without monarchical support, British politicians would not engage in a policy in favour of Hanover. It was not before the full establishment of the future George IV as Prince Regent and the defeat of Napoleon in Russia that Münster's and with it Hanover's fate would change once more.[108]

Although not in the same way as his predecessors, George III was crucial for the political survival of Hanover during the French

---

[105] George Canning to George III, in Aspinall, *The later correspondence*, No. 3915, p. 308 (footnote 1).
[106] Memorandum Münster, 29 March 1812, PRO London, FO 34/4.
[107] Memorandum Münster, December 1812, PRO London, FO 34/4.
[108] See the chapters by Christopher D. Thompson and Mjindert Bertram in this volume.

Revolutionary and Napoleonic Wars up to 1807. In opposition to the existing historiography, it is safe to argue for a special relationship between George III and his German dominions. Instead of dividing the 123 years of the dynastic union into the two parts before and after the accession of George III historians are well advised to consider the attitudes of each Hanoverian monarch individually in their full complexity.

5 The Hanoverian dimension in early nineteenth-century British politics

Christopher D. Thompson

> It might be very well to say, that Hanover and England were two separate kingdoms – that one had nothing to do with the other. This might be the case theoretically; but it never had been, it could not be so, practically... The policy pursued by the King of Hanover must, without strong proofs to the contrary, be considered as the policy of the King of England.
>
> Henry Lytton Bulwer MP, 2 August 1832.[1]

The Hanoverian dimension in British foreign policy and domestic politics during the final decades of the Personal Union has received little historical attention. The only historian to have specifically focused on the relationship between Britain and Hanover after 1815 confined his analysis largely to the realm of foreign policy and admitted the need for more research.[2] The absence of Hanover from general surveys of British domestic politics is perhaps understandable: the significance of the Personal Union in purely domestic British affairs was spasmodic and haphazard. Nevertheless there was a Hanoverian dimension to British domestic politics after 1815 which manifested itself in public attitudes towards the monarchy, catholic emancipation and the cause of liberty at home and abroad. Hanoverian issues were not constant themes in newspapers, periodicals and political caricature, but nor were they entirely invisible. The omission of the Hanoverian dimension by historians is particularly striking in areas where there seems to be a good prima facie case for taking the Personal Union into consideration. For example, recent royal biographies of George IV and William IV – kings of both Britain and Hanover – mention Hanover only when it forms an

---

[1] 2 August 1832, *Hansard's Parliamentary Debates 3rd Series* (London, 1833), vol. XIV, p. 1039.
[2] W. D. Gruner, *Großbritannien, der Deutsche Bund und die Struktur des europäischen Friedens im frühen 19. Jahrhundert. Studien zu den britisch-deutschen Beziehungen in einer Periode des Umbruchs 1812–1820* (2 vols., Munich, 1979); Gruner, 'England, Hannover und der Deutsche Bund 1814–1837', in: A. M. Birke and K. Kluxen, eds., *England und Hannover. Prinz-Albert-Studien 4* (Munich, London, New York, Oxford and Paris, 1986), pp. 81–126, especially pp. 83–4.

unavoidable part of the biographical narrative.[3] The Hanoverian connection is never permitted to assume any analytical significance. Yet it is hard to see how a complete account can be provided of George IV's or William IV's attitude to kingship in general, or of the transition to constitutional monarchy in Britain in particular, without at least some consideration of the actions of these monarchs in Hanover. The Personal Union is as unavoidable in assessing the strength of personal monarchy in this period as in the eighteenth century. The Hanoverian dimension has also been neglected in debates on British national identity in the early nineteenth century. Linda Colley's influential study on the forging of the British nation closes in 1837, but not because any significance is attached to the end of the Personal Union in that year: the close of the British monarchy's independent German political connections is not mentioned at all.[4] Even historians sympathetic to a reassessment of the Personal Union in the eighteenth century have expressed scepticism about whether this can be repeated for the nineteenth.[5] This chapter challenges such a view.

Yet the historiographical cupboard is not entirely bare. German historians – Hanoverian ones in particular – have appreciated the significance of the Personal Union. Both older and newer accounts of the history of the Kingdom of Hanover engage with several individual aspects of the relationship with Britain.[6] Understandably, however, the perspective taken has been a Hanoverian or German rather than British one. The classic works on British foreign policy in this era by Charles Webster and Harold Temperley have also paid due attention to the Hanoverian dimension, as has some more recent work on Anglo-German relations in the early nineteenth century.[7]

---

[3] E. A. Smith, *George IV* (New Haven and London, 1999); P. Ziegler, *King William IV* (London, 1971).

[4] L. Colley, *Britons. Forging the nation 1707–1837* (New Haven and London, 1992), p. 1.

[5] J. Black, *The Hanoverians. The history of a dynasty* (London and New York, 2004), pp. 191–2.

[6] W. v. Hassell, *Geschichte des Königreichs Hannover, 1. Teil: Von 1813 bis 1848* (Bremen, 1898); M. Bertram, *Das Königreich Hannover. Kleine Geschichte eines vergangenen Staates* (Hanover, 2004). See also W. R. Röhrbein and A. v. Rohr, *Hannover im Glanz und Schatten des britischen Weltreiches. Die Auswirkungen der Personalunion auf Hannover von 1714 bis 1837* (Hanover, 1977).

[7] H. W. V. Temperley, *The foreign policy of Canning 1822–1827* (London, 1925); C. K. Webster, *The foreign policy of Castlereagh 1815–1822* (London, 1925); Webster, *The foreign policy of Castlereagh 1812–1815* (London, 1931); Webster, *The foreign policy of Palmerston 1830–41* (2 vols., London, 1951); G. Lange, 'Die Rolle Englands bei der Wiederherstellung und Vergrößerung Hannovers 1813–1815', *Niedersächsische Jahrbuch für Landesgeschichte* 28 (1956), 73–178; Gruner, 'England, Hannover und der Deutsche Bund'; B. Simms, ' "An odd question enough." Charles James Fox, the crown and British policy during the

During the nineteenth century the Personal Union operated in principle as precisely that. The British and Hanoverian governments were distinct. On an official level contact between British and Hanoverian personnel took place only with royal permission. However, this was difficult to maintain if British and Hanoverian policy diverged because at the same time – paradoxically – there was an expectation of both policy consistency between the two states given their common sovereign and the priority of British interests. It became increasingly difficult to hide divergences of Hanoverian and British policy from public scrutiny. British action on behalf of Hanover was constitutionally suspect. It was certainly open to political exploitation if uncovered. Growing public scrutiny therefore reduced the scope for gaining monarchical favour through pro-Hanoverian policies. Finally, given the greater power of the king in Hanover than Britain, policy inconsistencies implied conflict between the king and his British ministers.

The remainder of the chapter is divided into four sections. First the attitude of the royal family – the embodiment of the Personal Union – towards Hanover is assessed. The Personal Union set the limits for the identification of the royal family with Britain. The second section examines the role of Hanover in purely domestic politics, focusing on catholic emancipation, but also the default position of Hanover in the British public sphere. Thirdly, the significance of Hanover in British foreign policy under Castlereagh, Canning and Palmerston is explored, particularly the interaction of foreign and domestic politics. Finally the close of the Personal Union is considered.

I

Given the nature of the connection between Hanover and Britain, it is unsurprising that the strongest affection for Hanover existed within the royal family. George III tried to ensure that his sons were aware of their German ancestry and family dominions by sending them to live in Hanover early in their lives. Prince Frederick (later duke of York) was appointed bishop of Osnabrück as an infant and moved to Hanover in 1781. Prince William (later Clarence) spent two years in the Electorate in the mid-1780s, while Princes Ernest (Cumberland), Augustus (Sussex) and Adolphus (Cambridge) were sent to Göttingen to complete their education in 1786. Although George III was unable to send his eldest son to Germany, he was anxious to ensure that the Prince of Wales learnt

Hanoverian crisis of 1806', *Historical Journal* 38 (1995), 577–96; T. Riotte, *Hannover in der britischen Politik (1792–1815). Dynastische Verbindung als Element außenpolitischer Entscheidungsprozesse* (Münster, 2005).

German and acquired a knowledge of the constitution of both the Holy Roman Empire and the Electorate of Hanover (as they then were). The success of this endeavour manifested itself in his son's choice of interior decoration. The vertical windows of the conservatory at Carlton House contained not only the coats of arms of all the sovereigns of England and Princes of Wales, but also those of the electoral princes of the House of Brunswick.[8] The royal dukes formed part of the Hanoverian faction in British politics, guarding its interests.[9] In 1814, according to Princess Lieven, Clarence was preoccupied with the future of Hanover to the exclusion of all other political issues.[10] The Prince Regent, urged on by Cumberland, was anxious to visit Hanover soon after its liberation. He was prevented from doing so only by a combination of Napoleon's return and the reluctance of his British ministers to seek the necessary parliamentary approval for the Prince Regent to leave the country.[11] While Jeremy Black is correct in asserting that the later Hanoverians may not have 'needed' to take an interest in Hanoverian affairs in the way the first two Georges had done, they were nevertheless actively interested in their German possessions.[12]

After the end of the Regency and following the near collapse of relations between George IV and his ministers over the Queen Caroline affair, the king was able to visit Hanover in autumn 1821. Although members of the royal family had lived in Hanover on and off since 1781, most recently the dukes of Cambridge and Clarence, this was the first visit by the ruler of Hanover since the final visit of George II in 1755. Sandwiched between trips to Ireland and Scotland – which had been even more neglected by their sovereigns than Hanover – the visit was an important part of the development of a peripatetic monarchy, which was subsequently emulated by King Ernst August in Hanover and Queen Victoria in Britain. Curiously, Linda Colley fails to mention the Hanoverian visit despite its clear relevance to her arguments about royal travel associating the monarchy with the nation.[13]

The king's presence in his ancestral lands was met with elaborate ceremony and jubilation by the population. Sir William Knighton, George IV's private secretary, was impressed by the devotion of the crowds but horrified by the quality of the roads.[14] The visit did not provoke the level of criticism in the British public sphere that had

---

[8] Smith, *George IV*, pp. 11, 29.   [9] Simms, 'Hanoverian crisis of 1806', pp. 583–4.
[10] Ziegler, *William IV*, p. 113.   [11] Webster, *Foreign policy of Castlereagh 1812–15*, p. 30.
[12] Black, *Hanoverians*, p. 192.   [13] Colley, *Britons*, pp. 233–5.
[14] Lady Knighton, ed., *Memoirs of Sir William Knighton* (2 vols., London, 1838), vol. I, pp. 165–79.

accompanied the travels of George I and II. *The Times*, for example, reported the visit without passing judgement.[15] However, at least one satirist noticed the contradictions of the king's image.[16] The print 'Travelling in Germany' showed George IV recruiting Hanoverians into the army through the excessive taxation of John Bull. Loyal and cheering moustachioed Hanoverians catch the gold thrown from the royal carriage. The artist successfully combined traditional fears about standing armies and the use of German troops by Hanoverian monarchs, as well as a more contemporary concern about the militarism of the continental powers. But in addition to the revival of the eighteenth-century critique of the Personal Union as a drain on English resources, the cartoonist took the opportunity to satirise the king's multiple identities through the observations of three Hanoverian bystanders. One says that George IV is indeed a Hanoverian, which is reflected in the German style of the monarch's clothing in the print, another that the king has claimed to be Irish, a third that some years back he had declared that, of his brothers, only he and William were not Germans.

The Hanoverian connection necessarily prevented a complete apotheosis of the royal family as the embodiment of British identity. Particularly during the difficult transition to peace after 1815, supporters of retrenchment tended to focus their ire on the military budget and the civil list. These two things were connected by the Germanness of the royal family. Whigs and Radicals warned against the dangers of militarism which was associated with Germany and a foreign form of government: absolutism. In a debate on the military budget, Henry Brougham warned his 'royal master' that 'this was not a country in which the constitutional system and habits were to be encroached upon by the prejudices, tastes, or views of a military monarch ... that this country was England not Germany'.[17] The association of royalty with the military – a pan-European phenomenon – was politically risky in Britain.

The Hanoverian connection was a useful stick with which to beat the monarchy. Hanover and its white horse often appeared in political prints satirising various aspects of the Napoleonic wars. With the resumption of peace in 1815, Hanoverian interests no longer appeared in caricatures as

---

[15] *The Times*, 20 October 1821.
[16] W. Heath, 'Travelling in Germany' (pub. 15 November 1821) located in British Museum Print Room, *A collection of caricatures, mounted in twelve folio volumes, transferred from the B.M.L.* (press-mark Tab. 524), vol. XI, p. 156. See also M. D. George, *Catalogue of political and personal satires preserved in the department of prints and drawings in the British Museum*, vol. X 1820–7 (London, 1952), no. 14254.
[17] 26 February 1816, *Parliamentary debates from the year 1803 to the present time* (London, 1816), vol. XXXII, p. 862; Gruner, 'England, Hannover und der Deutsche Bund', p. 94.

a secret motivation behind British policy. Instead Hanover was portrayed most frequently as an exit strategy for the monarch or his conservative political allies. Typically a signpost is marked 'To Hanover', or a character in the print declares his intention to travel there. Hence Hanover appeared in caricatures concerning the Queen Caroline fiasco in the early 1820s, catholic emancipation in the late 1820s and the progress of the Reform Bill in the early 1830s.[18] These prints were not complete fantasies; George IV certainly contemplated retirement to Hanover during the emancipation crisis in 1829, threatening at an audience with Eldon on 9 April 1829 to leave for Hanover and never return.[19]

Sir David Wilkie's epic painting *Chelsea Pensioners reading the gazette of the Battle of Waterloo* forms the centrepiece of Linda Colley's conclusions about the formation of British identity through war: 'one man's very perceptive interpretation of both the variety and the roots of Britishness'.[20] Yet discussion of the presence in the picture of a moustachioed German soldier 'of the Hanoverian Legion, a corps distinguished at Waterloo', is omitted.[21] Until 1837 the Hanoverian dimension in British politics undermined the completion of the monarchy's identification with British nationalism. Had Queen Victoria not reconnected the British monarchy to Germany through her marriage to Albert, the significance of this would be more apparent.

II

While there was an underlying awareness of the Personal Union in the British public sphere, it cannot be claimed that there was any significant degree of interest in or knowledge of Hanoverian affairs. In 1831–2 and 1837–8, the only two periods when Hanover received sustained attention in British newspapers and periodicals, the extent to which British people were ignorant of Hanoverian conditions was often noted. Hanover was primarily connected with the royal family. It was a frequent literary conceit to refer to the intimate relations between the king of Hanover and the king of Britain. The dispute in the late 1820s between Duke Charles of Brunswick and George IV, who in his capacity as king of

---

[18] See M. D. George, *Catalogue of political and personal satires preserved in the department of prints and drawings in the British Museum*, vols. IX–XI 1811–32 (London, 1949–54), especially 12077, 12234, 12537, 13896, 13974, 13986, 14254, 15690, 15704, 15865, 17082, 17100, 17212–3, 17220, 17255.
[19] D. G. S. Simes, 'The Ultra Tories in British politics, 1824–1834' (unpub. DPhil thesis, Oxford, 1974), p. 422.
[20] Colley, *Britons*, pp. 364–7.
[21] A. Cunningham, ed., *The life of Sir David Wilkie with his journals, tours and critical remarks on works of art; and a selection from his correspondence* (3 vols., London, 1843), vol. II, p. 76.

Hanover had acted as regent for Charles during his minority, was observed with amusement. *The Times* called on the king of England to intervene with the king of Hanover to prevent any threat to the peace of Europe.[22] Purely Hanoverian news was given no special emphasis. The negotiation of the 1819 constitution in Hanover passed almost unnoticed. Attention was only given if there appeared to be a British interest at stake or British political angle. The only evidence of a common non-political bond between Hanover and Britain appeared in relation to the severe flooding of Hanoverian coastal regions in February 1825. The duke of York set up a subscription in Britain for the benefit of the victims of the catastrophe to parallel the duke of Cambridge's efforts in Hanover.[23]

In domestic British politics the Personal Union received only spasmodic and haphazard attention. However, it did play a small role in arguably the most important political issue of the late Hanoverian period, namely catholic emancipation. The theoretically confessional basis of German territorial organisation was permanently destroyed by the Napoleonic wars. The two largest gains for Lutheran Hanover were the Roman Catholic bishoprics of Osnabrück and Hildesheim. The Confederal Act creating the German Confederation granted full religious toleration and civic equality to the three main German Christian denominations: Roman Catholicism, Lutheranism and Calvinism. This was confirmed in the Hanoverian constitution granted in December 1819 by the Prince Regent and on behalf of George III. Roman Catholics were permitted to sit in both chambers of the Hanoverian Assembly of Estates. Thus the Prince Regent had granted in Hanover what he withheld in Britain.

Tellingly, this anomaly does not appear to have been noticed for some time. After 1815 German states entered negotiations with the papacy over the reorganisation of Roman Catholic bishoprics within the German Confederation. In March 1824 a papal bull was issued which dealt with the Hanoverian bishoprics of Osnabrück and Hildesheim. Nearly a year later in late February 1825 Lord Liverpool and George IV exchanged correspondence following the publication of – in the words of the king – an 'absurd note' from an official Hanoverian source on this matter. George IV was anxious to reassure his British ministers that the agreement with the papacy was merely a legacy of the Congress of Vienna (which was basically true), and that his views on the issue of emancipation in Britain remained entirely unaltered. Liverpool reassured the king, but

---

[22] *The Times*, 26 December 1827, 25 August 1829.   [23] *Ibid.*, 21 and 23 March 1825.

stated that 'it was certainly most unfortunate that such an official paper as that to which your Majesty refers should have been sent forth to the world at a moment when it might be subject to such a misapprehension in this country'.[24]

In a long memorandum dating from that year on the case of the Roman Catholics in Ireland, Wellington noted the impact of the affair. The opinions of those opposed to the Roman Catholic claims had been shaken by it, the duke believed. He regretted the indiscreet and unnecessary publication by the Hanoverian government: 'such publication was not necessary; and should not have been made without previous communication with this government'. Although the case of the Roman Catholics in Hanover and Ireland were as different 'as any two cases of the same denomination can be', Wellington felt that

> we must not conceal from ourselves, that the adoption of this arrangement by his Majesty, as King of Hanover, has affected many well judging persons upon the Irish Roman Catholic question; and has tended, both in and out of Parliament, to occasion in some and to augment in others, the apathy upon the question of which the opposers of the Roman Catholics have had so much reason to complain. At all events this Hanoverian arrangement deprives the opposers of the Roman Catholic cause of all arguments founded on the repugnance of his Majesty and of the Royal Family to farther concession.[25]

Since Pitt had agreed, upon returning to office in 1804, not to press emancipation on George III, royal opposition had been an important consideration for moderate and pragmatic opponents of Roman Catholic claims, so Wellington was right to be concerned.

Wellington did not elaborate on the differences between the cases of the Roman Catholics in Hanover and Ireland. However, John Wilson Croker, like Wellington a reluctant emancipationist, recorded a conversation held with the duke of Clarence in 1828 in which Clarence 'observed on the inconsistency of the King refusing in Ireland what he granted in Hanover. I said the cases were not quite the same. The King held Hanover by hereditary right, but England only by the Protestant Settlement.'[26] This was technically correct but hardly politically convincing, except to a Tory Ultra, which Croker was not. Furthermore it drew

---

[24] Münster to Wellington, 23 February 1825, George IV to Liverpool, 25 February 1825, Liverpool to George IV, 25 February 1825, in Wellington, 2nd duke of, ed., *Despatches, correspondence, and memoranda of Field Marshal Arthur Duke of Wellington, K.G.* (15 vols., London, 1867–71), vol. II, pp. 413, 418.

[25] Memorandum on the case of the Roman Catholics in Ireland, *ibid.*, p. 593.

[26] Cited in J. C. D. Clark, *English society 1660–1832* (2nd edn, Cambridge, 2000), p. 555. For the similarity of Croker and Wellington's outlook, see W. Thomas, *The quarrel of Macaulay and Croker: politics and history in the age of reform* (Oxford, 2000), p. 41.

attention to the fact that half of the identity of the king was potentially arbitrary and despotic.

Roman Catholic campaigners for emancipation were particularly attracted to the Hanoverian argument. The 'Address of the Catholics of Ireland to the People of England' (1826) made use of Hanover twice: first as an example, alongside Prussia, of the invalidity of the dual allegiance argument used by opponents of emancipation; secondly, alongside Canada, as an example of the dignity of Roman Catholics who would not submit to be excluded from politics, implicitly asking why the Irish were different.[27] Eighteen months later *The Times* adopted in an editorial the argument that the emancipation of the Roman Catholics in protestant Germany – Hanover and Prussia specifically – had not proved dangerous.[28] In 1828 Daniel O'Connell, the leader of the Roman Catholic Association, asserted that the British government had been using the Hanoverian envoy to the Holy See in order to press for a concordat with the papacy. Wellington, now prime minister, successfully requested that George IV permit him to discuss the matter with Count Münster, the Hanoverian minister, so that a full public denial supported by a statement from the Hanoverian envoy in question could be issued.[29]

For opponents of catholic emancipation on principle – the so-called Tory Ultras – the Personal Union was significant because of its origins. They emphasised one half of the point made by Croker to Clarence: the House of Brunswick ruled in Britain by virtue of the Act of Settlement which had been passed specifically to exclude Roman Catholics from the throne. If Roman Catholics were now to be permitted involvement in politics, on what basis did that put the position of the House of Brunswick? This was of particular concern to royal opponents of emancipation such as George IV and the Duke of Cumberland.[30] The argument carried some weight. *The Times* admitted the 'natural prepossession' of any prince of the House of Hanover to oppose catholic claims, but not to the exclusion of all other dangers and considerations.[31] It also manifested itself in the formation of Brunswick clubs in 1828–9 to defend the Protestant Constitution at the instigation of leading Ultra politicians.[32] However, this attempt to associate the anti-emancipation cause with loyalty to the royal family was open to attack. *The Edinburgh Review*

---

[27] *The Times*, 21 December 1826.   [28] *Ibid.*, 7 May 1828.
[29] Wellington to George IV, 25 November 1828, Münster to Wellington, 15 January 1829, Wellington, *Despatches*, vol. V, pp. 285, 450.
[30] Smith, *George IV*, p. 193.   [31] *The Times*, 12 February 1829.
[32] Simes, 'The Ultra Tories in British politics', pp. 346–9. See also G. I. T. Machin, *Catholic question in English politics, 1820–1830* (Oxford, 1964), pp. 133–40.

lambasted the opponents of emancipation for their false appropriation of the Houses of Orange and Brunswick and the name of Pitt the Younger.

As *Brunswickers*, they assume the right of imposing their own corporation bigotries upon an illustrious family, in contradiction to that liberty of conscience which is now the common law of Germany, and in contradiction to the domestic example, of equality before the law, which the King of Hanover has so lately set to his relation, the King of England.[33]

The Hanoverian connection, therefore, could possess political significance in British domestic politics although there were few issues where this was the case. The Personal Union was recognised across the political spectrum to require some degree of consistency between Hanoverian and British policy. Any divergence was open to exploitation. Given this political reality, ministers grumbled about the absence of communication between the Hanoverian and British governments and even their inability to supervise Hanoverian policy, despite this contradicting the constitutional theory of the Personal Union.

III

The Personal Union could not be ignored in the foreign policy arena. Consequently, the British politicians most involved in the Hanoverian connection were foreign secretaries. The experiences of the three longest-serving foreign ministers of the period – Castlereagh, Canning and Palmerston – demonstrate that the Personal Union remained a significant foreign policy factor. The Hanoverian connection offered some benefits, but its fullest exploitation was difficult because of the purely personal nature of the union and the non-interventionist tenor of British policy after 1815. Meanwhile tensions between Hanoverian and British interests and between monarch and foreign secretary were increasingly difficult to hide from public gaze.

When Castlereagh became foreign secretary in 1812, the Personal Union was crucially important for providing him with intelligence about the European situation. Paradoxically, the Hanoverian connection proved diplomatically most useful to Britain at a time when Hanover had ceased to exist. Despite the dismemberment of Hanover in 1807, its diplomatic network continued to operate. By contrast Britain's had virtually collapsed. The correspondence between Count Münster in London and the Hanoverian residents at Vienna and Berlin provided a

---

[33] 'The last of the catholic question – its principle, history, and effects', *Edinburgh Review*, 29 (March 1829), p. 223.

means to keep Britain in touch with the two German powers even at the height of Napoleon's power.[34] During the peace negotiations in 1814 and 1815 Castlereagh rated Münster more highly than his British subordinates, the earl of Aberdeen, the earl of Cathcart and Sir Charles Stewart. Münster formally represented Britain on the two commissions appointed in Paris in May 1814 to negotiate the territorial and financial scope of the settlement.[35] At this level, the Hanoverian connection offered practical advantages, provided that the monarch and foreign secretary remained on good terms.

The close cooperation of Hanover and Britain dated back to 1806 when Prussia had occupied and annexed the Electorate. In a major departure from traditional British foreign policy, the government had insisted on the restoration of Hanover in its negotiations with both Prussia and France. As Brendan Simms has argued, this reflected the wishes of George III, the pressure exerted by the Hanoverian faction headed by Münster and the desire of Charles James Fox to shore up royal support for the government. At the same time the extent to which British policy was driven by Hanoverian interests remained intentionally ambiguous in public.[36]

Münster's achievement was substantial for Hanoverian restoration remained a settled aim of British foreign policy. However, he was not satisfied. The impact of Napoleon was revolutionising the map of central Europe and he wanted to ensure that, following the defeat of Napoleon, a restored Hanover would not miss out on territorial aggrandisement. Now Münster pressed the case for Hanoverian expansion, but on this score there was no consensus among British politicians. Nevertheless, Münster was successful. Hanover did gain substantial territory at the Congress of Vienna, and without British diplomatic support it is inconceivable that this should have occurred.

Restrictions of space do not permit a detailed discussion of these developments, but a number of points stand out.[37] Gruner is correct in his conclusion that in the eventual peace settlement Hanoverian interests did not override British ones and that the expansion of Hanover could be and was defended in terms of British interests. But Lange's more detailed narrative suggests that the Hanoverian faction identified by Simms as existing in 1806 continued to operate thereafter. At a number of moments Hanoverian interests were pursued by British diplomats at the expense of British ones, notably during the negotiations of the Prussian subsidy

---

[34] Webster, *Foreign policy of Castlereagh 1812–15*, pp. 29, 45–6.
[35] *Ibid.*, pp. 264, 267, 274, 280.   [36] Simms, 'Hanoverian crisis of 1806'.
[37] See Lange, 'Die Rolle Englands'; Gruner, 'England, Hannover und der Deutsche Bund'.

treaty in 1813, in which the only substantive political points concerned Hanoverian expansion. Sir Charles Stewart, the British negotiator with the Prussians, expressed the hope that he had 'pleased Carlton House on the Hanover points without militating general interests'.[38] At that time it would not have been easy to justify Castlereagh's policy solely in terms of British interests. Castlereagh feared public exposure and was economical with the truth in his reports to both parliament and the cabinet. Officially Hanoverian interests were not pursued. At this time, news did not leak, although a few years before Canning had expressed concerns about this possibility, and Stein, a Prussian politician aware of the constitutional delicacies, threatened to expose Castlereagh's Hanoverian predilections as a negotiating ploy.[39] New research is needed to see how significant Castlereagh's conversion to the Hanoverian cause was in securing the foreign secretary's position vis-à-vis the Prince Regent. Like Fox, he had opposed Hanoverian interests prior to 1806.[40] Castlereagh was probably less dependent on royal favour for his position than Fox which may explain why Münster compared his support for Hanover unfavourably to Fox's. But no member of the cabinet was friendlier to Hanover than Castlereagh in this period. He supported Hanover as far as possible, though this was sometimes not very far at all, and more than necessary.

From the end of 1815 to Castlereagh's suicide in 1822, Hanover played little or no role in British foreign policy.[41] The doctrine of non-intervention applied to Hanover as much as any other state. This was put to the test following the assassination of a Russian agent and playwright named Kotzebue by a German nationalist student in March 1819. At Metternich's instigation, the chief ministers of the German Confederation, including Münster as representative of Hanover, met at Karlsbad and consented to the passage of repressive confederal legislation. Castlereagh was sympathetic to Metternich in private, but drew back from violating the principle of non-intervention by offering the public support that Metternich desired.[42] The ministerial conference at Karlsbad coincided with the Peterloo Massacre in August 1819. Lord Liverpool's administration responded with repressive legislation itself, so any objections to Metternich's behaviour would have appeared

---

[38] Sir Charles Stewart to Edward Cooke, 19 June 1813, quoted in Webster, *Foreign policy of Castlereagh 1812–15*, p. 132.
[39] Lange, 'Die Rolle Englands', pp. 77–8, 88, 92, 99, 106, 110–18, 126–7, 147–52.
[40] Simms, 'Hanoverian crisis of 1806', pp. 573–4; Lange, 'Die Rolle Englands', p. 79.
[41] Though see Gruner, 'England, Hannover und der Deutsche Bund', pp. 97–8.
[42] Webster, *Foreign policy of Castlereagh 1815–1822*, pp. 194–5; Lange, 'Die Rolle Englands, p. 114.

hypocritical, and in fact the conservative British government was appalled by the challenge to order manifesting itself all over Europe.[43]

The Whig and Radical opposition did take some notice of these events. *The Times* denounced the Hanoverian censorship edict and also reported on a public meeting at Truro in which the Prince Regent *of Hanover* was accused of being in league with continental sovereigns in a conspiracy against liberty which would soon extend to Britain.[44] However, the government's critics did not need to focus on the Karlsbad Decrees. There was no divergence between British and Hanoverian policy and the actions of Liverpool's administration at home were so outrageous in non-Tory eyes that events in Germany were politically superfluous.

For Canning the Personal Union was a mixed blessing. Upon his return to the foreign office in 1822 the Hanoverian connection threatened to destroy his position. Thereafter it offered some benefits, but no major advantages. Canning's appointment had been forced upon George IV by the weight of the cabinet. Canning had supported George's estranged wife, Caroline of Brunswick, and the king believed that he would pursue a 'liberal' course in Europe which risked British isolation and possibly European war. For the next three years George IV intrigued against his own foreign secretary. The Personal Union was the chief weapon in the king's armoury because, acting in his capacity as king of Hanover, George IV could discuss international relations with the ambassadors of other states without the knowledge or constraint of the responsible British minister. Without the Personal Union, the development of George's cottage clique or coterie – so-named after the Windsor cottage where their meetings took place – would have been much harder if not impossible.

On his appointment Canning was not granted access to the Hanoverian diplomatic correspondence. Consequently George IV was frequently as informed if not better so than his foreign secretary. George's most authoritative modern biographer has tended to dismiss the significance of the cottage clique, characterising its existence as a means for a frustrated monarch to let off steam.[45] This interpretation is a necessary one for Smith, as admitting any significance for the cottage clique would undermine his portrayal of George IV as a willingly constitutional monarch. Temperley, however, believed that 'there was a real danger that a double system of foreign policy might be pursued'.[46] It seems implausible that foreign envoys – the Lievens, Esterhazy, Neumann and Polignac – should

---

[43] Gruner, 'England, Hannover und der Deutsche Bund', pp. 101–2, 123.
[44] *The Times*, 1 and 23 November 1819.   [45] Smith, *George IV*, pp. 227–8.
[46] Temperley, *Foreign policy of Canning*, pp. 240, 257n.

have devoted so much time to helping George let off steam if they did not perceive a genuine possibility of influencing and learning about British policy. Even if all the foreign ambassadors were deluded about the significance of their conversations with the king, the existence of the coterie influenced their reports and the understanding of foreign states about British policy and hence had an impact on international relations.

One of Canning's most important legacies was the opening up of foreign policy to public scrutiny through speeches inside and outside parliament and the publication of diplomatic despatches. This approach was forced upon Canning by the need to counter the king's double dealings through the Personal Union. At the start of 1825 the conspiracies against Canning began to collapse. The coterie had been unable to dislodge the foreign secretary, largely because he retained the complete confidence of the indispensable Lord Liverpool. In addition, Canning's foreign policy was very popular. Had he been forced to resign, Canning told Granville, he would have declared openly in the House of Commons: 'that I was driven from office by the Holy Alliance, and further, that the system, which I found established of personal communications between the sovereign and Foreign Ministers, was one under which no English Minister could do his duty'.[47] It is doubtful whether the Personal Union could have survived such an outcome. For as Canning also remarked:

I wonder whether he [Metternich] is aware that the private communication of foreign ministers with the King of England is wholly at variance with the spirit, and practice too, of the British Constitution ... the custom introduced in the time of my predecessor survives only by sufferance, and would not stand the test of parliamentary discussion.[48]

A tension existed between the theory of Personal Union, which the king had not contravened, and British constitutional liberty.

The transformation of George IV's attitude to Canning was marked by the closure of any possibility of a double foreign policy. On 13 October 1825 Canning reported to Granville that the king had begun showing him the Hanoverian diplomatic correspondence, gleefully and significantly asking '*Comprenez-vous?*'[49] Canning soon came to the same conclusion as Castlereagh about its superiority to British despatches.[50] In the short term he was able to turn the tables on Metternich by using the Hanoverian diplomatic network as a tool for his own purposes.[51]

---

[47] Canning to Granville, 11 March 1825, cited in *ibid.*, p. 248.
[48] Canning to Granville, 4 April 1825 in A. G. Stapleton, *George Canning and his times*, p. 433.
[49] Temperley, *Foreign policy of Canning*, p. 250.
[50] *Ibid.*, pp. 271, 287.   [51] *Ibid.*, pp. 250–5, 257n.

On only one occasion – on current knowledge – did Canning seek to use the Personal Union directly for the benefit of British policy. The circumstances in which this request was made and the nature of the Hanoverian response elucidate why the Personal Union was increasingly useless as an instrument of British policy. In 1824 the independence of Portugal – Britain's longest ally – was threatened by internal unrest and external intervention from French-influenced Spain. The Portuguese government demanded the despatch of British forces to Portugal. The British envoy wrote a despatch to Canning supporting the proposal on the basis that the French envoy had offered French troops in order to expand French influence at the expense of British. This despatch arrived shortly after Canning received a formal request from the Portuguese government on 29 June 1824. Canning was furious, believing that it was a French trap, because France knew that Britain had no troops available to send and was in any case unable to do so without parliamentary approval. Britain was now placed in an embarrassing position regardless of the answer given: either Portugal would have to be abandoned; occupied in concurrence with France and the continental powers, thereby associating Britain with their schemes; or occupied unilaterally, which could initiate a European war.[52]

The use of Hanoverian troops offered a means to escape the dilemma. George IV agreed to the British cabinet's request to send Hanoverian troops if necessary. The duke of Wellington advised the king about a range of matters connected with the proposal from the choice of Hanoverian general to the size – 6,200 – of the force.[53] However, the operation ran into a number of obstacles. News of the Hanoverian preparations leaked to the press on 3 July. *The Times*'s editorial condemned the operation a few days later. The reasoning was unrelated to the issues of the Personal Union, instead the editorial opposed intervention on principle before engaging in a sustained diatribe on the evils of standing armies, whether British or Hanoverian. However, it was argued that the use of Hanoverian troops would not necessarily save Britain from involvement because if Prussia used the opportunity to resurrect her designs on Hanover, then suddenly Hanover would be found to be as dear to British interests as – echoing Pitt the Elder – 'Hampshire'.[54] The legitimacy of using Hanoverian troops in defence of British interests was not considered, indeed a subsequent editorial, written after confirmation that Hanoverian troops would not be sent, assumed in passing that

---

[52] *Ibid.*, pp. 201–3.
[53] Wellington to George IV, 1 July 1824, in Wellington, *Despatches*, vol. II, p. 281.
[54] *The Times*, 8 July 1824.

Hanoverian forces were 'disposable by England' – an example of the way in which the Hanoverian connection was seen in *practice* as more than personal and British-led.[55]

More importantly, negotiations with the Hanoverian government stalled. Wellington advised George IV that the Portuguese should pay for everything and that a Hanoverian should be appointed to negotiate terms with the Portuguese government, 'possibly' aided by British mediation.[56] The king instructed Wellington to correspond with Münster on the proposed deployment. Wellington told Münster that the question of whether the deployment of the Hanoverian forces was convenient or constitutional was solely a matter for the king's German servants. However, Wellington ruled out the proposal – apparently originating from the Hanoverian chargé d'affaires – that Britain and Hanover negotiate terms and then Britain negotiate with Portugal, as the whole point of using Hanoverian troops was to avoid the need to summon the British parliament in order to agree to extra expenditure. The British government could not place itself in a position whereby it was responsible for recovering costs from Portugal. Similarly the British ministers could not guarantee a treaty between Hanover and Portugal as that too would require the recall of parliament and hence a delay.[57]

By this stage, however, Canning had secured an assurance that France would not intervene and therefore the Portuguese request for troops could be rejected. This episode reveals much about the Hanoverian connection. First, the use of Hanoverian troops was forced on Canning by circumstance. Secondly, difficulties quickly surfaced once the question of using Hanoverian troops was mooted. The link between Hanoverian and British policy was maintained solely by the king. His British and Hanoverian advisers scrupulously pursued their understanding of British and Hanoverian interests respectively. Hence, in Wellington's letter to Münster, the option was explicitly left open for Hanover to refuse to help at all. The Hanoverian government was understandably reticent about deploying Hanoverian troops in Portugal without any British guarantees about the recovery of the costs. Yet it was the informality and absence of guarantees that had attracted the British cabinet to the Hanoverian solution. Once the British government committed itself either to negotiating on Hanover's behalf, or guaranteeing a treaty with Portugal for Hanover's benefit – arguably the proper procedure for a transaction between two states linked solely in a Personal Union – then

---

[55] *Ibid.*, 28 July 1824.
[56] Wellington to George IV, 2 July 1824, in Wellington, *Despatches*, vol. II, p. 282.
[57] Wellington to Münster, 13 July 1824, in *ibid.*, pp. 287–8.

the benefits of the strategy would disappear. The British parliament would have to sanction any treaty committing the British government to such expenditure. But it was precisely a wish to avoid the delay of summoning parliament and the potential embarrassment of a failure to gain approval from the retrenchment-minded House of Commons that pointed ministers in Hanover's direction in the first place.

While the proposal to deploy Hanoverian troops in Portugal raised constitutional difficulties for British ministers, the divergence in Hanoverian and British policy in the early 1830s over the so-called Liberal Movement was far more public and hence possessed far greater political significance. The controversy exposed not just the difficulty of maintaining a purely Personal Union, but also the intimate connection between foreign and domestic politics and the increasing significance of public opinion to politics. George IV had used the Hanoverian diplomatic service to demonstrate to foreign powers his unhappiness with the policies pursued by Canning. In 1832, however, the differences between the king of Hanover and the British government over the Liberal Movement in Germany resulted in a far more public demonstration of the divergence between William IV and Palmerston.

The origins of the controversy lay in the July Revolution of 1830 in Paris. This had stimulated political disturbances across Germany and in several states conservative administrations were replaced by (more) liberal ones and a variety of reforms introduced. Hanover followed this pattern with a short-lived revolt in the university town of Göttingen in January 1831 which led to the resignation of Münster and the introduction of constitutional reform and peasant emancipation.[58] *The Times* welcomed the news from Göttingen ('as promising a little rebellion as could be wished'), argued that Hanover had been misgoverned, attacked Münster and stated that 'a liberal and humane Monarch who gives his willing sanction to reform in this country, cannot be inattentive to a call upon him for a similar boon from a state which was the cradle of his ancestors'.[59] The cause of reform in Hanover and Britain seemed for the reformist *Times* to be linked by the attitudes of William IV.

Conversely any signs of renewed conservatism in Hanover had implications for Britain. The Hambach Festival, a political demonstration held on 27–8 May 1832 in the Bavarian Palatinate, provided Metternich with an opportunity to act against the revival of German liberalism and nationalism. He engineered the agreement of the German Confederation to a

---

[58] Bertram, *Königreich Hannover*, pp. 45–50.
[59] *The Times*, 27 January 1831, p. 2. For coverage of Münster's resignation, see 28 February, 14 and 28 March 1831.

new set of repressive measures known as the Six Articles on 28 June. Acting in his capacity as king of Hanover, William IV instructed the Hanoverian ambassador to the *Bundestag* to vote for the Six Articles. By the end of July news of the Six Articles entered the public sphere.

It was scarcely possible for William IV to have chosen a more sensitive moment to make this political move. Although the Reform Act had received the royal assent on 7 June, the relationship between the king and his ministers was clearly tense. In early May, William's prevarication about peer creation had forced Grey's resignation. The king had unsuccessfully attempted to engineer a Tory administration under Wellington which would pass a more moderate reform measure. Previously popular, William was struck by a stone at Ascot on 17 June. This can hardly have increased William's confidence in his ministers as the passage of the Reform Act was supposed to have reduced the revolutionary threat. The attitudes of the king towards his British ministers and to reform were now far less clear.

Furthermore, since May the press had contained a number of articles drawing attention to the negative effects of the Hanoverian connection. First, a story emerged about the involvement of Baron Ompteda, the new Hanoverian minister in London, in various political intrigues affecting British foreign and domestic policy.[60] Barely a week later an article on German affairs drew attention to the paradoxes – in German eyes – of William IV's government in Britain and Germany, asking 'how is it possible that the King of England, who governs there the freest people in Europe, can tolerate, in his native dominions, the most abject despotism?'.[61]

On 12 June *The Times* reported on both the Hambach Festival and the opening of the Hanoverian Assembly of Estates. The former was praised, the latter condemned. The new Hanoverian constitution was dismissed by *The Times* on the basis of the royal rescript to the Assembly of Estates which explicitly referred to the need to avoid political arrangements 'suited only to republics' and the statement that freedom of the press would exist, but subject to laws enacted to prevent its abuse and the stipulations of the German Confederation: 'So the press in Hanover is to be under the superintendence of the German Confederacy, – that is, the Holy Alliance! From this the spirit and character of the whole constitution may be easily conjectured.'[62]

More articles on Hanoverian politics followed. A letter to *The Times* focused on the arrest of Poles in Göttingen and noted that

---

[60] *The Times*, 23 May 1832, pp. 5, 6. [61] *Ibid.*, 31 May 1832.
[62] *Ibid.*, 12 June 1832, p. 4.

the administration of Hanover, in its domestic relations, may be considered as acting quite independently of our own, and that the Ministers here, therefore, should hardly be held responsible for the misdeeds of their brethren in Germany; still the character of our common Sovereign must necessarily suffer from such an act of injustice committed in his name, and especially in a country where his power, as is well known, is almost absolute.[63]

On 25 June *The Times* reported on the new Hanoverian constitution arguing that the government's proposals had failed to meet the expectations of the people. The report drew particular attention to the king's attitude and noted that his amendments were 'dated from Windsor Castle, May 11, while Lord Grey had resigned office, and signed by Baron Ompteda'. This was scarcely relevant given the theory of the Personal Union. But the point was made in order to try to exculpate the king's reputation by suggesting that he had been without the protection of Grey from evil, reactionary and *Hanoverian* councillors, 'for it is generally known and generally believed that His Majesty is really a friend of liberal institutions and of liberal ideas'.[64] At this stage reformers had not completely written off royal support.

This was the context in which news broke of the Six Articles and the support of William IV for these measures. The position of the king of Hanover was immediately seen as significant, as much so as the articles themselves.[65] *The Times* described the Six Articles as 'monstrous' and illegal. Responding to a suggestion in the *Journal des Debats* that England had a special role in protecting the smaller German states by virtue of the kingdom of Hanover, *The Times* virtually denied the connection declaring that 'thank God, Hanover is no kingdom of ours' and eagerly anticipated the end of the Personal Union at the death of William IV. In eighteen months, the newspaper's position on the Personal Union had changed dramatically and did so in tandem with its understanding of the king's position. *The Times* argued that the British parliament would require some explanation of Hanover's behaviour at the Diet.

It is obvious that ostensibly the British Ministers are no ways accountable for the acts of the Hanoverian Government, and that as to official explanations, Lord Grey will have none to offer. But we do believe that no British Minister of Lord Grey's Cabinet will hesitate to pronounce his entire disavowal of all sympathy with the spirit of those proceedings at Frankfort... If Germany be trampled on as

---

[63] *Ibid.*, 20 June 1832, p. 5. The letter provoked a reply defending the Hanoverian government, see 21 June 1832, p. 3.
[64] *Ibid.*, 25 June 1832, p. 3. After news broke of the Six Articles, it was rumoured that the king had consented to Metternich's measures during the May interregnum as well, see 26 July 1832, p. 3.
[65] *Ibid.*, 21 July 1832.

Poland has been, while Great Britain and France look on like unmoved spectators at a disgusting drama, the next act of the piece will not have Germany for its theatre.[66]

A few days later *The Times* drew its own conclusion from the events of the past three months. Arguing that war was imminent due to the clash of the 'divine right of Kings to govern as badly as they please' and the 'social right of citizens to be governed beneficially and justly', the newspaper pointed to the various corners of Europe where the battle of these principles was taking place. The French and Belgian Revolutions and the English Reform Bill were 'declarations of war against the divine right doctrine of the Potentates of St Petersburgh, Hanover, and Berlin'.

Against the Reform Bill, proposed, recommended, and finally passed into law by the King of ENGLAND, the King of HANOVER issues letters of marque and reprisal by a State paper, signed in his name at Frankfort, wherein he stigmatises the first principle of all free government as revolutionary, puts down, as rank treason, the liberty of the press, and transfers universally from representatives of the people to the Crown and its Ministers, the privilege of imposing taxes, and all control over the public money.[67]

Hanover now kept company with Russia, Prussia and Austria as the bogeymen of liberal propaganda.

The contradictions of William IV's position were satirised in print on 1 August. In a double page spread print, the left-hand side depicts the 'King of H—v—r', the right-hand side the 'King of Br—t—n'. On the left, William IV sits on his throne as King of Hanover. At the dais a forlorn female figure in a torn gown – identifiable as Liberty by her broken spear and cap – pleads with the king: 'O save me, save poor Liberty. Metternich & the Prussians after despoiling and starving, now threaten me death itself.' But William IV waves her away, replying: 'Hence mischievous Wretch, I perfectly agree with all they propose.' On the right, however, the situation is reversed. William IV kneels before Liberty enthroned as Britannia and says: 'Should I be suspected of mediating anything against your August Goddessship, I should be unworthy the honour of Kissing as I now do the awful tip of your sublime toe.'[68] The extremely public gulf between William IV's positions as king of Britain and king of Hanover reeked of hypocrisy.

This was the context in which Palmerston made his famous declaration to the House of Commons condemning the Six Articles and stating that

---

[66] *Ibid.*, 23 July 1832, p. 4. See also 25 July 1832, p. 2.   [67] *Ibid.*, 27 July 1832, p. 2.
[68] *M^cleans Monthly Sheet of Caricatures No 32 ... 1 August 1832*, p. 2. See George, *Catalogue of political and personal satires*, vol. XI, 17212–3.

constitutional states were the natural allies of England.[69] Two radical MPs, Henry Lytton Bulwer and Joseph Hume had moved a motion calling on William IV to oppose actions of the German Confederation which damaged the liberty and independence of the German people. Lytton Bulwer's speech denied that the theory of the Personal Union held true in practice.[70] For Hume, differentiation between the actions of the king of Hanover and king of England was all very well, but 'the majority of persons would not be able to appreciate the justice of such a distinction'.[71] The foreign secretary responded by emphasising that he could not be held responsible for the actions of the king of Hanover. Like Canning, it was necessary for Palmerston to adopt the tactic of announcing British foreign policy publicly in the House of Commons in order to distinguish the stance of ministers from the king. The speech was a conscious strategic move for the debate was so thinly attended that Palmerston could have had the House counted out had he so desired. However, his declamation in favour of constitutional states as allies was also necessary to cover up the weakness of his response to Lytton Bulwer and Hume on the issue of the Personal Union. If the motion was addressed to the king of Hanover, Palmerston argued it was inappropriate, if addressed to the king of England, he opposed it merely because the actions of the German Confederation were insufficient to justify intervention by Britain as a signatory of the Vienna Settlement.[72] Yet Palmerston vigorously opposed the Six Articles. The ambassadors of the Eastern powers had successfully persuaded Ompteda to advise William to support the resolution. The king did not need much persuading and Palmerston's protests to his royal master had come too late.

Palmerston then drafted a despatch to be communicated to the smaller German states which condemned the Six Articles as contrary to the confederal constitution. Grey, after altering parts of the draft, submitted it to William IV for approval. William drew up a long reply objecting to the despatch on the grounds that its contents were not in accordance with the opinions he had already expressed as king of Hanover. William was determined to support the monarchical principle and queried whether it was really desirable for the power of the press to grow in Germany to the extent it had done so in Britain.[73]

The king's reference to his position as king of Hanover prompted discussion between Grey and Palmerston about the nature of the Personal Union and their response to the king. Palmerston's reply to

---

[69] 2 August 1832, *Hansard's Parliamentary Debates*, vol. XIV, p. 1045.
[70] See fn. 1 above.   [71] *Ibid.*, p. 1062.   [72] *Ibid.*, pp. 1046, 1067.
[73] Webster, *Foreign policy of Palmerston*, p. 231.

William argued that his intention was conservative because he wished to defend existing institutions from arbitrary attack. In relation to Hanover, Palmerston argued the traditional constitutional theory of the Personal Union, namely that Britain and Hanover were recognised across Europe as possessing little in common apart from their sovereign. Consequently it was only natural that their interests should differ: 'to expect that Hanover should submit her policy to the decision of Great Britain or that Great Britain should make hers follow the guidance of the Hanoverian Cabinet would be to require that, which would be equally repugnant to the feelings of both nations'. However, in this instance there was, Palmerston claimed, an identity of interest between British and Hanoverian councillors since both desired to preserve the status quo in Germany. Palmerston called for better communication between the two parties, which, he claimed, would not violate the doctrine of non-intervention.[74]

To Grey, Palmerston was able to express his full irritation:

With regard to his difficulty in doing anything as King of England which is not consistent with what he has done as King of Hanover, the answer is, that if the politics of the two countries are to be thus bound together, England being the most powerful and important is entitled to lead Hanover, and not Hanover to lead England; that if the English Government is to be tied by that which the Hanoverian has done, they ought to be previously consulted, and to have a voice in the deliberation. But neither you nor I could venture to tell Parliament that the European policy of England must be shackled and governed by decisions taken by the Hanoverian Cabinet without our knowledge or concurrence. Such a doctrine would go further than anything else to shake the root of the Hanoverian family in this country.[75]

In reply, Grey concurred: 'Our conduct must be regulated by English principles and English interests, and we cannot be diverted from the line prescribed by these, because Hanover has taken a different course.'[76]

Better communication did result to some extent. Palmerston and Grey were able to influence the instructions sent to the Hanoverian government prior to a confederal ministerial conference towards the end of 1833. They urged William to resist any alterations to the confederal constitution and warned that Hanover could not expect British support if such conduct led to an attack on her liberties. But William IV argued that he made no claim on Britain to defend Hanover, thereby reversing

---

[74] Palmerston to William IV, 5 August 1832, in Webster, *Foreign policy of Palmerston*, Appendix A, pp. 799–800.
[75] Palmerston to Grey, 3 August 1832, in *ibid.*, Appendix B, p. 819.
[76] Grey to Palmerston, 3 August 1832, in *ibid.*, Appendix B, pp. 829–30.

the policy of his father, and indeed cited the Napoleonic War as demonstrating Britain's inability to defend Hanover. Consequently he had to ally Hanover with Austria and Prussia, the only powers capable of defending Hanover from attack. William did convey Palmerston's criticisms to the Hanoverian government and appointed Ompteda to attend the ministerial conference rather than those originally chosen.[77] However, Ompteda slavishly supported Metternich's proposals and it was only through Bavarian opposition that Metternich failed to achieve all he wanted. William's preferences were also expressed by conferring membership of the Hanoverian Guelphic Order on the Austrian ambassador to the Bundestag.

It was in the light of these experiences that Palmerston welcomed the end of the Personal Union in 1837, for with the accession of Victoria,

> the Hanoverian Dynasty, & the German prejudices which belonged to it, & which for a century have embarrassed & impeded our March both at home & abroad will cease. The Sovereign of England will no longer be hampered by considerations belonging to the petty state of Hanover; & I believe that since the accession of George the 1st, these German politics have more or less continually had their influence on the Councils of England.[78]

However, his inability to understand William IV's genuine fears and concerns over the future of Hanover reflected Palmerston's general failure to comprehend the situation of the lesser German states and the anxieties of their governments.[79] Palmerston's jubilation at the end of the Hanoverian connection reflected the difficulties posed by a political situation in which monarch and foreign minister disagreed and these differences could not be hidden from the public eye.

IV

The Personal Union ended with the death of William IV on 20 June 1837. It passed almost without comment from either side. People looked forward rather than back: in Hanover to the permanent return of the sovereign after so many years' absence, in Britain to the new reign of a young queen. However, the Personal Union did not sink without trace. In the first few years after 1837 the possibility remained open that the Personal Union would return in the event of Victoria's death without heirs. The death, following the birth of a stillborn baby, of Princess Charlotte in

---

[77] *Ibid.*, pp. 364–5.
[78] Palmerston to Lamb, 12 June 1837, quoted in Gruner, 'England, Hannover und der Deutsche Bund', p. 125.
[79] Gruner, 'England, Hannover und der Deutsche Bund', p. 120.

November 1817 provided an ominous precedent. It was no wonder, therefore, that the actions of the heir to the throne, the duke of Cumberland and now King Ernst August of Hanover, were the subject of close British attention.

Upon his arrival in Hanover, the new king declared that he did not consider himself to be bound by the constitution passed by his predecessor in 1833. This action was interpreted by Liberals across Europe as reactionary, illegal and anti-constitutional. Meanwhile, the death of William IV necessitated a general election back in Britain. While it is well known that the government campaign relied on much repetition of the new queen's name, the negative flip-side of this tactic has not been noticed. The Whigs identified themselves with Victoria and the Tories with Ernst August. The conservative-leaning media denounced the negative campaigning. As the now Peelite *Times* put it:

> The Whigs prove dexterous in their abuse of Royal names to evil and dishonest objects. They begin by twisting the name of Queen VICTORIA into a chaplet wherewith to decorate their own ungraceful brows. They next press that of the King of HANOVER into their service, as an engine of calumny against their political rivals in this country.[80]

The tactic was effective in so far as few British Conservatives possessed the skill or knowledge to mount a defence of Ernst August's actions. The impact was sufficient for the Conservative leadership to distance themselves from Ernst August and refuse him any assistance in making his case before the British public.[81] The controversy returned when Ernst August formally annulled the 1833 constitution by royal decree in November 1837 and – in a *cause célèbre* – dismissed seven Göttingen University professors who protested against his actions.[82] Only after the marriage of Victoria to Albert and the production of a string of healthy children in the 1840s did Hanoverian affairs become of no consequence to British politics. At the level of foreign relations, Britain and Hanover drifted apart rapidly, largely due to poor personal relations between Ernst

---

[80] *The Times*, 18 July 1837, p. 4. See also, 'The Late Election', *Fraser's Magazine* 16 (September 1837), 269–70; 'The Elections', *Blackwood's Edinburgh Magazine* 42 (September 1837), 301.

[81] Instead it was claimed that the situation was unclear and/or it had nothing to do with the Conservative leadership in Britain. See *The Times*, 18 July 1837, p. 4, 19 July 1837, p. 4, 22 July 1837, p. 4, 1 August 1837, p. 5, 2 August 1837, p. 5.

[82] For criticisms of Ernst August, see 'History of Hanover', *London & Westminster Review* 30 (October 1837), 198–216; 'The Hanoverian Coup d'Etat', *British & Foreign Review* 6 (January 1838), 269–338. For defences, see *The Times*, 15 November 1837, p. 4, 16 November 1837, p. 4, 17 November 1837, p. 2; 'Hanoverian Constitution', *Foreign Quarterly Review* 20 (January 1838), 378–402.

August and Victoria and disputes over questions of precedence and family heirlooms.[83]

The end of the Personal Union in 1837 was the result of dynastic accident not conscious political action. It may well not have been mourned, but it is mistaken to view the decades prior to its end from this perspective. Palmerston's epitaph on the Personal Union reflected particular and contingent political circumstances: most importantly the difficulties of his relationship with William IV. Castlereagh certainly, and Canning on balance, fared better in their relations with William's predecessor. The Personal Union worked best for Britain when its operation was not exposed to public or parliamentary scrutiny. This reflected the contradiction in British attitudes towards the Personal Union which oscillated from the expectation of British management of Hanoverian policy to denials of any influence or responsibility. But scrutiny was becoming more and more difficult to avoid. For the last three decades of its existence, the end of the Personal Union seemed dynastically imminent because of the place of first Princess Charlotte and then Princess Victoria in the line of accession. Had this not been the case, then British politicians would have had to consider the Personal Union as a case for reform.

Brendan Simms concluded from his study of the Hanoverian crisis of 1806 that 'it is time to put the Hanoverian dimension back into the political history of later Hanoverian Britain'.[84] This chapter can only claim to have partly picked up the gauntlet in its survey of the terrain. Some areas, such as the British use of Hanover to influence the development of the Prussian-led German Customs Union, have not been touched upon. However, it has hopefully been established that the Hanoverian connection offers an excellent lens through which to view many aspects of the political history of this period.

---

[83] See P. H. H. Draeger, 'Great Britain and Hanover, 1830–66', (unpub. PhD thesis, Cambridge, 1997), pp. 168–9, 173.
[84] Simms, 'Hanoverian crisis of 1806', p. 595.

6 The end of the dynastic union, 1815–1837

Mijndert Bertram

Britain's special relationship with Hanover during the last two decades of the Personal Union has so far been seriously neglected by British historians. A typical example is Norman Gash who, in his presentation of the history of the United Kingdom in the nineteenth century,[1] regarded as a standard work, never mentions Britain's continental partner at all. More recent biographies of George IV[2] and William IV[3] do little to remedy this. Elsewhere there are a few comments, for example on the connection between Hanoverian customs policy and British trade interests.[4] The first to attempt a fundamental reassessment of Hanover's importance to Britain was Jeremy Black, in his work on the Guelph dynasty on the British throne.[5] It is to be hoped that this paradigm change has produced an achievement that will inspire further studies.

On the German side the list of relevant literature is not a great deal longer. Both older and more recent works on the history of the kingdom of Hanover do, however, at least mention individual aspects of its relationship with Britain.[6] The repercussions of the Personal Union for Hanover are illustrated in an essay that emerged as a by-product of an exhibition in Hanover's Historical Museum in the mid-1970s.[7] George IV's visit to his German kingdom in October 1821 was already documented in minute detail by contemporaries – albeit restricted to an

---

[1] Norman Gash, *Aristocracy and people* (2nd reprint, London, 1983).
[2] Christopher Hibbert, *George IV* (Harmondsworth, 1976); E. A. Smith, *George IV* (New Haven and London, 1999).
[3] Philip Ziegler, *King William IV* (London, 1971); Tom Pocock, *Sailor king. The life of King William IV* (London, 1991).
[4] John R. Davis, *Britain and the German Zollverein, 1848–66* (Houndmills and London, 1997).
[5] Jeremy Black, *The Hanoverians. The history of a dynasty* (London and New York, 2004).
[6] William von Hassell, *Geschichte des Königreichs Hannover*, 1. Teil: *Von 1813 bis 1848* (Bremen, 1898); Mijndert Bertram, *Das Königreich Hannover. Kleine Geschichte eines vergangenen deutschen Staates* (2nd edn, Hanover, 2004).
[7] Waldemar R. Röhrbein and Alheidis von Rohr, *Hannover im Glanz und Schatten des britischen Weltreiches. Die Auswirkungen der Personalunion auf Hannover von 1714 bis 1837. Beiträge zur Ausstellung* (2nd edn, Hanover, 1977).

account of his itinerary.[8] In addition Wolf D. Gruner deals with the relationship between Britain and Hanover in terms of foreign affairs, concentrating on the Congress of Vienna of 1814–15.[9] Apart from that, general required reading also produces a few further references.[10] The attempt made here to outline the Hanoverian dimension of British foreign policy between 1815 and 1837 is also based on archive material such as the files of the German Chancery in London,[11] and the papers of its long-time head, Count Ernst Friedrich Herbert von Münster (1766–1839).[12]

Münster plays a key role in the relationship between Hanover and Britain. Appointed head of the Chancery in 1805, and also Hanoverian Minister to the Royal House, he was regarded by its members not only as the leading statesman in their country of origin, but also as an intimate advisor and helper in many private and semi-private affairs. As well as George III (1738–1820), Queen Charlotte (1744–1818) and the two oldest princes – George (1762–1830), the heir to the throne and Friedrich (1763–1827), duke of York, held him in particularly high esteem. His wife later reported on his relationship with the royal family that the princesses had often said: 'Our father liked him so much, had such confidence in him, wished always to have him in the family, that we looked at him as one of our brothers.'[13]

Münster's social diary also shows how close his relationship was with the monarch's family. According to this weekly routine, for instance in 1809, seldom varied.[14] Every Sunday he travelled or rode to Windsor where he usually remained until Wednesday before returning to London. On Sundays he reported to the king. Then in the evening there was often a concert. Mondays and Tuesdays began with attendance at the chapel. He went for walks, and more often rides, with George III, who was

---

[8] Heinrich Dittmer, *Authentische und vollständige Beschreibung aller Feyerlichkeiten, welche in dem Hannoverschen Lande bey der Anwesenheit Seiner Königl. Majestät Georgs des Vierten während dem Monate October 1821 veranstaltet worden sind* (Hanover, 1822).

[9] Wolf D. Gruner, *Großbritannien, der Deutsche Bund und die Struktur des europäischen Friedens im frühen 19. Jahrhundert. Studien zu den britisch-deutschen Beziehungen in einer Periode des Umbruchs* (2 vols., typed copy, Munich, 1979); Gruner, 'England, Hannover und der Deutsche Bund 1814–1837', in: Adolf M. Birke and Kurt Kluxen, eds., *England und Hannover* (Munich, London, New York, Oxford and Paris, 1986), pp. 81–126.

[10] For example: Ernst von Meier, *Hannoversche Verfassungs- und Verwaltungsgeschichte 1809–1866* (2 vols., reprint of 1st edn, Leipzig 1898/99, Hildesheim and New York, 1973); Hilde Arning, *Hannovers Stellung zum Zollverein* (PhD Diss. Göttingen, 1930).

[11] Niedersächsisches Hauptstaatsarchiv Hannover (henceforth: NHStA Hann.), Hann. 92.

[12] Ibid., Dep. 110. Since there is no modern biography of Münster the standard texts are still Ferdinand Frensdorf, 'v. Münster', in: *Allgemeine Deutsche Biographie*, vol. XXIII (reprint of 1st edn of 1886, Berlin 1970), pp. 157–85; Carl Haase, ed., *Das Leben des Grafen Münster (1766–1839). Aufzeichnungen seiner Gemahlin Gräfin Wilhelmine, geb. Fürstin zu Schaumburg-Lippe* (Göttingen, 1985).

[13] Haase, ed., *Das Leben des Grafen Münster*, p. 29.   [14] NHStA Hann., Dep. 110, A 503.

already blind, and with his daughters, and his day ended playing cards for small sums with the king and his wife, and Princess Augusta Sophia (1768–1840).

At this time – Napoleon was at the height of his power and only unshakeable optimists dared to hope that an end to French rule on the continent of Europe might be in sight – plans were already being made in London for a post-war order for Germany in general and Hanover in particular. The driving force behind these ideas was Count Münster. From England he fought for the liberation of his homeland by constantly urging those British politicians responsible to continue the war, despite numerous setbacks, while at the same time using his manifold connections to keep the spirit of resistance alive on the continent. For a time he toyed with the idea (linking up with the Merovingian period) of founding a great Guelphic empire called 'Austrasia' that would stretch from the Elbe to the Schelde.[15]

After the disaster of the French campaign in Russia and Prussia's re-entry into the circle of European great powers, ambitious ideas of this sort had to be put on the shelf. In the end the only recompense for British subsidies was a declaration by Prussia in the Treaty of Reichenbach (1813) that it wished to help Hanover increase its territory by 250–300,000 inhabitants. The fact that the Principality of Hildesheim was specifically mentioned here did mean that a goal of Guelphic territorial policy aspired to for hundreds of years was attained. But it was not enough to secure Hanover, as was intended, especially against Prussian ambitions.

Under these circumstances Münster's only option was to work towards establishing a general association of all German states, which would be strong enough to keep the cohesion of its members intact internally and externally, but would not interfere unduly in their affairs. In short: the old *Reich* should be recreated and given some new powers, mainly in military affairs and the administration of justice. As a concession to the *Zeitgeist* and recognising the justified wishes of the Germans, who had answered their princes' call to arms – indeed in some cases had risen up even before the call came – Münster also envisaged the establishment of regional and central corporative representative bodies. However, he was by no means dogmatic about all this, but constantly followed the guiding principle that he expressed in a letter to Freiherr vom Stein: 'Let us not strive for what may theoretically be desirable if it means losing what we can practically achieve.'[16]

---

[15] Bertram, *Das Königreich Hannover*, pp. 30–1.
[16] NHStA Hann., Dep. 110, A 118, Münster's letter to Stein of 4 January 1813 (copy).

In fact, however, despite the exceptional degree of confidence placed in Münster by both George III and the Prince of Wales, who took over the Regency in 1811 when his father finally succumbed to his metabolic disease, he did not have a completely free hand in formulating his policy. Even if he had an elevated position compared to that of his ministerial colleagues – recognised by them though not institutionalised[17] – his plans and drafts still needed the approval of the king so that they retained the character of an instruction, and acquiring this approval was by no means a mere formality. Given the time-period under consideration here, it is perhaps sufficient to restrict ourselves to the case of the Prince Regent when considering this issue more closely.

Prince George, whose extraordinary talents were matched by striking weaknesses, took over the office of Regent with the intention of leading the government of the two Houses of Guelph in exactly the same way as his father had done, since he regarded himself purely as a stand-in until such time as his father recovered.[18] Before long, however, this resolution solidified into a stubborn conservative attitude. Long after it had become obvious that George III had no hope of recovering, the regent still had doubts about his right to make long-term plans for the lands inherited from his father while the king was still alive.[19]

The prince's disinclination to make any territorial or constitutional changes to the states entrusted to him was a quantity that his Hanoverian ministers could by no means ignore. George took an active part in determining the fate of his father's subjects, ordered Münster to report to him on Hanover's affairs – irregularly, but often and in detail[20] – read with interest the reports sent by the count of his journeys to the continent[21] and usually made his decisions once he had weighed up for himself the proposals made to him.[22] Anyone who wanted to voice an opinion on Hanoverian affairs could not allow his recommendations to

---

[17] *Ibid.*, Dep. 110, A 223, letter by the minister Friedrich Franz Dietrich von Bremer to Münster of 9 April 1813.

[18] Smith, *George IV*, p. 283.

[19] NHStA Hann., Dep. 110, A 52, letter from Geheimer Kabinettsrat Best to Münster of 21 Feburary 1815.

[20] This becomes apparent, for example, from a study of Münster's social diary, *ibid.*, Dep. 110, A 504–6.

[21] *Ibid.*, Dep. 110, A 80, letter from Geheimer Kabinettsrat Best to Münster of 4 October 1814.

[22] *Ibid.*, Dep. 110, A 52, letter from Best to Münster of 13 February 1815 and the Prince Regent's decree to the Count of 21 February 1815; *ibid.*, Dep. 110, A 178, letter from minister Ernst von Hardenberg to Münster of 4 February 1815; *ibid.*, Hann. 92, No. 236, Regent's decree to the ministry in Hanover of 19 October 1819.

exceed what the regent was prepared to accept in order to maintain the situation he had inherited.

If Münster thus prescribed the direction in which he was to orientate his political plans, he certainly did not have to betray his own convictions in order to bring his concepts for the reorganisation of Hanover into line with the Prince's conservative attitudes. They shared the view that it was not so much a question of reshaping as of reviving the old, traditional state of affairs, in other words, of integrating Hanover into the old *Reich*, which would have slightly extended powers.

But what did all these ideas look like from a British point of view? Let us look at the situation there: after the defeat of Napoleon Britain was a saturated power.[23] Its trade and colonial interests were more or less unrivalled, apart from competition in North America from the USA, which was becoming established. From the European continent, however, no danger threatened as long as the two militarily strong powers on the flanks, France and Russia, could be kept in check. The key element in a security system for the whole of Europe, as envisaged by British Foreign Minister Castlereagh (1769–1822), was a new federal system for Germany which integrated Prussia and Austria and balanced them against one another.[24] France's expansionist ambitions were to be blocked by Prussia's territories on the Rhine, while Austria's Lombardy and Venice would fulfil the same function south of the Alps. This blockade had outposts, to some extent, in the shape of the new Kingdom of the Netherlands in the north and Piedmont-Sardinia in the south east.

Under these conditions rounding off Hanover was not a high priority for British diplomacy. On the contrary, the British regarded Hanoverian desires in this respect as less important than making concessions to Prussia so that the Hohenzollern monarchy would be willing to compromise on the question of Saxony.[25] After initial differences of opinion regarding the line to be taken at the Congress of Vienna on this issue, Münster accepted Castlereagh's point of view that it was more important for Hanover to be secure than to expand as far as possible. So along with Hildesheim they contented themselves with acquiring East Friesland, which increased Hanover's territory along the North Sea coast and gave it a border with the Netherlands, and other smaller territories, while more ambitious dreams of Ravensburg and Minden remained unfulfilled. It was vital for Britain's exports of colonial goods and industrial products

---

[23] Gash, *Aristocracy*, pp. 283–5.
[24] Gruner, *Großbritannien, der Deutsche Bund und die Struktur des europäischen Friedens*, vol. I, pp. 5, 91, 171–2.
[25] *Ibid.*, vol. I, pp. 195–6, 390 and 396–7.

that Hanover's connection to central and southern Germany remained unimpeded in order to preserve the transit route.[26]

Another issue on which the head of the German Chancery had to bow to the situation at hand was that of re-establishing the old *Reich*. In Vienna Münster quickly realised that this was not going to happen. Since, as a consequence, no more emperors would be elected, the status of an Electorate no longer made any sense. So on 12 October 1814 Münster made the declaration, subsequently endorsed by the Prince Regent, that Hanover had decided to take on the status of a kingdom.[27]

All in all it is clear that Castlereagh, who worked closely with Münster at the Congress of Vienna, certainly wished Hanover no harm, but also saw no reason to become involved on its behalf beyond what was needed to ensure its security. Protected by the German Confederation, the smaller of the two Ghelphic empires barely played any further role in Britain's foreign policy.

However, this did not mean that London completely neglected the crown's German possessions. It had long been recognised that a portrait of the ruler in an armchair there was no longer a sufficient representation[28] of the royal house.[29] So a plan was formed to send one of the royal princes to Hanover and Count Münster had already decided on his favourite: Duke Adolphus Frederic of Cambridge (1774–1850), George III's youngest son.[30]

However, one of the duke of Cambridge's brothers threatened to thwart Münster's plans. Duke Ernest Augustus of Cumberland (1771–1851) had been to the continent in the spring of 1813, in order to be present at the liberation of his family's ancestral lands. Now he had hopes of being appointed as the crown's permanent representative there. Münster, however, was not keen on the idea. Cumberland was strong-willed, energetic and ambitious. Apart from that he held unmoveable, ultra-conservative views, which meant that he already regarded the chief minister's moderate reform plans as too far-reaching. Eventually Münster got his way. At his insistence the duke of Cambridge was appointed as military governor, a man who unlike his older brother had limited ambitions and could easily

---

[26] Arning, *Hannovers Stellung*, p. 16.   [27] Bertram, *Das Königreich Hannover*, p. 33.
[28] This is what had happened during the long abseneces of the ruler or his representative: Heide Barmeyer, 'Hof und Hofgesellschaft in Niedersachsen im 18. und 19. Jahrhundert', *Niedersächsisches Jahrbuch für Landesgeshichte* 61 (1989), 92–3.
[29] Mijndert Bertram, 'Der "Mondminister" und "General Killjoy". Ein Machtkampf im Hintergrund der Ernennung des Herzogs Adolph Friedrich von Cambridge zum Generalgouverneur von Hannover (1813–1816)', *Niedersächsisches Jahrbuch für Landesgeschichte* 65 (1993), 213–62.
[30] NHStA Hann., Dep. 110, A 244, Münster's letter to minister von Bremer of 23 April 1813.

be manipulated. Ernest Augustus had no option but to return to England disgruntled, while in December 1813 Adolphus Frederic took over an office that gave him a striking title, but very little responsibility. As regards the ministry, in which he was only in charge of military affairs, he was not granted any particular privileges.

This was typical of Münster's statecraft. Utterly convinced of the indivisibility of monarchical power he insisted to the end of his career that Hanover should be ruled from the seat of the ruler, i.e. from England. Transferring sovereign rights to a governor, the ministry or a corporate representative body was out of the question. Thus Münster excluded the most effective means of removing those inhibitions imposed by the Personal Union. The focus of the government's attention was not transferred to Hanover, even if the dynasty was at last represented in its German territories for the first time since the Prince of Wales, Frederic Louis, was recalled in 1728.

Hanover's finances were in a disastrous state due to the long period of war and occupation. In order to consolidate the position an agreement on debts and taxes was needed. There did not seem to be any point, however, in negotiating with seven or eight different provincial diets, as had been the case hitherto. So, in accordance with the principles put forward by Count Münster at the Congress of Vienna, a central representative body was convened, committed to the two modern principles of representation: overall responsibility and freedom of instruction.[31] The duke of Cambridge opened this general assembly on 15 December 1814. The words he used on this occasion raised high expectations: 'If it is a question of sacrificing individual rights, bear in mind that the Prince Regent first gave up rights which others consider to be an essential part of royal dignity when he called to be for him what parliament is in our brother-land Great Britain: a high council of the nation.'[32]

This could only be interpreted as meaning that the Hanoverian assembly should play the same role as parliament played in Britain. And indeed the new body subsequently developed its own dynamics, which far exceeded the government's expectations. For example, contrary to all tradition it concerned itself with the internal affairs of the armed forces, insisted that its negotiations be made public, and proposed the introduction of a civil code, similar to that in France. Of special significance,

---

[31] Mijndert Bertram, *Die erste oder provisorische Allgemeine Ständeversammlung des Königreiches Hannover und ihre definitive Organisation (1814–1819)* (Hanover 1986).
[32] NHStA Hann., Hann 92 No. 227, 'Anwort des Herrn Herzogs von Cambridge, Königl. Hoheit auf die Rede des erwählten Präsidenten der allgemeinen Stände-Versammlung'.

however, was that it called into question the fact that the owners of feudal estates were exempt from ground tax. According to the assembly this was no longer in keeping with the spirit of the times.

Faced with this threat to their age-old privileges, ultra-conservative members of the nobility tried to persuade the head of the German Chancery that the assembly, in its current form, represented an instrument of revolutionary forces. Graf Münster, under the influence of reactionary attitudes that had set in all over Germany, eventually accepted this argument and decided to prevent the upheaval of the old system that was supposedly threatened. So the general assembly was dissolved in the autumn of 1819 and replaced by a *Landtag* consisting of two chambers. Its two parts – and this was a unique phenomenon in German constitutional history – had completely equal rights and could therefore block one another when differences of opinion arose. This meant that the government's decision ultimately prevailed.[33] Moreover, the landowning aristocracy were given a majority of votes in the First Chamber, giving this body an instrument by which to defeat any resolution it opposed.

Once the assembly had been effectively muzzled, attempts at parliamentarisation in Hanover came to a sorry end. Public interest in the assembly's negotiations dwindled. A complacent peace settled over the country. Below the surface, however, dissatisfaction with the political and social situation was brewing, and was to erupt in the not too distant future.

While the country's constitutional system was brought into line with a generally reactionary attitude, the structure of the army developed in a different direction. The original intention was that the King's German Legion (KGL) should form the core of the new army. This legion was founded in 1803 and consisted overwhelmingly of émigré Hanoverians. It served under the British flag and had fought against the French in all European theatres of war, from Pomerania to Portugal and from Zeeland to Sicily.[34] But the Hanoverian formations brought together between 1813 and 1815 stood in its way. So when the legion was dispersed in the spring of 1816 only a portion of its members, mostly the excellent cavalry and artillery, could be taken on. Nonetheless, the tradition of the whole KGL, in other words a British tradition, lived on in the Hanoverian army as long as it continued to exist.

---

[33] Bertram, *Die erste oder provisorische Allgemeine Ständeversammlung*, pp. 292–304.
[34] Bernhard Schwertfeger, *Geschichte der Königlichen Deutschen Legion 1803–1816* (2 vols., Hanover 1893/95); Mike Chappell, *The King's German Legion* (2 vols., Oxford 2000).

With only limited means available, new ways had to be found for building up the armed forces.[35] General conscription had already been introduced in November 1813. In addition thirty territorial reserve battalions were formed, to exist alongside the field battalions made up of professional soldiers. Each field battalion was combined with three territorial reserve battalions to form a regiment, so that the territorials – unlike in Prussia for example – were a solid component of the regular army.

In determining the future size of the armed forces an important question was that of their status in the state. Some of the army leaders harboured ambitions of influencing the affairs of government and substantially increasing the number of troops compared with the period before 1803.[36] There was even talk of transforming Hanover into a military state.

The driving force behind such efforts was General Friedrich von der Decken (1769–1849) who had been charged with organising the peacetime army and who used his great influence over the duke of Cambridge to achieve his goals. In future Adolphus Frederic should no longer just bear the nominal title of military governor, but should head the government as viceroy, while von der Decken saw himself as war minister, pulling all the strings in the background. Here, however, he came into conflict with Count Münster whose dominant position he could not seriously threaten. What is more, the general assembly refused to increase the military budget beyond what had already been approved. So in the end the general had to shelve all his ambitious plans. In 1816 the duke of Cambridge was indeed given another title: not that of viceroy, but that of a governor general. All this meant in practice was that he was formally allowed to chair the ministry in civilian matters as well. Münster saw to it that Adolphus Frederic's eldest brother, the Prince Regent, never granted him any real authority.

It was not long before the army organisation put in place after the liberation of Hanover proved to be quite inadequate. For one thing the armed forces were still too numerous, and therefore too expensive for the depleted country to maintain. What is more, the short annual periods when the territorial reserves were drilled did not provide satisfactory training. So in 1820 the number of troops was reduced from 30,801 to 20,912. At the same time both the territorial reserves and the field

---

[35] Richard W. Fox, 'Konservative Anpassung an die Revolution: Friedrich von der Decken und die hannoversche Militärreform 1789–1820. Eine Untersuchung der Rolle des Militärs in Staat und Gesellschaft', *Niedersächsisches Jahrbuch für Landesgeschichte* 34 (1973), 171–273.

[36] Bertram, 'Der "Mondminister" und "General Killjoy" '.

battalions were abolished. They were replaced by integrated regiments made up exclusively of respectable Hanoverian citizens – both volunteers and conscripts. Military service was supposed to be regarded, in principle, as the duty of every citizen.

In keeping with the new image of the soldier conjured by compulsory military service – no longer a mercenary but a citizen in uniform – King George IV (1762–1830) declared, at the request of the assembly, that the army would never be used in the interests of a foreign power.[37] This assurance acquired concrete significance when in 1824 Portugal's independence was threatened by France's ally, Spain, and by internal unrest.[38] When asked for assistance the British government had the idea of sending a Hanoverian relief corps of 6,200 men into the fray.[39] Although George IV was initially enthusiastic about this plan it was never carried out since the Hanoverian ministry under Count Münster raised objections[40] and the British cabinet rejected it because of the costs involved and for fear of a diplomatic incident with France.[41] This created a precedent that henceforth was to obstruct all similar plans.[42] The times when Hanoverians would have fought for the British empire in faraway lands were long gone.

After reigning for almost sixty years King George III died on 29 January 1820. The Prince Regent succeeded him as George IV. Unlike his father, who throughout his long life never left England, the new ruler became an avid traveller in order to visit his various realms. In August and September 1821 he visited Ireland. Then he set sail for Hanover.

On 6 October 1821 a British sovereign set foot on Hanoverian soil for the first time since George II's last visit in 1755.[43] Four days later the king was received in the capital with great ceremonial and extreme rejoicing by the people. His notoriously excessive lifestyle and less than attractive appearance did nothing to diminish the people's devotion to the House of Guelph. The only source of regret was that he had to return home early on 29 October due to an attack of gout, without visiting Celle and other places where preparations had been made for his arrival.

---

[37] NHStA Hann., Dep. 110, A 185, undated note by Count Münster.
[38] Gash, *Aristocracy*, p. 289.
[39] NHStA Hann., Dep. 110, A 185, letter from the Geheime Legationsrat Carl Friedrich v. Stralenheim to Count Münster of 2 July 1824.
[40] *Ibid.*, report by the ministry to George IV of 19 July 1824, Münster's draft.
[41] *Ibid.*, letters from Stralenheim to Münster of 13 and 20 July 1824, and an undated letter from him to Münster.
[42] *Ibid.*, letter from Stralenheim to Münster of 23 July 1824.
[43] Dittmer, *Authentische und vollständige Beschreibung*, pp. 83–294.

Unlike the visits by George I and George II to the continent the visit in 1821, as far as we know, did not give rise to any criticism in England. Admittedly a meeting with Metternich evoked memories of previous precedents in which Britain was, for a time, to some extent ruled from Hanover. But the Austrian chancellor did not really come in order to see the king, but to confer with foreign minister Castlereagh, now the 2nd marquess of Londonderry,[44] who was travelling in the king's entourage. There was therefore no question of the monarch behaving in an unconstitutional manner.

Count Münster had prepared George IV's visit to Hanover down to the last detail. The head of the German Chancery was, in any case, still very much in control.[45] His proximity to the throne meant that his power to exert influence was far greater than any of the other ministers. He generally laid down the guidelines by which the country was ruled in the name of the king, and he was the man to approach with reports, petitions and applications. What is more, he continued to enjoy the king's favour. He belonged, for example, to the so-called 'cottage clique', an informal group of friends that George IV invited to join him at the Royal Lodge in Windsor.[46]

However, Münster was increasingly alienating himself from the country whose affairs he controlled. He was so remote from it that he came to be called the 'minister on the moon'.[47] It was only in 1824 and again in 1826 that he travelled to Hanover for any length of time and was able to form his own impression of the situation there. Apart from that he became more and more dependent on the information given to him in London. This clearly did not give him adequate insight, and he failed to assess certain developments accurately.

This was particularly true of the growing dissatisfaction beyond the sea and the fact that it was increasingly directed against Münster. It was mainly caused by the peasants' lack of adequate representation and by the worsening situation of the rural population. The latter was the first to reach the political agenda.

In February 1829 the Osnabrück Deputy Johann Carl Bertram Stüve (1797–1872) presented a demand to the Second Chamber of the assembly for a general system of land redemption. Although this met with consent in the Second Chamber, it was rejected by the aristocratic majority in the First Chamber. So Stüve then turned to the public. In a piece written at the beginning of 1830 entitled 'Über die Lasten des Grundeigentums und Verminderung derselben in Rücksicht auf das

---

[44] Black, *The Hanoverians*, p. 164.   [45] Bertram, *Das Königreich Hannover*, pp. 44–5.
[46] Hibbert, *George IV*, p. 687.   [47] Fox, 'Konservative Anpassung', p. 216.

Königreich Hannover' he drew attention to the critical social situation threatening the country as a result of the progressive impoverishment of broad sections of the population. As a remedy he recommended the abolition of the services and duties that burdened land ownership to make way for a free economy. At first there was not much reaction to Stüve's proposals. Soon, however, there was to be a turn of events that shed new light not only on the question of land redemption. Far-reaching changes were about to take place, in terms of both personnel and of substance.

On 26 June 1830 George IV died of an enlarged heart. Since he had no direct descendants, the crown passed to the oldest of his surviving brothers. This was Duke William of Clarence. William IV was much more liberal than his predecessor. Even before he ascended the throne, as a member of the House of Lords he had supported the abolition of legal and political discrimination against the catholics. He was also open-minded about the popular demand for electoral reform to expand parliament's representational basis.

Having a king of this sort, who had also been in Hanover from 1785 to 1787 and again in 1818–19 and therefore had first-hand knowledge of the situation there,[48] allowed the opposition in Hanover to hope that their aspirations and ideas would no longer fall on deaf ears.[49] And times were changing: in July 1830 King Charles X of France, hated for his tyranny, was overthrown. A month later there was an uprising in Brussels that led to the secession of Belgium from the Netherlands, and soon afterwards there were also disturbances in Saxony, Brunswick and Hesse.

In order to prevent the revolutionary movement from spilling over into southern Hanover, where the rural population was particularly oppressed, the government summoned troops there. Nonetheless an anonymous pamphlet started to circulate, entitled 'Anklage des Ministeriums Münster vor der öfftenlichen Meinung'. In it the distant head of the German Chancery was held personally responsible for everything that was wrong in the country.

Things got the furthest out of control in Göttingen. Here more than 2,000 citizens and students joined together to form a 'National Guard', to underpin their demand for an assembly freely elected by all classes of society. A community council made up of members of the crowd took the place of the magistrate and the 'Anklage des Ministeriums Münster', along with calls to join the uprising, were distributed amongst the inhabitants of the surrounding area.

---

[48] Ziegler, *King William IV*, pp. 45–53, 125–7.
[49] Bertram, *Das Königreich Hannover*, pp. 45–8.

The authorities reacted harshly to these events. The governor general and the ministry demanded that the town be subjugated. An army of 7,000 men encircled Göttingen. The commander of these troops gave the rebels twelve hours in which to lay down their arms. Now the leaders of the rebellion saw that their cause was lost and sought to take flight. The magistrate took back his office and informed the military commander that the community council, which had constituted itself without authority, had been dissolved. Thereupon the troops entered the town without encountering any resistance.

A few days later the duke of Cambridge started to travel round the areas in the south of the kingdom where disturbances had occurred. Now he discovered for the first time that in some cases petitions addressed to him had been withheld by police officials and that other petitions had remained unanswered by the king. He became convinced that many of these complaints were justified and publicly promised to attend to the matter.

The governor general held his word: on 3 February 1831 he sent two high-ranking civil servants to England with a memo asking for the reforms he considered urgently needed. Now that he had heard his brother's views, on 12 February the king informed Count Münster, who with the help of his wife had once even undertaken to find the king a bride,[50] that in the light of the changes about to take place he could not expect to remain in his current position. This hint was enough to end the career, after more than twenty-five years in office, of one of the most significant statesmen ever to have been part of the government of Hanover. Without hesitation, Münster agreed to retire, which William allowed him to do with immediate effect – sweetening the pill by bestowing on him the British Order of the Bath, into whose civilian department he was the very first foreigner to be accepted. A short time later the count left England and withdrew from public life. His successor in London, Ludwig Karl Georg von Ompteda (1767–1854),[51] had no influence on the king worth mentioning, and simply liaised with the ministers in Hanover.[52]

The path was now clear for far-reaching reforms. The first sign of the king's will to instigate change was his appointment of the duke of Cambridge as viceroy by a decree of 14 February 1831.[53] This promotion was intended 'to give more unity and power to the highest state authority there, so that in important or particularly urgent cases they can proceed

---

[50] NHStA Hann., Dep. 110, A 19, Wilhelmine Countess of Münster to Duchess Louise of Sachsen-Meiningen, 19 February 1818.
[51] Ferdinand Frensdorff, 'v. Ompteda', in: *Allgemeine Deutsche Biographie*, 24 (reprint of 1887 1st edn, Berlin, 1970), pp. 355–8.
[52] v. Hassell, *Geschichte des Königreichs Hannover*, p. 319.
[53] v. Meier, *Hannoversche Verfassungs- und Verwaltungsgeschichte*, vol. I, pp. 201–6.

without waiting for Our special orders'.[54] In practical terms, however, as William declared shortly thereafter, this simply meant that if danger were imminent the viceroy could act independently and, if need be, against the majority vote of the ministry.[55] As a general rule – apart from a few insignificant instances – all he did was report to the king and receive his instructions. Thus there was not much change from the system of government established in 1714. However, the appointment of a viceroy was of high symbolic value and in Hanover work did now indeed begin on formulating two extensive laws.

The first was a written constitution. Tied to the historical–organic concept of the state, as prevailed in Great Britain, the ministry, under Münster's leadership, had always put forward the view that it was impossible to lay down the complex interrelations between monarch and subjects in their entirety and with lasting effect in a constitutional act. On the initiative of the Second Chamber of the assembly, however, a start was now made on drafting such a constitution. After two years of negotiations William IV finally announced on 26 September 1833 the 'Grundgesetz für das Königreich Hannover', which introduced the Estates' legislative and budgetary law as well as limited ministerial responsibility. Hanover thus joined the ranks of Germany's constitutional monarchies.

The second major reform whose legal basis was created during William IV's reign was the abolition of the peasants' services and duties that were still widespread. This complicated issue also required long negotiations between the ministry and the assembly, but on 23 July 1833 a system of land redemption was agreed upon, which ultimately made it possible for the peasants to work efficiently and productively.

William IV consented to both these reform measures. That his willingness to accept reform had its limits was shown, however, when in his capacity as king of Hanover and in opposition to the British foreign minister Palmerston (1784–1865), he approved the resolutions of 28 June 1832, by which the German Bundestag accepted the so-called 'Six Articles' intended to restrict freedom of the press and to prevent any further liberal developments in the individual German states.[56] To annoy Palmerston still further he even bestowed on the Austrian and Prussian envoys to the Bundestag, for their services in bringing about these resolutions, Hanover's highest honour, the 'Guelphen-Orden'.[57]

---

[54] NHStA Hann., Hann 92, No. 20, William IV's decree to the ministry of 14 February 1831.
[55] *Ibid.*, William IV's decree to viceroy and minister of 3 April 1831.
[56] Ziegler, *King William IV*, pp. 230–1.
[57] v. Hassell, *Geschichte des Königreichs Hannover*, p. 355.

There was another area in which the Hanoverian government stuck to a conservative line. This was the kingdom's foreign-trade relations. While the attempt to create larger economic spheres had already led to a Customs Union between Bavaria and Wüttemberg in 1828, and the Grand Duchy of Hesse formed a Customs Union with Prussia, Hanover stayed out of it all. This was still true after the German Customs Union was founded on 1 January 1834. Between the Ems and the Elbe the low duties that favoured the import of British colonial and finished products were retained, thereby hindering the emergence of a local industry.[58] The reason for this policy was not so much to accommodate Hanover's partner in the Personal Union. Rather the idea, first, was to prevent the emergence of new social classes and an increase in the conflict potential inherent in this.[59] Secondly, it can also be seen as a reflex reaction to Prussia's hegemonic ambitions, the economic dimensions of which were also feared. So Hanover continued to function as a bridgehead for British trade in Germany while on the other side of the Channel Hanoverian exports to Britain – mainly farm products and oak for ship-building – were subjected to just the same protectionist British customs laws as those of the other states – despite the dynastic connection. This led to a very disadvantageous cash-flow situation in the country's economy and it ended up in debt.

Britain, quite understandably, constantly supported the preferential treatment it received from Hanover. After all Britain's main interest was in retaining, if possible, a customs-free path to southern Germany, especially to the towns where the great trade fairs were held, Leipzig and Frankfurt am Main.[60] For this reason Britain favoured the *Mitteldeutscher Handelsverein*, founded at Hanover's instigation, whose main purpose was to counteract further expansion of the Prussian Customs Union.[61] Accordingly Palmerston used diplomatic channels to second Hanover's objection in the German Bundestag when Electoral Hesse left the *Handelsverein* to join the Customs Union. Nonetheless it would be wrong to think that in the customs question Hanover simply followed in Britain's slipstream, which is how German historiography, with its focus on Prussia, has presented it so far.[62] It would be more appropriate to talk of parallel interests. Even after the Personal Union had ended it was still several years before Hanover joined the Prussian-led Customs Union.

---

[58] Röhrbein and Rohr, *Hannover im Glanz und Schatten*, pp. 69–70.
[59] Bertram, *Das Königreich Hannover*, pp. 41–2.
[60] Arning, *Hannovers Stellung zum Zollverein*, p. 31.
[61] v. Hassell, *Geschichte des Königreichs Hannover*, pp. 350–1.
[62] Davis, *Britain and the German Zollverein*, pp. 4–5.

When William IV died on 20 June 1837 without any legal offspring a situation arose that Hanover had been anticipating for some time. In Hanover the crown could only pass to a woman if there were no men left in the family. In Britain, on the other hand, succession was direct, regardless of gender. So it came about that Princess Victoria (1819–1901), daughter of the late Duke Edward of Kent (1767–1820), the king's next-oldest brother, ascended the throne, while on the continent her uncle Ernest Augustus (1771–1851) took up the reins of government.

After almost 123 years the Personal Union ended without any great fuss, indeed without anyone taking much notice on either side of the Channel. During the last two decades of their special relationship, if not before, Britain and Hanover had developed away from, rather than towards one another. The end of the dynastic connection merely put the constitutional seal on a process that had set in long ago in the sphere of practical policies.

During the first few years after 1837, however, the possibility continued to exist that the Personal Union might be revived should Queen Victoria die without issue.[63] The British viewed this prospect with horror since King Ernest Augustus, who belonged to the House of Lords as the duke of Cumberland, had already made himself widely hated by the ultra-conservative speeches he gave there. This aversion became even more pronounced when he started his rule in Hanover with an act regarded by many contemporaries in the whole of Europe as a reactionary coup d'état: the abolition of the state's basic law of 1833. It was not until Edward, Prince of Wales (1841–1910), was born that the prospect of this unpopular succession evaporated. After that the House of Hanover increasingly lost significance for the United Kingdom. Leaving the Regency to his son, who had already gone blind at a young age,[64] King Ernest Augustus travelled to England in 1843. He was greeted with antipathy by large sections of the population and given a reserved reception at court.[65] However, this was little more than a minor episode.

The title duke of Cumberland was withdrawn from the great grandson of this king who was so unpopular in England as a result of his role in the First World War. On the other hand the Guelphs were able to fight for legal recognition of their British citizenship.[66] They are still in line to the throne, to some extent, but are a long way down the list. Indeed, after the

---

[63] Black, *The Hanoverians*, pp. 211–12.
[64] v. Hassell, *Geschichte des Königreichs Hannover*, p. 477.
[65] G[eoffrey] M[alden] Willis, *Ernest Augustus. Duke of Cumberland and King of Hanover* (London, 1954), pp. 340–52.
[66] Information provided verbally by HRH Heinrich Prince of Hanover on 28 October 2004.

Second World War in north-west Germany the rumour started to circulate that Lower Saxony, via the marriage of a prince of the House of Hanover to a British princess, should become a 'kingdom affiliated to England'.[67] Needless to say, re-establishment of the Personal Union in this form was never a political reality.

What course history might have taken had the dynastic connection not been broken in 1837 is, of course, a matter of pure speculation, but it is extremely interesting. The present head of the House of Guelph would rule the United Kingdom as Ernest Augustus V (born 1954). It seems unlikely that in 1866 Prussia would have dared to annex German possessions of the British crown, which is what actually happened to Hanover, then isolated from Britain. Under such circumstances the First World War, and therefore also the Second World War, are unlikely to have happened. The far-reaching implications of this are a matter for conjecture. We can assume, however, that the world today would look quite different.

---

[67] Reinhard Bein and Bernhardine Vogel, *Nachkriegszeit. Das Braunschweiger Land 1945 bis 1950. Materialien zur Landesgeschichte* (Braunschweig 1995), p. 12.

7 The university of Göttingen and the Personal Union, 1737–1837

Thomas Biskup

The British literary critic and historian of the Enlightenment, Robert Shackleton, once called Hanover 'an outpost of English civilization',[1] and the university town of Göttingen in particular, in the south of the Electorate, did indeed like to bask in the reflected glory of British power and English fashion like other outposts of the empire. At the nearby spa of Pyrmont, in the Waldeck principality, the Göttingen merchant Knierim established a stall where only English products were offered, and the university town itself celebrated English victories in the colonies with illuminations: 'Göttingen is Londres *en miniature*', wrote Caroline Michaelis – daughter of the eminent theologian Johann David Michaelis – following Rodney's naval victory over the French in 1782; indicating, incidentally, with her use of French that other points of reference remained important for the cosmopolitan university town. According to the Göttingen theologian and historian Ludwig Timotheus Spittler, English influence went beyond fashion, and affected what today would be called norms and values: 'We like to consider ourselves half-English here, and certainly not just in fashion, dress, and manners, but in character.'[2] Historians of the German Enlightenment and of the history of science have confirmed this view. In particular, it has been emphasised how Göttingen functioned as a gateway for the influx of British political and social thought, and as a place where *Anglophilie*, the German image of Britain as a model of political 'freedom', economic prosperity, and sociable culture, was shaped.[3] Little is, however, known about the role

---

[1] Michael Maurer, *Aufklärung und Anglophilie* (Göttingen, 1987), p. 44.
[2] Both quotations taken from Götz von Selle, *Die Georg-August-Universität zu Göttingen 1737–1937* (Göttingen, 1937), p. 186.
[3] Selle, *Die Georg-August-Universität*, pp. 115–204; Hermann Wellenreuther, 'Göttingen und England im 18. Jahrhundert', in *250 Jahre Vorlesungen an der Georgia Augusta 1734–1984* (Göttingen, 1985), pp. 30–63; Maurer, *Aufklärung*; Theodor Wolpers, 'Göttingen als Vermittlungszentrum englischer Literatur im 18. Jahrhundert', in: Reinhard Lauer, ed., *Philologie in Göttingen: Sprach- und Literaturwissenschaft an der Georgia Augusta im 18. und beginnenden 19. Jahrhundert* (Göttingen, 2001), pp. 90–136. For a survey of the Göttingen

Göttingen played for *Britain*, and it remains to be seen whether historians are right to brand 'cultural exchange' between Britain and Göttingen as a one-way road, or whether one should not rather speak of a 'special relationship' between Göttingen and Britain within the European republic of letters.[4]

The history of science has long recognised that early modern scholarship was a European phenomenon, which cannot be grasped by 'national' limitations.[5] During the half-century from the 1660s when London's Royal Society formed the avant-garde of Europe's growing network of academies, international epistolary exchange formed the bedrock of scholarship in all fields despite persisting confessional divides and emerging national rivalries. Indeed, historians of science have pointed out that it was international exchange as the complement to national institution-building which made England's leading role in the 'Scientific Revolution' of the seventeenth century possible at all.[6] For the century following Newton's death, it is the connections between British and French scholars which have found particular scholarly attention, whereas the connections between the academic cultures of England and Germany during this period have remained largely unexplored.[7] Even the two eminent natural scientists, Johann Reinhold Forster and his son Georg, who accompanied

---

historiography, see now Nicolas Rupke, 'The Göttingen location', in: Rupke, ed., *Göttingen and the development of the natural sciences* (Göttingen, 2002), pp. 19–32, esp. pp. 20–7, which also highlights the anti-semitic and nationalist slant of Selle's commemorative volume for the University's bicentenary in 1937.

[4] Hans Hecht, ed., *Briefe aus Georg Chr. Lichtenbergs englischem Freundeskreis: Aus den Handschriften des Lichtenberg-Archivs*, (Göttingen, 1925), and Hecht, *T. Percy, R. Wood und J. D. Michaelis: Ein Beitrag zur Literaturgeschichte der Genieperiode* (Stuttgart, 1933), are rare exceptions. In his statistical work on British students at Göttingen, Stewart points out that 'there would indeed seem to be sufficient evidence to explore the influence Göttingen had on their subsequent scientific productivity', Gordon M. Stewart, 'British students at the University of Göttingen in the eighteenth century', *German life and letters* 33 (1979), 30.

[5] David Lux and Harold Cook, 'Closed circles or open networks? Communicating at a distance during the Scientific Revolution', *History of Science* 36 (1998), 200–1. For Göttingen's role within the European republic of letters, see the survey provided by Hartmut Boockmann, *Göttingen – Vergangenheit und Gegenwart einer europäischen Universität* (Göttingen, 1997). Wellenreuther, 'Göttingen und England', highlights that Göttingen professors saw their English partners as members of an international community of scholars rather than as representatives of another nation.

[6] Michael Hunter, *Establishing the new science: the experience of the early Royal Society* (Woodbridge, 1989); Andrea Rusnock, 'Correspondence networks and the Royal Society, 1700–1750', *British Journal for the History of Science* 32 (1999), 155–69.

[7] Maurice Crosland, 'Anglo-continental scientific relations c.1780 – c.1820, with special reference to the correspondence of Sir Joseph Banks', in R. E. R. Banks, B. Elliott, J. G. Hawkes, et al., eds., *Sir Joseph Banks: a global perspective* (London, 1994), pp. 13–22.

Cook on his second South Sea voyage, have found only scant attention.[8] Contemporaries, however, were well aware of the importance of German scholars: the leading Whig physician, advocate of 'pneumatic' medicine and one-time Oxford don Thomas Beddoes was by no means untypical in his assessment of German scientists 'whom he considered as, both in talents and industry, greatly superior to the French'.[9] By the late 1780s when Beddoes planned a trip to north Germany (but was prevented by his appointment at Oxford and then by the ensuing political turmoils of the 1790s), north German scholarship was almost synonymous with the university of Göttingen. Founded as late as 1737, Göttingen had already by the time of its fiftieth anniversary reached an almost unrivalled status among German, and indeed European, universities.

Wider trends in historiography are partly to blame for the neglect of the role German scholars played in the scientific world of eighteenth- and early nineteenth-century Britain: until quite recently, the Royal Society and much of eighteenth-century natural science in general, have been characterised as a dull and comfortable old regime of scholarship administration crippled by patronage and corruption, dominated by well-connected aristocrats such as Sir Joseph Banks, and populated by scholars who were keen on 'improving' the state of knowledge through the collecting and classifying of artefacts and specimens, rather than embarking on Newton-style, 'ground-breaking' innovations themselves.[10] This view has been challenged in the last decade, and historians of science now acknowledge that the natural sciences of the later eighteenth century were crucial for the formation of the highly professionalised, specialised and institutional world of science of Victorian Britain. The burgeoning historiography on the role empire played has especially contributed to this reassessment. Thus, the colonies turn out to have been far more influential in shaping British life than has long been allowed for, and it is now being highlighted how economic, social, and cultural exchange with Britain's far-flung colonial possessions contributed to the integration of the first British

---

[8] Standard works in English are still Leslie Bodi, 'Georg Forster, the "Pacific expert" of eighteenth-century Germany', *Historical Studies: Australia and New Zealand* 8 (1957–9), 345–63, and Michael E. Hoare, *The tactless philosopher: Johann Reinhold Forster (1729–1798)* (Melbourne, 1976).

[9] Quoted in John Edmonds Stock, *Memoirs of the life of Thomas Beddoes, M. D., with an analytical account of his writings* (London, 1811), p. 18: 'His admiration of foreign scientific characters was confined to the Germans.' This may, however, be changing, as Michael Kempe, *Wissenschaft, Theologie, Aufklärung: Johann Jakob Scheuchzer (1672–1733) und die Sintfluttheorie* (Epfendorf, 2003), suggests putting much emphasis on Scheuchzer's English connections.

[10] This view is summarised by Rusnock, 'Correspondence networks', p. 155.

empire.[11] Here, the 'periphery' suddenly appears as crucial for the formation of attitudes, values and identities at the 'centre', and in pointing out how, for instance, encounters with the islanders, or the flora and fauna, of the Indian and Pacific Oceans shaped notions of 'Europeanness' and 'otherness', history of science has been at the forefront of this enterprise.

The focus, however, has almost exclusively been on British overseas possessions in America and India whereas the less exotic Electorate of Hanover has largely remained excluded from the 'new' British history. Yet Hanover was arguably an important part of the empire too; and Göttingen has hitherto played a marginal role in the histories of eighteenth-century British science and scholarship. In Roy Porter's *British Enlightenment*, for instance, neither Göttingen nor other German universities figure at all. His version of the 'creation of the modern world' thus appears – in this respect strikingly old-fashioned – as a product of *British* curiosity, commerce, and enterprise.[12] Similarly, the British Museum exhibition and catalogue on the 'discovery of the world', while acknowledging the central role of empire for the development of the sciences from the later eighteenth century, remains curiously uninterested in the question of how the knowledge making possible the 'discoveries' of the period was actually produced, which institutions were drawn upon, and how Britain was integrated into the European republic of letters.[13] In this last respect, the concept of 'centers of calculation', forwarded by network theorists who argue that the information – reports, images and specimens – flowing back from various parts of the empire was transformed into knowledge back home in London, may reach its limits:[14] by putting the emphasis on the interrelationship between colonial 'periphery' and imperial 'centre', or between indigenuous peoples and British explorers, studies of scholarly exploits in the empire tend to underestimate the importance of other European centres.[15]

---

[11] David Hancock, *Citizens of the world: London merchants and the integration of the British Atlantic community, 1735–1785* (Cambridge, 1995) conversely highlights the influence London as a trading metropolis had on the American colonies; Linda Colley, *Britons: forging the nation, 1797–1837* (New Haven, 1992), pp. 101–46; Linda Colley, *Captives. Britain, empire and the world, 1660–1850* (London, 2002).

[12] This has already been pointed out by Clarissa Campbell Orr, 'The late Hanoverian court and the Christian Enlightenment', forthcoming in Michael Schaich, ed., *Monarchy and religion*.

[13] Roy Porter, *Enlightenment: Britain and the creation of the modern world* (London, 2001); Kim Sloan, ed., *Enlightenment: discovering the world in the eighteenth century* (Exhibition cat., London, 2003).

[14] Bruno Latour, *Science in action: how to follow scientists and engineers through society* (Cambridge, MA, 1987).

[15] Even the otherwise admirable David Philip Miller and Peter Hanns Reill, eds., *Visions of empire: voyages, botany, and representations of nature* (Cambridge, 1996), almost exclusively focuses on the discussion *within* the British, and Swedish, communities of scholars, thereby marginalising French and German contributions.

In this context, the notion of a 'network of networks', which has been suggested by historians analysing international scholarly correspondences, can be helpful as it puts the emphasis on the interdependence of various networks spread all over Europe which through Imperial extensions may well reach beyond the borders of Europe.[16] If we want to know more about the patterns of scholarly exchange and cooperation shaping the scientific vision of the Enlightenment, it seems appropriate to take up the approach of embedding science in the history of communication as propagated so effectively by Martin Gierl, who, in his analysis of early enlightened discourse in Germany, has shifted the emphasis away from the contents, and instead emphasised the central function of scholarly exchange in establishing a network of academics who were prepared to engage in debates over contested points, rather than in mutual accusations of heterodoxy and adherence to the 'wrong' system of belief.[17] As David S. Lux and Harold J. Cook have pointed out, in particular the international character of the 'new science' emerging in the seventeenth century can only be grasped by paying close attention to 'the ways in which matters of fact were communicated'.[18]

At the centre of this chapter will thus be an analysis of the network of scholarly correspondences, rather than an analysis of their publications. Such an approach, making use of the correspondences of several Göttingen scholars and their English partners, which are preserved in the libraries and archives of Göttingen, London, and Oxford, contributes to uncovering a dimension of the Anglo-Hanoverian Personal Union which has been buried by the national historiographies of scholarship and science that prevailed for much of the nineteenth and twentieth centuries. How this network was formed and how it operated was always dependent on the particular political, cultural and socio-economic factors of the Anglo-Hanoverian Personal Union. After all, the making of knowledge is no transcendental process taking place in a disembodied space of thoughts and ideas, but is always dependent on the local, regional, or national scientific cultures. As Steven Shapin rightly maintains, it is important to avoid both the scylla of localism and the charybdis of transcendentalist conceptions of truth; looking at the ways in which the Anglo-Hanoverian union provided a unique transnational framework

---

[16] Quoted recently with respect to the Göttingen professor of medicine, Albrecht von Haller's position within the European republic of letters by Urs Boschung, 'Göttingen, Hanover, and Europe: Haller's correspondence', in Rupke, ed., *Göttingen and the development of the natural sciences*, p. 44.
[17] Martin Gierl, *Pietismus und Aufklärung: Theologische Polemik und die Kommunikationsreform der Wissenschaft am Ende des 17. Jahrhunderts* (Göttingen, 1997).
[18] Lux and Cook, 'Closed circles or open networks?', p. 181.

The university of Göttingen 133

for scholarly 'curiosity' may thus also allow us to provide a novel geographical perspective on eighteenth-century scholarship.[19]

In this context, two historians have in recent years begun to reassess Göttingen's position within the Hanoverian monarchy: John Gascoigne, in his study of the long-standing president of the Royal Society, Sir Joseph Banks, has contributed to reintegrating Göttingen into the orbit of British science by pointing to his German connections, and Clarissa Campbell Orr has emphasised how many Göttingen scholars formed part of Queen Charlotte's intellectual circle.[20] An exhibition of Göttingen's University Library has also pointed to the manifold connections between Göttingen and Britain.[21] This chapter wishes to take this thread up, and to suggest that far from being a remote 'outpost' of English civilisation, Göttingen was instead at the centre of English science and scholarship in the second half of the eighteenth and during the first years of the nineteenth century. It may have played a limited role as a training ground for members of the *British* elite, but it did provide the expertise in natural sciences, oriental studies and philology needed by *England* which lacked the academic institutions necessary to make sense of the scientific exploits in the decades following the Seven Years Wars. The necessity to communicate over a large distance did not mean that these scholars could not form quite a close-knit community.[22] Sharing interests and common goals, and establishing close contacts on individual as well as institutional levels with London's scientific and political elites, Göttingen contributed to shaping the British capital's scholarly life into the nineteenth century through the exchange of letters, books, specimens and pupils, collaboration from editing books to organising large-scale expeditions, the professional training of British scholars, and the export of Göttingen graduates to occupy important positions at the scholarly institutions that were emerging in the first decades of the nineteenth century.

The university of Göttingen was established in 1737 with two primary aims, one domestic, and one 'international': like other German universities

---

[19] Steven Shapin, 'Placing the view from nowhere: historical and sociological problems in the location of science', *Transactions of the Institute of British Geographers* 23 (1998), 5–12.
[20] John Gascoigne, *Joseph Banks and the English Enlightenment: useful knowledge and polite culture* (Cambridge, 1994), pp. 149 et passim, and Gascoigne, 'Blumenbach, Banks, and the beginnings of anthropology in Göttingen', in Rupke, ed., *Göttingen and the development of the Natural Sciences*, pp. 86–98; Clarissa Campbell Orr, 'Queen Charlotte and the republic of letters', in Campbell Orr, ed., *Queenship in Europe, 1660–1815: the role of the consort*, pp. 368–402. See also Campbell Orr, 'Late Hanoverian court'.
[21] See the exhibition catalogue Elmar Mittler, ed., *'Eine Welt allein ist nicht genug': Großbritannien, Hannover und Göttingen 1714–1837* (Göttingen, 2005), which also contains a number of essays on the Personal Union as well as on academic relations.
[22] Lux and Cook, 'Closed circles or open networks?', p. 179.

established in the early modern period, it functioned as a training ground for Hanoverian civil servants and clergy, but it was also aimed at increasing Hanover's influence within the Holy Roman Empire, and at raising the profile of George II as a *German* ruler, in particular vis-à-vis neighbouring Prussia. Plans to establish a Hanoverian university had been discussed for some time, but what really got the university project off the ground was the expansion of Hanover in the 1710s, and the accession of a new King-Elector in 1727. The acquisition of Bremen and Verden in the wake of the Great Northern War had led to an increasing demand for clergy and civil servants, which made the continued sharing of the declining university of Helmstedt with the Wolfenbüttel line of the House of Brunswick-Lüneburg difficult. In a memorandum outlining the university project, the Hanoverian librarian and historian Johann Daniel Gruber thus argued that both the needs of the newly expanded Electorate's 'Landes-Kinder' *and* the prestige of the King-Elector demanded a university: if almost all imperial princes had their own universities, Gruber wrote, rising Hanover certainly needed 'such a jewel'.[23] After all, there were already thirty-two universities in the empire, and a university and/or academy of sciences was a prerequisite for any German ruler to be taken seriously as a patron of the arts and sciences.

The constitution as well as geographical location of Hanover's new university (in the south east of the territory) clearly indicated that Göttingen was supposed to replace the Hohenzollerns' Halle as Germany's leading 'enlightened' university. It was 'modern' in the sense that Gerlach Adolph von Münchhausen, the leading Hanoverian minister who directed the project from the start, and later became the university's curator, asserted tight government control over its doings while simultaneously keeping it free from church interference: a typically 'enlightened' policy also pursued by other German governments throughout the eighteenth century.[24] Deliberately attracting students from all over Europe, but in particular from other German states, irrespective of their denomination, Göttingen was designed to extend Hanoverian influence throughout the empire and beyond through its teachings. Göttingen had indeed a high proportion of

---

[23] 'Ein solch Kleinod', as Gruber wrote. His 'Präliminaria, so vor Anrichtung der neuen Universität zu berichtigen sein werden', dated 16 September 1732, as well as the royal charter, dated 7 December 1736, drafted by Gruber as well, are reprinted in Rössler, *Gründung der Universität Göttingen* (Göttingen, 1855), from p. 10.

[24] For instance in the duchy of Brunswick where the government tried to wrest the territory's schools from church control, and subject it to government authority, in the 1780s, see Hanno Schmitt, *Schulreform im aufgeklärten Absolutismus: Leistungen, Widersprüche und Grenzen philanthropischer Reformpraxis im Herzogtum Braunschweig-Wolfenbüttel 1785–1790* (Weinheim, Basel, 1979).

non-Hanoverian students; in medicine, between 50% and 75% of doctoral students came from outside the Electorate, and a tenth of these was from outside the Holy Roman Empire.[25] To attract the future decision-makers and their advisers as students, Göttingen was marketed as a morally safe, disciplined, and rather expensive university where students could gain professional training as well as a gentlemanly education: 'applied sciences' was the buzzword. Thus, the *Short account of his Majesty's late journey to Goettingen, and of the state of the new University there*, published in 1748 ostensibly to attract English students, boasted that Göttingen was not governed by 'bare theory', but by 'the practice of sciences'.[26]

Educating the future elites of the empire and beyond was one thing, but Göttingen was also more directly used as a propaganda platform: in the poems published on occasions such as royal birthdays, anniversaries, or the opening of new university buildings, as well as in publications sent out to other academic institutions, George II was branded as a tolerant yet effective prince who had Germany as a whole, rather than the limited professional and confessional demands of his territory, at heart.[27] The ceremonial visit George II paid to his foundation after the end of the War of the Austrian Succession, accompanied by the duke of Newcastle, demonstrates how Göttingen could be used this way. Orchestrated by Münchhausen, the 1748 visit was documented in a 227-page Festschrift compiled by Göttingen's star professor of theology, Johann Lorenz Mosheim to guarantee maximum circulation. He emphasised the King-Elector's Protestant and 'North European' credentials as a no-nonsense ruler who would not interrupt the university's business but came to see the university 'functioning' by witnessing the conferment of degrees and the change of the prorectorate.[28] In the speeches, poems, and the

---

[25] Ulrich Tröhler, *Vom Medizinstudenten zum Doktor: Die Göttinger Medizinischen Promotionen im 18. Jahrhundert. Sozialhistorisch-vergleichender Überblick* (Göttingen, 1993), p. 17.

[26] [Anon.], *A short account of his Majesty's late journey to Goettingen, and of the state of the new University there. In a letter to my Lord*** (1748), no page numbers – For the Göttingen professor Michaelis, the *Cameralnutzen* a university provided its home country with was a crucial argument he discussed right at the start of his survey of German protestant universities, see Johann David Michaelis, *Räsonnement über die protestantischen Universitäten in Deutschland* (4 vols., Frankfurt-on-Main, 1768–76), vol. I, sections 2–11.

[27] A poem published on behalf of the university to celebrate George II's 1736 birthday called the king Britain's pride and Germany's protector: 'Durchlauchtigster August/ Der Teutonen Schutz/ Der Britten Lust', taken from *Allerunterthänigste Glückwünsche der Göttingischen Musen an Georg den Andern, als Königlich Majestät Dero Hohes Geburts-Fest den 10. November 1736 celebrierten* (Göttingen, 1736), quoted in Wellenreuther, 'Göttingen und England', p. 41.

[28] Johann Lorenz Mosheim, *Beschreibung der grossen und denckwürdigen Feyer die bey der allerhöchsten Anwesenheit des allerdurchlauchtigsten, grossmächtigsten Fürsten und Herren, Herren Georg des Andern, Königes von Grosbritannien, Frankreich und Irrland, Beschützers*

iconography of the two triumphal arches which had nonetheless been erected, the recent military victories on the continent, in Britain and at sea figured prominently: one inscription of the triumphal arch erected by the university read 'Germania liberata ad Dettingam', linking German 'freedom' and the King-Elector's victory at Dettingen over the French in 1743. The victory over the Jacobites at Culloden in 1746 as well as the Royal Navy's victories over the French in 1747 are also brought into the context of German peace and the European balance of power, the 'aequilibrium europae restitutum', as another inscription read.[29] The 'aequilibrium europae' as safeguarded by the British king in general played a prominent role in the university's teachings: the philosopher Ludwig Martin Kahle's *La balance de l'Europe considerée comme la règle de la paix et de la guerre* (Göttingen, Berlin, 1744) as well as other speeches and occasional writings emanating from Göttingen indicate that during George II's reign, Göttingen's academic staff considered the Personal Union almost exclusively in terms of the balance of power.[30] Throughout the 1748 visit, George was portrayed as being able to liberate Germany from the French yoke with the help of his British power base, and thus implicitly contrasted favourably with Frederick II of Prussia, who at the time was still an ally of the French, who had marched yet again through South Germany and Bohemia during the War of the Austrian Succession. The layout and use of Göttingen thus seem to have addressed the specific problems created by George II's continued absences from Hanover, which seriously affected the Hanoverian court's effectiveness as a centre of diplomatic activity and propaganda within the Empire; it was Göttingen university which as a centre of scholarship, print culture, and international exchange as well as a stage for ceremonial occasions took over some of the tasks the Hanoverian court was unable to fulfil.

The inability of Britain to provide protection during the Seven Years War when Göttingen was repeatedly occupied by French troops appears to have diminished George II's reputation within the university: in the disputations on the causes and effects of the Seven Years War published anonymously after peace had been concluded, the Göttingen professor Samuel Christian Hollmann went as far as to accuse the British of winning the war in the empire at the cost of the Electorate.[31] Indeed, this indicates wider change: if

---

des Glaubens, Herzoges zu Braunschweig-Lüneburg, des Heil. Röm. Reiches Ertzschatzmeisters und Churfürsten, auf deroselben Georg Augustus hohen Schule in der Stadt Göttingen im Jahr 1748. am ersten Tage des Augustmonates begangen ward (Göttingen, 1749), p. 8.

[29] Mosheim, *Beschreibung*, p. 19.
[30] See Wellenreuther, 'Göttingen und England', pp. 41–4.
[31] 'Des Königs Teutsche Unterthanen haben daher zum Theil, nebst ihren Alliirten, den armen Hessen, fast mit Haut und haar für die Engelländer bezahlen müssen', in *Lob des*

occasional poems and festive speeches prior to 1756 had emphasised the king's role as protector of Göttingen's interests, this changed markedly after 1756 when even on occasions such as the 1787 anniversary, praise of the King-Elector – who between 1748 and 1821 did not visit the university in person – was much less prominent.[32] This, however, should not necessarily be taken as a sign of declining royal protection, or an awareness of its importance on the side of Göttingen's professors;[33] rather, the relationship between university and King-Elector took on a new shape in the years following the Seven Years War, and this had to do both with George III's policies and attitudes, and with changes in the world of academia.

First of all, the university's public presentation underwent a transformation, as Göttingen university's fiftieth anniversary in 1787 demonstrates. The enlightened university professors and their superiors in the Hanoverian administration were proud to have managed, as the theologian Gottfried Leß remarked in his anniversary sermon, the transition from baroque barbarity to the noble dignity of well-educated people. Looking back on public university events in the early days, Leß damned them in good Enlightenment manner as morally dangerous and economically wasteful, characterised by 'swarming bacchants and senseless people' who were causing 'tumult in the lecture halls, rudeness and barbarity in the streets, screaming and dreadful hurly-burly during day-time and horror and devastation at night'.[34] According to Leß, in contrast, the 1787 anniversary was celebrated modestly, peacefully, in a happy harmony of all ages, classes, and indeed genders, and in such a way as to honour scholarly merit, not social rank; Pütter made the same point.[35] Quite in accordance with this view, George III figures in Pütter's university history not as a ceremonial visitor like his grandfather, but as the royal protector with scholarly leanings who contributed several hundred

Krieges: In einigen Gesprächen entwickelt (2 vols., Frankfurt-on-Main and Leipzig, 1765–70), vol. II, p. 412; on the authorship, see Albrecht Schöne, ed., *Die Universität Göttingen im Siebenjährigen Kriege: Aus der handschriftlichen Chronik des Professor Samuel Christian Hollmann (1696–1787)* (Leipzig, 1887), p. 42. The book's title 'Praise of war' is, of course, to be understood ironically.

[32] Wellenreuther, 'Göttingen und England', p. 49.
[33] Wellenreuther, 'Göttingen und England', *ibid.*, sees the king's diminished role in public statements as a sign of a dissociation of university and monarchy.
[34] Thus Gottfried Leß in his sermon given at the occasion of the university's 50th anniversary, looking back on the way university celebrations had been handled from the 1730s, quoted in Pütter, *Versuch eimer academischen Gelehrten-Geschichte von der Georg-August Universität zu Göttingen* (Göttingen, 1765), vol. II, p. 408.
[35] *Ibid.*, p. 409 – although the festive procession of university members itself was strictly gendered, one of the anniversary's highlights was the conferment of a doctoral degree on Dorothea Schlözer, daughter of the Göttingen professor of history, who thus became one of Germany's first female PhDs.

specimens from Cook's three South Sea voyages to the university museum and to the botanical garden; all sorts of astronomical instruments, which he was keen to collect himself, to the observatory; and who sent his own three sons to Göttingen to strengthen the ties between his 'family' and the university.[36] On the king's explicit order, his sons were taught by the theologians Leß and Johann David Michaelis as well as the classicist Christian Gottlob Heyne, who in addition chose new German-language publications for the king's library at Buckingham House.[37] Had George II's main merit been to have left the university in the hands of able men, his successor 'gave many examples of thoughtfulness, grace, and generosity of [his] immediate, high person'.[38]

It was not only the flattery that had changed over time: George II had used his foundation to promote himself as a German ruler, but his grandson George III rather considered Göttingen as the German pole of an Anglo-Hanoverian community of scholars sharing his interests in the sciences, but also in theology. He was particularly interested in bolstering scholarship which opened up new branches of knowledge yet remained socially conservative, which contributed to 'improving' society while remaining ideologically close to the established Church and the 'state'. Indeed, in the decades following the Peace of Paris which confirmed Britain's eminence in global politics, Göttingen became something of Britain's 'imperial university': for George III as well as for other members of the British elite, following the 'progress' made in the sciences, collecting documents and monuments of the past as well as specimens from the recent colonial conquests was more than an aristocratic fashion; it was an attempt to make sense of Britain's novel position as a great power by exploring its place in the world as well as its place in history. For Göttingen professors, the Seven Years War marked the time when Britain was transformed from powerful partner guaranteeing the balance of power and peace in Europe, into master of an empire which allowed a glimpse of the world at large. As Hermann Wellenreuther has pointed out, England was the lens through which Göttingen professors came to

---

[36] Most of the royal gifts were ethnographic, such as a Tahitian funeral dress, a tattoo apparatus, and an idol from Owhyhee, see Pütter, *Versuch*, vol. II, pp. 234, 255, 267–70. The observatory's Herschel telescope, Adams microscope and three clocks were all royal gifts; one clock was given by Queen Charlotte. On the king's enthusiasm for collecting in particular technical instruments, see now Jane Roberts, ed., *George III and Queen Charlotte: patronage, collecting and court taste* (Exhibition cat., London, 2004), pp. 287–302.

[37] See Campbell Orr, 'Queen Charlotte'. In this context, Arnold Herm, Ludwig Heeren, *Christian Gottlob Heyne. Biographisch dargestellt* (Göttingen, 1813), p. 341, speaks of a handwritten letter by Queen Charlotte preserved at Göttingen, which, however, I have been unable to identify.

[38] Pütter, *Versuch*, vol. II, p. 12.

The university of Göttingen 139

see the world in the decades after c. 1760.[39] Simultaneously, however, it was Göttingen which helped England make sense of her own imperial experiences.

Before the Seven Years War, Göttingen does not appear to have been much noticed at all in the United Kingdom: only twenty-three students from England and nine from Scotland matriculated before 1756, most of them after George II's well-publicised 1748 visit which also marked the end of the series of wars which had started with the War of the Polish Succession, and may well have been an impediment to the arrival of English students.[40] From 1763 to 1800, however, Göttingen emerged as the most important university outside the British Isles (with the partial exception of the Dutch universities) for English students, for whom the universities of Oxford and Cambridge, which had lost much of their scientific vigour and were crippled by church dominance, offered little in much-debated subjects such as medicine, botany, classics, and orientalism; fields Göttingen was particularly strong in. Of the 228 students from Britain up to 1800, the English were, with 171, the largest group, followed by 32 Scots and 25 students from Ireland.[41] Medicine and law attracted particularly many British students. Imperial law was one of the biggest subjects at Göttingen, and qualified students for diplomatic service within the Holy Roman Empire where a sound knowledge of the constitution's legal framework was the indispensable basis of all diplomacy. Members of the aristocracy thus tended to study law as part of their

---

[39] 'England wurde nach 1760 zum Mittler der Welt schlechthin', Wellenreuther, 'Göttingen und England', p. 60.
[40] Only five students from Britain had been enrolled prior to 1750. For the numbers, see Stewart, 'British students', p. 25; Harald Ssymank, 'Engländer und Amerikaner auf der Universität Göttingen im ersten Jahrhundert ihres Bestehenes', *Göttinger Blätter für Geschichte und Heimatkunde Südhannovers*, N. F. 2/4 (1938), pp. 15–31, provides only a preliminary survey.
[41] Stewart, 'British students', p. 25, who relies on the matriculation lists reprinted in Götz von Selle, ed., *Die Matrikel der Georg-August-Universität zu Göttingen 1734–1837* (Hildesheim, Leipzig, 1937). The number of British students actually *studying* at Göttingen, however, must be put slightly lower as Stewart does not consider that a number of high-ranking visitors – mostly members of the royal family – only signed the matriculation book for ceremonial purposes when passing through Göttingen; thus the dukes of York and Gloucester in 1765 and 1769 respectively, Frederick, Bishop of Osnabrück in 1781, but also the duke of Newcastle in 1748. See Pütter, *Versuch*, vol. I, p. 15, note a, and Pütter, *Versuch*, vol. II, pp. 15–16, notes b and d. As an analysis of Selle, *Matrikel*, demonstrates, the number of British students declined slowly after 1800 until the French occupation of 1806 made the situation entirely untenable: in 1801, six Britons matriculated (pp. 412–42), in 1803, 1804, and 1806 only one each year (pp. 437, 452, 465), and none in 1807. In 1814 only three Britons enrolled at the university (pp. 531–7), and Göttingen never regained its previous popularity with British students: in 1815, only three Britons matriculated (pp. 547–58), two in 1820 (pp. 621–42), and when the Personal Union ended in 1837, only one was left (p. 935).

preparation for further service, whereas the professional classes rather sent their sons to Göttingen to receive a state-of-the-art medical training. With Albrecht von Haller and Johann Friedrich Blumenbach, Göttingen boasted two of the most famous teachers of medicine of the whole of Europe. In the quarter-century prior to 1800, medicine alone boasted no fewer than 30 British students, most of whom enrolled at Göttingen to do research following an Oxford, Cambridge, or Edinburgh education.[42]

From the 1760s on, some of George III's confidants and courtiers had sent their sons to Göttingen: Lord Boston's son William Irby and Robert Adair, son of the king's physician, both studied at Göttingen.[43] Their cases suggest that far from starting a new trend, the king perhaps rather followed a trend set by other members of his court as well as his German relations (the princes of Hesse-Cassel had been sent to Göttingen in the 1750s)[44] when sending his three younger sons to Göttingen in 1786. Considering that both Bute and George's father had had little to do with Göttingen, and had rather emphasised the *British* aspects of his education, it is probable that the king's increasing interest in Göttingen from the 1770s was rather due to the influence exerted by his German-born consort and their circle of virtuosi and gentlemen-collectors, ranging from the physician John Pringle to the botanist Joseph Banks, who were fascinated by the latest findings in the natural sciences which were so well represented at Göttingen. With Pringle, his friend Benjamin Franklin, Robert Lowth, bishop of Oxford, and the Oxford bible scholar Benjamin Kennicott, several members of the the king's and queen's learned circle had been elected into Göttingen's Royal Society of Sciences in 1766; Pringle and Franklin had even visited the university.[45] After the disappointments and domestic turmoil during the American War of Independence, George III in general showed greater interest in his German territories; indeed, he twice threatened to abdicate and move to Hanover.[46] Once having recognised Göttingen's potential, the king then undertook his own efforts to bring Hanoverian and British scholars together, complaining repeatedly that Göttingen was not appreciated

---

[42] Stewart, 'British students', p. 29.
[43] Irby matriculated in 1768, Adair in 1778, see Stewart, 'British students', pp. 33–4, and Campbell Orr, 'Queen Charlotte', p. 387 and n. 68.
[44] The princes William, Carl and Frederick of Hesse, George II's grand-children, studied at Göttingen 1754–6. See Johann Stephan Pütter, *Versuch*, vol. I, p. 15.
[45] Pütter, *Versuch*, vol. II, pp. 281–3.
[46] Sigisbert Conrady, 'Die Wirksamkeit König Georgs III. für die hannoverschen Kurlande', *Niedersächsisches Jahrbuch für Landesgeschichte* 39 (1967), 150–91.

enough by his British subjects.[47] Apart from contributing to the university collections, the royal *Rector magnificentissimus* also repeatedly intervened in university politics, and showed particular interest in his two main fields of interest, applied sciences and theology, stimulating a prize essay competition in the latter, pressing agricultural sciences upon the university, and closely following the progress of astronomy and physics Göttingen was famous for. The physicist Georg Christoph Lichtenberg, founder of the university's collection of scientific apparatus, was repeatedly invited to the court of St James's where the king was building up a collection of such instruments himself. Not only did George III send his three younger sons to study at Göttingen in 1786; his brothers Edward, duke of York, and William, duke of Gloucester had visited the university as early as 1765 and 1769, and his sister Augusta, then hereditary princess of Brunswick-Lüneburg, visited the university library when she travelled through Göttingen in 1778.[48] Before matriculating in 1786, Adolphus Frederick had already been to Göttingen in 1781.[49] These royal visits mirror an intensification of scholarly connections between Göttingen and England in the 1770s and 1780s when the number of English students at Göttingen peaked, and the king's astronomer, William Herschel, as well as the professors of astronomy at Oxford and Cambridge, Thomas Hornsby and Edward Waring, were elected into Göttingen's Royal Society of Sciences.[50]

Despite Lichtenberg's complaints that supervising English students was often enough limited to 'taming' students notorious for their fondness of alcohol,[51] the Göttingen education with its emphasis on social

---

[47] 'Die auswärtigen, insonderheit Englischen Gelehrten erfahren von den Arbeiten der Deutschen Gelehrten, u. so auch der Göttingischen, so gar weniges; und Ihro Maj. unsrer gnädigster König haben selbst zu äusern geruhet: Sie hörten von Deutschen Fremden viel Gutes von Göttingen, aber seine Engländer wüßten nichts von seinen G.[öttinger] Professoren', the philologian Christian Gottlob Heyne wrote to Albrecht von Haller in 1775, see Frank William Peter Dougherty, ed., *Christian Gottlob Heyne's Correspondence with Albrecht and Gottlieb Emanuel von Haller*, vol. I (Göttingen, 1997), no. 99, pp. 172–3.

[48] Pütter, *Versuch*, vol. II, pp. 15–16, notes b and c. York signed the university book on 23 August 1765, Gloucester on 14 August 1769. See also Abraham G. Kästner, *Nachricht von demjenigen, was bey höchster Gegenwart des Herzogs von York zu Göttingen vorgegangen* (Göttingen, 1765), and *Göttingische Gelehrte Anzeigen* (GGA) 1765, pp. 817–20; for Gloucester, see GGA 1769, p. 889.

[49] Pütter, *Versuch*, vol. II, p. 16, n. d.

[50] Herschel and Waring were elected in 1786, Hornby in 1776, see Pütter, *Versuch*, vol. II, p. 282.

[51] Of all the non-Hanoverian groups of students, in particular the English had to be 'menagirt', as government authorities articulated it, with the Hanoverian *Geheimer Rat* following all movements of English students with particular care, see Stefan Brüdermann, *Göttinger Studenten und akademische Gerichtsbarkeit im 18. Jahrhundert* (Göttingen, 1990), p. 144.

skills and sound scholarship, its atmosphere of religious toleration and scientific 'progress', could offer qualifications which made the young and aspiring Robert Adair interesting for his patron Charles James Fox. His stint there equipped him to undertake a diplomatically delicate tour of Germany and Russia in the 1790s, and later qualified him for diplomatic posts in Vienna and Berlin. Canning's and Pitt's attacks on Adair in the *Anti-Jacobin* invariably included side-swipes at the supposedly rebellious atmosphere of Göttingen University.[52] Rebellious, however, Göttingen certainly was not in the decade of the French Revolution; even riots such as the 1790 'exodus' of students entirely conformed to early modern rituals of protest against mistreatment by the authorities.[53] Josiah Dornford, who had gone to Göttingen from Trinity College, Oxford, and later became inspector of the army accounts in the West Indies, not only published an English translation of Johann Stephan Pütter's *Historical development of the present political constitution of the Germanic empire* in three volumes, but also a pamphlet supporting the Pitt administration in 1793, thus belying rumours of the revolutionary spirit of former Göttingen students. As a result of the uncertainty following the outbreak of the revolutionary wars, the number of British students at Göttingen declined briefly in 1793–4, but picked up again quickly in the second half of the 1790s.[54] After the conclusion of the peace of Basle, Hanover had become part of the Prussian-protected neutrality zone in north Germany which remained a haven of peace and economic prosperity in war-torn Europe until 1803–6. After the fall of the Netherlands, the Dutch universities were out of reach, but for the British, the space for continental travel was generally much curtailed. For most young *British* travellers, France was out of bounds, and the 'Grand Tour' almost impossible; Göttingen benefited from this, and for a few years even took the place of Paris and Rome as a source of inspiration for English poets, such as Wordsworth and Coleridge. With its rich collections in old

---

[52] In *The Anti-Jacobin*, no 30, 1798, Adair is satirised as love-sick prisoner Rogero from the 'University of Gottingen', see Charles Edmonds, ed., *Poetry of the Anti-Jacobin: comprising the celebrated political and satirical poems* (London, 1890), pp. 201–18, in particular Rogero's Göttingen song, which was composed by Canning and Pitt, pp. 215–16. For Adair, see also William Prideaux Courtney, rev. H. C. G. Matthew, 'Adair, Sir Robert', in H. C. G. Matthew and Brian Harrison, eds., *Oxford Dictionary of National Biography*, vol. I (Oxford, 2004), pp. 189–90.

[53] See Stefan Brüdermann, *Der Göttinger Studentenauszug 1790: Handwerkerehre und akademische Freiheit* (Göttingen, 1991).

[54] In 1793–4, only four British students matriculated in two years, but in 1795, the number rose to eight per annum again, c. 3% of all matriculations that year, a proportion similar to the years 1786–91. Numbers taken from Selle, *Matrikel*, pp. 342–412; and Stewart, 'British students', pp. 36–9. See also Friedrich Saalfeld, *Geschichte der Universität Göttingen in dem Zeitraume von 1788 bis 1820* (Hanover, 1820), p. 29.

manuscripts, proximity to old towns such as Goslar, and set of young authors like August Schlegel, it was a convenient place from which to explore 'Romantic Germany'. When Coleridge was in Göttingen in 1798–9, he discovered medieval German literature for himself, copying manuscripts which he later took back to England.[55] With a fellow physician studying at Göttingen, Charles Henry Parry, he walked in the Harz mountains, by then famous through Goethe's writings as a site of mystic nature. Much as the Romantics criticised elements of an Enlightenment they deplored as merely rationalist, they developed their art out of an intense engagement with the latest results of 'enlightened' sciences, such as Michaelis's early steps toward comparative philology, or Blumenbach's research into poisons which inspired some of the poems of Thomas Lovell Beddoes, the poet and son of the physician Thomas Beddoes, who studied at Göttingen with Blumenbach. Early nineteenth-century poets, and in particular the first generation of English Lake poets, have usually been associated with British empiricism on the one hand, and German idealism on the other, but if we consider that Göttingen, after all, was a bastion of Immanuel Kant's critics, such as Georg Heinrich Feder or Christoph Meiners; and that philology, orientalism and medicine were crucial for the development of the Romantic movement in both Germany and Britain, we should perhaps reassess these stereotypical categorisations.

The Göttingen–Britain link, however, was at no stage a mass phenomenon. Relatively few members of Britain's establishment studied there, and Göttingen never took the place of the ancient English universities as the main training ground for Britain's elite. Of the c. 300 students enrolling each year at Göttingen from the 1770s, only 5 to 15 were British, and they did not even always represent the largest group of non-German students. It was British *scholarship* which benefited most from the Göttingen connection, through the cooperation of leading scholars and the ensuing influx of former Göttingen students, both British and German. How under the king's patronage, and with the help of the Personal Union's diplomatic and communicative infrastructure, this Anglo-Hanoverian community of scholars operated, will in the following be demonstrated through the examples of the theologian and orientalist Johann David Michaelis and the anthropologist Johann Friedrich Blumenbach.

Personally pious and interested in theology bridging the divide between Anglicanism and Lutheran orthodoxy, theological questions were of

---

[55] Alice D. Snyder, 'Books borrowed by Coleridge from the Library of the University of Göttingen, 1799', *Modern Philology* 25 (1928), 377–80, mentions fourteen books in this field.

particular importance to George III, head of the church in both Hanover and England.[56] The response of Frederick II to Holbach's radical critique of religion shows that at a time when in all European states the church was a main pillar of the social and political order, the debates on scripture could not be ignored by *any* ruler, whatever his personal stance on religion was. How in the face of radical scepticism as epitomised by Voltaire, and materialism as advocated by La Mettrie or Holbach, any notion of 'truth' in the Bible could be salvaged was thus a crucial problem not only for theologians and their colleagues in related fields.[57] Keen to shore up a modernised version of orthodoxy (an enterprise which with the outbreak of the French Revolution only gained importance), George III and his queen found allies at Göttingen's faculties of philosophy and theology which were famous for supporting *Neologie*, the modernising Lutheran theology of the later eighteenth century. In particular Michaelis's annotated bible translations for interested non-experts (*'Ungelehrte'*), which were – in true Enlightenment spirit – designed to make accessible to a wider audience what had hitherto only been published in Latin, were the basis of Michaelis's reputation with the royal couple who read avidly and widely in theology.[58] As soon as the first parts of Michaelis's Old Testament had appeared, the queen's physician, Sir John Pringle – son of a baronet and president of the Royal Society from 1771 – brought them to the attention of Queen Charlotte, who commented on them favourably.[59] This pattern was continued over the following decade, with Pringle acting as a go-between for Michaelis and the royal couple, who later also entrusted their three younger sons to the orientalist. Using his influence with the royal couple to promote Michaelis's interests, Pringle nevertheless had to manoeuvre carefully to avoid transgressing borders, and was keen to draw a line when it came to influencing the king in matters of *university business*, such as appointments at Göttingen. Pringle repeatedly rejected requests by Michaelis as well as

---

[56] Campbell Orr, 'Late Hanoverian court'. The role of protestantism prior to 1761 has recently been highlighted by Hannah Smith, 'The idea of a protestant monarchy in Britain 1714–1760', *Past and Present*, 185 (2004), 91–118.

[57] Even Frederick the Great considered attacks on biblical authority as dangerous, and he went to great lengths to refute Holbach's *Système de la nature* (1770), see Theodor Schieder, *Friedrich der Große: Ein Königtum der Widersprüche* (1983, reprint: Berlin, 1998), pp. 369, 371.

[58] See Graham Jefcoate, '"Most curious, splendid and useful": the king's library of George III', in Sloan, ed., *Enlightenment*, pp. 38–45.

[59] Pringle to Michaelis, 2 June 1769, Johann Gottlieb Buhle, ed., *Literarischer Briefwechsel von Johann Daniel Michaelis* (3 vols., Leipzig, 1794–6), vol. II, no. 28, pp. 228, 250, 271.

by the president of Göttingen's Royal Society of Sciences, Albrecht von Haller, to further their causes with the king and queen as he thought it improper as a courtier to meddle in politics:[60]

> As to the cause of Your late discontent, which You communicated to me, I could not pretend, to enter upon that with His Majesty; it would have approached much to the medling in business ... Such points can only be entered upon by His Hanoverian Ministers; as what concerns this country, can only be touched by his English Ministers.

With Albrecht von Haller and Johann David Michaelis, Pringle's two most important correspondents were Göttingen men; he in turn was their most important correspondence partner in Britain.[61] The connection had been established by Burckhard von Behr, head of the German Chancery from 1762 to 1770.[62] Encouraged by Behr, Pringle and his friend Benjamin Franklin travelled to Göttingen in 1766, and over the following decade Michaelis came to be integrated into the orbit of English scholarship and into the circle of antiquaries close to the court.[63] Putting bible studies on a scientifically sound footing was an eminently political project which stood at the crossroads of several disciplines, and English scholars who belonged to the king's and queen's scholarly circles were Michaelis's most important group of non-German contacts. They stood at the forefront of the reappraisal of biblical and mythological texts, which was one of the most discussed problems of the later eighteenth century, signalling a major shift in the representation of the past.[64] Scripture or Homer's *Iliad* were not taken as a source book to 'real' events of the past any more; rather, scholars came to see these texts as sources from which the ancient mindset could be reconstructed. The letters exchanged by Michaelis and Pringle on the prophecies of Daniel, which were central to those

---

[60] Pringle to Michaelis, 14 February 1771, Buhle, *Literarischer Briefwechsel*, vol. II, p. 272. Similarly, Pringle wrote to Haller on 28 June 1768, referring to Haller's envisaged return to Göttingen, which was a matter of prolonged negotiations between Haller, Pringle, the university, and Bernese authorities. The letter is printed in Sonntag, *John Pringle's correspondence*, p. 19. Otto Sonntag, ed., *John Pringle's correspondence with Albrecht von Haller* (Basel, 1999), no. 39, pp. 111–12.

[61] Johann David Michaelis, *Lebensbeschreibung, von ihm selbst abgefasst, mit Anmerkungen von Hassencamp. Nebst Bemerkungen über dessen literarischen Charakter von Eichhorn, Schulz* (Rinteln, Leipzig, 1793), p. 104; Sonntag, *John Pringle's correspondence*, p. 11.

[62] Michaelis highlights Behr's role in his autobiography, see Michaelis, *Lebensbeschreibung*, pp. 103–4.

[63] Pütter, *Versuch*, vol. II, p. 281. They were among the first dozen of non-German members ever admitted.

[64] See Ulrich Muhlack, *Geschichtswissenschaft im Humanismus und in der Aufklärung: Die Vorgeschichte des Humanismus* (Munich, 1991); Hans-Jürgen Schings, ed., *Der ganze Mensch: Anthropologie und Literatur im 18. Jahrhundert: DFG-Symposion 1992* (Stuttgart, 1994).

discussions, were published in 1773.[65] With the bible scholar Benjamin Kennicott he corresponded on questions of text variations, with Robert Lowth on Hebrew poetry, with Jacob Bryant on mythology, with Robert Wood on questions of Near-Eastern archaeology, and with Jean-André De Luc on new developments in earth science.[66] With the Polish-born orientalist and preacher at the Dutch chapel at St James's, Charles Godfrey Woide, who had worked with Reinhold Forster and was also a corresponding member of Göttingen's Royal Society of Sciences,[67] Michaelis exchanged a detailed correspondence on the *Lexicon Aegyptiaco-Latinum* which the French scholar La Croze had drawn up, but never finished. Woide edited it with additional material from the Berlin court preacher Scholtz, adding notes and indexes based on Michaelis's advice.[68] For Lowth, Woide, Wood, and Bryant, Michaelis was a source of constant information, and they integrated his comments and annotations into their published lectures, books and articles. Michaelis's identification with his English partners in turn went so far that he commented on Lord North's resignation: 'suddenly we found ourselves in opposition'.[69] When Michaelis's son, a doctor,

---

[65] Johann David Michaelis, John Pringle, *J. D. Michaelis Epistolae de LXX Hebdomadis Danielis, ad D. J. Pringle* (London, 1773).

[66] Of the nineteen letters exchanged between Michaelis and Kennicott, and preserved at the Staats- und Universitätsbibliothek Göttingen (SUB Gö), 2° Cod. Mich. 325, Bl. 112–46, only one is printed in Buhle, *Literarischer Briefwechsel*, vol. III, no. 62, pp. 216–18. For the Bryant correspondence, see the four letters in SUB Gö, Cod. Mich. 321, two of which are reprinted in Buhle, *Literarischer Briefwechsel*, vol. III, nos. 43, 60. For Lowth, *ibid.*, nos. 57–8, vol. III, nos. 16–17, 53 – Kennicott, for instance, presented his new edition of the Old Testament to the royal couple in 1789, and after his death his widow remained close to the court, living in Windsor, see Campbell Orr, 'Late Hanoverian court', p. 23. Kennicott and Michaelis, however, fell out after Michaelis criticised the former's bible edition for being based on a too limited source base. Michaelis was central to De Luc's discussion of geology and revealed religion, see Clarissa Campbell Orr, 'Queen Charlotte, "Scientific Queen"', in Campbell Orr, ed., *Queenship in Britain 1660–1837: royal patronage, court culture and dynastic politics* (Manchester, 2002), pp. 237, 244–9.

[67] Pütter, *Versuch*, vol. II, p. 284.

[68] *Lexicon Aegyptiaco-Latinum, ex veteribus illius linguae monumentis summo studio collectum et elaboratum a Maturino Veyssière la Croze. Quod in compendium redegit Christian Scholtz. Notulas et indices adjecit Carolus Godofredus Woide* (Oxford, 1775). Most of the 13 letters Michaelis received from Woide between April 1772 and May 1775, which are reprinted in Buhle, *Literarischer Briefwechsel*, vol. III, nos. 18–30, pp. 43–114, originated in this context. Twenty-nine letters from Woide are reprinted in Buhle, vol. III. For Best's role, see *ibid.*, pp. 56, 79, and Graham Jefcoate, 'Best, Wilhelm Philipp', in *Oxford Dictionary of National Biography*, vol. V (Oxford, 2004), pp. 526–7. For Woide's life, see W. P. Courtney, Rev. S. J. Skedd, 'Woide, Godfrey', in *Oxford Dictionary of National Biography*, vol. LIX (Oxford, 2004), p. 948, and the remarks by Forster in Buhle, *Literarischer Briefwechsel*, vol. III, no. 94, p. 351. On Woide's friendship with Forster, see also Hoare, *Tactless philosopher*, passim.

[69] Michaelis, *Lebensbeschreibung*, p. 133.

travelled to England *en route* to America in 1778, he was introduced to society by Pringle, Bryant and Woide as well as the Forsters; Georg Forster in turn visited Michaelis in Göttingen.[70] Among Woide's patrons were George III, Robert Lowth and Lord North,[71] but Woide was also a link to Sir Joseph Banks, through whose recommendation he came to serve as assistant librarian at the British Museum from 1782. By the 1790s, Michaelis's name was so established that Herbert Marsh advertised his letters to Archdeacon Travis as a work 'by the translator of Michaelis'.[72]

Establishing a comprehensive picture of ancient cultures through the study of geography and botany, and the examination of monuments, travel reports, and ethnographic comparisons, gave scholarly *expeditions* a crucial function. Leading here were British and German scholars: the British, after all, had the political clout, financial resources, and logistics to send ships and people to the Near East, while back in their studies, German professors had, of course, developed the exploration of foreign countries into a science of its own.[73] Michaelis had written a classic in the field, the 348-page *Fragen an eine Gesellschaft gelehrter Männer*, which set the standard for decades.[74] It was his method, rather than his theological stance, which made him so interesting for the amateur-classicists and explorers organised in the Society of Dilettanti and the Asiatic Society who took his writings as manuals when organising expeditions to Greece and Turkey, but also to the Far East in the 1760s to 80s.[75] Michaelis's *Orientalische Bibliothek*, the first scholarly journal dedicated to oriental

---

[70] Bryant to Michaelis, 10 October 1778, Buhle, *Literarischer Briefwechsel*, vol. III, no. 43, pp. 143–4; Woide regularly reported back to Michaelis on his son's progress, see *ibid.*, nos. 44–6, pp. 149–54. For the 'exchange of sons', as Reinhold Forster called it, see Ludwig Uhle, *Georg Forster: Lebensabenteuer eines gelehrten Weltbürgers (1754–1794)* (Göttingen, 2004), pp. 110, 123.

[71] Woide to Michaelis, 8 April 1774, Buhle, *Literarischer Briefwechsel*, vol. III, no. 25 p. 88. On this occasion Woide made North acquainted with articles on Coptic language from Michaelis's *Orientalische Bibliothek* as nothing similar could be found in England ('da hier in England von den Koptischen Sachen nichts Gedrucktes bekannt ist').

[72] [Herbert Marsh,] *Letters to Mr. Archdeacon Travis, in vindication of one of the translator's notes to Michaelis's introduction, and in confirmation of the opinion, that a Greek manuscript, now preserved in the Public Library of the University of Cambridge, is one of the seven, which are quoted by R. Stephens at I. John V.7. with an appendix* (Leipzig, 1795).

[73] For a survey of ethnography, see now Wolfgang Petermann, *Die Geschichte der Ethnologie* (Wuppertal, 2004).

[74] Johann David Michaelis, *Fragen an eine Gesellschaft gelehrter Männer, die auf Befehl Ihro Majestät des Königes von Dännemark nach Arabien reisen* (Frankfurt-on-Main, 1762). When embarking on his South Sea voyage in 1772, Georg Forster brought a copy aboard Cook's *Resolution*. Woide to Michaelis, 26 June 1772, Buhle, *Literarischer Briefwechsel*, vol. III, no. 19, p. 55, and Forster to Michaelis, 10 July 1772, *ibid.*, no. 98, p. 374.

[75] Hecht, *T. Percy, R. Wood und J. D. Michaelis*, pp. 64–5.

studies, also served as a model for the *Asiatick researches* published by the Asiatic Society, which Sir William Jones and the inevitable Sir Joseph Banks were involved in.[76] In particular with the Society of Dilettanti, a productive collaboration was established. Having explored Baalbek and Palmyr himself, Wood also organised several of the Society's expeditions, and contributed to several of its publications; he did not feel confident enough, however, to publish his book on Homerian Greece without the advice of the most respected scholar in the field, whose commentaries on Lowth and whose *Fragen* he had long admired; various political posts he was employed in kept him away from his book project as well. It was only after the prolonged cooperation of Wood and Michaelis, with texts being sent to Göttingen via Pringle, who here comes into the picture again as a mediator between Göttingen and London,[77] that Wood's *Essay on the original genius of Homer* was published; a book which, together with the German Johann Joachim Winckelmann's works on Greek art, contributed so much to making Greece the central point of reference for literature, education and the arts in later eighteenth- and nineteenth-century Europe.[78]

Under Pringle's successor at the presidency of the Royal Society, the emphasis of Anglo-Hanoverian cooperation switched to the exploration of territories beyond the Mediterranean. In particular from 1786, Johann Friedrich Blumenbach and Joseph Banks, the Lincolnshire baronet who had participated in Cook's first journey to the Pacific, established a pattern of cooperation which went even further than the Pringle–Michaelis link.[79] Banks wrote few books and published only a small number of papers, but exerted enormous influence over decades through his proximity to king and court, offices, and extensive correspondence.[80]

---

[76] Garland Cannon, 'Sir William Jones, Sir Joseph Banks, and the Royal Society', *Notes and Records of the Royal Society in London* 29, 2 (1979), 221, 223.

[77] Hecht, *T. Percy, R. Wood und J. D. Michaelis*. Wood calls Pringle 'our good freind' [sic!], p. ix. SUB Göttingen, 2° Cod. Mich. 325, Bl. 330/8, and Cod. Mich. 321, Bl. 117.

[78] Hecht, *T. Percy, R. Wood und J. D. Michaelis*, p. 26; Dennis R. Dean, 'Bryant, Jacob', in *Oxford dictionary of national biography*, vol. VIII (Oxford, 2004), pp. 393–5, fails to mention Bryant's German connections at all. After Wood's death, Bryant continued the work until publication in 1774–5. For Bryant's connections to George III, see Roberts, *George III and Queen Charlotte*, pp. 232–4.

[79] Banks was also elected into Göttingen's Royal Society in 1779, see Pütter, *Versuch*, vol. II, p. 282. For the start of their correspondence, see Thomas Bendyshe, ed., *The anthropological treatises of Johann Friedrich Blumenbach, late professor at Göttingen and court physician to the king of Great Britain, with memoirs of him by Marx and Flourens, and an account of his anthropological museum by Professor R. Wagner, and the inaugural dissertation of John Hunter, MD on the varieties of man* (London, 1865), p. 31, n. 2.

[80] The Banks correspondence amounts to more than 20,000 letters, see Harold Carter, 'Introduction', in Neil Chambers, ed., *The letters of Sir Joseph Banks: a selection, 1768–1820* (London, 2000), p. xvii.

His connections at court, and access to resources, were of particular interest to Blumenbach, whose research interests went far beyond what had hitherto been considered the domain of medicine: he made Göttingen a centre of ethnography, and was a key figure in the establishment of the new science of anthropology, acquiring a famous collection of human skulls from all over the world with the help of Banks. Banks also contributed more than 200 plants from the South Sea to Göttingen's Botanic Garden; Göttingen's botanic and ethnographic collections – divided into the departments of natural history of mankind, fauna, flora, minerals according to Blumenbach's handbook – were indeed largely based on the findings of Cook's voyages.[81] Blumenbach, in turn, helped categorise and analyse the enormous collections Banks had amassed in his house in Soho Square; he contributed papers read at the Royal Society, and published books on the basis of Banks's contributions.[82] Together with Banks, he organised a series of expeditions into Africa and Arabia in the 1790s and early 1800s, such as Friedrich Hornemann's exploration of Sudan, and Johann Ludwig Burckhardt's journeys into Arabia. After several London-organised expeditions had failed, Banks had turned to Blumenbach for advice, and they devised a new pattern: Blumenbach chose able Göttingen students and provided them with a special linguistic, geographical and mathematical training before sending them to London, whence they were shipped off to Africa or Arabia, financed and equipped by the African or Asiatic Societies. Less spectacular than Mungo Park's famous journey, these Göttingen-trained experts were, however, much more effective in terms of producing knowledge, and the travel reports they sent back, and which were published by the London Societies, formed the basis of further explorations in the nineteenth century.

The Blumenbach–Banks connection generally served as a catalyst of the latest products of German academia into English life. Like Michaelis,

---

[81] Pütter, *Versuch*, vol. II, p. 256 – Banks's main field of interest was botany rather than ethnography, and he used his other collections largely for the upkeep of exchanges with other scholars, see Harold B. Carter, *Sir Joseph Banks (1743–1820): a guide to biographical and bibliographical sources* (London, 1987), pp. 259–60. See also Gascoigne, *Joseph Banks*, pp. 150–5, and David Philip Miller, 'Joseph Banks, empire, and "centers of calculation" in late Hanoverian London', in: Miller and Reill, eds., *Visions of empire*, pp. 29–30.

[82] When Blumenbach was in London in 1791, for instance, and had the opportunity of opening six mummies, he continued to discuss the topic in his ensuing correspondence with Banks reprinted in Bendyshe 1865, pp. 145–276, in part 'Introductory letter to Sir Joseph Banks'. See also his 'Observations on some Egyptian mummies opened in London. Addresssed to Sir Joseph Banks. Read April 10, 1794', *Philosophical transactions of the Royal Society of London*, vol. LXXXIV, pp. 177–95.

the charismatic Blumenbach managed to convert talented students from all subjects to his fields of interest, such as George Bellas Greenough: following a Cambridge education, he had come to Göttingen in 1798 to study law, but was so impressed by Blumenbach that he switched to geology (another field of Blumenbach's interest). Having returned to London in the early 1800s, he founded the Geological Society, which he presided over for decades. The German Carl Ludwig Giesecke had similarly come to Göttingen to study law, but turned to mineralogy under Blumenbach's influence; he later became professor of mineralogy at the Royal Dublin Society. The Brunswick-born mineralogist Carl Dietrich Eberhard Koenig had also been a pupil of Blumenbach's, on whose recommendation he was employed to reorganise Queen Charlotte's collections in 1800. Through Blumenbach, he also met Sir Joseph Banks, whose librarian he became on finishing the royal job. As happened so often, a position in the Banks household was a stepping stone to an official position in the British world of science, and Koenig became keeper of the Natural History Department at the British Museum in 1813, and keeper of the Mineralogical and Geological Branches in 1837, which had been reorganised along Göttingen lines according to Blumenbach's version of natural history.[83] Together with the Museum's principal librarian Joseph Planta, another Göttingen *alumnus* whose father had already been an assistant librarian at the museum, and whose sisters were sub-governesses to the royal princesses,[84] Koenig was one of the men who oversaw the British Museum's transformation into an institution both popular and scientifically up-to-date when during the first decades of the nineteenth century, the collections were extended, rearranged, catalogued, and the new buildings planned and built which replaced the crumbling Montagu House. The band of Göttingen mineralogists Greenough, Koenig and Giesecke was instrumental in establishing geology as an independent specialist science in the first decades of the nineteenth century, which provoked an enduring conflict with Banks, who rather wished to keep all the sciences under the umbrella of his Royal Society.[85] This is testimony

---

[83] Edward Edwards, *Lives of the founders of the British Museum* (Reprint of 1870 edn: Bristol, 1997), pp. 532, 575; P. R. Harris, *A history of the British Museum Library 1753–1973* (London, 1998), pp. 36, 48, 171.

[84] On Planta, see Harris, *History*, pp. 62–65, and Harris, 'Planta, Joseph', in *Oxford Dictionary of National Biography*, vol. XLIV (Oxford, 2004), pp. 519–21. Planta did spend a stint at Göttingen, but he was not matriculated, see Harris, 'Planta', p. 520, and Selle, *Matrikel*. For his sisters' court connections, see Jill Shefrin, *Such constant affectionate care: Lady Charlotte Finch, royal governess and the children of George III* (Los Angeles, 2003), p. 56.

[85] Martin Rudwick, 'The foundation of the Geological Society of London: its scheme for co-operative research and its struggle for independence', *The British Journal for the History of Science* 4 (1963), 325–55.

to the fact that there was no coherent 'Göttingen faction' in Britain's scientific community, but that by the early 1800s, a Göttingen education or Göttingen contacts were almost a precondition for scholars in the natural sciences who wished to play a prominent role on London's scientific stage. As the cases of Michaelis and Wood as well as Blumenbach and Banks suggest, the British 'virtuoso' tradition went hand-in-hand with German academic culture. They were different enough to be complementary while drawing on a compatible social background which was a prerequisite for scholarly relations among equals. German professors, who were usually in the employment of land-locked states, were keen to exploit the archaeological, botanical or ethnographical expeditions organised by London's scholarly societies. In particular after 1763, the undisputed naval power Britain came to occupy something of a monopoly when it came to organising overseas expeditions. While Michaelis had still organised his Arabian expedition of 1761 with the help of the Danish court, all post-war explorations of the Near East and the South Sea were arranged through the London link.[86] Protagonists of London's scholarly life in turn, such as Wood and Banks, who had little time for scholarly analysis in their busy lives as leading members of society and politicians as well as amateur collectors, left to Göttingen professors the task of incorporating their rich collections into a 'body of theory which would make sense of their significance',[87] and of making them relevant to the European republic of letters. Thus Blumenbach, on the basis of Banks's steady flow of information, developed his theory on the variety of species which went far beyond Linné's classification, and remained a standard work until Darwin.[88] Few Britons of the later eighteenth century, in contrast, were eminent as scientists in the sense of classifying and interpreting the new findings which were being made at the time – which, as Roy Porter wrote, 'encapsulates the limitations of the British, amateur, decentralized naturalist tradition'.[89]

The distinction, so central to eighteenth-century scholarship, between 'fieldwork' on the one hand, and analysis of the information gathered on

---

[86] For a recent general assessment of the naval aspects of empire, see Jeremy Black, *The British seaborne empire* (New Haven, 2004). For the role of the navy for scholarly exploits, see David Mackay, 'Agents of empire', pp. 38–57. The triangular links of dynasty and patronage between Britain, Hanover and Denmark are now discussed in Campbell Orr, 'Queen Charlotte'.

[87] Gascoigne, *Joseph Banks*, pp. 158–9.

[88] Blumenbach, *De Generis Humani Varietate Nativa, editio tertia, praemissa est epistola ad virum perillustrem Josephum Banks, Baronetum, Regiae Societatis Londini Praesidem* (Göttingen, 1795).

[89] Roy Porter, *The making of geology: earth science in Britain 1660–1815* (Cambridge, 1977), pp. 169–70.

the other, is usually employed to characterise the agents spread all over the British empire to send information back to Britain on the one hand, and Banks and other England-based scholars on the receiving end on the other.[90] After all, knowledge – as epistemologists such as Herder maintained – is not just made by collecting specimens and describing phenomena encountered in explorations or experiments, but by analysing and reflecting this wealth of information in the study; as was expressed by the classic distinction between classifier and collector, or – as Herder put it – *Reisender* on the one hand, and *Stubengelehrter* on the other.[91] However, the picture of knowledge-making in the empire becomes less clear-cut than this dichotomy suggests if one considers that at least within the Anglo-Hanoverian community of scholars, it was rather the English side as a whole who functioned as 'collectors' and 'gatherers', and their German cooperators who as *Stubengelehrte* analysed their findings. Indeed, Cook's and Banks's generation of sea-voyaging explorers was criticised as early as 1800 for simply gathering whatever botanical, ethnographic or geographical material they happened to come by during the expeditions sent out by the Admiralty to secure the empire's vital naval routes. In a lecture delivered at the Berlin Academy in 1806, following the return from his five-year expedition to Central and South America, Alexander von Humboldt thus firmly put English scholars into the category of 'travelling naturalists' who neglected research into nature's fundamental forces which constituted truly scientific endeavour.[92] For English virtuosi such as Banks, respected scholars such as Blumenbach were thus crucial for acquiring the academic credibility that was necessary to maintain one's position in the world of European scholarship. In the decades around 1800, the age of amateur collectors in the vein of

---

[90] David Mackay, 'Agents of empire: the Banksian collectors and evaluation of new lands', in: Miller and Reill, eds., *Visions of empire*, pp. 38–57.

[91] Simon Schaffer, 'Visions of empire: afterword', in: Miller and Reill, eds., *Visions of empire*, pp. 340–1. The distinction between fact-gatherer and natural philosopher is still prominent in John Herschel, *A preliminary discourse on the study of natural philosophy* (1830, reprint: Chicago, 1987), p. 289. On Herder's distinction, and the explorer Carsten Niebuhr's critique, see Martin Krieger, 'Zwischen Meldorf und Bützow: Carsten Niebuhrs Korrespondenz mit Oluf Gerhard Tychsen', in: Josef Wiesehöfer/Stephan Conermann, eds., *Carsten Niebuhr (1733–1815) und seine Zeit: Beiträge eines interdisziplinären Symposums vom 7.–10. Oktober 1999 in Eutin* (Stuttgart, 2002), pp. 341–61.

[92] 'Little has been done by traveling naturalists for the physical description of the earth, or rather for the physics of the globe (physique du monde), because almost all of them are concerned exclusively with the descriptive sciences and with collecting, and have neglected to track the great and constant laws of nature manifested in the rapid flux of phenomena.' Quoted, and translated, in Michael Dettelbach, 'Global physics and aesthetic empire: Humboldt's physical portrait of the tropics', in: Miller and Reill, eds., *Visions of empire*, p. 260.

Sir Hans Sloane was slowly coming to an end, and academic respectability was increasingly being conveyed through publications as well as membership of learned societies and academic institutions. As Banks was to experience himself when the Paris *Académie des Sciences* discussed his election for the first time in 1784, and rejected him, his strong domestic position as manager of science would not necessarily impress foreign scholars who would have rather liked to see publications of his as proof of his scientific standing.[93] Having, for instance, Blumenbach profusely acknowledge the crucial role Banks had played for the development of his theory in the important 3rd edition of 1795 of his *De generis humani varietate nativa*, and thus appearing to deal with one of Europe's most eminent scientists on an equal footing, can thus also be seen as a measure to counter doubts about his scholarly reputation.[94] This also highlights the necessity to further broaden the picture, and integrate the scientific exploration of empire more systematically within a European history of science where exchange between European scholars remained as important as the interaction between 'centre' and 'periphery'.

Although it is easy to emphasise the differences between the scholarly cultures of England and Germany, there was, in fact, a huge stock of similarities between the cult of the 'virtuoso' on one side of the Channel, and the 'polite professor' on the other side. The latter had been developed by the Halle professor Christian Thomasius in the decades around 1700, and made 'good manners' and 'a perfectly polished behaviour' prerequisites for the success of any enlightening effort among the powerful. Michaelis, who during his England trip had been more impressed by the London court preacher Ziegenhagen than by the Oxford dons, combined the Halle type of worldly scholar with English elements, lecturing on the Old Testament with a rapier at his side and translating English literature, such as Richardson's *Pamela*. After all, both the urbane professor and the polite gentleman were variants of the *honnête homme*, the pan-European ideal of a sociable person maintaining integrity while pursuing rational pleasures. Its English version was epitomised by wealthy amateur collectors such as Joseph Banks.[95] Successful German professors, however, could reside in no less a gentlemanly manner: Michaelis's grand Göttingen house served as a scholarly *salon* where the famous professor gave his lectures and received prominent visitors,

---

[93] In 1787, Banks was elected anyway, see Miller, 'Joseph Banks', p. 21.
[94] Blumenbach, *De generis humani varietate nativa*, 'Introductory letter to Sir Joseph Banks', and *passim*; in particular, pp. 11, 271, 274.
[95] Robert Huxley, 'Natural history collectors and their collections: "simpling macaronis" and instruments of empire', in Sloan, ed., *Enlightenment*, pp. 88–90.

ranging from Lessing and Goethe to the British royal princes. The house also generated an additional income as it comprised a purpose-built wing with student rooms, which proves Michaelis to have been a polite scholar–entrepreneur if there ever was one.[96]

Notions of civility and politeness formed the bedrock of Anglo-Hanoverian cooperation, which in this age of personal, rather than institutional, communication was necessarily dependent on social prestige and trust; the latter, in this era of global exploration, became a key word for the conduct of any scholarship, and the enormous number of forgeries in this period – from archaeological artefacts to fossils – testifies to its importance.[97] In particular in botany and ethnography, the pictorial or verbal representation of unclassified plants or unfamiliar tribes was essential: as the credibility of reports and pictures depended on the authority of the people who communicated them, the prestige of the scholars involved as well as that of their institutions was crucial. 'Sedentary' scholars such as Michaelis and Blumenbach thus preferred to rely on observers they knew well, and notions of gentlemanly honour and integrity formed the basis of this trust.[98]

Gentlemanly codes of conduct were not only necessary for communication between scientists, but also for maintaining scholarship in negotiations with courts, councellors, diplomats, and military personnel; the case of Queen Charlotte's reader De Luc – appointed to a chair at Göttingen in 1797 as a 'cover' for a diplomatic mission to Berlin – highlights yet again how the roles of courtier, diplomat and professor could intersect.[99] In particular during the turbulent periods of the Seven Years War and the Napoleonic Wars, 'politeness' turned out to be essential for the conduct of scholarship, and the very survival of the university; it was the precondition for the semi-diplomatic role scholars had to take on in their dealings with rulers and generals: like Banks, who negotiated with kings and princes to organise explorations or to place protégés, Michaelis and Blumenbach had to be diplomats as well as scholars when in 1757, 1760–1, 1803, 1806–7, and 1812–13, French or Allied troops repeatedly occupied, or threatened to occupy, Göttingen. Eminent professors then entered into negotiations with foreign generals and politicians: on behalf of the Hanoverian government, Blumenbach negotiated

---

[96] For the Michaelis house, see Ida Hakemeyer, *Das Michaelis-Haus zu Göttingen* (Göttingen, 1947), in particular p. 13.

[97] 'Without the ability to place trust in reports of matters of fact that had not been personally experienced by people like oneself, the new philosophy would have remained fragmented and isolated in local social and geographical spaces', David and Cook, 'Closed circles or open networks?', p. 181.

[98] Shapin, 'Placing the view', p. 8.   [99] See Campbell Orr, 'Queen Charlotte', pp. 388–91.

with General Mortier in 1802 and 1805, with Napoleon in 1806, and with Bernadotte in 1812.[100] When the Napoleonic kingdom of Westphalia, which incorporated Göttingen as well as much of southern Hanover, threatened to abolish all universities within its borders, diplomatic tools had to be oiled again. For Göttingen professors, quite as for most German civil servants in this time of upheaval, loyalty to their institution always superseded loyalty to the Hanoverian monarchy.[101] Using their international connections and prestige, Banks and Blumenbach in conjunction even managed to secure a French passport for the Göttingen graduate Friedrich Hornemann who on his way to Africa had to cross France, of all times, when Napoleon was preparing his Egyptian campaign.[102]

Cooperation and exchange were prerequisites for eighteenth-century scholarship, as Pütter, in his history of Göttingen university, highlights with reference to the case of Michaelis and his oriental studies.[103] Like London's merchants in business, the members of this Anglo-German community of scholars were transnational agents in an international academic environment.[104] In the decades following the Seven Years War, not only did Britain's American, Indian, and African possessions come to be integrated with the British Isles much more deeply than previously through an improved infrastructure with frequent voyages across the oceans, more regular postal services, and a much expanded exchange of goods and news, but so did North Germany. This allowed letters, drafts, books and specimens to be exchanged quickly and in great numbers over the North Sea. In the shape of the German Chancery, the Personal Union provided a regular, reliable and above all cheap channel of communication. It was possible to reply to letters even within a fortnight, and books ordered in Göttingen or London could arrive at the other end of the link within five weeks.[105] The systematic development of the Anglo-Hanoverian connection by individual scholars into a high-speed link used for the transmissal of massive amounts of data thus complemented the university policy of acquiring the latest German

---

[100] Blumenbach's role is underestimated by Saalfeld, *Geschichte*, pp. 45–9, who rather puts the emphasis on Heyne. Compare, however, Hermann Thiersch, *Ludwig I. von Bayern und die Georgia Augusta* (Berlin, 1927).
[101] Schöne, *Die Universität Göttingen*, p. 59, and the correspondence of Michaelis and the French Marshall Broglie reprinted in Buhle, *Literarischer Briefwechsel*, vol. II, nos. 7–9, pp. 17–19.
[102] Gascoigne, *Joseph Banks*, p. 243.   [103] Pütter, *Versuch*, vol. I, pp. 6–7.
[104] To adapt a phrase taken from Hancock, *Citizens of the world*, p. 20.
[105] Graham Jefcoate, 'Wilhelm Best und der Londoner Buchhandel: ein deutscher Diplomat im Dienste der Universitätsbibliothek Göttingen im 18. Jahrhundert', *Leipziger Jahrbuch zur Buchgeschichte*, 6 (1996), 201.

and foreign-language publications, for instance in history, within weeks of their publication; the rapidity of epistolary exchanges is testimony to the importance both Göttingen and London scholars put on gaining, assessing and forwarding information quickly. For them, as well as for merchants and diplomats who needed to be kept abreast of the latest developments, speed mattered.[106] As much scholarship remained dependent on informal reports on lectures or bits of information snapped up at *soirées*, Göttingen and London scholars could hence be ahead of the rest of the academic pack: through the reports of the uniquely placed Pringle, Michaelis thus managed to acquire the results of James Bruce's expedition to Ethiopia sixteen years before they were finally published in 1790, with a preface by Blumenbach in the German edition.[107] First announced in the *Gentleman's Magazine* in 1773, Bruce's report was a much awaited event as he had previously published only small parts in the *Philosophical Transactions* and the supplements to Buffon's *Natural History* and other scattered places.[108] William Bruce, in the *Asiatick researches* (vol. I, 1788), speculated on what Bruce might have to contribute to the long-discussed problem of the sources of the Nile. Pringle in turn made Bruce aware of Michaelis's work on North Africa and Arabia, who then integrated it into his published travel record. The picture we gain from analysing the Anglo-Hanoverian community of scholars thus suggests that as late as 1800, letter-based communication in the sciences, far from being an old-fashioned mode of communication which was being replaced by printed journals (and *Fachzeitschriften*) and the 'public sphere' in the course of the eighteenth

---

[106] 'Göttingen readers had access to English and German texts quite literally within weeks of their first appearance', Graham Jefcoate, 'Göttingen University Library and the acquisition of historical books in the eighteenth century', *Factotum: Newsletter of the XVIIIth century STC* 37 (1993), 25. For the importance of speed in early modern scholarship, see Lux and Cook, 'Closed circles or open networks?', p. 201.

[107] James Bruce, *Travels to discover the source of the Nile: in the years 1768, 1769, 1770, 1771, 1772, and 1773* (Edinburgh, London, 1790). The German translation – annotated by Blumenbach – appeared in the same year under the title *Reisen zur Entdeckung der Quellen des Nils in den Jahren 1768, 1769, 1770, 1771, 1772, und 1773: in fünf Bänden von James Bruce von Kinnaird, ins Teutsche übersetzt von J. J. Volkmann und mit einer Vorrede und Anmerkungen versehen von Johann Friedrich Blumenbach* (Leipzig, 1790). For the disputes surrounding Bruce's claim to have discovered the source of the Nile, see the editor's introduction in Herbert Gussenbauer, ed., *James Bruce: Zu den Quellen des Blauen Nils. Die Erforschung Äthiopiens 1768–1773* (Stuttgart, Vienna, 1987), pp. 12–16 – 'The global explorations of the 1760s and 1770s that loom large in Pringle's letters also fascinated contemporaries from many segments of society. Few individuals, however, were so well placed as Pringle to hear about these exploits.' Sonntag, *John Pringle's correspondence*, p. 12.

[108] Blumenbach, 'Vorrede', p. xii.

century, on the contrary remained central to scholarly collaboration throughout the period.[109]

For the upkeep of communication, the German Chancery's civil servants were more important than the ministerial level as they were often based in London more permanently and had excellent connections within court, government and leading London circles. The London *Geheimer Kanzleisekretär* Wilhelm Philipp Best and his son Georg August thus acted as London agents of Göttingen University from 1752: Göttingen professors frequently discussed university affairs with Best father or son, who would then act on their behalf either at court or in Hanover;[110] the fact that Georg August Best was elected into the Royal Society in 1782 highlights the importance the diplomatic link also had for London's scholarly circles.[111] Best also directly corresponded with explorers sent out by the Anglo-Hanoverian network, for instance with Friedrich Hornemann, for whom he acted as an agent sending money, and forwarding letters, to his family in Hildesheim.[112] Best's access to diplomatic mail was primarily used to convey books and send letters.[113] In particular at times when even the generally supportive George III was annoyed to find his messengers abused as porters struggling with bulky manuscripts or crania of South Sea chiefs, and tried to curb their overuse by 'his' scholars, civil servants like Best with their direct access to diplomatic channels were crucial for the upkeep of communications.[114] After all, sending letters overseas was otherwise an extremely expensive business, and even Pringle as the king's physician could not obtain permission

---

[109] See, in contrast, Richard Sorrenson, 'The ship as a scientific instrument in the eighteenth century', in: Henrika Kuklick and Robert E. Kohler, eds., *Science in the field* (= *Osiris: a research journal devoted to the history of science and its cultural influences* N. S., 11, Chicago, 1996), p. 221: 'By the end of the seventeenth century the language of one science, geography, routinely pervaded the language of all the sciences. Investigators made "discoveries", which were published in "journals".' The continued importance of epistolary exchanges for the 'Anglo-Swiss connection' of the early eighteenth century is maintained by Kempe, *Wissenschaft, Theologie, Aufklärung*, pp. 79–109.

[110] Pringle to Haller, 9 September 1768, on Haller's proposed return to Göttingen, Sonntag, *John Pringle's correspondence*, no 41, pp. 114–15. Michaelis corresponded with Best extensively, see Buhle, *Literarischer Briefwechsel*, vol. I, nos. 70–8.

[111] Jefcoate, 'Wilhelm Best', p. 207.

[112] Rolf Schulte, 'Friedrich K. Hornemann (1772–1801): Annäherung an einen Hildesheimer Afrikaforscher', in: Herward Sieberg and Jos Schnurer, eds., *'Ich bin völlig Africaner und hier wie zu Hause ...' F. K. Hornemann (1772–1801), Begegnungen mit West- und Zentralafrika im Wandel der Zeit. Hildesheimer Symposion 25.–26.9.1998* (Hildesheim, 1999), pp. 29–57, esp. pp. 33, 39.

[113] John Pringle acknowledged this crucial role when writing to Michaelis on the services 'of good Mr. Best', who 'has constantly shewn a readiness, to convey every thing to You, that could give You pleasure, and I take him to be much your friend'. Pringle to Michaelis, 8 February 1774, in: Buhle, *Literarischer Briefwechsel*, vol. II, no. 51, pp. 374–5.

[114] Chambers, *The letters of Sir Joseph Banks*, pp. 157–8.

to make use of official dispatches for his correspondence with the Swiss Haller.[115] No wonder that Göttingen professors were keen to strengthen these channels by marrying into Hanover's leading families, the *Hübsche Familien*, which also provided the staff of the German Chancery: Blumenbach and Heyne were thus linked to Georg Friedrich Brandes, who controlled university politics and was well connected in Britain; Michaelis married his daughter Caroline to the son of his Göttingen colleague Georg Ludwig Böhmer, whose wife was daughter of a London *Wirklicher Geheimer Sekretär* and in addition closely related to the Bests.[116] This system of communication was as personalised and family-based as were scholarly networks and university–government relations in general: just as the Anglo-Hanoverian network of scholars could only be as successful as it was due to the longevity of its protagonists Michaelis, Heyne and Blumenbach on the German side, and Pringle, Bryant and Banks on the English, it also helped that the communication channels between London and Göttingen were upheld by Best father and son (between 1746 and 1806) for six decades without interruption.[117] The Anglo-Hanoverian community of scholars thus appears to have operated not dissimilarly from other communities, whether diplomats or merchants, who communicated over long distances, and were only occasionally able to solidify their epistolary exchanges with personal meetings.[118]

In the later eighteenth century, the Hanoverian university was nicknamed 'Göttingische Gelehrten Colonie',[119] but this term characterised Göttingen's international eminence as a centre of scholarship, attracting professors and students from 'the most diverse parts' of Europe, not any place on the periphery of the British empire. Göttingen was not an imperial 'outpost', but part of an extended 'network of Anglo-Hanoverian networks' which taken together formed a centre of calculation. The Napoleonic

---

[115] Sonntag, *John Pringle's correspondence*, p. 43.

[116] For the Mejer–Best connection, see Joachim Lampe, *Aristokratie, Hofadel und Staatspatriziat in Kurhannover: Die Lebenskreise der höheren Beamten an den kurhannoverschen Zentral- und Hofbehörden* (Göttingen, 1963), vol. I, p. 246, and vol. II, pp. 28, 38. For the Brandes family's English connections, see F. Frensdorff, 'Georg Brandes, ein hannoverscher Beamter des 18. Jahrhunderts', *Zeitschrift des Historischen Vereins für Niedersachsen* 76, 1, (1911), pp. 1–57, esp. p. 12. The crucial role of the *Wirkliche Geheime Sekretäre* in the German Chancery is highlighted by Uta Richter-Uhlig, *Hof und Politik unter den Bedingungen der Personalunion zwischen Hannover und England* (Hanover, 1992), pp. 164–70.

[117] Jefcoate, 'Wilhelm Best', p. 200: 'Kontinuität war offensichtlich ein wichtiger Faktor für den Erfolg der administrativen Vereinbarungen, die man für den Ankauf der Bücher getroffen hatte, und Best spielte hierbei eine entscheidende Rolle.'

[118] The role of personal visits is however emphasised by Lux and Cook, 'Closed circles or open networks?', p. 202.

[119] Saalfeld, *Geschichte*, pp. 2, 6.

occupations of the early 1800s put an end to this community which had managed to keep in touch over large distances but remained, after all, dependent on regular, quick, and 'dense' communication. When Napoleon's brother Jérome became ruler of the newly created kingdom of Westphalia, the university of Göttingen was not dissolved, as had been planned and feared at first, but it survived, and quite successfully so.[120] As soon as the French left Göttingen in 1813, British royal visits were taken up again: the duke of Cambridge came as early as November 1814, on which occasion he received an honorary doctorate as well as the honorary presidency of Göttingen's Royal Society of Sciences, and the dukes of Cumberland and Clarence paid visits in 1815 and 1819 respectively; in 1821, George IV in person visited Göttingen.[121] This flurry of royal activity did, however, not indicate a return of Göttingen to the unique role it had previously played for Britain, and of the confluence of several developments, I wish to highlight three. First of all, Göttingen lost the unique position it had occupied within Germany: had it been *the* university of the age of Enlightenment, it suddenly saw itself confronted by a whole row of new universities set up in Berlin, Bonn and Munich in the two decades from 1810; universities which were products of Humboldt's neo-humanist rather than Münchhausen's ageing Enlightenment spirit, and intellectual powerhouses where the kingdoms of Prussia and Bavaria for the first time ever managed to concentrate most of their intellectual resources. Old universities, such as Freiburg and Heidelberg, were also reformed.[122] The political context was changing rapidly as well: in the increasingly repressive political atmosphere of the German Confederation, provocative scholars who maintained semi-political international networks, and even edited political journals, such as the historian August Ludwig Schlözer, were seen with little enthusiasm. In particular the Karlsbad Decrees of 1819 undermined exactly the sort of open-minded, politically aware scholarship Göttingen had been famous for. Next, the world of British science was also changing. Blumenbach, of course, continued to attract British students until his death in 1840 – he taught at Göttingen for no fewer than 118 semesters – but for institutional as well as epistemological resasons, the central role of the English gentleman-scholar was coming to an end; after Banks's death in 1820, no president of the Royal Society could gain a position similar to his

---

[120] As even Saalfeld, *Geschichte*, p. 13, must acknowledge as late as 1820. Jérome visited Göttingen no fewer than five times between 1808 and 1813 (as opposed to the two visits of George II (1748) and George IV (1821)), see *ibid.*, p. 20. On Heyne and Müller, see *ibid.*, pp. 17–18, and Heeren, *Christian Gottlob Heyne*.
[121] Saalfeld, *Geschichte*, p. 22.
[122] James D. Copp, *The forgotten reforms: non-Prussian universities 1797–1817* (Ann Arbor, 1980).

again. Due to the illness of George III, and despite George IV's ceremonial visit to Göttingen in 1821, the university after 1814 never enjoyed the kind of royal patronage again which had been so important from the 1770s onward. Ironically, the king who never visited Göttingen thus turns out to have been the most important monarch for the development of the Göttingen–London link. Finally, from the 1820s on, Britain also began to reform its existing, or build up new, scientific institutions which made Göttingen's role increasingly redundant.[123] By the late 1830s, the university of London was up and running, and even Oxford and Cambridge had begun to reform their curricula.[124]

As far as Göttingen's role for Britain is concerned, the end of the dynastic union in 1837 was thus of less importance than the upheaval provoked by the dismissal of seven liberal professors by the new king, the Göttingen graduate Ernest Augustus, suggests; by 1837, Göttingen had indeed become peripheral to British science. It was also in these decades that the early modern pattern of transnational cooperation and exchange, which characterised even 'imperial' sciences in Britain, fell victim to the construction of 'national' scientific cultures; part of a wider process which has been called the 'nationalisation' of culture, and which was speeded up by the Napoleonic Wars. Contemporaries of Michaelis and Blumenbach were well aware of the contributions non-British scholarship made to the sciences in England although in times of war, their role could become a matter of contention.[125] When the above-mentioned *Anti-Jacobin* drama written by Canning in 1798 was performed in 1811 at London's Haymarket Theatre, a particularly nationalist prologue was added to 'this night's Anglo-German Horse-Play', which praised Johnny Bull and his constitution for having 'recovered half from foreign quacks'.[126] However, by considering Göttingen's role for British scholarship, it has hopefully become possible to question the national historiographies of science and scholarship written from the nineteenth century on, to reintegrate other European centres of science into the history of British scholarship, and to reassess ways in which the early modern republic of letters shaped 'modern' and 'national' institutions of science much more than has hitherto been acknowledged.

---

[123] A process heavily influenced by Humboldt's novel concept of university education, see Marc Schalenberg, *Humboldt auf Reisen? Die Rezeption des "deutschen Universitätsmodells" in den französischen und britischen Reformdiskursen (1810–1870)* (Basel, 2002).
[124] See Negley Harte, *The university of London 1836–1986* (London, 1986), pp. 74–93; Peter Searby, *A history of the university of Cambridge*, vol. III (Cambridge, 1997), pp. 433–71.
[125] Banks, who maintained that science and scholarship should not be affected by international crises or war, was repeatedly accused of a lack of patriotism, in particular during the revolutionary and Napoleonic Wars, see Crosland, 'Anglo-continental scientific relations'; Gascoigne, *Joseph Banks*, esp. pp. 243–7.
[126] Edmonds, *Poetry of the Anti-Jacobin*, p. 218.

8   The confessional dimension

Andrew C. Thompson

Confession was vitally important to both Britons and Hanoverians in the eighteenth century. Probing the nature of confessional relationships throws light on several aspects of the Hanoverian connection, as this chapter illustrates. The chronological focus is predominantly on the reign of the first two Georges. The power of confession, for reasons discussed subsequently, changed in the middle decades of the eighteenth century. This chapter also considers the idea of the 'protestant interest' and how this affected the nature of interactions between Britain and Hanover.

Studying confession indicates an area of common interest and experience between Britain and Hanover. This may seem surprising, given that the official confession of Hanover was Lutheranism and Britain was confessionally diverse, with an established Presbyterian church in Scotland and an Episcopalian in England and Ireland. Some argued that there was an incompatibility between the Lutheranism of the Hanoverian electors and the creed of their new British subjects, although this usually reflected a particular political position. On the other hand some wanted to look beyond narrow confessional boundaries and stress either the similarity of Lutheran and Anglican beliefs or the value of shared protestant experience and heritage.

Both Hanover and confession featured prominently within partisan political debate in Britain. However, confession also impinged on foreign policy making. Common values implied a unified protestant outlook in European affairs. Supporters of the Hanoverian dynasty sought to justify policy by stressing ideas of protestant interest and the essential similarity of British and Hanoverian concerns. This, in turn, raises the question of how appropriate it is to talk about separate and distinct 'national interests' in this period. In one sense emphasising a common protestant interest was simply a rhetorical strategy but such strategies can of themselves be revealing.

Acknowledgement: I would like to thank all the participants in the 'Hanover in British History, 1714–1837', two day conference at Peterhouse, September 2004, for the helpful discussion of the original version of this chapter. The dissertation on which the present piece is based was funded by an AHRB studentship. Continental dates are given New Style and British dates Old Style.

Confession was important to what might broadly be called loyalist or monarchical argument in the first half of the eighteenth century, although loyalism has tended to be marginalised within the existing literature.[1]

Mention of justifications of policy and rhetorical strategy also raises questions of identity. One area in which this was obviously important was in relation to the monarch. The Act of Settlement (1701) had vested the succession in the Electress Sophia and 'the heirs of her body, being protestants'.[2] Both Hanoverian monarchs' self-portrayal as protestants and why they chose to do this are interesting.[3] Protestantism was an essential component of the Hanoverians' claim to the throne so it is unsurprising that it featured prominently in official pronouncements in favour of the Hanoverians and against the Stuarts. Yet this was not purely a British concern. Being protestant was also popular with the German subjects of the first two Georges and it was a useful tool in the still highly confessionalised politics of the Holy Roman Empire.[4]

Both Britons and Germans had expectations about how a protestant prince should act. Policy was shaped not simply by the personal preferences of the monarch but also by the structural circumstances of power relations within the Holy Roman Empire and the nature of the Hanoverian claim to the British thrones. Ideas can sometimes shape behaviour. Debates about confession and the protestant interest also impinge on the well-known debate, considered in several other chapters in this volume, about the relative merits of a continentalist or a 'blue-water' strategy.

Evidence for the importance of confession takes several forms. It is possible to indicate occasions where a confessional motivation can be observed behind a particular policy. Good examples can be found in cases of intervention in favour of persecuted protestants.[5] However,

---

[1] While the importance of loyalism is now routinely stressed in accounts of Britain in the 1790s, to explain the limits of E. P. Thompson's 'failed revolution' thesis, much recent work on the early eighteenth century has sought to stress the importance of opposition to the Whig oligarchy from either Jacobitism or patriot ideas. See Paul K. Monod, *Jacobitism and the English people* (Cambridge, 1989); Christine Gerrard, *The patriot opposition to Walpole* (Oxford, 1994) and Kathleen Wilson, *The sense of the people* (Cambridge, 1995).

[2] 12 & 13 Gul. III, ch. 2. The full text of the act can be found in *English Historical Documents: volume VIII, 1660–1714* ed. Andrew Browning (London, 1953), pp. 129–34.

[3] Aspects of this theme have been discussed in Hannah Smith, 'The idea of a protestant monarchy in Britain, 1714–1760', *Past and Present* 185 (2004), 91–118.

[4] Jürgen Luh, *Unheiliges Römisches Reich: der konfessionelle Gegensatz 1648 bis 1806* (Potsdam, 1995).

[5] Three of the most prominent examples of persecution in the first half of the eighteenth century were the expulsion of Calvinists from the *Heiliggeistkirche* in Heidelberg in 1719, the 'massacre' at Thorn in 1724 and the expulsion of protestants from the territories of the archbishop of Salzburg in 1731. These incidents are considered fully in Andrew C. Thompson, *Britain, Hanover and the protestant interest* (Woodbridge, 2006), chs. 3–5.

confession also operated at other levels. Analysing public expectations and the worldviews and assumptions of both rulers and ruled reveals the depth of concern with confession. It is important initially, though, to consider historiographical issues and explain why the importance of confession has not been fully appreciated previously.[6] There are both English and German trends counting against such an appreciation. The English trends should be considered first.

I

As in so much else, Whig historiography has a great deal to answer for. A major aspect of the Whig narrative was to emphasise how 1688 and the Glorious Revolution ushered in an era of constitutional monarchy, the growth of parliamentary sovereignty and general progress.[7] Much historical attention was consequently lavished on such figures as Robert Walpole, Henry Pelham and William Pitt the Elder. All, to a greater or lesser extent, were representatives of the new era because they ruled from the House of Commons. This was, of course, important because the future of British political development 'obviously' lay in the great reforming parliaments of the nineteenth century and the growth of democracy.

The problem with such 'one eye on the present' history is that it not only minimised the role of the House of Lords, from which many members of eighteenth-century administrations were still drawn, but it virtually ignored the monarchy.[8] It might be called the phenomenon of the 'missing monarch' – it was difficult to tell a tale of the growth of the power of the Commons if it was acknowledged that the monarch still enjoyed considerable privileges and power. This is important for present purposes because one of the key areas in which the importance of confessional influence can be seen is through the foreign policies of George I and George II. Whiggish accounts of foreign policy tended to minimise the influence of the monarch so, by extension, awareness of

---

[6] Jeremy Black has, however, reflected on confessional issues on several occasions: see Jeremy Black, 'The catholic threat and the British press in the 1720s and 1730s', *Journal of Religious History* 12 (1982–83), 364–81; Black, *British foreign policy in the age of Walpole* (Edinburgh, 1985), ch. 6 and Black, 'Confessional state or elect nation? Religion and identity in eighteenth-century England', in: Tony Claydon and Ian McBride, eds., *Protestantism and national identity* (Cambridge, 1998), pp. 53–74.

[7] This is the thrust of G. M. Treveylan, *History of England* (London, 1926), pp. 472–6.

[8] The fact that neither Charles, 2nd Viscount Townshend nor George II have been the subject of modern scholarly biographies whereas books on both Robert Walpole and Pitt the Elder are legion is further evidence of this trend.

confession was lost as well.⁹ Moreover, later Whig historiography also tended to reinforce a perception of English exceptionalism and difference.¹⁰ England had always been distinct from the continent and pursued her own unique agenda of imperial and colonial expansion, even before 1688. Ironically, the latter emphasis had been more characteristic of Tory and radical Whig positions in the early eighteenth century. Given that the present argument stresses the role of cooperation and fellow feeling between Britain and Hanover for appreciating the value of confession, such an emphasis on English exceptionalism is unhelpful.

Neither George I nor George II were seen as personally very moral by the Victorians. In contrast with the monogamous (and more British) George III, both George I and George II kept mistresses. Morality is not the same as religion, but it is relatively easy to equate the two and assume that because one is not 'moral', then one is not likely to be 'religious'.¹¹ Confession, however, is something slightly different again and confessional concerns could operate independently of personal convictions.

Add on, finally, the more recent trend to see the eighteenth century as a century of Enlightenment and the Enlightenment being profoundly anti-Christian, at least in Peter Gay's influential redaction, and it quickly becomes clear why the eighteenth century might not be the first place that a British historian would look for the importance of confession and the protestant interest. The problems are aptly summarised in the words of one historian:

> It is a time-honoured contention – consecrated in our Universities by a long succession of examination questions – that wars of religion ceased with the treaty of Westphalia, and that wars of commerce took their place. The contention is not in itself quite accurate, and if it implies that religion ceased in 1648 to be a

---

[9] This imbalance has been partially redressed by Ragnhild Hatton, *George I: elector and king* (London, 1978). For George II's centrality for the formulation of foreign policy (and government more generally), see Jeremy Black, 'George II reconsidered. A consideration of George's influence on the control of foreign policy, in the first years of his reign', *Mitteilungen des österreichischen Staatsarchivs* 35 (1982), 35–56 and Aubrey Newman, *The world turned inside out: new views on George II* (Leicester, 1987).

[10] This refers to later eighteenth-century and early nineteenth-century historians, rather than the contemporary Whig supporters of George I and George II. Contrast T. B. Macaulay, *The history of England from the accession of James II*, ed. C. H. Firth (6 vols., London, 1913–15), V, ch. 19 with C. H. Firth's comments on Macaulay's insularity in Firth, *A commentary on Macaulay's History of England* (London, 1938), pp. 249–57.

[11] Little is known about the personal religious beliefs of either George I or George II. Georg Schnath argues that, in contrast to the more worldly and cosmopolitan approach of his father, George I took confession seriously and maintained an orthodox Lutheran belief. Georg Schnath, *Geschichte Hannovers im Zeitalter der neunten Kur und der englischen Sukzession, 1674–1714* (4 vols., Hildesheim, 1938–82), III, p. 61.

substantial force in inter-state relations, it is demonstrably untrue. Possibly by the middle of the eighteenth century 'the Protestant cause' had become a stereotyped formula in the diplomatic language of certain states, but it was a formula whose value lay in its appeal to public opinion, and this rendered it worth while to pay more than lip-homage to the phrase.[12]

Sir Richard Lodge made this comment in his Ford Lectures on Britain and Prussia, published in 1923. Although Lodge, in the rest of his introductory remarks, exemplifies some of the Whiggish tendencies mentioned earlier, it is perhaps an indication that neglect of confession also has a great deal to do with more general secularisation.

Lodge's mention of wars of religion also provides a neat link to some more Germanic historiographical concerns. The German term '*konfessionelles Zeitalter*' ['confessional age'] refers to the period from the Religious Peace of Augsburg (1555) to the end of the Thirty Years War and the conclusion of the Peace of Westphalia (1648). For traditional German historiography, 1648 marked the end of confession as a vital explanatory factor in history.[13] Consequently claims for the importance of confession thereafter have met with a degree of scepticism. The Peace of Westphalia was meant to have settled confessional conflict. The problem with this view is twofold. First it assumes that because conflict had been brought within a legal framework, disputes between catholics, Calvinists and Lutherans disappeared. They did not. Rather confrontation moved from the battlefield to the Diet and the Court Room. Secondly, the Westphalian settlement attempted to set in stone the confessional situation within the empire, taking 1624 as the fairest snapshot (the *Normaljahr*) and then attempting to turn the clock back to 1624 when it came to the confessional character of churches and territories. A combination of the Counter-Reformation and Louis XIV made it difficult to maintain the status quo.[14] Before the Thirty Years War the confessional balance of the electors within the empire was almost equal. The Lutheran elector of Saxony and the Calvinist electors of Brandenburg and the Palatinate faced the Habsburg kings of Bohemia and the archbishops of Mainz, Trier and Cologne. Things had changed dramatically by 1700. Catholic Bavaria had become a secular elector whilst the Palatine title had devolved on a catholic branch of the family in 1685. The elector of Saxony, Augustus the Strong, had converted to Catholicism to ensure

---

[12] Richard Lodge, *Great Britain and Prussia in the eighteenth century* (Oxford, 1923), p. 3.
[13] A recent recapitulation of this view can be found in Michael Maurer, *Kirche, Staat und Gesellschaft im 17. und 18. Jahrhundert* (Munich, 1999), p. 17. See also Ernst Walter Zeeden, 'Zur Periodisierung und Terminologie des Zeitalters der Reformation und Gegenreformation', in Zeeden, *Konfessionsbildung* (Stuttgart, 1985), pp. 60–6.
[14] W. R. Ward, *Christianity under the ancien régime* (Cambridge, 1999), pp. 3–7.

his election to the Polish throne in 1697, although his Saxon territories remained protestant. Added to this, Louis XIV had invaded the empire and in the Peace of Ryswick (1697) he had won the concession that any churches that he had given to catholics would be retained by them, regardless of what the Westphalian settlement said. Thus, although George I's father, Ernst August, was raised to electoral status in 1692 and therefore a slight shift back in favour of protestants took place, the outlook for protestants in the empire was discouraging.

There are two further noteworthy aspects of German historiography. The first is part of the larger Borussian myth. According to late nineteenth-century German historiography of the *kleindeutsch* school, Prussia had always been eventually destined to lead Germany.[15] One aspect of this view was that Prussia, stretching back at least to the days of the Great Elector in the seventeenth century, had always been the unchallenged leader of German Protestantism. This view found extension in aspects of *Ostforschung* in the early twentieth century where Prussia's fraternal protection was argued to have extended to protestants throughout central and eastern Europe.[16] Naturally such views left little space for Hanover. Hanover was the newcomer to the electoral college, not even raised to electoral status until the late seventeenth century and certainly not nearly as powerful or influential as Prussia in the nineteenth century. Hanover had, after all, been on the losing side in the Austro-Prussian War in 1866. Yet the myth does not bear close scrutiny, at least not for the period with which this chapter is primarily concerned. Hanover was not as important as Prussia in the seventeenth century but the territorial consolidation that George I's father and uncle pushed forward had increased the size of the Hanoverian army considerably by the start of the War of the Spanish Succession.[17] More crucially, the Personal Union that came into being in 1714 linked Hanover to an established great power, something that Prussia was not until at least 1742. If anything Hanover was the more obvious choice as leader of German Protestantism in the first half of the eighteenth century and the sources bear this out.

Mention of sources raises a final historiographical point. Confessional tensions within the empire were played out at the Imperial Diet in Regensburg. Traditionally the empire in general and the diet in particular were seen by Borussian historians as empty talking shops. Over the last twenty years, with a decline in confidence in the nation-state and an

---

[15] Such works as Johann Gustav Droysen's monumental *Geschichte der preußischen Politik* (14 vols., Leipzig, 1855–86) should be viewed as part of this tradition.
[16] This theme is explored in Michael Burleigh, *Germany turns eastwards* (Cambridge, 1988).
[17] Peter H. Wilson, *German armies* (London, 1998), p. 162.

increased interest in ideas of federalism, the historiographical evaluation of both institutions has become more favourable.[18] An increasing number of studies have taken the politics of the diet at Regensburg seriously. The material published by the diet itself reveals the importance of confessional concerns. This also comes across forcefully in Hanoverian archival material relating to the diet which, unlike much of the Hanoverian foreign policy material, survived both British bombs and the flood of 1946.

II

The term most frequently used now in the literature to describe the arrival of George I and his family on the British thrones in 1714 is the Hanoverian succession. Contemporaries used different terminology. They talked almost exclusively of the protestant succession.[19] The phrase immediately indicated that what was important about George I was not where he was born but the religion he confessed. 1714 was the third occasion since 1603 when faith had been placed above birth in the calculations of the English political nation in determining their monarch. Only a cursory glance at the troubles of the British Isles in the seventeenth century reveals how important confession was. The origins of the Whig and Tory parties in the 1680s lay in the struggle about whether it was appropriate to disqualify someone from succeeding to the throne on religious grounds.[20] The arrival of William of Orange in 1688 was partly triggered by the birth of a legitimate male heir to James II, thus creating the possibility of a permanent change in royal confession. After the Glorious Revolution, measures were quickly put in place to protect the protestant succession. The Bill of Rights (1689) excluded catholics and those married to catholics from the succession and this was confirmed in 1701 by the Act of Settlement.

So what did the Hanoverians think about the protestant succession? Ernst August initially displayed little interest in the question, partly because he was more concerned to achieve electoral status, partly because the claim was his wife's (she was a granddaughter of James I), and partly because whilst Anne and her son the duke of Gloucester lived, the

---

[18] There are now a number of works arguing for the vitality of both the empire and the diet at Regensburg. See Karl Otmar von Aretin, *Das alte Reich, 1648–1806* (3 vols., Stuttgart, 1993–7); Karl Härter, *Reichstag und Revolution, 1789–1806* (Göttingen, 1992); Georg Schmidt, *Geschichte des alten Reiches* (Munich, 1999) and Maiken Umbach, ed., *German federalism: past, present and future* (Basingstoke, 2002). Umbach, in particular, is keen to see the federal traditions of the empire as an alternative to the nation-state tradition.

[19] Schnath, *Geschichte Hannover*, iv, p. 435.

[20] Tim Harris, *Politics under the later Stuarts* (London, 1993), chs. 3–4.

prospect of succeeding to the British thrones remained distant.[21] Moreover Ernst August was not nearly as close to William III as his brother, Georg Wilhelm, the duke of Celle. Things had changed by 1700. The duke of Gloucester had died, as had Ernst August. Sophia was now, after Anne, William III's nearest protestant relative and the future George I had been drawn by his uncle and father-in-law, Georg Wilhelm of Celle, into William III's circle.[22]

One of the chief reasons for the closer relationship between William and the elector of Hanover was the struggle against Louis XIV. Louis, it was argued, posed a fundamental threat to both 'the liberties of Europe' and the 'protestant interest'.[23] It is easy to see why. Louis's aggression and ambition suggested that he posed a threat to other states. The revocation of the Edict of Nantes (1685) indicated that he was neither a supporter of religious toleration nor Protestantism. Huguenot exiles took the message of the dangers that Louis posed with them when they left France. Thus in the protestant Swiss Cantons, protestant Germany, the Low Countries and Britain there was a strong and well-organised pressure group to speak out against Louis as a tyrant and potential universal monarch.[24]

The idea of universal monarchy is an important component in understanding contemporary protestant worldviews. The universal monarch desired limitless dominion and tyranny. Historically, the Assyrians, the Persians, the Greeks and the Romans had all aspired to universal monarchy but, more recently, the idea was associated with Emperor Charles V, Philip II of Spain and, of course, Louis XIV.[25] These last three were all catholic and in many ways could be counted as bogeymen amongst protestants. Universal monarchy fitted very neatly into a nexus of

---

[21] Schnath, *Geschichte Hannovers*, iv, pp. 4–5.
[22] *Ibid.*, pp. 9–10; Hatton, *George I*, pp. 82–6.
[23] Thompson, *Britain, Hanover and the protestant interest*, ch. 1.
[24] See Robin Gwynn, 'The Huguenots in Britain, the "Protestant International" and the defeat of Louis XIV', in Randolf Vigne and Charles Littleton, eds., *From strangers to citizens* (Brighton, 2001), pp. 412–24.
[25] One example of a contemporary usage of this scheme is Charles Davenant, *Essays upon I. the Ballance of Power. II. The right of making war, peace and alliances. III. Universal Monarchy* (London, 1701). John Robertson has explored the implications of ideas of universal monarchy in two important articles. See John Robertson, 'Empire and union: two concepts of the early modern European political order', in: Robertson, ed., *A union for empire* (Cambridge, 1995), pp. 3–36 and Robertson, 'Universal monarchy and the liberties of Europe: David Hume's critique of an English whig doctrine', in: Nicholas Phillipson and Quentin Skinner, eds., *Political discourse in early modern Britain* (Cambridge, 1993), pp. 349–73. For a different approach to the nature of universal monarchy, see Steven C.A. Pincus, 'The English debate over universal monarchy', in: Robertson, ed., *Union for empire*, pp. 37–62. The use of the term in the seventeenth century is covered in Franz Bosbach, *Monarchia Universalis: ein politischer Leitbegriff der frühen Neuzeit* (Göttingen, 1988).

protestant ideas about what catholics were like: they sought dominion over others, they were intolerant, they were persecutors and bigots and wanted to destroy protestants – in English domestic discourse, these ideas were encapsulated in the notion of 'popery and arbitrary government'. Universal monarchy was in many ways the analogue of these ideas in the sphere of foreign affairs.

So how was universal monarchy to be stopped? One solution was to create a foreign policy based upon the idea of a balance of power. It was the duty of the other states of Europe to stop one state from becoming overly powerful. The means to do this was through systems of alliances. In practical terms this might mean that on certain occasions it was necessary to swap sides to ensure that shifts in the balance of forces between states did not lead to a more general imbalance. Many British thinkers and indeed figures throughout Europe argued that Britain had a special role to play in preserving the balance.[26] Thus in the immediate aftermath of the Treaty of Utrecht (1713), when French power was in decline while Louis XV was a minor, Austria posed a greater threat to the balance of power than France. It therefore made sense to be more anti-Austrian and pro-French. The situation changed during the 1730s and by the 1740s France was once more perceived as the greater threat.

From the confessional point of view, the balance of power offered the chance to protect Protestantism from the perceived threat of extermination by aspirant popish universal monarchs. This way of looking at the world was reinforced from a number of directions. Prior to the rise of Prussia, it was difficult for protestants to see anything but a catholic threat to the liberties of Europe and the protestant interest. Moreover, instances of persecution continued to happen in places like Hungary, Poland, Savoy, France and within the Holy Roman Empire.[27] Cases of persecution were well documented and spread quickly because not only did

---

[26] In addition to the work by Davenant (fn. 24), similar sentiments can be found in William Gibson, *A history of the affairs of Europe, from the peace of Utrecht to the conclusion of the Quadruple Alliance. With a treatise of the religious and civil interests of Europe* (London, 1725), p. 11. See also Jens Metzdorf, *Politik – Propaganda – Patronage: Francis Hare und die englische Publistik im spanischen Erbfolgekrieg* (Mainz, 2000), ch. 5 for a discussion of Francis Hare's use of such thinking. Hare was a Whig cleric and pamphleteer. For examples of non-British work arguing in a similar vein see Ludwig Martin Kahle, *La balance de l'Europe considerée comme la règle de la paix et de la guerre* (Berlin and Göttingen, 1744) and Johann Jacob Schmauß, *Einleitung zu der Staats-Wissenschaft, und Erleuterung des von ihm herausgegebenen Corpus Juri Gentium Academici* (2 vols., Leipzig, 1741–60). Both Kahle and Schmauß were academics at the university of Göttingen so their use of arguments popular in Britain is unlikely to have been coincidental.

[27] A flavour of continuing British interest in cases of the persecution of continental protestants, often triggered by requests for help, can be gained from the following references: Rochford to Newcastle, Turin, 22 April 1752, British Library [hereafter BL], Add. Mss.

Huguenots establish tight business networks after their expulsion from France but these networks could also be used to distribute news; and news of persecution was grist to the protestant mill.

Ideas of universal monarchy and the balance of power were central to the sense of expectation that (particularly) British commentators placed on the new Hanoverian monarchs. Defending the protestant religion was not solely a domestic concern. It had European dimensions as well. Put another way, Protestantism was important not only because it had created the right to the throne for George I; it brought with it concomitant responsibilities. A sense of responsibility and expectation was not simply derived from British sources. A desire to defend confessional interests was just as strong (and probably lasted even longer) in Hanover. In June 1714 George's Hanoverian privy council had urged him to send his eldest son to Britain to secure the protestant succession. They painted the advantages of being British monarch in vivid colours: it provided the means to preserve the balance of Europe, European liberties and the protestant religion.[28] Hanoverian officials were acutely aware of how much additional power the British throne could bring to bear on protestant concerns within the empire. *Schützer des Glaubens* – Defender of the Faith – was quickly added to the list of titles that Hanoverian officials routinely included at the head of letters from their royal and electoral master. One reason for doing this was that the British connection provided the Hanoverians with new-found leverage within the still highly confessionalised politics of the Imperial Diet at Regensburg.

The 1648 settlements had provided that confessional issues would be resolved by direct negotiation between protestants and catholics at the diet. This contrasted with usual arrangements whereby decisions were made through the three colleges of electors, princes, and cities. In the context of an ever-increasing number of princes succumbing to the temptations of patronage that conversion to Catholicism offered (it opened up the vast field of the *Reichskirche* for one), protestants at the diet were under pressure in the early eighteenth century. Claiming that a particular issue was confessional, and thus being able to invoke the provisions about direct negotiation, offered the chance to even up the

---

32835, fols. 100–1 expressing concern about protestants in Savoy; Villettes to Newcastle, Bern, 25 April 1752; *ibid*, fols. 129–30 about a dispute between catholic and protestant cantons in Switzerland and Villettes to Newcastle, Bern, 27 May 1752, BL, Add. Mss. 32836 fols. 179–81 which provides further news on the dispute between the cantons and details protestants escaping from France and seeking refuge in Lausanne.

[28] *Gutachten der Geheime Räte über die dringende Notwendigkeit, den Kurprinzen zur Rettung der Sukzession nach England zu schicken*, 5 June 1714 [Report of the Privy Council on the urgent necessity of sending the electoral prince to England to rescue the succession]. The document is reprinted in Schnath, *Geschichte Hannovers*, iv, pp. 743–6.

The confessional dimension   171

odds in a situation of declining numerical strength. Protestants and catholics at Regensburg coordinated their activities through the *Corpus Evangelicorum* and the *Corpus Catholicorum*. The leadership or directorate of the protestants had traditionally been in the hands of Saxony, as the senior protestant Electorate. However, after August the Strong's conversion, although August had left *Reichspolitik* in the hands of his Saxon *Räte*, questions were still asked about the appropriateness of a continued Saxon directorate. The obvious replacements for Saxony were Brandenburg-Prussia, with its long protestant traditions, or Hanover. What Hanover lacked in longevity of electoral rank, it more than made up for by the connection with Britain.[29] Rudolf von Wrisberg, the Hanoverian representative in Regensburg from 1714 to 1726, was particularly adept at making use of the British connection to persuade his fellow protestants of the wisdom of any given course of action. He was instrumental in bringing about an agreement for closer cooperation between Lutherans and Calvinists within the empire in 1722 and he corresponded with a number of well-known theologians and churchmen, such as Gerard Molanus, William Wake, Jean Alphonse Turrettini, Mattheus Pfaff and Daniel Ernst Jablonski about religious matters.[30] Wrisberg was also responsible for negotiating an agreement with the Prussians about a proposal to alternate the directorate of the *Corpus Evangelicorum* between Prussia and Hanover.[31] He then used the prospect of invoking the agreement to persuade the Saxons to press the emperor for greater concessions to protestant demands. The same tactic was repeated by one of his successors in 1733.[32] Wrisberg, like the privy councillors in 1714, also sought to emphasise protestant responsibilities in his correspondence with the king. If Hanover wanted to improve its power–status within the empire, then it was important to be seen to be the leader of the protestants.[33] Not only would this encourage support from the smaller protestant princes but it would mean that catholic powers, like Bavaria, would develop a healthy

---

[29] Andreas Biederbeck, *Der deutsche Reichstag zu Regensburg im Jahrzehnt nach dem spanischen Erbfolgekrieg 1714–1724* (Düsseldorf, 1937), p. 74.
[30] See, for example, Wrisberg to George I, Regensburg, 1 February 1720, Niedersächsisches Hauptstaatsarchiv, Hanover [hereafter NdHStA], Calenberg Brief [hereafter CB] 11, 2978, fols. 242–4. Wrisberg's involvement in the 1722 agreement can be seen in Wrisberg to George I, Regensburg, 23 February 1722, NdHStA, CB 11, 2294:I, fols. 313–15.
[31] Adolph Frantz, *Das katholische Directorium des Corpus Evangelicorum* (Marburg, 1880), pp. 77–96, 137–58.
[32] See the exchange between George II and his Geheime Räte: George II to Geheime Räte, St James's, 13 February 1733, Geheime Räte to George II, Hanover, 6 March 1733 and George II to Geheime Räte, St James's, 24 April 1733, NdHStA, CB 11, 1628, fols. 99–100, 103–5 and fol. 116.
[33] NdHStA, CB 11, 1652 is a detailed memo from c. 1720 that sets out how George I can use his power 'à la tête de tout le Parti Protestant' (fol. 1v).

respect for Hanoverian demands. Confession might, therefore, be seen as an important element of 'soft power' in the eighteenth-century empire.[34]

This aspect of confession, and its relation to dynastic concerns, was certainly not lost on George I or George II. For the eighteenth-century monarch, royal marriages offered the means of furthering political ends and dynastic ambitions. Choice of partner for royal children was critically important, just as the existence of children was vital for preserving the succession (this was, incidentally, an additional advantage that the Hanoverians enjoyed – there was never any real doubt about the existence of a legitimate heir). Three examples illustrate the links between marriage and confession.

The first is a story of failure. In 1725 the French government suggested a marriage between Louis XV (then still a minor) and Princess Anne, one of the daughters of the Prince of Wales (the future George II). George I was unenthusiastic about the idea, as the duke of Newcastle, secretary of state for the Southern Department reported to Sir Robert Walpole's brother Horace, a British diplomat in Paris. The king, 'who upon all occasions prefers the Religion and Interests of his people to all other Considerations', had told Broglie, the French ambassador, that 'however acceptable such a marriage would be upon many accounts, the Objection of Religion was such, that he could by no means entertain any Thought of it'.[35] Newcastle and Townshend, secretary of state for the Northern Department, were happy to confirm subsequently that George was unlikely to change his mind.[36] The event made a considerable impression on Newcastle, as he noted a week later. He had never seen George 'more determined in any one point than in this; and it is wonderful, that any person who knows the King's Goodness for his people and zeal for the Protestant Religion and Interest, should ever have imagined it possible for His Majesty to have been in any other way of thinking'.[37] The French proposal attracted considerable comment in European courts. Prussian ministers had heard rumours that an announcement of the marriage was imminent. Du Bourgay, the British extraordinary envoy in Berlin, had received several enquiries about it so he asked Townshend whether there was any truth in the rumours. Townshend responded that George was surprised that anyone could believe that he would 'sacrifice his Religion

---

[34] The relative merits of both hard and soft power in international relations are discussed in Joseph Nye, *The paradox of American power* (Oxford, 2002), ch. 1.
[35] Newcastle to H. Walpole, Whitehall, 1 March 1725, BL, Add. Mss. 32742, fol. 308r.
[36] *Ibid.*, fol. 308v.
[37] Newcastle to Walpole, Whitehall, 11 March 1725, BL, Add. Mss. 32742, fol. 429r.

for any worldly Interest or procure the advancement of his family at the expense of his conscience'.[38]

The second example concerns Anne's actual marriage to William of Orange-Nassau in 1734. Contemporary opinion praised this union for securing the protestant interest. The renewed links between Britain and the United Provinces also strengthened the claims of the maritime powers to be defenders of both the balance of power and Protestantism, although it should be noted that British support for the Orangists, which this match was perceived by the Dutch patriots to exemplify, was not without its problems.[39] Not all matches proved to be as successful in religio-political terms. Another of George II's daughters, Mary, had married Frederick, the Landgrave of Hesse-Kassel's heir in 1740. Mary's marriage was far from happy. In 1754 it emerged Frederick had converted to Catholicism. This caused consternation in London. Newcastle wrote to Joseph Yorke, British minister in The Hague, to solicit Dutch support for a guarantee for protestants in Hesse-Kassel, adding that 'surely the Repu[blic]k will not refuse to concur in any Guaranty, in which the Protestant Religion is so much concern'd. It would be shameful, if it did.'[40] Yorke replied that the Princess Royal, as Anne was still invariably known by British correspondents, was glad that George was determined to act and concluded 'Her Royal Highness may certainly depend upon all Ranks of People in this Country, where the interest of Religion is concern'd, & she can't pay her Court more than by exerting herself upon the occasion'.[41] Anne herself sought divine blessing for both her sister's children and Protestantism more generally and hoped that God would 'deliver my poor sister from the dangers with which that unworthy Prince Frederick has sought to ensnare her'.[42]

III

Thus far confession has been discussed as a sphere of agreement and cooperation. It is important to recognise that there were also areas where confession was a source of dispute and contention. The first occurs in the confessional aspect (or rather lack of it) to more general challenges to the

---

[38] Townshend to Du Bourgay, Whitehall, 30 March 1725, PRO, SP 90/18.
[39] See Veronica Baker-Smith, *A life of Anne of Hanover, Princess Royal* (Leiden, 1995), pp. 38–40.
[40] Newcastle to Yorke, Newcastle House, 1 November 1754 BL, Add. Mss. 32851, fol. 124r.
[41] Yorke to Newcastle, the Hague, 5 November 1754 private, *ibid.*, fol. 146.
[42] Quoted in Veronica Baker-Smith, 'The daughters of George II: marriage and dynastic politics', in: Clarissa Campbell Orr, ed., *Queenship in Britain, 1660–1837* (Manchester, 2002), p. 202.

Hanoverian regime. Recent research has shown both the extent and variety of opposition to the Whig oligarchy. For George I and George II the most profound challenge came from those alternative sovereigns, the Stuarts. For Jacobite polemicists there were a number of potential lines of attack against the Hanoverians: they were foreign and so could not understand true English liberties; moreover they were accustomed to absolute rule in their German territories so could not accommodate themselves to English practice; as Lutherans, they could neither understand nor properly defend the Church of England.[43] Much of this argument hovers round confessional issues. It either tries to claim that nationality is more important than religion for a monarch, thus redeeming the Stuarts, or it attempts to argue that the Georges were not real protestants, or not in a Church-of-England sense.[44] These accusations were worrying enough to prompt a Hanoverian cleric, Balthasar Mentzer, to publish a lengthy defence of Lutheranism to disprove the charge that it was too close to popery.[45] Attempting to claim that the Hanoverians were not appropriate defenders of the Church of England was, in many ways, a difficult case to make. It was, after all, James II's Catholicism that had proved so unpalatable for many of his subjects. The attempts to draw attention away from this confessional problem reveal the extent to which it was important to deal with confessional issues.

There were various other tactics that could be used to muddy the confessional waters. One, particularly prominent in the 1710s, was to complain about the plight of Sweden. After 1715 Hanover became actively involved in the Great Northern War on the side of Sweden's

---

[43] Such arguments are articulated in Mathias Earbery, *An historical account of the advantages that have accru'd to England, by the succession in the illustrious House of Hanover* (London, 1722) and Earbery, *The second part of the advantages that have accrued to England by the succession in the Illustrious House of Hanover* (London, 1722). For an overview of Jacobite rhetoric, see Monod, *Jacobitism*, pp. 28–38.

[44] There had been initial concern in 1714 about whether it would be possible for a Lutheran to defend the Church of England. See the exchanges in Thomas Brett, *A review of Lutheran principles* (London, 1714), *A letter to the author of the history of the Lutheran church, from a country school-boy* (n.p., n.d. [1714]), *The Lutheran liturgy: now us'd by the Protestants in the reformed churches of Germany, prov'd to agree with the rites and ceremonies in the several offices of the Book of Common Prayer* (2nd edn, London, 1715), *Two letters to the Right Honourable the Lord Viscount Townshend: shewing the seditious tendency of several late pamphlets; more particularly of, A review of the Lutheran principles, by Thomas Brett; and of A letter to the author of the Lutheran church, from a country school-boy. By a presbyter of the Church of England* (London, 1714).

[45] Balthasar Mentzer, *A vindication of the Lutheran Religion, from the charge of popery* (London, 1720). Mentzer was ordained in 1714 at the Hamburg Church in London. He subsequently became a *Hofprediger* in Hanover. See Rudolf Steinmetz, 'Die Generalsuperintendenten in Calenberg', *Zeitschrift der Gesellschaft für niedersächsische Kirchengeschichte* 13 (1908), 153–66.

enemies.[46] This, argued George's opponents, was deeply disturbing. Sweden, the country of Gustavus Adolfus and guarantor of the Westphalian settlements, was under attack from Hanover, Denmark, Prussia and Russia, concerned only with their own selfish ambition. What price now the protestant interest?[47] A real supporter of the protestant interest would be doing everything within their power to save Sweden and certainly not be allowing it to be dismembered – interestingly once Russia had become the chief threat in the Baltic, there was a greater emphasis in official discourse on the value of Sweden for broader protestant alliance systems. Carteret told Sir John Norris in August 1719 that 'the scales of the North are in your hand. You can cast the balance as you please. The cause of Liberty and the Protestant Religion will be served by rescuing this brave nation [Sweden] and I know by experience how true a friend you are to those sentiments both at home and abroad.'[48]

Another way to break up a simple sense of confessional unity was to link support for protestants abroad to domestic partisan concerns. In September 1719, Calvinists in Heidelberg were expelled from the church they shared with the catholics by the Elector Palatine. The incident caused a huge furore within the contemporary public sphere. The event provoked a series of diplomatic responses, led by George I, and ushered in a period of what one recent historian has called a 'reconfessionalisation' of imperial politics.[49] In March and April 1720, the Jacobite printer and publisher Nathaniel Mist attacked the Palatine protestants in *The Weekly Journal, or Saturday's Post*. On 5 March 1720, he noted that 'the Presbyterians, Dissenters, or, as they call themselves, the Reformed at Heidelberg' continued to insist obstinately on the return of their church and revenues.[50] Mist's description is revealing because he constantly sought to link the Palatine protestants with English dissenters and their supposedly anti-monarchical principles. These were not the sort of

---

[46] The best study in English remains J. F. Chance, *George I and the Northern War* (London, 1909).
[47] See Earbery, *Second part*, p. 14. Bolingbroke (or St John as he then was) had made similar points about the need to defend Sweden before Hanover had even become involved in the Great Northern War. See St John to Robinson and Strafford, Whitehall, 26 March 1713, BL, Add. Mss. 31138, fol. 120v.
[48] Carteret to Sir John Norris, Stockholm, 31 August 1719, BL, Add. Mss. 22511, fol. 44r. I owe this reference to Brendan Simms. For the broader impact of British intervention on politics in the period, see John J. Murray, *George I, the Baltic and the Whig Split of 1717* (London, 1969).
[49] For 'reconfessionalisation' see Gabriele Haug-Moritz, *Württembergischer Ständekonflikt und deutscher Dualismus: ein Beitrag zur Geschichte des Reichsverbandes in der Mitte des 18. Jahrhunderts* (Stuttgart, 1992), pp. 140–54. The manifold implications of the Heidelberg crisis are explored in Thompson, *Britain, Hanover and the protestant interest*, ch. 3.
[50] *The Weekly Journal, or Saturday's Post*, 5 March 1720, 66, p. 392.

people that good Anglican protestants should be supporting – they were rabble-rousers and sectarians, as dangerous as those English protestants who had caused the disruptions of the 1640s and 1650s. By aiding such people, the monarchy was associating itself with a dangerous and partisan cause.

This example of a partisan twist to inflections of the protestant interest is far from unique. Claims and counterclaims about which version of foreign policy most accurately embodied protestant principles were tossed back and forth frequently in pamphlet debates in the 1720s and 1730s. They even surfaced in debates about the value of taking Hessian troops into British pay. Opposition writers argued that Hessian forces could only serve Hanoverian ends. One ministerial writer responded to this charge by claiming that the Hessians were not needed 'for the Sake of a small German Duchy [Hanover], but in reality for the Safety of the whole Protestant Interest Abroad, which is strictly speaking our own safety'.[51] It is possible to identify two poles or versions of protestant interest between which authors could position themselves. At one extreme there were those who claimed, like Mist and other Jacobites, that Hanoverian monarchs actually endangered the protestant interest with their foreign Lutheranism, their lack of sympathy for the Church of England and their interest in aggrandising Hanover through attacks on protestant powers, like Sweden. Such people would tend also to be Tories and advocates of a 'blue-water' strategy. The concern for Sweden's fate is interesting. Swedish protestants were 'safe' in a way that the protestant Dutch and the protestant Hanoverians were not. Supporting Sweden was a way to appear to back Protestantism more generally without having to accept the association of foreign rule in Britain that both the Dutch and Hanoverians brought to mind. Protestant solidarity was thus not placed above British independence. On the other hand, there were continentalists amongst the Whigs who conceived of Protestantism as a broad church, capable of encompassing Anglicans and dissenters at home, and Calvinists and Lutherans abroad. They had little problem with accepting that a protestant foreign policy might entail involvement in European affairs. Moreover, Hanover was worthy of British protection for no other reason than that it was a fellow protestant territory.[52] Both common confession and a shared monarch meant that Hanover was worth defending.

---

[51] *A defence of the measures of the present administration* (London, 1731), p. 24.
[52] See the ministerial pamphlet *Observations upon the treaty between the crowns of Great-Britain, France, and Spain, concluded at Seville on the Ninth of November, 1729, N.S.* (London, 1729), pp. 26–7.

George I had always taken his role as confessional guardian seriously. George II continued this pattern in the early years of his reign, although he was slightly more reluctant to use British diplomats for confessional ends than his father.[53] For various reasons, the situation began to change in the 1740s. Analysis of fast sermons published during the War of the Austrian Succession suggests that the period of warfare dramatically accelerated tendencies towards a growth in proto-national sentiment. The comparison made by many clerics between the ancient Hebrews and the modern Britons subconsciously undermined a wider sense of confessional solidarity with Hanover. The emphasis now was much more on the superiority of British institutions and civil and religious liberties. This has not appeared *ex nihilo* but the war was important for the process.[54]

Attitudes at the top of the British administration were perhaps also turning against continental involvement. The Lord Chancellor, Philip Yorke, earl of Hardwicke and Henry Pelham were less than enthusiastic about British commitments in Europe. Newcastle remained committed to his version of the 'Old System', based on support for Austria. However continental politics in a confessional mould had been made much more complicated by Frederick the Great's explosion on to the international scene. Frederick was the ultimate *Realpolitiker*. When the earl of Hyndford attempted to explain to Frederick in late 1741 that his actions in Silesia were endangering the protestant religion and the liberties of Europe by permitting the rise of France, Frederick responded that 'As for the matter of Religion that is the least concern of Princes'. Hyndford was brave enough to respond that 'altho' some protestant princes had not so much of it as to make them bigots, yet that was not the case with the Catholicks, whose religion very often got the better of their interest, and I leave Your Majesty to judge what may be the consequence when these principles act together'.[55] This, in a nutshell, indicates the difference between the old world and the new – older confessional concerns and Frederick's calculated *raison d'état*. It was the inability of Frederick to play his allotted role in the confessional scheme, that of valiant seconder to George II's lead, that led, amongst other things, Newcastle to argue in the 1750s that the Austrians had done more to support the protestant succession than the Prussians.[56] Frederick's appointment of a Jacobite George Keith, the Earl Marischal, as his envoy to Paris in 1751 did little

---

[53] See Thompson, *Britain, Hanover and the protestant interest*, pp. 130–2.
[54] *Ibid.*, pp. 222–8.
[55] Extract from Hyndford to Harrington, BL, Add. Mss. 23809, fol. 289r.
[56] Reed Browning, *The Duke of Newcastle* (New Haven, 1975), p. 161.

to convince already distrustful British ministers that the king of Prussia had not abandoned both sound policy and his co-religionists.[57] George's German ministers were slower to see how things were developing. In 1748 Gerlach Adolf von Münchhausen was still reminding Newcastle of the dangers that France posed for the empire and for Europe.[58] One aspect of this danger was religious. Münchhausen also pressed Newcastle during the latter's efforts to secure the election of a king of the Romans to sort out protestant complaints about the mistreatment of protestants in the *Erbländer* and elsewhere.[59]

Perhaps there had been a parting of the ways between elite and popular concern with confession. While Manfred Schlenke has shown how well Frederick did as popular protestant hero in the Seven Years War (one of the few occasions when the major protestant powers allied against the major catholic ones),[60] British administrative opinion was no longer thinking in such strictly confessional terms. With this change, one of the firmest connections between Britain and Hanover had been eroded.

IV

This did not mean that confessional concerns disappeared completely with the death of George II. While it has been traditional to portray George III as more 'British' than his immediate predecessors, Grayson Ditchfield has recently pointed out that it is vital not to make too much of George III's comment that he gloried in the name of 'Briton'.[61] Ditchfield devotes a chapter to George III's position as a European monarch and another to his religion and he mentions that the defence of the protestant interest was included in George's first speech from the throne in relation to the aims of the Seven Years War.[62] Ditchfield rightly remarks that the lack of a scholarly biography of George II makes it difficult to assess the degree of continuity either side of 1760.[63] Nevertheless George III's

---

[57] Lodge, *Great Britain and Prussia*, p. 78.
[58] See Münchhausen's memo for Newcastle, BL, Add. Mss. 38215, fol. 249.
[59] G. A. Münchhausen to Newcastle, Hanover, 8 June 1750, BL, Add. Mss. 32821 fol. 281. A 'Note touchant les Griefs du Corps Evangelique dans l'Empire' (dated 4 June 1750) follows on fol. 283.
[60] Manfred Schlenke, 'England blickt nach Europa: Das konfessionelle Argument in der englischen Politik um die Mitte des 18. Jahrhunderts', in P. Kluke and Peter Alter, eds., *Aspekte der deutsch-britischen Beziehungen* (Stuttgart, 1978), pp. 24–45 and Schlenke, *England und das friderizianische Preussen, 1740–1763* (Munich, 1963).
[61] Grayson Ditchfield, *George III: an essay in monarchy* (Basingstoke, 2002), p. 23.
[62] *Ibid.*, p. 77, although this may reflect the continuing influence of the Old Corps Whigs prior to the 'massacre of the Pelhamite innocents'.
[63] *Ibid.*, p. 12.

strong association with the Church of England in particular, which Ditchfield identifies as a point of difference from previous generations,[64] made the sort of broadly protestant identity described for the first half of the eighteenth century more problematic. The Anglican church no longer saw itself as connected to the mainstream of European Protestantism as it had previously.[65] The conflict in America also contributed to a process of mutual alienation between George III and his dissenting subjects.[66]

Yet the spread of Enlightenment had not removed the need to think about confessional concerns within mainland Europe. Confession was still a source of dispute within the Holy Roman Empire. George III caused a confessional storm of sorts when he made clear his desire to elect his infant son Frederick as bishop of Osnabrück in 1764.[67] The terms of the Peace of Westphalia had provided for an alternation of rule in Osnabrück between a catholic bishop and a secular protestant prince from amongst the Guelphs. The catholic bishops had tended to come from the Wittelsbach clerical dynasties that dominated the Rhine bishoprics in the early modern period. Clemens August of Bavaria, the archbishop and elector of Cologne, had died in 1761. Clemens August's successor had to come from George III's family but the election of a minor, as Frederick was, caused problems, particularly in relation to a regency for Osnabrück and control of the Osnabrück vote at Regensburg.[68] Both the Hanoverian and Prussian representatives in Regensburg mobilised the *Corpus Evangelicorum* to ensure that it would be George and not the cathedral chapter that would maintain control of the Osnabrück vote. Such overtly confessional behaviour made it difficult for the emperor to maintain a position of confessional neutrality and inhibited Joseph II's plans for imperial reform.[69]

Aretin's discussion of the empire from the 1760s to the 1780s suggests that Hanover was now more overtly protestant and aggressive in its attitude towards imperial politics than Prussia.[70] It is not at all clear how far such attitudes were mirrored amongst British politicians and how far they were even aware of the Hanoverian stance. Aretin attributes the Hanoverian stance to an attempt to split Austria away from alliance

---

[64] *Ibid.*, p. 78.
[65] Although W. R. Ward, 'The eighteenth-century church: a European view', in: John Walsh, Colin Haydon and Stephen Taylor, eds., *The Church of England, c. 1689–c. 1833* (Cambridge, 1993), pp. 285–98 is a reminder that a 'party of openness' wished to connect Anglicanism to continental Protestantism, even if its influence was declining.
[66] Ditchfield, *George III*, p. 105.   [67] Aretin, *Das alte Reich*, III, p. 136.
[68] Jonathan B. Knudsen, *Justus Möser and the German Enlightenment* (Cambridge, 1986), pp. 69–81.
[69] Aretin, *Das alte Reich*, III, pp. 136–7.   [70] *Ibid.*, p. 114.

with France,[71] which would probably have also benefited Britian. Yet Hanoverian and British interests could also conflict. As Tim Blanning has shown, the *Fürstenbund* of 1785 can be viewed as an attempt by George III to pursue a largely Hanoverian policy directed against Joseph II's attacks on the integrity of the empire, in contradistinction to the desire of such British politicians as Francis, Marquess of Carmarthen, to secure an Austrian alliance.[72] The language of foreign relations was now far more related to secularised conceptions of the balance of power than to the combination of balance of power and protestant interest that had held sway in the first half of the eighteenth century. Hanoverian officials might still hope for a united protestant front in North Germany, combining Hanover and Prussia against the perceived tyranny of Joseph II but it was not to be.[73] Frederick was an advocate of *raison d'état*.[74] He had also not forgotten George III and Bute's hasty efforts to bring the Seven Years War to a conclusion and remained wary of British motives.

If foreign affairs no longer provided such an easy conduit for confessional influence to cross the Channel, there remained other areas of importance. The Enlightenment is one of these. Clarissa Campbell Orr has assembled a persuasive case for viewing both George III and his wife, Charlotte of Mecklenburg-Strelitz, as part of a north European protestant Enlightenment. Charlotte's interest in geology was part of a wider anti-deist campaign.[75] With her extensive patronage networks and interest in dynastic affairs, Charlotte's concern to promote Enlightenment stretched beyond her London circle to encompass both Hanover, while her brother was serving as governor there, and the university of Göttingen.[76] Campell

---

[71] *Ibid.*, p. 139. Dissolving the Austro-French alliance was certainly something both Britons and Hanoverians wanted but it is less clear how Hanover's strong protestant line might have achieved this.

[72] T. C. W. Blanning, ' "That horrid Electorate" or "ma patrie germanique"? George III, Hanover and the *Fürstenbund* of 1785', *Historical Journal* 20 (1977), 311–44.

[73] For an analysis of the *Fürstenbund* that stresses both Hanover's importance and the continuing centrality of confession, despite the bi-confessional nature of the alliance itself, see Dieter Stievermann, 'Der Fürstenbund von 1785 und das Reich', in: Volker Press, ed., *Alternativen zur Reichsverfassung in der Frühen Neuzeit* (Munich, 1995), pp. 209–26 especially p. 219.

[74] At least one British commentator had realised this very early in Frederick's reign. The dissenting divine Thomas Bradbury commented in a sermon from 1745 that it was a great shame that someone who had written so well against Machiavelli should be such an excellent student of his teaching. See Thomas Bradbury, *The sin and punishment of Edom; Considered and applied, in a Sermon on the Fast-Day, January 9, 1744–5* (London, 1745), p. iii.

[75] Clarissa Campbell Orr, 'Queen Charlotte, "Scientific Queen" ', in Clarissa Campbell Orr, ed., *Queenship in Britain, 1660–1837: royal patronage, court culture, and dynastic politics* (Manchester, 2002), p. 236.

[76] Clarissa Campbell Orr, 'Charlotte of Mecklenburg-Strelitz, queen of Great Britain and electress of Hanover: northern dynasties and the northern republic of letters', in Clarissa Campbell Orr, ed., *Queenship in Europe, 1660–1815* (Cambridge, 2004), pp. 378, 387.

The confessional dimension 181

Orr argues that both king and queen wanted to link the monarchy to a type of Enlightenment that sought to synthesise revealed religion with science and ethics and opposed the materialism and skepticism so often associated with the French Enlightenment. The sources for this synthesis included British authors, as well as Lutherans from Hanover and Calvinists from Geneva.[77] Even if Hanoverian influence over matters confessional had been reduced in a strictly political sense, cultural influence persisted.

V

Historians have often suggested that the decline of interest in confession was linked to some sort of modernisation. Secularisation is usually taken to be one of the identifying features of the modern world.[78] As such, it could be argued that Britain modernised faster than Hanover. Previous sections of this chapter have shown how confessional concerns persisted in Hanover in the 1750s and beyond, while British politicians were increasingly unwilling to look at the world in such terms.

Yet a final example calls such a simplistic identification of Britain with progress and Hanover with backwardness into question. George III stood firm and refused to contemplate catholic emancipation. His refusal precipitated Pitt the Younger's resignation in March 1801. George III was unwilling to break his coronation oath. Despite his earlier differences with his father, the Prince Regent also moved away from his former Whig supporters and became an opponent of emancipation.[79] Yet, despite royal resistance and the best efforts of the ultra Tories, the issue would not go away. This is not the place to consider the high-political crisis that eventually led to what J. C. D. Clark has termed the 'sudden collapse' of the protestant constitution in any detail.[80] Yet in 1828 the duke of Clarence, the future William IV, commented to J. W. Croker, the secretary to the Admiralty and Tory intellectual, that he had 'observed an inconsistency of the King's refusing in Ireland what he granted in Hanover'. Croker responded that the cases were not the same: Hanover was held by hereditary right but Britain 'only by the

---

[77] Clarissa Campbell Orr, 'The late Hanoverian court and the Christian Enlightenment', in Michael Schaich, ed., *Monarchy and religion* (Oxford, forthcoming).
[78] Max Weber's famous remark that the Enlightenment was part of the 'disenchantment of the world' is usually taken as the basis for such views. For a recent defence of the links between secularisation and modernity, see the introduction to Steve Pincus and Alan Houston, eds., *A nation transformed: England after the Restoration* (Cambridge, 2001).
[79] E. A. Smith, *George IV* (New Haven, 1999), ch. 12 details this transformation.
[80] J. C. D. Clark, *English society* (2nd edn, Cambridge, 2000), part VI.

Protestant settlement'.[81] Civil rights had been granted to catholics in Hanover in the Napoleonic period and not withdrawn after 1815.[82] Rather than being the cause of all Britain's woes, Hanover could also be advanced as a model to be emulated (and even by Tories).

The importance of religious concerns for understanding eighteenth-century British history is now widely acknowledged by historians. This chapter has shown how confession was a matter of more than merely insular concern. It was intimately connected to debates about the nature of the monarchy and the importance of the protestant succession. This, in turn, had implications for the conduct of foreign affairs and the ways in which ministerial foreign policy was justified. While both Hanover and confession were staples of partisan political discoure, the extent to which the Personal Union could be justified on the basis of shared protestant concern, at least in the first half of the eighteenth century, needs to be remembered. The nature of the link changed after the 1750s, yet the more 'British' George III did not simply ignore either Hanover or confession. The heady mixture of monarchical identity and political dispute indicate why the confessional dimension merits serious scholarly attention.

---

[81] Quoted in Clark, *English society*, p. 555.
[82] Reinhard Oberschelp, *Niedersachsen, 1760–1820* (2 vols., Hildesheim, 1982), II, pp. 263–4. Article 16 of the *Deutsche Bundesakte* (8 June 1815) secured civil rights across the entire German Confederation for religious groups.

9 Hanover and the public sphere

Bob Harris

The importance of attitudes during the early-Hanoverian period towards the Anglo-Hanoverian union and its consequences for Britain – suspected as well as real – has long been recognised by historians.[1] Nevertheless, our knowledge of these remains uneven, with some episodes and periods having been much more closely studied than others. Little work exists on public and press responses to war and British diplomacy in the Baltic between 1716–20, which raised very directly the threat of Hanoverian subversion of British interests and policy.[2] Similarly, press coverage of foreign policy and related issues in the early 1720s, later 1730s and early 1750s has received only cursory attention. It is notable that Gibbs's discussion of attitudes to Hanover in the early Hanoverian period concentrates very heavily on the 1740s.[3] Yet the prominence of Hanover as a topic of public and political debates in this decade was unusual, reflecting a unique combination of circumstances: a series of issues and events which brought into unusually sharp focus Hanoverian influence on British interests; an absence of other issues competing for political attention (there is a strong contrast here with the later 1710s); a ruthless parliamentary opposition willing to stir up public opinion on the issue (again in contrast at least to some elements of opposition in 1717–18); and a large cross section of public opinion alienated, indignant and angry

---

[1] See, *inter alia*, Richard Pares, 'American versus continental warfare, 1739–1763', *English Historical Review* 51 (1936), 429–65; R. Harris, *A patriot press: national politics and the London press in the 1740s* (Oxford, 1993), especially ch. 4; G. C. Gibbs, 'English attitudes towards Hanover and the Hanoverian succession in the first half of the eighteenth century', in: A. M. Birke and Kurt Kluxen, eds., *England and Hanover* (Munich, 1986), pp. 33–50.

[2] Some details can be gleaned from J. J. Murray's *George I, the Baltic and the Whig split of 1717: a study in diplomacy and propaganda* (1969); J. F. Chance, *George I and the Northern War* (1909). See also Jeremy Black, 'Parliament and the political and diplomatic crisis of 1717–18', *Parliamentary History* 3 (1984), 77–101; Nicholas (Nick) Harding, 'Dynastic union in British and Hanoverian ideology, 1701–1803' (unpublished PhD thesis, Columbia University, 2001), ch. 2. I am grateful to Dr Harding for allowing me to read a copy of his thesis when preparing this paper.

[3] Gibbs, 'English attitudes towards Hanover'.

about the lack of substantive political change which followed Walpole's fall from power. If, from the British perspective, the War of the Austrian Succession, at least between 1742 and 1744, could be portrayed as an unnecessary war, no one said the same thing about the Seven Years War. The latter was, as one contemporary put it, 'a war truly NATIONAL'.[4]

If some periods and episodes have yet to be systematically researched, other areas have attracted strictly limited discussion. What did British people know about Hanover and Hanoverian foreign policy? Some years ago, Uriel Dann argued, with reference to the anti-Hanoverian outcry of the early 1740s, that the British knew little and cared less; domestic factors were uppermost in their minds.[5] Frauke Geyken's conclusion is equally straightforward: 'there was for an Englishman of the eighteenth century no good reason to take any interest in Hanover, whether economically, or politically, or least of all culturally'.[6] The intense xenophobia of the English public has been emphasised by several historians, as it was by writers at the time, although the latter were very often spokespersons for nations which found themselves at particular moments special objects of English hostility.[7] As a factor shaping public attitudes towards the Hanoverian connection, national prejudice was clearly very important, although such prejudice was hardly a monopoly of the English or British, as Linda Colley has recently reminded us.[8] Perhaps we need to disentangle more carefully in this context, as I shall argue below, different levels of debate. There is also the question of who cared about Hanover and Hanoverian influence, apart from a small group of politicians and a political nation mainly based in and around London with an apparently

---

[4] *A letter addressed to two great men* (1760), p. 17.
[5] Uriel Dann, 'Hanover and Great Britain 1740–60' (DPhil thesis, University of Oxford, 1980), pp. 97, 117.
[6] Frauke Geyken, 'The German language is spoken in Saxony with the greatest purity of English: images and perceptions of Germany in the eighteenth century', in: Joseph Canning and Hermann Werllenreuther, eds., *Britain and Germany compared: nationality, society and nobility in the eighteenth century* (Göttingen, 2001), p. 59. I am grateful to Dr Brendan Simms for drawing this source to my attention.
[7] See e.g. Linda Colley, *Captives: Britain, empire and the world 1600–1850* (2003 edn), p. 105; Gerald Newman, *The rise of English nationalism: a cultural history 1740–1830* (1987), especially ch. 4; Paul Langford, *A polite and commercial people: England 1727–1783* (Oxford, 1987), pp. 320–3; J. S. Bromley, 'Britain and Europe in the eighteenth century', *History* 66 (1981), 394–412; *A compleat view of the present politicks of Great Britain in a letter from a German nobleman to his friend at Vienna* (1743); *A letter from Hanover, shewing the true cause of the present broils of Germany, and confusions of Europe* (1744); L'Abbé Le Blanc, *Letters on the English and French nations* (2 vols., 1747), I, 13, 24–7, 180–1; *A letter from a member of parliament in London to his friend in Edinburgh, relating to the present critical state of affairs, and the dangerous antipathy that seems daily to increase between the people of England and Scotland* (1763), pp. 12–13.
[8] Colley, *Captives*, p. 104.

insatiable appetite for news and comment on foreign affairs. How Hanover and Hanoverian influence were regarded in Edinburgh or Dublin has never been explored. Echoes of metropolitan debates on Hanover can be found in Scottish sources, reflecting the links which existed between the main Scottish political factions and parties and politicians in London.[9] Dublin newspapers regularly drew on English sources, and Dublin publishers reprinted pamphlets originally published in London.[10] What we do not currently know is whether the circulation of material in Scotland and Ireland touching on the Hanoverian connection was more than occasional, or how it was responded to.

In a short paper, it is not possible to furnish anything like complete answers to these questions. The aims, therefore, are more modest. The first section traces the course and fluctuating importance of debates about the role of Hanover and Hanoverian influence between the Hanoverian accession and death of George II. As Prince of Wales, George III was strongly critical of his grandfather's attitude towards his German territories, a stance in which he was confirmed by deep dislike for Pitt the Elder, whom he regarded as having betrayed his friendship and trust after the formation of the Pitt–Newcastle ministry in 1757. On his assumption of the throne, he was determined to liberate Britain from its continental commitment in the Seven Years War. His accession marks as a result a new phase in the history of the Hanoverian connection, and is thus a sensible end point for this paper.[11] The second section examines the main characteristics of press and public concern about the Anglo-Hanoverian union, and explores the question of why many contemporaries were so apparently ready to believe that Hanoverian interests were subverting British policy and interests. By way of conclusion, the final section offers a series of thoughts about the wider political significance of the early Hanoverian British public's preoccupation with Hanoverian influence.

However, before starting a word is needed about the evidence on which much of this paper is based. In seeking to reconstruct public attitudes in this period, we are heavily reliant on print – newspapers, pamphlets, ballads, and engraved cartoons. While there is a consensus about the strong expansion and vitality of the early Hanoverian press, certainly between 1725 and around 1740, there is less agreement about

---

[9] See e.g. *A letter from a freeholder in the county of Edinburgh, to his friend in Edinburgh* (Edinburgh, 1743), p. 8; *The ambition and avarice of H[anove]r, the CAUSE of this present war* (Edinburgh, 1744).

[10] For this, see e.g. Bob Harris, *Politics and the nation: Britain in the mid eighteenth century* (Oxford, 2002), pp. 200–2.

[11] G. M. Ditchfield, *George III: an essay in monarchy* (2002), ch. 2.

its influence.[12] Surviving information on circulation and readership, which is at best patchy, is well rehearsed elsewhere.[13] In the present context, what needs emphasising is, first, the diversity of forms of print which appeared on the Hanover question. This material ranged from lengthy, quite expensive pamphlets and prints to cheap, populist items such as ballads and dialogues, suggesting a discourse conducted at different social levels. Second, a significant number of pamphlets which looked closely at the issue of Hanoverian influence appear to have gained an unusually wide circulation. A complete list of these would be a lengthy one. Pertaining to only the mid-century, it would have to include Israel Mauduit's *Considerations on the present German war* (1760), which, at over 5,000, had one of, if not the, highest print runs of any pamphlet published during the early Hanoverian years; *The case of the Hanover forces in the pay of Great Britain* (1742); the second earl of Egmont's *Faction detected by the evidence of facts* (1743) – which incorporated a lengthy defence of the employment of Hanoverian troops in 1742 – and John Shebbeare's notorious *A sixth letter to the people of England on the progress of national ruin* (1757), each of which may have boasted circulations on a similar scale.[14] One anti-Hanoverian pamphlet published in Edinburgh in early 1744 noted:

One would have thought, after the DEFENCE OF THE PEOPLE, and several Pieces relating to the *Hanover* Forces in *British* pay, especially the FARTHER VINDICATION ... had been so long in almost every Hand, that there would have been no farther need to enlarge upon those subjects.[15]

A defence of the people was one of several ripostes to Egmont's *Faction detected*, while *A farther vindication of the case of the Hanover troops* was the third and final pamphlet written in the winter of 1742–3 by the Earl of

---

[12] For a summary, see Bob Harris, *Politics and the rise of the press: Britain and France, 1620–1800* (London, 1996), especially ch. 1. See also Jeremy Black, *The English press 1621–1861* (Stroud, 2001); Michael Harris, *London newspapers in the age of Walpole: a study in the origins of the modern English press* (London and Ontario, 1987); G. A. Cranfield, *The development of the provincial newspaper 1700–1760* (Cambridge, 1962); Marie Peters, *Pitt and popularity: the patriotic minister and public opinion during the Seven Years War* (Oxford, 1980). On prints, see Herbert M. Atherton, *Political prints in the age of Hogarth* (Oxford, 1974); Eirwen E. C. Nicholson, 'Consumers and spectators: the public of the political print in eighteenth century England', *History* 81 (1996), 5–21.
[13] See n. 12 above. See also Hannah Barker, *Newspapers, politics and English society 1695–1855* (2000), ch. 1.
[14] Karl Schweizer, 'Foreign policy and the 18th century English press: the case of Israel Mauduit's "Considerations on the present German war"', in: Stephen Taylor, Richard Connors and Clyve Jones, eds., *Hanoverian Britain and empire: essays in memory of Philip Lawson* (Woodbridge, 1998), pp. 198–209; Harris, *A patriot press*, pp. 65, 129–30; Harris, *Politics and the nation*, p. 90.
[15] *The AMBITION AND AVARICE OF H[ANOVER]*, p. 3.

Chesterfield and Edmund Waller on the taking into British pay of the Hanoverian troops. Concerted efforts appear to have been made to ensure that the dissemination of *The case of the Hanover forces*, the first of these, extended well beyond London.[16] There is even a tantalising hint that this occurred in the case of one famous anti-Hanoverian print produced in 1743, *The confectioner general setting forth the H[anoveria]n desert*, a biting attack on the favour supposedly shown by George II to his Hanoverian troops at the Battle of Dettingen.[17] The audience for the majority of topical political prints was probably confined to London, although the market for print engravings, including portraits of political figures, was British-wide at least by the early 1730s.[18]

Hanover's influence on British national interests was, unsurprisingly, a topic of public discussion before 1714, and it formed an important theme immediately following the accession of George I and during the 1715 rebellion, for the very good reason that the Old Pretender and his supporters chose to make it one.[19] It was, however, growing concern about British policy in the Baltic in the mid- to later 1710s, and George I's anxiety to incorporate the formerly Swedish territories of Bremen and Verden into his electoral lands, which first brought the issue into clear focus. During 1716, Count Karl Gyllenborg, Swedish minister in London, was very active in seeking to stir up parliamentary and public opposition to Britain's anti-Swedish stance, warning of the Russian threat to British interests in the Baltic and identifying Hanoverian ambitions as the true source of ministerial policy. As well as writing and arranging for the publication of several pamphlets, Gyllenborg regularly placed material in the Tory newspaper, the *Post Boy*, a paper said to favour the Jacobite and, in consequence of this, the Swedish cause.[20] On 29 September 1716, Gyllenborg, writing to Baron Goertz, a German nobleman in the Swedish service and, like Gyllenborg, a key figure in contemporary negotiations between the Swedes and the Jacobites, boasted of the 'universal approbation' which he had been informed had greeted his *An English merchant's remarks*, a pamphlet which, according to several

---

[16] Harris, *A patriot press*, p. 129.
[17] Lord Mahon, *History of England from the Peace of Utrecht to the Peace of Versailles, 1713–1783* (7 vols., 1858), III, Appendix, pp. vii–ix.
[18] See relevant comments in Diana Donald, *The age of caricature: satirical prints in the reign of George III* (New Haven and London, 1996), pp. 19–21, although much of her evidence comes from the end of the eighteenth century. See also Stana Nenadic, 'Print collecting and popular culture in eighteenth-century Scotland', *History* 82 (1997), 203–22.
[19] Harding, 'Dynastic union', chs. 1 and 2. See also the same author's contribution to the present volume.
[20] *An account of the Swedish and Jacobite plot with a vindication of the government from the horrid aspersions of its enemies* (1717), pp. 8–9, 34–40.

ministerial supporters, had been 'very industriously spread to confirm the faction in their bad opinion of the Government'.[21] Gyllenborg's activities were brought to a sharp halt in early 1717 when he was arrested and his papers seized by the ministry, in blatant violation of diplomatic immunity and international law, ostensibly because of his involvement in Jacobite conspiracy. Further pamphlets which focused specifically on the issue of Hanoverian influence on British policy in the Baltic appeared in 1717–18.[22] Ironically, it was an anti-Swedish propaganda drive in early 1717 by ministers and their supporters, aimed at shoring up support for their policies in the Baltic against the background of the Whig Split, and exploiting the discovery of the Jacobite 'plot' involving Gyllenborg, which seems to have stimulated the appearance of some of these.[23]

Criticisms made of the role of Hanover in 1717–18 anticipate important later lines of argument. In a pamphlet published in 1718, the Tory George Sewell drew on an earlier history of the 1701 Parliament by James Drake, which had portrayed foreign possessions as undermining Britain's special geographical advantages as an island in Europe and its natural insularity.[24] This insistence on Britain's supposed identity as a maritime nation was a recurrent feature of opposition writing on foreign affairs throughout the early Hanoverian period. Attacks on the Hanoverian dimension of foreign policy also quickly became interwoven with attacks on the maintenance of a standing army, portrayed as a potential instrument of German despotism.[25] William Shippen's intervention in a Commons debate on the standing army in 1717, in which he raised the spectre of German tyranny, famously saw him sent to the Tower, thereby at a stroke ensuring his speech uncommon notoriety and widespread circulation in printed form.[26] This strand of anti-Hanoverianism was

---

[21] National Archives, Kew, SP 107/2B/113, Gyllenborg to Goertz, 29 September 1716; *An account of the Swedish and Jacobite plot*, pp. 10–11, 34. See also *Observations on Count Gyllenborg's remarks upon Mr Jackson's memorial* (1717). Another pamphlet which has been attributed to Gyllenborg is *The Northern Crisis. Or, impartial reflections on the policies of the Czar* (1716), also published by Morphew.

[22] *The Gottemborg Frolick* (1718); *A true translation of Baron Bothmar's letter to Monsieur Schutz, 21 April 1717* (1717); *A letter from an unknown hand, to Mr Pettecum, the Holstein Minister, in answer to that of Mr Secretary Stanhope* (1717).

[23] For this campaign, see Murray, *George I, the Baltic, and the Whig Split*, pp. 285–6, 342–3.

[24] [Sewell] *The resigners vindicated, or the defection re-consider'd* (1718), quoted in Nick Harding, 'Sir Robert Walpole and Hanover', *Historical Research* 76 (2003), 167. The pamphlet was a riposte to *The defection consider'd, and the designs of those who divided the friends of the government, set in a true light* (1717).

[25] See e.g. *The necessity of a plot; or reasons for a standing army. By a friend to K. G.* (1718), especially p. 11. This pamphlet was the subject of legal action by the ministry.

[26] 'A speech against continuing the army, spoken the 4th of December 1717. By W[illiam] S[hippen]', printed as part of *Three speeches against continuing the army &c ... To which are added the reasons given by the Lords who protested against the bill for punishing mutiny and*

particularly associated with the Jacobites. The Jacobite author of the pamphlet entitled *To Robert Walpole* (1716), linked the breach of the Act of Settlement involved in alleged British support for Hanoverian aggrandisement – the act included a clause preventing Britain fighting wars on behalf of foreign territories without parliamentary consent – with the standing army in a wider critique of the threat which Hanoverian rule posed to English liberties. The warning was blunt: 'For if the Crown could violate that Act, before it was Possest of the Army that now is, it may with this vast Army, dissolve our whole Constitution'.[27] Similar warnings about the threat supposedly posed to English liberties by the union, and a German monarch who allegedly governed as an absolute ruler in Hanover, were contained in Francis Atterbury's *English advice to the freeholders of England* (1714) and Mathias Earberry's *An historical account of the advantages that have accrued to England, by the succession of the illustrious House of Hanover*, which was published in the aftermath of the South Sea crisis in two parts in 1721 and 1722 respectively. In both of these works, Hanoverian rule was portrayed as the source of corruption in British politics and as leading to the transfer of specie and British wealth to the Electorate.

Supporters of the ministry and the Hanoverian regime responded vigorously to these attacks. A defence of the acquisition of Bremen and Verden, published in 1717, stressed the advantages the transfer of territory would bring to British commerce. To underline the point, the Elbe and the Weser were portrayed as 'next to the Thames and the Severn ... of the greatest consequence to Britain, of any two Rivers in the known World, and through whose streams so great a part of our Riches flows continually home to us'.[28] Other writers emphasised the accession of strength which the Anglo-Hanoverian union supposedly brought to British influence and key national interests in Europe, including the defence of the 'Protestant interest'.[29] The protestant card was one which several subsequent defenders of the Hanoverian union would play,[30] reminding us of the continuing

---

desertion (1718). The pamphlet went through several editions, and was reissued in 1732. Shippen's speech continued to reappear in the opposition press into the 1750s. See e.g. *Old England, or the National Journal*, 28 October 1752; *True Briton*, 1 November 1752.

[27] *To Robert Walpole* (1716), pp. 2–3.

[28] *Some considerations upon his Majesty's message; and the duchies of Bremen and Verden* (1717), pp. 10, 13.

[29] *The state anatomy of Britain* (4th edn, 1717), especially pp. 53–4; *The juncture: or considerations on His Majesty's speech at the opening of the present session of parliament, November 21 1717* (2nd edn, 1718).

[30] See e.g. *The consequences of his Majesty's journey to HANOVER at this critical juncture considered in a LETTER from a member of parliament in town, to a noble duke in the country* (1740), especially pp. 10–11; *Observations upon the treaty between the crowns of Great Britain, France and Spain, concluded at Seville on the Ninth of November, 1729* (1729), especially p. 16; *A defence of the measures of the present administration* (1731), p. 23.

importance of, and interest in, confessional conflicts and identities in shaping popular responses to war and foreign affairs in this period. How persuasive and important this line of defence was is hard to say since the evidence is at best ambiguous. Whilst a high level of public interest in the fate of European Protestantism was sustained certainly into the early 1720s, denominational loyalties complicated the picture.[31] Dissenters were in general much more ready to identify with this interest than High Church members of the Church of England.[32] Prevailing patterns and configurations of international politics and diplomacy could, moreover, easily weaken appeals to the 'Protestant Interest'.[33] It may be for this reason that pro-ministerial writers tended rather, on the occasions they looked for general principles to defend policies, to talk in terms of the 'balance of power', a helpfully elastic concept which could, but did not have to, carry confessional connotations.[34] Very often, they simply stressed other, more immediate dangers to British interests, as they perceived or portrayed them, which included trade (the Imperial Ostend East India Company which threatened the interests of the English East India Company), British possessions (Gibraltar), areas of special strategic interest (the Low Countries), or Jacobite invasion plans.

Viewed from the perspective of the middle of the eighteenth century, the level of press interest in the 1710s in the impact of the Anglo-Hanoverian union on British foreign policy appears to have been quite limited. Gyllenborg's arrest, quickly followed by that of Goertz in the United Provinces, and publication of their correspondence kept the Jacobite threat to the Hanoverian and protestant succession squarely in the public eye. The international as well as domestic threat from Jacobitism formed a key plank in the defence of Stanhope's

---

[31] See the comment on the 'interest' and 'indignation' in Britain created by events at Thorn in 1724, in G. C. Gibbs, 'Britain and the Alliance of Hanover, April 1725–February 1726', *English Historical Review* (1958), 422. See also Jeremy Black, 'The Catholic threat and the press in the 1720s and 1730s', *Journal of Religious History* 12 (1983), 364–81.

[32] See various contributions and introduction in Tony Claydon and Ian McBride, eds., *Protestantism and national identity: Britain and Ireland, c.1650–c.1850* (Cambridge, 1998). Future work by Tony Claydon and Andrew Thompson promises to advance considerably our understanding of this dimension to public attitudes.

[33] Jacobite and Tory propagandists delighted in pointing out the contradictions between contemporary realities and a language of confessional interests as applied to international relations. It formed, for example, a major theme in the Jacobite essay paper, *The True Briton* (1751–3), which dwelt at considerable length on the circumstances of war and diplomacy in the later seventeenth and early eighteenth centuries, emphasising that the Grand Alliance could not be portrayed as a confessional alliance or the conflicts of that period as about religion.

[34] See, for a similar conclusion applied to an earlier period, Steven Pincus, ' "To protect English liberties": the English nationalist revolution of 1688–1689', in: Claydon and McBride, eds., *Protestantism and national identity*, especially pp. 95–102.

interventionist diplomacy in southern Europe in the later 1710s.[35] In opposition, Walpole and Townshend were cautious about supporting public attacks on Hanoverian influence.[36] Government pressure on the press may have been another important factor restraining criticism of Hanover; Gyllenborg makes several references in his letters to Goertz to the large sums he was compelled to devote to securing printers for his material, at one point commenting that it was necessary to 'win [*gagner*] the printers who risked a lot in printing material which was not to the taste of the government'.[37] John Morphew, printer of the *Post Boy* and of several anti-Hanoverian pamphlets, was prosecuted in 1717 for paragraphs on foreign affairs published in his paper, which may have induced him to adopt a more cautious stance from that point.[38] At the end of the decade, little attention appears to have been given to Hanoverian influence on the anti-Russian direction of policy, and in particular the issue of control of the Duchy of Mecklenburg in that context, which brought Russia and Hanover into conflict, although a memorial presented to George I by Peter the Great was published in London at the end of 1719 which focused directly on this question.[39] Nor was the formation of the Quadruple Alliance in 1718 and war against Spain, which commenced in that year, attacked on the grounds of Hanoverian influence, although this would happen later.[40] Domestic and religious issues – notably the Peerage Bill and, even more so, the Bangorian controversy and dissenting disputes over the subscription issue – excited, in any case, a great deal more press interest and argument.

The Baltic crisis did, nevertheless, have one very important longer-term effect on perceptions of Hanoverian influence, and it is here that its real significance lies in the present context. It helped to entrench further the notion of Hanover as an expansionist power. In the mid-eighteenth century, the tenacity of this view would detract from the

---

[35] See e.g. *A letter to a friend at the Hague, concerning the danger of Europe, and particularly of Great Britain, in case the Quadruple Alliance should not succeed* (1718).
[36] See Harding, 'Dynastic union', p. 118.
[37] NA, SP 107/2B/172, letter of 12/23 October 1716. See too 208–13, letter of 4 November 1716.
[38] Murray, *George I, the Baltic, and the Whig Split*, p. 346.
[39] *Memorial presented to the king of Great Britain on the part of his Czarish Majesty, at London, 14 December 1719* (1719). Also published as *A memorial presented to the king of Great Britain, by M. Wesseloski the Czar's resident at London ... His Majesty's answer to that memorial ... A letter from a gentleman at London to a friend in Holland, upon that memorial* (1720).
[40] See e.g. *The extraordinary craftsman* (1729), p. 13, where the author declared: 'But the destruction of that Fleet was the sole and principal occasion, which was not wrought by the Advice or Counsel of any *Englishman*, but by Foreigners who had influence enough in the late Reign, equal to Designs which no *Englishman* would or durst undertake.'

more fundamental condition of the Electorate – its vulnerability to military and diplomatic pressure, especially in view of the rise of Prussia and Russia as major military powers.

In contrast to the later 1710s, foreign policy was a major topic of public and press discussion between 1726 and 1731. This reflected the careful avoidance by Walpole of controversial domestic policies, but also the anti-Walpolian opposition's political strategy. The opposition press critique of ministerial foreign policy, mounted from 1726 in the influential weekly essay paper, the *Craftsman, or Country Journal* and a series of important pamphlets, generally avoided, however, direct reflection on Hanoverian influence on British interests. Instead, it focused on specific criticisms of diplomacy, the supposedly dangerous reliance on the defensive alliance with the French, which lasted until 1731, and on what was depicted as an inappropriately interventionist thrust to foreign policy.[41] Had Britain been dragged into a continental war in the mid- to later 1720s, things might have been different. Yet just as Walpole in opposition in 1717–18 had avoided attacking too openly the role of Hanover and Hanoverian influence, so did William Pulteney and most of his colleagues, extremely conscious no doubt of ministerial efforts to label their opposition as disloyal as well as factious. In 1727, following the accession of George II, the *Craftsman* talked of the 'foreign reign' and the 'new family' being no longer popular topics, asserting too the new king's British credentials in comparison to those of the pretender.[42] The most outspoken attacks on Hanoverian influence in this period, which arose in the context of the decision to retain Hessian troops in British pay in 1730 and 1731, were articulated in parliament, not in the press.[43] Prominent critics included the City MPs George Heathcote and John Barnard,

---

[41] See e.g. *A short view of the state of affairs, with relation to Great Britain, for the four years past* (1730); *A letter to Caleb D'Anvers, Esq; concerning the state of affairs in Europe as published in the Craftsman, January 4, 1728–9, By John Trott, Yeoman* (1730); *The observations on the Treaty of Seville examined* (1730); *The motives and designs of the Vienna alliance examined, &c* (1729); *The second craftsman extraordinary; being farther remarks on a pamphlet lately published, entitled, Observations on the conduct of Great Britain* (1729); *The craftsman extraordinary. Being remarks on a late pamphlet entitled observations on the conduct of Great Britain* (1729); *The craftsman extraordinary: containing an answer to the defence of the enquiry into the reasons for the conduct of Great Britain* (1729). For parliamentary attacks in 1726 on the Treaty of Hanover, see Gibbs, 'Britain and the Alliance of Hanover', p. 428.

[42] *Craftsman*, 4 November 1727.

[43] See J. Black, 'Parliament and foreign policy in the age of Walpole: the Case of the Hessians', in Black, ed., *Knights errant and true Englishmen: British foreign policy, 1660–1800* (Edinburgh, 1989), pp. 41–54. In 1726, when the opposition was still disorganised, isolated voices in parliament had also attacked the Treaty of Hanover (1725) as likely to involve Britain militarily in the defence of Hanover.

which may indicate the presence of stronger anti-Hanoverian sentiment in London at this time than commonly found expression in the *Craftsman* and other opposition journals.[44] In 1729, the press seems to have largely ignored the threat of war between Hanover and Prussia, which arose from disputes over Prussian recruitment on Hanoverian territories. Reichenbach, the Prussian envoy in London, had links, through the Tory, Lord Strafford, to the opposition, and a pamphlet on the subject was prepared and published in London in 1730 in advance of the parliamentary session.[45] The main battle lines of the session were drawn elsewhere, however, notably on France's failure to demolish fortifications at the port of Dunkirk in contravention of the Peace of Utrecht. In 1730–1, Walpole and his main spokesman in the press, William Arnall, were able to argue that Britain had an obligation and duty to defend Hanover against possible attacks because of the direction of Britain's foreign policy, without creating a great deal of controversy.[46]

Open concern about the role of Hanover was, therefore, usually absent from public and press debate between the mid-1720s and early 1730s. Yet, as with the Baltic crisis of 1717–18, this period has a deeper lying importance for public attitudes towards the Anglo-Hanoverian union. Opposition writers perpetuated very strongly the notion of a British or more usually English national interest which was basically isolationist. This was, for example, a central theme of Bolingbroke's 'Remarks on the History of England', published in serial form in the *Craftsman* during 1730–1. While most opposition attacks on the Walpolian regime drew a careful distinction between the monarch and his ministers, this was not always the case. Discussing the reign of Edward III, Bolingbroke noted:

The Nation had been miserably harass'd by civil wars and oppression of various kinds, when he [Edward III] came to the Crown. The Burthen of personal service, and Taxes raised to defend the Dominions, which his Predecessors held on the Continent, had exhausted all degrees of people. The mischief was so much resented by them, that Foreign Interest and Foreign Counsels must justly be reckoned among the principal causes of all the Disputes & even wars between them and their former kings.[47]

---

[44] For a report on the debate on 4 February 1730, which emphasises the ferocity of Heathcote's comments, see *Tory and Whig: the parliamentary papers of Edward, third earl of Oxford and William Hay, MP for Seaford, 1716–1753*, eds. Stephen Taylor and Clyve Jones (1998), pp. 243–4, letter from Edward Harley to Martha Harley, 5 February 1730.
[45] *A letter from an English traveller to his friend at London: relating to differences betwixt the courts of Prussia and Hanover* (1730).
[46] See especially Harding, 'Sir Robert Walpole and Hanover', pp. 172–82.
[47] *Country Journal, or the Craftsman*, 15 August 1730.

A form of 'Guarded Treason', as one writer termed it, oblique feints such as this infuriated ministers and their supporters.[48] The portrayal by Bolingbroke and others of Elizabeth I as a patriot monarch, a monarch who in her person, actions and policies managed to identify completely with the interests of her 'people', can only have further encouraged negative comparisons to the Hanoverian kings with their foreign interests and dominions.[49] At a different level, but equally importantly, the extent of debate on foreign policy in these years, the concerted effort by the Walpole ministry to explain and defend its policies and answer its critics in print, served to reinforce a belief that foreign policy was a natural and important area of public scrutiny.[50]

For the rest of the 1730s, the place of Hanover and Hanoverian interests in public and press debate remained basically unchanged. In the middle of the decade, Walpole's ability to keep Britain neutral during the War of the Polish Succession (1733–5) disabled any attack on ministerial foreign policy on the grounds of Hanoverian influence. Looking back from the perspective of 1742, Henry Bland, defending Walpole and his ministry, commented: 'I have observed that the whole *Posse* of *Craftsmen*, legislators and Auxiliaries were quite silent during the Existence of the late war between the Emperor and France.'[51] In 1739, British moves to ally with Denmark led to new criticism of Hanoverian influence on foreign policy. The attack appeared in the essay paper *Common Sense, or the Englishman's Journal*, a paper closely associated with the opposition Whigs, the earl of Chesterfield and George Lyttelton. Such notes, however, were drowned out by the upsurge from 1738 of popular agitation and fury about ministerial policy towards Spain and Spanish attacks on British traders in the Caribbean and, during 1739–40, the conduct of the war against Spain which broke out in October of the former year.[52]

---

[48] *Farther observations on the writings of the craftsman* (1731), p. 16.
[49] For Bolingbroke's political Elizabethanism, see especially Isaac Kramnick, *Bolingbroke and his circle: the politics of nostalgia in the age of Walpole* (Harvard, 1968). It remained a key theme in Patriot propaganda throughout the rest of the early Hanoverian period, for which see especially Christine Gerrard, *Patriot opposition to Walpole: politics, poetry, and national myth, 1725–1742* (1994).
[50] For Walpole's press strategy, see especially relevant comment in Michael Harris, 'Print and Politics'; Simon Targett, 'Government and ideology during the age of Whig supremacy: the political argument of Walpole's newspaper propagandists', *Historical Journal* 27 (1994), 289–318.
[51] *The conduct of the late administration* (1742), p. 58.
[52] *Memoirs and correspondence of George, Lord Lyttleton from 1734 to 1773*, ed. R. J. Phillimore (2 vols., 1845), I, p. 121.

Hanover and the public sphere   195

For much of the 1720s and 1730s, therefore, Hanover and Hanoverian interests were lesser themes in public debate, although they were never far from the surface of public consciousness. In this context, it is striking that Walpole and his supporters were keen to portray the Treaty of Seville with Spain in 1729, which threatened to alienate Austria, as a concrete example of George II favouring British interests over Hanoverian ones, although more often they asserted, as we saw earlier, that there was no conflict of interests, potential or actual.[53] In the subsequent two decades, the position was to change dramatically. The outbreak of the War of the Austrian Succession in October 1740, which Britain was drawn into in the following spring in an auxiliary capacity as an ally of Austria, placed Europe and European power politics once again at the very centre of public attention, where it remained for much of the following two decades. British intervention in the War of the Austrian Succession (1740–8) and subsequently the Seven Years War (1756–63) also made it inevitable that the role of Hanover and alleged Hanoverian subversion of British foreign and military policy and interests would re-emerge as important topics of public concern and discussion. What could not have been foreseen was just how far this was to occur.

From late 1742 until midway through 1745, the issue of Hanover and its influence dominated press and political debate, for long periods completely overshadowing consideration of other political issues. Part of the explanation for this predominance is, as referred to at the beginning of this paper, to be found in domestic political circumstances and conditions. The full causes lie, however, in the interaction between, on the one hand, domestic political conditions and circumstances and, on the other, an unprecedented and highly controversial series of events and measures, which severally and when viewed in combination brought into sharp relief the reality of George II's Hanoverian responsibilities and interests and their capacity to impinge on British interest and fortunes in war. The Hanoverian Neutrality of 1741 was the first concrete example of the ability of France to use Hanoverian vulnerability as a military and diplomatic lever against Britain. In late November 1741, Zamboni, the agent of Hesse-Darmstadt wrote to the Bavarian minister, Count Haslang, of public opinion in London being in patriotic uproar about the agreement.[54] In the case of the Hanoverian troops, the terms of service were

---

[53] *Observations upon the treaty between the crowns of Great Britain, France and Spain, concluded at Seville on the ninth of November, 1729 N.S.* (1729). This pamphlet was published in Edinburgh as well as London.
[54] Cambridge University Library, Cholmondeley (Houghton) MS, correspondence nos. 3107 and 3109.

unusually favourable, and the nature of their employment as much political as military, hence the opposition's jibe that Carteret was the 'Hanoverian troop master'.[55] Nor did opposition writers need to expend great effort to provoke popular indignation at the events of the military campaign of the summer of 1743 and in particular George II's 'obsessive concern' – the phrase is Uriel Dann's – for the Electorate's soldiers during the campaign.[56] Most influentially, a memorial issued by the earl of Stair on the resignation of his command in the Pragmatic Army quickly found its way into print in late 1743, probably through the influence of the earl of Chesterfield.[57] In this, Stair directly criticised the dependence on 'inferior channels' (i.e. the Hanoverians) after George II had joined the army in June.

The winter of 1743–4 saw anti-Hanoverian sentiment at a pitch of intensity unmatched during the rest of the early-Hanoverian period. The Rev. Dr Francis Ayscough, Clerk of the Closet to the Prince of Wales, claimed in early November 1743 that the outcry over the role of the Hanoverian troops exceeded those witnessed over Walpole's excise scheme in the mid-1730s and the convention of Prado in 1739.[58] The outcry extended beyond London and its immediate environs, although this was something disputed by at least one ministerial supporter speaking in parliament.[59] On 11 January 1744, Lord Tankerville wrote from Chillingham, in the north east: 'The Hanoverians made a great noise here, and there has not wanted proper emissaries to throw out every invective the heart of man can invent, and to make the *greatest of personages* [George II] appear as black and as odious to the people as possible.'[60] From Grantham in Lincolnshire, Sir John Cust, the pro-government MP for the town, was painted a similar picture by a local ally.[61] In the second half of 1744, the role of Hanover was kept in the forefront of public and press debate by a series of pamphlets produced by the Prussian envoy in London, Andrié, which alleged that renewed Hanoverian ambitions for territorial expansion in the German empire had in the summer of 1743

---

[55] Dann, 'Hanover and Great Britain', p. 102. [56] *Ibid.*, p. 104.

[57] The memorial was printed as an appendix to the populist and, in the view of ministers, seditious pamphlet, *A true dialogue between Thomas Jones, a trooper, late return'd from Germany and John Smith, a serjeant in the First Regiment of Foot Guards* (1743). It was also published separately as *The memorial of the E[arl] of S[tai]r* (1743).

[58] BL, Add MS 51,437 (Holland House Papers), fol. 50: Political Journal of Dr Francis Ayscough, 5 November 1743.

[59] Bodleian Library, Oxford, MS Don C 106 (Tucker Papers), fol. 154, John to Richard Tucker, 23 January 1744.

[60] BL, Add. Mss. 32,702 (Newcastle Papers), fol. 7: Tankerville to Newcastle, 11 January 1744.

[61] Jeremy Black, *Walpole in Power* (Stroud, 2001), p. 89.

constituted the major obstacle to the settlement of differences between Austria and Bavaria.[62] In the spring of 1745, further popular anger and alienation resulting from the failure of the Broad–Bottom ministry, formed in late 1744, to produce substantive political change, and military defeat in the United Provinces, notably at the Battle of Fontenoy in May 1745, provoked new, bitter attacks in the opposition press on Hanoverian influence and further calls for severing the Anglo-Hanoverian union.[63] It was only the outbreak of the Jacobite rebellion in the late summer of 1745 which finally silenced the critics in the opposition press of Hanoverian influence, although unsurprisingly many of the specific allegations about the role of Hanover and Hanoverian subversion of British interests made in the opposition press in the early 1740s found their way into Jacobite propaganda circulated during the rising, as well as into the dying speeches of several Jacobites executed after its defeat.[64]

Following the suppression of the 'forty-five', and for the remainder of the War of the Austrian Succession, much less was heard of Hanover and its influence on British foreign policy. In 1746, so confident was one pamphleteer of the transformation in popular and political mood brought about by the failed 'forty-five' that he urged the unique dependability of Hanoverian troops as allies of Britain and a bulwark against invasion. Their commitment to English liberty and independence was a consequence, in the first place, of their sharing the same monarch. In what was a strange inversion of the more common opposition argument that Hanoverian slavery was a threat to English liberties, their reliability was also attributed to their 'want' of liberty; those currently lacking freedom were unlikely agents, or so it was argued, of any attempt to deprive it from those who did possess it. The same author also declared, with an enthusiasm unmatched during the rest of the early Hanoverian period, that the interests of both nations were identical: 'Once cleared of prejudice and jealousy all distinctions will vanish, and we shall look upon Hanover to be as much a part of our political body as Ireland, and Hanoverians to be

---

[62] See R. Lodge, 'The Hanau controversy in 1744 and the fall of Carteret', *English Historical Review* 38 (1923), 509–31.

[63] Harris, *A Patriot Press*, pp. 185–8.

[64] *Considerations addressed to the publick printed by authority* (1745); *A collection of declarations, proclamations and other valuable papers, published by authority at Edinburgh in the years 1745 and 1746* (1748). 1745 also saw a further printing of Earberry's *An historical account of the advantages that have accrued to England by the succession in the illustrious House of Hanover. A true copy of the papers, wrote by Arthur Lord Balmerino, Thomas Syddal, David Morgan, George Fletcher, John Berwick, Thomas Deacon, Thomas Chadwick, James Dawson and Andrew Blyde, and delivered to the Sheriffs by them at the places of their execution* (1746); *A full and true collection of all the orders, proclamations and papers &c published by the authority of Charles, Prince of Wales, since his arrival in Scotland to this present time* (Glasgow, 1746).

much as entitled to our care and esteem as either the Scots or Irish.'[65] Given the Scotophobia and punitive legislation which followed the 'Forty-Five', this was perhaps an unfortunate parallel. In the later 1740s and early 1750s, an undercurrent of popular anti-Hanoverian sentiment continued to find sporadic expression.[66]

In the Seven Years War, subsidy treaties signed in 1755 with Russia and Hesse-Cassell revived debates about Hanoverian influence on British interests. These were explicitly designed to protect Hanover in the event of the growing conflict between Britain and France in North America spreading back to the continent. In early 1756, a defensive alliance was formed with Prussia for the same purpose. There was no repetition, however, of the intense preoccupation with the issue of Hanoverian influence which had marked the early phases of the previous war. One reason for this was that, unlike during the earlier war, there appears to have been near universal agreement about Britain's principal aim of the Seven Years War – to defend its North American colonies against French aggression; the war in Europe was for ministers and public alike a secondary matter.[67] Again unlike in the early 1740s, there was no dispute about the immediacy of the French threat to British security and interests, highlighted by the French invasion scare of 1756. In June 1756 the ally of Pitt the Elder, Thomas Potter, observed: 'The almost universal language is, opposition must be wrong when we are ready to be eat up by the French.'[68] Some of the criticism of the subsidy treaties was aimed not so much at the reasonableness of protecting the Electorate in circumstances when pursuit of British interests brought it under threat – the position which Walpole had defended in 1730–1 and which ministerial speakers urged in parliamentary debates on the treaties in 1755 – but the effectiveness and cost of the measures. This was the crux of the case made in a pamphlet entitled *Deliberate thoughts on the system of late treaties* (1756). Israel Mauduit was later to praise the pamphlet's author, Samuel Martyn,

---

[65] *An examination of the expediency of bringing over immediately the body of Hanoverian troops taken into our pay* (1746), p. 21.
[66] For contemporary comment on this, see Cumberland Record Office, Carlisle, D/Lons/W2/1/114 (Lonsdale Papers), Sir James Lowther to John Spedding, 2 April 1752, see too letter of 12 March. Anti-Hanoverianism was also a recurrent theme, unsurprisingly, in the Jacobite paper, *The True Briton*. See especially issues for 10 July, 11 September, 18 December 1751; 8 April, 20 May 1752; 7, 14 March 1753.
[67] See relevant comment on this in P. J. Marshall, 'Britain and the world in the eighteenth century: I Reshaping the empire', *Transactions of the Royal Historical Society* 6th series, (1998), VIII, p. 8.
[68] *Correspondence of William Pitt, Earl of Chatham* (4 Vols., 1838), I, p. 161: Potter to William Pitt, 4 June 1756.

Hanover and the public sphere   199

another ally of Pitt the Elder's, as 'an elder brother, and a much wiser [one]'.[69] Others urged, however, that Britain had no obligation or reason to defend Hanover, that the current war with France had nothing to do with the continent, and Britain should, therefore, confine itself to the colonial and maritime theatres. To do otherwise was to compromise once again the unique advantages conferred on Britain by its insular position.[70] Such arguments brought forth familiar counter-arguments from ministerial supporters about the scope and importance of Britain's commercial and political interests in Europe, the interdependency of continental and maritime military strategies, and the duty to protect the Electorate.[71]

Several other events during 1756–7 served further to fuel public and press interest in the Hanover issue. In the spring of 1756, Hessian and Hanoverian troops were brought over to Britain in response to the French invasion scare. In September of that year, there was what Marie Peters has described as a 'minor furore' associated with the release of a Hanoverian soldier following the theft of a handkerchief in Maidstone, an incident which some sections of the opposition sought to inflate into a major attack on the constitution and fabric of English liberty.[72] In September 1757, the duke of Cumberland, following the military defeat of his army of observation at Hastenbeck in July, negotiated neutrality for Hanover at the convention of Kloster-Zeven, a treaty subsequently repudiated by George II and his ministers. The neutrality convention was portrayed by some as the true cause of the dismal failure in the same month of the combined expedition to Rochefort in the Bay of Biscay, the first of several coastal raids during the war promoted by Pitt the Elder.[73]

---

[69] *Occasional thoughts on the present German war* (1761), p. 33.
[70] See especially *The Monitor, or British Freeholder*, 6, 27 September, 11 October, 1, 8, 15, 22 November, 6, 20 December 1755; *A constituent's answer to the reflexions of a member of parliament upon the present state of affairs at home and abroad* (1755).
[71] See e.g. *The important question, concerning invasions, a sea war, raising the militia and paying subsidies for foreign troops* (1755); *An appeal to the sense of the people on the present posture of affairs* (1756); *The conduct of the ministry impartially examined* (1756); *An impartial view of the conduct of the M[inist]RY, in regard to the war in America* (1756); *Occasional reflections on the importance of the war in America and the reasonableness and justice of supporting the king of Prussia* (1758).
[72] The phrase is Marie Peters's, in *Pitt and popularity*, p. 50. See also *England's warning: or a copy of a letter from a Hanoverian officer in England to his brother in Hanover. Found near Canterbury, translated from the German* (1756); [Edward Lancer] *Some particular remarks upon the affair of the Hanoverian soldier* (1757); *The Hanoverian treaty: or, Maidstone spectacle* (n.d. [1756]?).
[73] Quoted in Nicholas Rogers, *Whigs and cities: popular politics in the age of Walpole and Pitt* (Oxford, 1989), pp. 108–9. See also *The Monitor*, 15, 22 October, 5, 12 November 1757; *London Evening Post*, 11–13 October 1757.

According to Horace Walpole, it was a suspicion very widely entertained in the City of London.[74] Nevertheless, what needs to be stressed in the present context is that the role of Hanover and Hanoverian influence on British policy and conduct of the war were not the main factors shaping popular responses to the early phases of the Seven Years War. The loss of Minorca, strategically vital to naval control of the Mediterranean, to the French in the spring of 1756, generated much more controversy and public excitement.[75] It was also this military setback which served to galvanise, along with the early disappointments in the war in North America, a wider libertarian attack on the personnel and politics of Hanoverian rule in Britain, which included criticism of Hanoverian influence on British military and diplomatic policy, portrayed as the cause of current military impotence. John Shebbeare's *Letters to the people in England*, published between 1755 and 1757, represented the most influential vehicles for this attack, along with the weekly essay paper, *The Monitor, or British Freeholder*, established in 1755 under the patronage of West India merchant and City Alderman William Beckford, a paper to which Shebbeare was initially, and for a short time, a contributor.

In the later 1750s the sharp upturn in British military fortunes, especially in North America, served temporarily to allay the revived concerns about Hanoverian influence. The popularity and military achievements of Britain's main continental ally, Frederick the Great – depicted in many sermons and certain sections of the press as a protestant hero – also helped to mute wider criticism of Britain's continental commitment. As the costs of the war mounted, however, and the commitment to the war in Germany escalated, so debate about how the war should be fought was firmly rejoined. The issue became entangled too in the question of what sort of peace Britain should impose on France, and whether pursuit of German interests would undermine potential Britain gains during the war, an issue which became more pressing after 1760 as the Prussian military position deteriorated. Already in 1758, several voices were raising the possibility that at a future peace Britain would be forced to relinquish, as it had in 1748, Cape Breton, which it had just retaken from the French; the difference this time would be that it would not be to secure a British strategic interest, the Low Countries, but for the sake

---

[74] Horace Walpole to Henry Seymour Conway, 13 October 1757, quoted in Rogers, *Whigs and cities*, pp. 108–9.
[75] For a similar interpretation, see Rogers, *Whigs and cities*, especially ch. 3; Marie Peters, *Pitt and popularity*, *passim*; and, more recently, M. John Cardwell, *Arts and arms: literature, politics and patriotism during the Seven Years War* (Manchester, 2004), especially p. 118.

of Hanover.[76] Alluding to a similar possibility in relation to Quebec in the following year, Lord Chesterfield declared: 'God knows what consequences such a measure may produce; the germ of discontent is already great upon the bare supposition of the case; but should it be realised, it will grow to a harvest of disaffection.'[77]

The most influential contribution to these growing exchanges, and growing public disenchantment with the continental dimension to the war, was Mauduit's *Considerations on the present German war*, which appeared in November 1760. There were several aspects to his case against the German war, including a lengthy refutation of the notion that Britain had any duty or need to defend Hanover militarily. In Mauduit's eyes, British support for Prussia was simply fuelling civil war in Germany at great financial and personal cost to Britain; the German war was not, contrary to what its supporters asserted, and as Pitt was to urge retrospectively in 1761, a diversion aiding Britain's war in America by tying up French resources in Europe. The burden of the criticism was one of futility as well as extravagance; unlike between 1689 and 1713, there was no balance of power to defend in Germany.[78] At bottom, however, the *Considerations* represented a forceful restatement of a long established argument for maritime war and disengagement from the continent, an argument which rested ultimately on a series of assertions about the superior efficacy of a 'blue-water' strategy. 'There is', one contemporary wrote, 'nothing new in the arguments the author employs but they are handled in a manner not unlikely to raise a flame among the vulgar and abet the prejudices of many.'[79] Mauduit's critics equally offered little or nothing that was new in debates about military strategy.[80] What took the heat out of this debate, and the renewed concern about German interests, was George III's and Bute's dislike of the German commitment and the ending of the Prussian subsidy in 1762. Although there continued to be some weak echoes of earlier debates on Hanoverian

---

[76] *Examination of a letter published under the name of L[ieutenan]t G[enera]l B[lig]h and addressed to the Hon. W[illia]m P[it]t, Esq.* (1758), p. 25; *The honest grief of a Tory, expressed in a genuine letter from a Burgess of ——— in Wiltshire to the author of the Monitor, February 17 1759* (1759), pp. 15–16.

[77] Quoted in E. J. S. Fraser, 'The Pitt-Newcastle coalition and the conduct of the Seven Years' War, 1757–1760' (unpublished DPhil thesis, University of Oxford, 1974), p. 288.

[78] See too on this, *Thoughts on the present war and future peace; wherein our present measures and alliances, are candidly considered* (1760), especially pp. 24–5, where the author recommended the exchange of Silesia for the Austrian Netherlands to reconcile Austria and Prussia as a 'check for the Future the overgrown Power of France'.

[79] Symmer to Andrew Mitchell, 28 November 1760, quoted in Schweizer, 'Foreign policy and the 18th century English press', p. 204.

[80] *A vindication of the conduct of the present war in a letter to ******* (1760); *A full and candid answer to a pamphlet entitled considerations on the present German war* (1760).

influence in the pamphlet exchanges on the issue of peace at the end of the war, these were mostly subordinate to more general press attacks on Pitt's 'Patriot' credentials following his resignation in 1761.[81] The main burden of the debate on the peace also lay elsewhere – on how best permanently to secure British interests and security against any revived French threat and not squander the unparalleled opportunity which appeared to exist at the end of the war for achieving British security and prosperity.[82]

Having traced in outline the main shifts in the level and direction of public and press concern under the first two Georges about the impact of Hanover and the Anglo-Hanoverian union on British interests, we now need to turn to examine more closely the nature of this concern. Several historians have emphasised the unsophisticated, overtly populist character of much anti-Hanoverian polemic.[83] At one level, this simply reflected general characteristics of public discussion of and attitudes towards foreign policy. Much public commentary on foreign policy in the early Hanoverian period was fiercely nationalistic in tone, and also infused with a profound sense of national entitlement to international significance and power. Sometime in the 1740s, the Frenchman, the Abbé le Blanc, encapsulated the imagined superiority (quite literally) which underpinned much opposition polemic, when he wrote: 'If you credit the English, both the empire of the seas, and the right of holding the balance of Europe equally belong to them; and in their pretensions at least you find a proof of their power.'[84] On the other hand, anti-Hanoverian comment was frequently especially crude.

A recurrent trope in anti-Hanoverian polemic was the supposed contrast between, on the one hand, British liberty, prosperity and strength and, on the other, Hanoverian poverty and insignificance. Anti-Hanoverian writers vied with one another to describe the Electorate in ever more disparaging terms; 'a spot of German Furze and Heath' was how one of them put it.[85] Jacobites had pioneered this typology of denigration, not least in popular ballads, around the time of the Hanoverian accession.[86] Such stereotyping is perhaps best seen less as evidence of xenophobic prejudice – although it was that – than as symptomatic of a recurrent sense of national destiny

---

[81] Cardwell, *Arts and arms*, ch. 10.

[82] [George Heathcote] *A letter to the Right Hon. The Lord Mayor of the City of London. From an old servant* (1762), pp. 75–6; *A letter to a member of the Honourable House of Commons, on the present important crisis of national affairs* (1762), pp. 39, 44.

[83] See e.g. Gibbs, 'English attitudes towards Hanover', especially p. 45; Pares, 'American versus continental warfare', *passim*.

[84] Le Blanc, *Letters on the English and French nations* (2 vols., 1747), I, pp. 2–3.

[85] *Westminster Journal*, 13 October 1744.

[86] See e.g. *A dialogue between the Old Black Horse at Charing Cross, and the new one, with a figure on it in H[anove]r Square* (n.d., 1714–15).

thwarted or denied. The vehemence with which Hanover was denigrated tended to reflect the uncertainty and alienation with which individuals and groups excluded from power viewed Britain's condition at certain moments.[87]

If a great deal of anti-Hanoverianism was, therefore, another manifestation of the deep-rooted prejudices of the British political nation in this period, and perhaps an equally pervasive and troubling uncertainty about the condition and prospects of society and the nation, the issue of Hanoverian influence was always more than simply one about Britain's international fortunes and destiny. There was a well-known constitutional reason for this. The Hanoverian title to the throne was created by the Act of Settlement (1701), which included clauses aimed specifically at preventing foreign influence from dictating British policy. One of these preventing monarchs from travelling abroad without the permission of parliament was repealed in deference to George I in 1716. Both George I and George II visited Hanover on a regular basis during most of their reigns. In periods when British interests were perceived to be under immediate threat, and even on occasion when they were not, such trips highlighted, or seemed to do, the monarchs' lack of paternal feeling for their subjects and their interests. In 1737, the Sardinian envoy, Ossorio, reported that the opposition were thinking of proposing a parliamentary ban on George II going abroad. The timing almost certainly reflected the anger felt when the king spent over half a year, from the summer of 1736 to early 1737 in Hanover. (It was widely rumoured that the reason for this was the charms of his new mistress, Madame Walmoden.)[88]

It was, however, a clause which went unrepealed, which talked of the monarch not fighting wars on behalf of foreign territories without parliamentary approval, referred to earlier in the context of debates about the acquisition of Bremen and Verden, which engendered most debate. To some extent, the exchanges were actually about something else; the supposed ineffectiveness of the Act of Settlement was used to imply or assert the wider threat to British liberties associated with the corruption of parliament and politics under Hanoverian rule. 'These were the Articles', one writer declared, in a reference to both this and the clause banning the monarch from travelling abroad, 'which were calculated to preserve

---

[87] For a similar conclusion, made in a slightly different context, see Colley, *Captives*, p. 105, where she writes that such prejudices were as much a 'defence mechanism as an expression of serene superiority or considered aggression'.

[88] I owe the information on Ossorio to transcripts of his reports, held in the Archivio di Stato in Turin, made by Professor Jeremy Black. A parliamentary ban on royal travel was a political tactic or necessity which was also discussed in print in the early 1740s (*Westminster Journal*, 17 September, 13 November, 19 November, 24 December 1743).

British liberties and on the keeping of which the present glorious and august Family accepted the Throne.'[89] It was a radical Whig line of attack which, as we have already seen, was appropriated by Jacobites. Yet the same clause also provided an essential point of reference in the broader debate about what the Anglo-Hanoverian union meant both generally and for British foreign policy in particular. On this last issue, positions could vary quite widely, but at bottom they resolved into two starkly opposed viewpoints. A common assertion in opposition propaganda was that the meaning of the clause was simply that British and Hanoverian interests should and could be kept completely separate. 'The Act of Settlement', declared one pamphleteer, 'absolutely forbids our interfering upon any pretence whatever, with, or for H[anover].'[90] Such comments might well be seen as further evidence of a lack of realism which accompanied much of the debate about the role of Hanover and Hanoverian interests. As Richard Pares pointed out quite a few years ago now, the Act did not envisage or clarify responsibilities in circumstances where, as in 1741, Hanover found itself menaced because of its union with Britain and British policies and interests.[91] Supporters of ministers and the court urged that the clause did not disallow British action on behalf of Hanover, but that this simply required parliamentary sanction. As one of them urged, answering directly those who read the Act in a narrow contractual manner, the 'fundamentality' lay exactly in the words 'without parliamentary sanction'.[92]

Domestic divisions and concerns impinged on debates about Hanoverian influence in several other ways. Some public criticism of Hanover was principally factious in motivation. This was especially true of the opposition Whigs of the early 1740s. Their main vehicle in the press, apart from a series of important pamphlets, was the weekly paper, *Old England or the Constitutional Journal*, founded in the spring of 1743. The paper's anti-Hanoverianism was outspoken, populist and often savage, and it was little wonder that ministerial supporters depicted the contents of the paper as outright Jacobitism.[93] In reality, its stance was a radical or real Whig one, a stance often indistinguishable from Jacobitism. In late 1743, pleading the ineffectiveness of constitutional restraints on monarchical powers of making war and peace and treaty making, recalling the Exclusion Bills and heroic spirit of an earlier generation of

---

[89] *Westminster Journal*, 5 March 1743. [90] *The late minister unmask'd* (1742), pp. 15–16.
[91] Pares, 'American versus continental warfare', p. 447.
[92] *The occasional patriot, or an enquiry into the present connections of Great Britain with the continent* (1756), pp. 27–8.
[93] Public Record Office of Northern Ireland, T 3158, transcripts of Chatworth MS, 251, Hartington to Devonshire, 10 November 1743.

Whigs, one of the paper's writers urged the necessity of dissolving the Anglo-Hanoverian union; the alternative was poverty, international insignificance, and loss of liberty.[94] The insults supposedly heaped on British soldiers during the military campaign of 1743 were depicted as part of a wider campaign to suppress English liberties and public spirit.[95] It was an allegation which, according to the Jacobite Thomas Carte, had made Sir John St Aubyn, who made it in the course of a Commons debate on the Hanoverian troops, the 'darling toast of the City of London'.[96]

Similar lines of argument surfaced in the middle of the following decade in the anti-Hanoverian writings of Shebbeare and several other Tory patriots. The burden of complaint was not so much Hanoverian influence on the conduct of foreign policy, although that was an important dimension, but the impact of Hanoverian rule and policies on liberty and national spirit. The Game Laws, lack of a militia (before 1757), and introduction of German, including Hanoverian, troops into Britain were portrayed as aspects of a wider assault on English liberties and, as importantly, the public spirit which sustained and perpetuated them. Shebbeare, who portrayed Whig oligarchy as a system of tyranny more menacing than anything attempted under the Stuarts, was accused by one critic of 'senseless and virulent Jacobitism'.[97] In his *A third letter to the people of England*, published in 1756, he appeared to suggest that the Hanoverian troops brought over to England during the invasion scare of the spring of 1756 represented a greater threat to English liberties than catholic troops had done in the final months of James II's reign.[98] The obvious implication of such views was that if a revolution had been justified in 1688, then it was also legitimate under present conditions. In the infamous *Sixth letter*, published in the following year, he rehearsed criticisms of policy and politics under George I which had been aired by Earberry in 1722 and more recently in a series of pamphlets on the Hanoverian troops taken into British pay in 1742 by Chesterfield and Waller in the previous decade. British policy and interests had been subordinated to Hanoverian aggrandisement; British wealth and

---

[94] *Old England Journal*, 3 December 1743.
[95] *Old England Journal*, 12, 19 November, 3 December 1743.
[96] Quoted in Linda Colley, 'Eighteenth-century radicalism before Wilkes', *Transactions of the Royal Historical Society* fifth series, XXXI (1981), 8.
[97] *Fourth letter to the people of England* (1756), p. 7. See too, for similar accusations, *An answer to a pamphlet called a third letter to the people of England* (1756), p. 13; *A letter of consolation to Dr Shebbeare* (1758).
[98] *A third letter to the people of England on liberty, taxes, and the application of public money* (1756), pp. 14–15.

prosperity were depleted to secure this end. What was singular, however, was the question his reasoning provoked him into asking:

> What Evils a Stuart on the Throne of England would have produced, can be but a speculative Consideration at present; however, it may be perfectly discerned what are the Blessings which came with a North-East Wind from Germany, and the Effects of them were never more conspicuous than at this unparallel'd Moment.[99]

The possible meanings existed in the gap between what was said and implied, in what might be described as a 'conspiracy of meaning' between Shebbeare and his readers.

We might easily conclude, therefore, along with Dann and others, that anti-Hanoverianism had little or nothing to do with any real appreciation of the role of and dangers confronting Hanover, or indeed the dilemmas which faced ministers in the conduct of foreign policy created by the Anglo-Hanoverian union. Press interest in the issue was notably selective. Tensions, for example, between Hanoverian and British interests regarding policy towards Prussia in the later 1740s, went unremarked, as did many other aspects of policy where Hanoverian interests did have a direct and important bearing. Attacks were not based on real knowledge of the Electorate or its policies, but derived from a series of frameworks which were expressions of domestic political divisions and ideological traditions, some of which can be traced back to William III's reign and criticism of the 'Dutchifying' of Britain, as the popular lecturer Orator Henley once put it.[100] The question we need to ask, however, is a somewhat different one. The salient issue is why many contemporaries were so ready at certain moments to believe Hanoverian influence was damaging British interests overseas; it is to this question that this paper now turns.

Part of the explanation is again domestic in origin – the political sensitivity which surrounded Britain's relationship to the continent. To a considerable degree, the question of Hanoverian influence was, as already alluded to in several places, subordinate to this wider issue. The immediate points to be made here are twofold. First, the British in this period continued to see themselves as inhabitants of a state whose destiny, continued independence, and prosperity were principally determined by developments in Europe. Recent work on empire and its

---

[99] *A sixth letter to the people of England on the progress of national ruin: in which it is shewn, that the present grandeur of France, and calamities of this nation, are owing to the influence of Hanover on the councils of England* (1757), p. 38. Evidently, some ministerial supporters thought Chesterfield and Waller were implying the same thing in their pamphlets of the early 1740s. See especially William Hay's journal for 10 December 1742, in Taylor and Jones, eds., *Tory and Whig*, p. 186.

[100] BL, Add. Mss., 19,920, fol. 153.

importance in forging a sense of national identity in eighteenth-century Britain has tended to detract from this basic observation. As David Armitage has recently stressed, notions of empire, in any case, are better seen in terms of ideology rather than identity.[101] Even more significantly in the present context, what is striking is just how far most British people appear to have viewed the national interest in terms primarily of European power politics and rivalries. This remained true until relatively late – one could argue until the French reminded the British that they had an American empire, and of its potential strategic importance in the later 1740s and early 1750s.[102]

Secondly, isolationism was the natural instinct of Tory and much popular opinion, although this could be overridden, at least in the short term, by military success, as occurred, for example, briefly in 1743 after Dettingen or in the later 1750s amongst some Tory supporters of Pitt. The Augustan Tory party also bequeathed to the early-Hanoverian 'Country' opposition a deep-rooted suspicion of interventionist policies as serving primarily domestic political ends.[103] The move from arguing that interventionism was an instrument of corruption to its subserving Hanoverian goals was a relatively easy one to make. It was, for example, a prominent feature of Shebbeare's political writing, although in his case this was aided by an unusually pronounced paranoid style of argument.

The threat Louis XIV's France had posed to European peace and stability also naturalised a way of perceiving and portraying the national interest in Britain which was to prove remarkably enduring. Most obviously, it created a view or conception of French power as the main threat to Britain and its interests and European stability. Even in the 1720s, when Austria and, to a lesser degree, Spain appeared to constitute the immediate threat to these things, contemporaries found it difficult to free themselves of this way of seeing things. It also stood in the way of them in responding flexibly both to fluctuating and longer-term shifts in diplomatic conditions. This, in turn, seems to have made it very difficult for people to appreciate Hanoverian vulnerability, especially during the mid-eighteenth century when the French threat re-emerged as, for the British, the pre-eminent issue in international politics. Appeals to

---

[101] David Armitage, *The ideological origins of the British empire* (Cambridge, 2000), especially p. 195.
[102] See Harris, *Politics and the nation*, ch. 3. See also Langford, *A polite and commercial people*, pp. 172–3; Colley, *Captives*, pp. 160–1, 167.
[103] The classic statement of the Tory view, Swift's *The case of the allies* (1711), was reprinted in 1748 as a contribution to debates about peace or war at the end of the War of the Austrian Succession.

German unity (potential as much as actual) as a bulwark against French designs, which featured in much opposition propaganda – it formed, for example, a key element in Mauduit's *Considerations* – are principally explicable in such terms; during the 1740s, moreover, a ready explanation for German disunity in the face of French aggression was available in the form of Hanoverian ambition. Austrian anger about the Prussian seizure of Silesia in 1741 was never really appreciated, even after the diplomatic revolution of 1756, tellingly (mis)described by one paper as a 'monstrous offspring', monstrous in the sense of being unnatural.[104]

If contemporaries were habituated, therefore, to thinking in terms of unchanging national interests, they were also very familiar with the notion of 'hidden springs' at work in international diplomacy. The origins of this tendency were various. At one level, it was a further facet of the deep vein of suspicion about ministerial motivations which pervaded opposition writing.[105] It was also a reflection again of how far debates on foreign affairs overlapped with debates on domestic policy. The distinction between the two is in any case ultimately unsustainable. As emphasised at several points in this paper, the opposition critique of foreign policy throughout this period was in part predicated on the assumption that under Whig oligarchy it had been made to serve private, domestic ends. The realities of diplomacy also worked, however, to encourage a notion of undeclared as opposed to public motives in foreign policy. Diplomacy could not by its nature be fully public; there was frequently a gap, therefore, between the real motives behind diplomatic agreements and what ministers chose to emphasise to win political and public support for them.[106] Secret negotiations and treaties were common features of diplomacy, such as the supposed secret articles of the Treaty of Vienna or George I's letter to Philip V of Spain in 1721 apparently promising to secure parliamentary consent to the return of Gibraltar to Spain.[107] There was in this context an obvious and evident tension between strengthening expectations of transparency, fostered by an expanding,

---

[104] *The Monitor*, 19 March 1757.

[105] This feature of the Patriot tradition in political writing has been emphasised by American historians studying the ideological origins of the American Revolution. See especially Gordon S. Wood, 'Rhetoric and reality in the American Revolution', *William and Mary Quarterly*, 3rd series, 23 (1966), 3–32; Wood, 'Conspiracy and the paranoid style: causality and deceit in the eighteenth century', *William and Mary Quarterly*, 3rd series, 39 (1982), 401–41.

[106] See Gibbs's comments on this in his 'Britain and the alliance of Hanover', especially p. 418.

[107] For George I and Gibraltar, see Ragnhild Hatton, *George I* (2001 edn), pp. 228, 277. The secret articles of the Vienna treaty formed a key plank in ministerial defences of their response to it – the Treaty of Hanover.

politically involved press, both domestic and international, and foreign policy and war as aspects of royal prerogative. Because of this, and the effects it had on the information available to illuminate foreign affairs, contemporaries were usually forced to construct explanations for events with only partial information. This, however, only emphasised the scope which existed for speculation or, to view it more charitably, deductive reasoning in this sphere.

There was also an important, often neglected and little researched international dimension to public debate about foreign policy in this period. Domestic debates on international politics were linked to a wider international public sphere of discussion about foreign policy which emerged in the seventeenth century and which continued to develop thereafter. It was a sphere structured by a range of publishing practices, such as having a work printed first in French or German and published or sold in the United Provinces, from where it was imported into England. It was through this route that some notably subversive works reached London, including, with reference to the main theme of this paper, Karl Ludwig von Pöllnitz's *Histoire secrette de la Duchesse d'Hanover, epouse de Georges Premier, roi de la Grande Bretagne*, a work which the Walpole ministry strove to prevent circulation of in 1732.[108] (An English translation appeared in 1743.) A crucial phase in the development of this international public sphere was the expulsion of the Huguenots from France in the 1680s, their subsequent diaspora and role as propagandists and brokers of information.[109] Diplomatic information and documents circulated in large quantities, often through international gazettes founded by Huguenot exiles and published in the United Provinces and elsewhere on the frontiers of France. British ministers frequently had cause to complain of information published in such sources. In 1728, for example, reports in the Hamburg press that George II did not oppose the Danish East India Company led to a formal representation to the Danish ministry. The British diplomatic representative at Copenhagen was instructed to wait 'on the Great Chancellor to let him know the evil tendency of printing such falsities, which, if spread here by ill-disposed persons, are enough to inflame the Parliament and the nation, as if the King were indifferent to a point which so nearly

---

[108] Jeremy Black, 'A failed attempt at censorship: the British diplomatic service and Pollnitz's *Histoire secrette de la Duchesse d'Hanover*', *Quaerends* 8 (1988), 211–17.
[109] Joseph Klaits, *Printed propaganda under Louis XIV* (Princeton, 1976); Elizabeth L. Eisenstein, *Grub Street abroad: aspects of the French cosmopolitan press from the age of Louis XIV to the French Revolution* (Oxford, 1992).

concerns the trade of his subjects'.[110] Through the medium of print, European governments also argued their case in front of the tribune of international public opinion. From one perspective, the famous 'Hague Letter' episode of 1731 was a symptom of this set of realities in that the conductors of the *Craftsman* were able to urge in their defence, albeit with no evident influence on the courts, the degree to which the second Treaty of Vienna was already public knowledge.[111]

Focusing more narrowly on the domestic sphere, it is also worth pointing out that the vast majority of pamphlets published on foreign policy issues in this period were not simply or even mainly populist in nature. Rather the reverse, for they were, in most cases, detailed, often quite lengthy, closely argued narratives which focused on facts, or what the authors took to be facts. They were also aimed as much at parliamentary as public opinion (however we might define the latter). The annual cycle of publication closely followed parliamentary sessions, and there are frequent examples of their having had a considerable influence on the terms of parliamentary debates.[112] Opposition writers especially commonly made exaggerated claims, but they were not always wrong in their facts and they did not only appeal to prejudice. Even Pares, whose judgement of the quality of public debate on foreign affairs in this period is generally a strongly negative one, acknowledges that anti-Hanoverian propaganda was a mixture of '*true facts*' (my emphasis) and 'extraordinary rant'.[113]

What of the broader significance of debates about the role of Hanover and Hanoverian interests on British politics and interests during the early Hanoverian period? That they served to confirm the first two Georges' lack of apparent Britishness is obvious. This, in turn, powerfully inhibited, although it did not entirely prevent, the Hanoverian monarchy from exploiting the potential which existed for popular protestant monarchy in Britain in this period, a potential which, ironically given how events turned out, was momentarily glimpsed in the effusion of positive sentiment towards George II created by the initial news of the victory at Dettingen in 1743. On 24 June of that year, the duke of Newcastle wrote in a letter marked private to Lord Carteret, then in Germany with

---

[110] NA, SP 75/51, Lord Townshend to Johann Hermann, 7 May 1728, quoted in Jeremy Black, 'In search of a scandalous pamphlet: Sir Robert Walpole and the attempt to suppress the publication of opposition literature in the united provinces', *Publishing History* 25 (1989), 6.

[111] *Craftsman*, 30 January 1731.

[112] See emphasis given to this in Schweizer, 'Foreign policy and the 18th century English press', *passim*.

[113] Pares, 'American versus continental warfare'.

George II: 'It is impossible to describe the General satisfaction, and joy, that appear everywhere, and what particularly affects all honest men, is the share, the King has personally had in this great Action.' Tellingly, the opposition in the autumn of 1743 sought to spread rumours that George II had not been present at the battle.[114] There is plenty of evidence for the unpopularity of both George I and II, often at quite low social levels. The conviction or suspicion that their monarchs lacked paternal feeling for their subjects appears to have been a powerful contributory factor to this.[115] That this did not become a more powerful nutrient of Jacobitism was only owing to the Stuarts' and Stuart court's own suspect Britishness, although some interesting efforts were made to counteract this in Jacobite propaganda.[116]

Viewed from a longer-term perspective, criticism of Hanoverian influence reinforced the long-term process by which the office of monarchy in Britain (and indeed Europe) came to be seen as separate from the person of the monarch, a process which French historians describe as the 'de-sacralisation' of monarchy.[117] Ironically, in Britain, it was the legitimist cause, Jacobitism, a cause which came increasingly from the early 1720s to wear a republican mask, which played an important role in this process. During the Hanoverian regime's greatest crisis – the Jacobite rebellion of 1745–6 – the burden of the defence was, first, the record of the Hanoverians in protecting and promoting British liberties, Protestantism and prosperity and, secondly, that their elevation to the throne had been determined by the object of securing these ends. The Hanoverian monarchy was pre-eminently a monarchy which existed for the 'public good', and on such terms it was to be judged. As one Whig urged in 1718, 'they [the Hanoverian dynasty] can plead nothing for what they enjoy or claim, but by fundamental and positive laws'. The same writer also pointed out that 'the subject's interest in his Liberty and Property is conveyed unto him

---

[114] These rumours seem to have been quite widely circulated by opponents of the ministry and the Hanoverian regime after the battle, for which see the comments of William Hay on the eve of the parliamentary session of 1743–4 in Taylor and Jones, eds., *Tory and Whig*, p. 188.

[115] See *Lord Hervey's Memoirs*, II, p. 223, for comment on public hostility to George II when he was caught in a storm returning from the Electorate in the summer of 1737. See too Philip Woodfine, *Britannia's glories: the Walpole ministry and the 1739 war with Spain* (Woodbridge, 1998), pp. 129–30.

[116] See e.g. *An authentick account of the conduct of the young chevalier, from his first arrival in Paris, after his defeat at Culloden, to the conclusion of the Peace of Aix-La-Chapelle* (1749), which asserted that it was in France's interest to ensure that there was not a Stuart restoration, and which also sought to demonstrate the Young Pretender's identification with English interests, reputation and honour.

[117] See e.g. Roger Chartier, *The cultural origins of the French Revolution* (Durham, NC, 1991), ch. 6.

by the same Terms and Channels, and fenc'd unto him with the same Hedges and Pales'.[118] This conviction or political doctrine, as we might call it, was the reason why defence of the Anglo-Hanoverian union could, on occasion, prove so problematic for Whig ministers.

Anti-Hanoverian feeling was not always what it seemed, and, as we have seen, on occasion it was undoubtedly stirred up for factious motives. Yet what may be of surprise here is not that Jacobites were responsible for some important anti-Hanoverian writing, but that they were, after the early 1720s, not responsible for more, although this reflects the wider collapse of a popular Jacobite press in the early 1720s.[119] The imagery of disparagement exploited in attacks on Hanover and Hanoverian influence was very often, so far as its genealogy is traceable, Jacobite in origin, but by the mid-century most anti-Hanoverian writers were not supporters of the Stuarts. There were exceptions, although they were relatively few in number, as I have argued elsewhere.[120] There may be other examples still to be discovered. A cheap ballad attacking the Hanoverian neutrality of 1741 which is undoubtedly of Jacobite inspiration and provenance survives, for example, in the special collections of the St Andrews University Library.[121] Shebbeare may be an exception too, although he, like many others in the mid-1750s, and notwithstanding his 'conspiracies of meanings', was able to invest great hopes for political renovation in Pitt the Elder. At the accession of George III, he transferred very readily his wider hopes for national revival on to the new king, whom he hailed as a true patriot monarch.[122] In the early 1740s, it was opposition Whigs who produced the most vehement and outspoken attacks on Hanoverian influence, attacks which, as mentioned at the outset of this paper, helped fuel yet another surge of optimism amongst Jacobites, already buoyed up by the war in Europe and the potential for Jacobite meddling in European power politics which this created. In the event, such hopes were misconceived in that the beliefs and prejudices which fed opposition to and suspicion about Hanoverian influence could just as well be mobilised in opposition to the Jacobite cause. This, after all, was exactly what did happen in 1745–6.

---

[118] *The juncture: or considerations on His Majesty's speech*, p. 27.
[119] See especially Paul Chapman, 'Jacobite political argument, 1714–1766' (unpublished PhD thesis, Cambridge University, 1983).
[120] See the comments on this, in my *Politics and the Nation*, pp. 38–40.
[121] *A Poem* (1742) [Typ. BG D45XC, 199,723]. This sold at 1d.
[122] Margaret Avery, 'Toryism in the age of the American Revolution: John Lind and John Shebbeare', *Historical Studies* 18 (1978), 24–36.

10 Dynastic perspectives

Clarissa Campbell Orr

I

The Anglo-Hanoverian connection began partly, and ended solely, for dynastic reasons. After the Glorious Revolution Britain needed to preserve the protestant succession, the new parliamentary constitution, and strategic alliances against French support for the Jacobite claims. The failure of the protestant Stuart line in 1701 led to the succession being vested in the granddaughter of James I, Sophia, Dowager Electress of Hanover, and her protestant descendants. As well as these dynastic links, Hanover had been part of the grand alliance formed against France in 1689, and again during the War of the Spanish Succession. The link came to an end because Hanoverian succession law, favouring male over female descent wherever possible, meant the claims of Queen Victoria's oldest uncle Ernest duke of Cumberland took precedence there when she ascended the British throne. Political and strategic considerations were not significant: this was purely a family matter.

How can dynastic perspectives suggest an agenda for contemporary historical research? It is not a concept which has received much recent attention by academic Anglo-American historians dealing with the long eighteenth century, and there is virtually no recent historiography devoted to it, though it has been an integral strand to the revival of interest

---

I am grateful to the Central Fund for Sabbaticals at Anglia Ruskin University, under whose auspices research for this chapter was completed, and to Séan Lang, Alison Ainley and Rohan McWilliam for taking over my teaching and administrative responsibilities so cheerfully. I am also immensely appreciative of the advice and comments of the editors, of my fellow-contributors, Thomas Biskup, Andrew Thompson and Hamish Scott – who also guided me to the relevant papers in the National Archives Kew (NA) and British Library on the Bavarian issue – together with those of Nigel Aston, Andrew Hanham, Veronica Baker-Smith and Tim Blanning. Derek Beales encouraged me to look at Frederick the Great in his own words, and Peter Wilson added insights from his encyclopaedic knowledge of the *Reich*. More distantly I must thank Graham O'Neil and Jarl Kreimeier for introducing me to the eighteenth-century architectural legacy of the Holy Roman Empire, a wonderful stimulus for understanding its dynastic and political particularity. Genealogies have been consulted in *Europäische Stammtafeln, Neue Folge*, Band I: *Die Deutschen Staaten*, Marburg, 1980.

in court studies since the mid-1990s.[1] Of course dynasticism has to be invoked to explain the composition of states such as the Habsburg Monarchy, or the background to the War of the Spanish Succession: but the tendency in mainstream works is to define it in a limited, instrumentalist way, centred on an individual male ruler, with little attention to his family and related dynastic links, or sympathy for the dynastic mindset.[2] Herbert Rowen's 1980 essay on proprietary dynasticism suggested it needed exploring in the Enlightenment, even though criticism of the concept became increasingly voiced, but his suggestion has not been systematically followed up. Historians have tended instead to concentrate on the changes brought about in the course of the century, rather than on continuities.[3] The outstanding exception to this is Peter Wilson's subtle evaluation of competing strategic and dynastic elements in *Reich* princely politics.[4] While pinpointing at what point in the later part of the eighteenth century the European dynastic state gave way to the modern one is beyond the scope of this essay, it does suggest the continuing salience of dynastic thinking and motivation.

There are at least three principal, interrelated ways to consider dynastic perspectives. First, there is the sense in which individual rulers need to be considered in the light of their dynasty, conceived not just biographically, but as part of a dynastic system and project to advance their status and protect their interests; in short, as a particular kind of family business. Ragnhild Hatton's biography of George I is a model of this dynastic understanding.[5] Accruing territory came about partly through dynastic means; marriage into a family might mean, eventually, a fortunate inheritance, as the examples of Habsburgs and Hohenzollerns attest. These perspectives emerge strongly in some of the essays in *Royal and republican sovereignty in early modern Europe*.[6]

---

[1] Hamish Scott, *The emergence of the eastern powers 1756–1775*, Oxford 2001 and Jeremy Black, *Kings, nobles and commoners: states and societies in early modern Europe: a revisionist history* (London, 2004), especially p. 68, integrate dynastic perspectives much more into international relations and the nature of the European state, building on their earlier work where the concept of the nation-state still lingered.

[2] Anthony Upton, *Europe 1600–1789* (London, 2001), p. 328, typifies this with his definition of 'dynastic competition [exerting] its murderous imperative over rulers'.

[3] Herbert H. Rowen, *The king's state, proprietary dynasticism in early modern France* (New Brunswick, NJ, 1980). James J. Sheehan, *German history 1770–1866* (Oxford 1989), discusses the spectrum of *Herrschaft* from modest seigneur to grand prince but is more interested in defining the forces making for change than examining the continuing salience of courts and dynasties in the second half of the eighteenth century. I would argue for the persistence of the dynastic mentality alongside enlightened state-building.

[4] Peter Wilson, *German armies: war and German politics 1648–1806* (London, 1998).

[5] Ragnhild Hatton, *George I, elector and king* (London 1978).

[6] G. C. Gibbs, R. Oresko and H. M. Scott, eds., *Royal and republican sovereignty in early modern Europe* (Cambridge,1997), especially essays by Robert Oresko and Rohan Butler.

Considering the dynastic strategy of a ruler has several useful consequences. One is that it necessitates a polycentric approach, a look at both the ruler and his – occasionally her – consort, but also his siblings, parents and children and their respective marriage partners. What provision does the head of the family make for second sons and younger brothers? As well as formal secundigenitures, these males can occupy important military or ecclesiastical positions; for German princes the institutions of the *Reich* were especially useful in providing niches. In turn this means looking at both female as well as male members of a ruling dynasty and their respective roles and functions. As well as the dynastic capital a consort brings, the enquiry can broaden into looking at her representational role, cultural contribution, her success or failure in producing living heirs and spares, in educating and marrying them.[7] The consort may have a crucial role as Regent when an heir is under age, or the ruler ill or absent: Caroline of Ansbach was Regent for George II during his visits to Hanover. A consort can enhance the moral or religious reputation of a dynasty; conversely, her misconduct can damage its reputation. Male adultery had less damaging consequences morally but a powerful mistress or an ambitious morganatic wife could create a damaging court faction.[8]

Secondly, looking at dynasties reinforces the contingency of history. The biological accident of a failure of an heir can have massive implications for the success of a state and for its international relations. This is an obvious truism for the eighteenth century when so many wars – of the British, Spanish, Austrian and Bavarian succession – were fought at least ostensibly over dynastic inheritances. The Bavarian succession claims show clearly the extent to which the eighteenth-century Electorate was scarcely a state, more a congeries of feudal entitlements, and suggest how uneven was the evolution of hereditary dynastic possessions into a modern state before the end of the *Reich* in 1806. The composition of the Electorate of Hanover as a series of hereditary duchies interrupted territorially by the lands of the elder branch of the dynasty in Brunswick-Wolfenbüttel was typical of the component parts of the Holy Roman Empire. Mark Greengrass's anthology on the composite states of the seventeenth century stresses their character as a composite legal entity, a perspective that needs following through into the eighteenth,

---

[7] T. C. W. Blanning, *The culture of power and the power of culture, old regime Europe 1660–1789* (Oxford, 2002), briefly examines electoral Saxony's dynastic strategy in order to explore its consequent representational strategy, his main focus: pp. 62–3.
[8] These issues form the substance of C. Campbell Orr, ed., *Queenship in Europe 1660–1815: the role of the consort* (Cambridge, 2004).

notwithstanding the growth of more formal institutions of bureaucracy, revenue raising and military organisation.[9]

Dynastic marriages served diplomatic purposes, by cementing new alliances or maintaining them in good order. It can therefore be equally important to know the marriages which were planned but never took place as well as those that did. For a consort, the important issue is how far she adopts her marital court as the primary locus of her interest, and how far she is supposed by her parental family to represent their interests. Marie Antoinette was supposed to represent Austrian interests at Versailles after the Diplomatic Revolution created the Franco-Austrian alliance in 1756.[10] Frederick the Great's minister Count Finckenstein accounted for his master's rejection of French overtures in March 1778, by explaining to the British ambassador that 'the King of Prussia could place very little confidence in that Court, while the Emperor's sister was upon the throne, at the head of a powerful party attached to the House of Austria'.[11]

Thirdly, insofar as the ruler and his court is the pinnacle of society, exploring dynastic perspectives can also enable us to see how far the court is successful at managing crown–elite relations and integrating elites from different constituent parts of a dynastic state.[12] The polycentric character of courts means that more household positions are potentially available to give to diverse members of these elites to increase these integrative functions. The further implication is that we need to consider how far dynastic thinking permeates society, creating generations of court and office holders in service to a particular monarch.[13] There is much more work to do in looking horizontally and vertically at family networks, to incorporate both a gendered and a comparative European perspective to this. The anatomy of female participation in ancien régime British politics offered by Anna Clark, Judith S. Lewis, Elaine Chalus and Naomi Tadmor constitutes a major reinterpretation integrating gender and dynasties for

---

[9] Mark Greengrass, ed., *Conquest and coalescence* (London, 1991).
[10] Thomas Kaiser, 'Who's afraid of Marie Antoinette? Diplomacy, Austrophobia and the queen', *French History* 14, 3 (2000), 241–71.
[11] NA, SP 90/102, Hugh Elliott to the Earl of Suffolk, 28 March 1778.
[12] This is of course the major theme of R. J. W. Evans, *The making of the Habsburg monarchy, 1550–1700* (Oxford, 1979). The Habsburg situation is often seen as an exception within Europe, because of its obvious character as a dynastic agglomeration, whereas it may be more likely that most states only differed in degree, not kind, from the Habsburg monarchy, as French historians such as Mettam are beginning to suggest.
[13] For British history, the *History of parliament* and R. O. Bucholz and J. C. Sainty, *Officials of the royal household 1660–1837* (2 vols., London, 1997) are available as prosopographical tools.

Britain,[14] while Lawrence Baack has evaluated the Bernstorffs of Hanover who also served in Denmark.[15] Thomas Biskup's chapter shows the importance of scholarly and clerical dynasties.

Because of Britain's own historiographical tradition of English exceptionalism, institutionalised within most university history departments where there are historians of Britain (sometimes only of England) as distinct from historians of Europe, most thinking about the nature of the eighteenth-century British state has stayed within an insular context.[16] Jonathan Clark's interventions, for instance, have provoked debate on Britain's character as an ancien régime, but this has not involved any European comparative element; neither examination of dynasty, nor court. Comparisons have been more thoroughly pursued along the Atlantic axis.[17]

In what follows I want to suggest how the revival of interest in dynastic perspectives and court studies can add to our understanding of how the Hanoverian electors, in conjunction with their consorts, juggled their multiple roles as kings of Great Britain, German territorial princes, and members of the Holy Roman Empire, and how the union coincided with or diverged from their usual marriage strategies. In particular I will suggest how dynastic perspectives shed some new light on the Bavarian War of Succession, and the increasing rapprochement between George III and 'his Prussian majesty' during the early years of the American War of Independence, even though the king's British imperial role was of paramount importance and his attention to German matters was relatively

---

[14] Anna Clark, *Scandal: The sexual politics of the British constitution* (Princeton and London, 2004); Judith S. Lewis, *Sacred to female patriotism* (London, 2003); Elaine Chalus, *Elite women in English political life c. 1754–1790* (Oxford, 2005); Naomi Tadmor, *Family and friends in eighteenth century England: household, kinship and patronage* (Cambridge, 2001). Architectural historians often shed light on family strategy over the long term in studying the physical headquarters of a family.

[15] Lawrence J. Baack, 'State service in the eighteenth century: the Bernstorffs in Hanover and Denmark', *The International History Review* 1, 3 (1979), 323–43; John Rogister, 'Queen Marie Leszczynska and faction at the French court' in *Queenship in Europe*, illustrates dynastic office-holding in the queen's household; Edgar Melton, 'The Prussian Junkers' in: H. M. Scott, ed., *The European nobilities*, vol. II (London 1995), discusses Prussian service traditions among the nobility. Architectural historians often shed light on family strategy over the long term in studying the physical headquarters of a family; see John Martin Robinson, *Temples of delight: Stowe landscape gardens* (London 1990), as well as John Beckett's political and social study, *The rise and fall of the Grenvilles, Dukes of Buckingham and Chandos* (Manchester, 1994).

[16] Exceptions include the historians Derek Jarrett, Nicholas Henshall, Jeremy Black and Nigel Aston.

[17] J. C. D. Clark, *English Society 1660–1832, religion, ideology and politics during the ancien régime* (2nd edn, Cambridge, 2000). Clark has also edited the *Memoirs and speeches of James, 2nd Earl of Waldegrave* (Cambridge 1988).

limited. This draws on the published correspondence of George III, in conjunction with the manuscript correspondence of his wife, Charlotte of Mecklenburg-Strelitz, with her brother Charles; on state foreign office papers; on letters between British diplomats, and on the published correspondence of William IV of Orange and Frederick the Great of Prussia.

II

The marriage strategies of the House of Brunswick-Lüneburg were already determined before it became apparent that the last protestant Stuart, Queen Anne, would have no surviving heirs. The 1701 Act of Succession came after a lengthy period when the dynasty had concentrated its efforts into creating primogeniture, streamlining four duchies into one, and attaining electoral status.[18] Its marriage policy must therefore be seen in the context of a fluid familial and territorial situation, and also that of the ambitions of the other two protestant Electorates of the Holy Roman Empire, Saxony and Brandenburg, who could provide suitable marriage partners but were also competing in the same dynastic pool. This included the senior branch of the House of Guelph, that of Brunswick-Wolfenbüttel, who resented Hanover's elevation to the Electorate, the dukes of Mecklenburg, the dukes and landgraves of Hesse, and, both within and outside the empire, various branches of the Holstein-Gottorp dynasty in Denmark and in Schleswig-Holstein. The decision of Augustus II of Saxony to convert to Catholicism in 1697 in order to become king of Poland restricted the dynastic pool for the protestant Guelphs and Hohenzollerns to the lesser Saxon duchies in the non-electoral, Ernestine line, while the now catholic Wettins were able to marry into the French and Habsburg royal houses and attain catholic prince-bishoprics.[19] This interlinking of three catholic dynasties created a competitive catholic phalanx claiming the Bavarian lands after the electoral line failed in 1777. The three ambitious Electorates needed the cooperation and approval of the Holy Roman Emperor, if new titles were to be recognised or inheritance rights modified: each was able to attain a royal crown, or the prospect of one, between 1697 and 1701. Furthermore, the catholic conversion of the Saxons left the Electorates of Hanover and Brandenburg competing for leadership of the Corpus

---

[18] My account relies on Hatton, *George I*, ch. 2. See also George Schnath, *Geschichte Hannovers im Zeitalter der neunten Kur und der englischen Sukzession 1674–1714* (5 vols., Hildesheim, 1938–82).

[19] Helen Watanabe-O'Kelly, 'Religion and the consort: two electresses of Saxony and queens of Poland (1697–1757)' in Campbell Orr (ed.), *Queenship in Europe*, pp. 252–75.

Evangelicorum, just when Britain's own protestant succession was in need of protection. Dynastically then the Hanoverians had to plan and act, as it were, in three dimensions – as Hanoverian electors, building up their territories and consolidating their *Landeshoheit*; as imperial princes, consolidating their status as electors within the *Reich*, their strategic links within the evangelical union and with other princes, and dealing with their rivals; and as British monarchs ruling three imperfectly integrated kingdoms.

The marriage strategies of George I's family were compatible with but not identical to those of the Stuarts, and like them they had rival catholic claimants: George I's brother Maximilian William converted, as did his uncle John Frederick. He married one daughter, Charlotte Felicitas, into the House of Modena, and the other, Wilhelmina Amelia to Joseph of Austria, Emperor 1705–11. The elder Brunswick-Wolfenbüttel line had one convert catholic ruler in the person of Anton Ulrich (sole ruler 1704–14), whose granddaughter Elisabeth-Christine also converted on her marriage to Archduke Charles, later Emperor Charles VI. Until 1706 this elder Brunswick line was not reconciled with the cadet branch over its primogeniture policy, but once achieved the reconciliation facilitated marriages between the two Guelph houses, especially as Anton Ulrich's conversion was not imitated by his successors.[20]

The Electorate's concentration of power in the hands of one ruling duke was personified in the marriage arrangements of George William and Ernest Augustus, who paired their children, respectively Sophia Dorothea and George (later Britain's George I). This was a marriage made to help electoral consolidation in 1682, when claims to the British throne were remote. The failure of this marriage at a personal level created the possibility that Sophia Dorothea would become a magnet for either Hanoverian or Jacobite reversionary claims, and her life was closely circumscribed. George's subsequent liaison with Melusine von der Schulenburg, almost certainly regulated by a morganatic but secret marriage which produced three 'nieces', meant the entourage he brought to England seemed decidedly strange: morganatic marriages were not practised in Britain. In terms of public court ceremonial he had no consort but appeared to have two mistresses – the second being his half-sister from his own father's morganatic marriage. When he quarrelled with his son George Augustus Prince of Wales the latter benefited from having a living wife and able political partner, Caroline of Brandenburg-Ansbach, who, with their children, was able to present a more 'normal'

---

[20] Wilson, *German Armies*, pp. 97–8, 163.

family pattern. These irregularities and quarrels hindered uncritical acceptance of the Brunswick-Lüneburgs as the new British monarchs.[21]

The attainment of electoral status had been achieved with the political support of the Brandenburg family. This was reflected in two generations of Hanover/Brandenburg–Prussian marriages: that of Sophia Charlotte, sister of George I, to Frederick, son of the 'Great Elector' and the first king in Prussia, and that of their children, the two cousins Sophia Dorothea of Hanover and Frederick William I of Brandenburg-Prussia (see Table 10.1).[22] The Hohenzollerns also had a pattern of marriage with the House of Orange, territorial neighbours of their duchies of Cleve and Mark, further facilitated by their common Calvinism.[23] The Great Elector was an uncle by marriage of William of Orange/William III; his grandmother and mother were also Dutch. From the British crown's side, the Stuarts had already made two Dutch marriages in the seventeenth century, those of Charles II's sister Mary and his niece Mary, co-ruler with William III after the Glorious Revolution. There was therefore a potentially useful three-way connection between Brunswick-Lüneburg in both its British and electoral capacity, to the Houses of Orange and Hohenzollern. However the Hohenzollerns until Frederick II were also aligned with France and then the emperor, a consequence of Brandenburg's precarious state after the Thirty Years War and its subsequent need for imperial recognition of the royal crown in Prussia. Their link to the Brunswick-Wolfenbüttel family branch, with its Habsburg marriage, was just as useful to them as any links to the Brunswick-Lüneburgs.

Hanoverian dynastic assets could sometimes be used to promote British foreign policy and vice versa; the link with the House of Orange would be repeated with the marriage of George II's daughter Anne to Stadholder William IV. In contrast, Stuart marriages with the Danish ruling family initially presented more of a problem for George as elector and designated heir to Queen Anne. Her husband was George of Denmark, but Hanover was allied with the dukes of Holstein, rivals to the royal Danish crown in the complicated territorial mix of the Schleswig-Hostein duchies. The Electorate was at war with Denmark in 1700. However Britain needed a Baltic ally to protect her naval supplies and after the Peace of Travendal knocked Denmark out of the Great Northern War and neutralised her conflict with the Electorate, it became

---

[21] Hatton, *George I*, chs. 2 and 5; and Andrew Hanham, 'Caroline of Brandenburg-Ansbach and the "Anglicisation" of the House of Hanover' in: Campbell Orr (ed.), *Queenship in Europe*, pp. 276–99.

[22] Melusine's family came from the Altmark, the core of Brandenburg, which also helped gain Hohenzollern support for electoral recognition: Hatton, *George I*, p. 48.

[23] They would inherit East Frisia and the enclave of Neuchâtel in Switzerland in 1744 through this connection.

easier to foster a British-Danish alliance. As for Hanover, once she had gained Bremen and Verden from Sweden, alliance with her former rival for this territory, the increasingly weaker Danish crown, gradually became feasible.[24] In 1743 George II married his daughter Louisa to Fredrik V of Denmark, where she became very popular;[25] at the time of her marriage there were commercial disputes with Britain, so it was actually more acceptable in electoral than British terms. Indeed, the marriage needs to be seen in the context of George II's search for continental allies after 1740 to act as a counterweight to Prussia. Frederick II's immediate attack on Silesia after inheriting the crown inaugurated his disturbance of the balance within the Holy Roman Empire. Moreover the Danes were not helpful allies against the Jacobite threat and accepted French subsidies to remain neutral.[26] This was also a link effected in spite of competition from the prolific Hohenzollerns, since Frederick II of Prussia was trying to marry one of his sisters to the Danish crown prince.[27] Stuart Anglo-Danish links had transmuted into useful Danish-Hanoverian ones.

Although George I's marriage had been made with electoral dynastic interests chiefly in mind, his son's marriage was made in the full knowledge that the dynastic union with Britain would be a reality. Recent appraisals by Hanham and Marschner have underlined the important role played by Caroline of Brandenburg-Ansbach as Princess of Wales and queen in 'anglicising' the Brunswick-Lüneburgs as a British dynasty. This process was reflected partly in Caroline's activities as a connoisseur, collector and bibliophile, where her acquisitions and arrangements were designed to create links back to the Stuart ancestry of Sophia, and even further, to the marriage of the great Brunswick Emperor Henry the Lion to the Plantagenet Princess, Matilda.[28] Indeed Caroline's dynastic career illustrates the importance of women as dynastic matchmakers, who could

---

[24] See Hatton, *George I*, idem, *Charles XII* (London, 1969), and John J. Murray, *George I, the Baltic, and the Whig Split of 1717* (Chicago and London, 1969).

[25] Michael Bregnsbo, 'Danish absolutism and queenship: Louisa, Caroline Matilda, and Juliana Maria', in *Queenship in Europe*, pp. 344–67.

[26] Veronica Baker-Smith, 'The daughters of George II' in: C. Campbell Orr, ed., *Queenship in Britain: royal patronage, court culture, and dynastic politics* (Manchester, 2002), p. 203; W. Mediger, 'Great Britain, Hanover and the rise of Prussia', in: R. Hatton and M. S. Anderson, eds., *Studies in diplomatic history* (London, 1970).

[27] Baker-Smith, 'Daughters', p. 200; Serge Rivière, ' "The Pallas of Stockholm": Louisa Ulrica of Prussia and the Swedish crown', in: Campbell Orr, ed., *Queenship in Europe*, pp. 322–43.

[28] Christine Gerrard, 'Queens-in-waiting: Caroline of Anspach and Augusta of Saxe-Gotha as Princesses of Wales', in: Campbell Orr, ed., *Queenship in Britain*, pp. 143–61; and Joanna Marschner, 'Caroline of Anspach and the European princely museum tradition', in *ibid.*, pp. 13–42. See also Hannah Smith, 'The idea of a protestant monarchy in Britain 1714–1760', *Past and Present* 185 (November, 2004), 91–11, and Stephen Taylor, 'Caroline ... queen of Great Britain and Ireland', *Oxford DNB* (2004).

222   Clarissa Campbell Orr

Table 10.1. *The House of Hohenzollern and its links to the House of Brunswick*

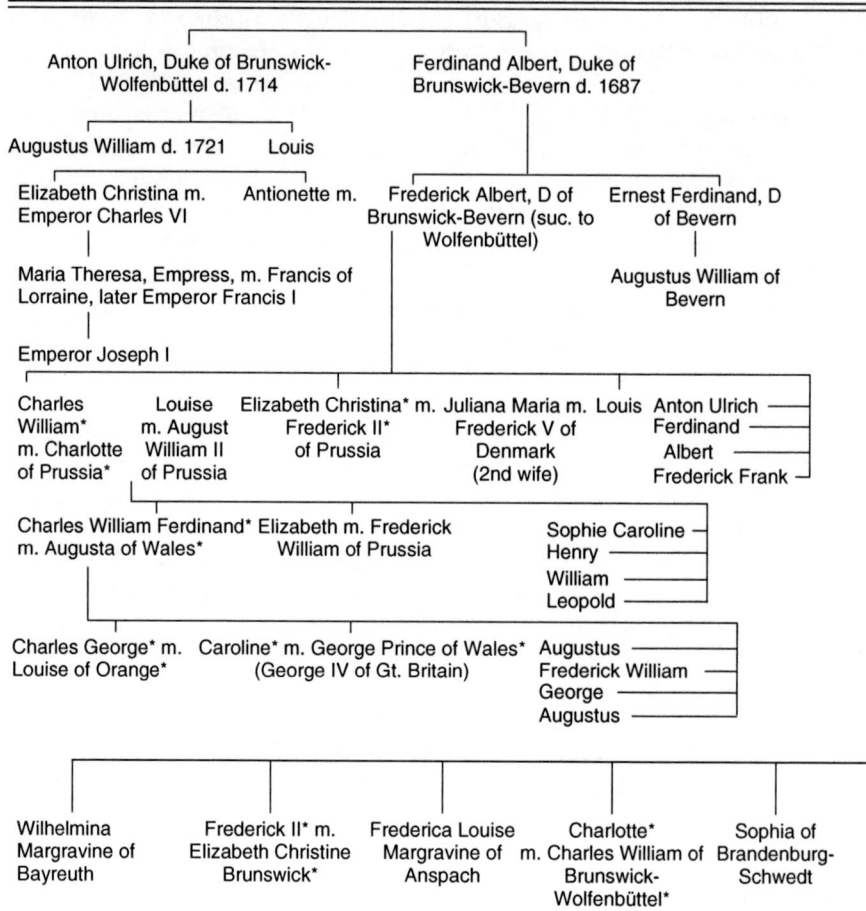

Note:
*Asterisk denotes people appearing twice.

Dynastic perspectives

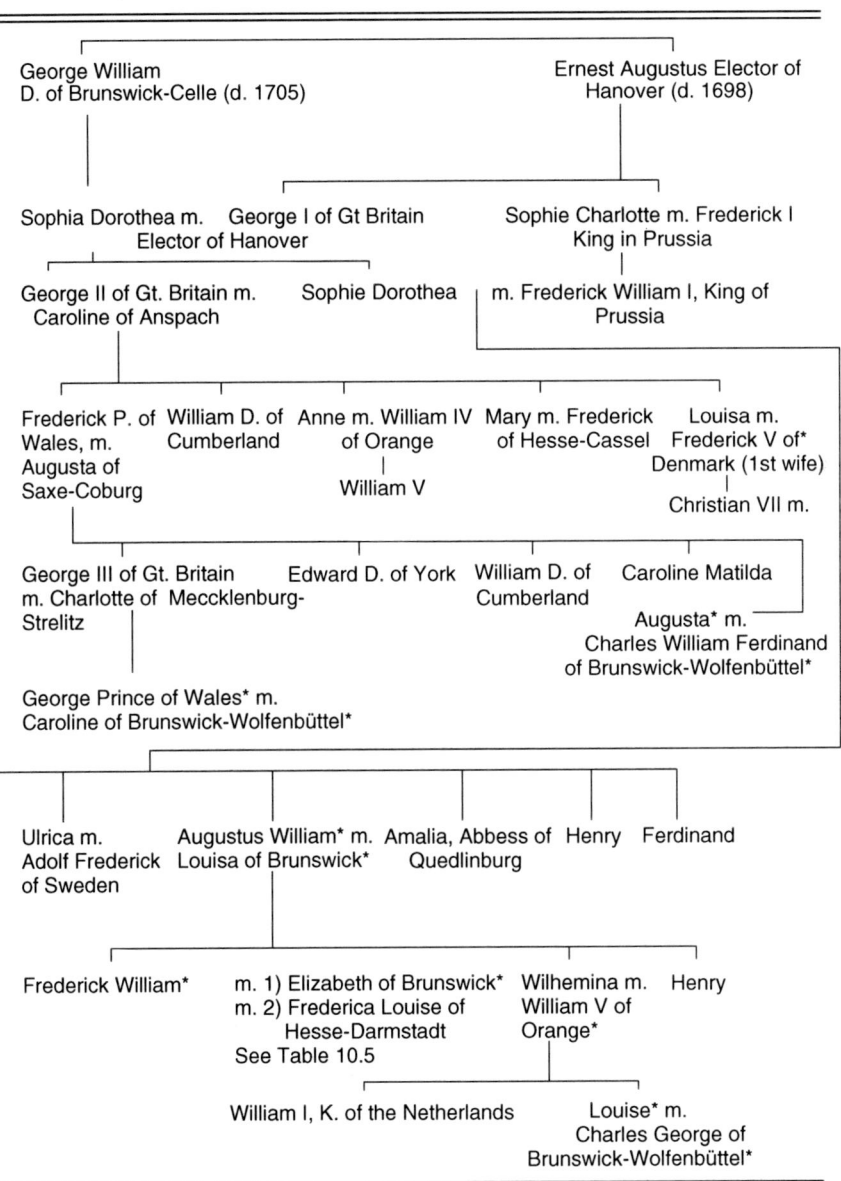

groom suitable princesses for the marriage market and show them how to assist in advancing the prestige and popular image of an upwardly mobile dynasty.[29] Caroline was of joint Saxon and Brandenburg descent; she therefore represented the third-generation Hanover-Brandenburg alliance. Her father, John Frederick Margrave of Brandenburg-Ansbach, was from a cadet branch of the Hohenzollerns; her mother, Eleonore of Saxe-Eisenach, married as her second husband Elector John George IV of Saxony. This was a protestant dynastic marriage designed to strengthen the coalition against Louis XIV, before the Saxon-Polish Personal Union dictated catholic conversion of John George's brother and heir. As an orphan, Caroline became the ward of George I's sister Sophia Charlotte, electress of Brandenburg and first queen in Prussia, and her husband Frederick I. Unlike either her step-uncle Augustus of Saxony, Wilhelmina Amelia of Brunswick-Calenberg, or Elisabeth-Christine of Brunswick-Wolfenbüttel, she resisted the option of converting to Catholicism. She rejected the courtship of Archduke Charles, so when she married the future George II she brought the cachet of staunch Protestantism with her to dynastic union – which was seen largely in terms of the protestant succession at this time.[30] She also benefited from her years in Berlin and Hanover by being with two generations of strong-minded, cultured, intellectually curious, Hanoverian women, who had manoeuvred George Augustus skilfully into a position in which he found it natural to propose to Caroline.

III

Determined and ambitious though she was, however, it was not immediately open to Caroline or her husband to decide the marriage policy of their children. As Hatton has shown, George I gave early attention to the problems created by the Personal Union, and formulated a plan to split the succession between any male great-grandchildren born to his grandson, Frederick, with the eldest keeping the British crown and the second son the electoral bonnet.[31] He took steps to have this agreed with the Holy Roman Emperor and with the Brunswick-Wolfenbüttel line. Alternatively, he considered the suggestion of George Augustus and Caroline that their eldest son, Frederick, should keep the Electorate, and the crown be invested in their second son, William, born and bred in England. George I's will was suppressed by George II, and his son Frederick, Prince of Wales, did not live long enough to discuss with his

---

[29] In what follows I draw on Hanham, 'Caroline' and Smith, 'Idea'.
[30] See chapter by Andrew Thompson.   [31] Hatton, *George I*, pp. 162–9, 271–2.

own heir, the future George III, George II's alternative strategy for the dissolution of the Personal Union, which would have required both Frederick and his son to accept the Electorate and renounce in advance the kingdom, and necessitated the agreement of the emperor as well as the Brunswick-Wolfenbüttel dukes.

In parallel with these succession plans George I, in conjunction with his daughter Sophia Dorothea, wife of Frederick William I of Prussia, also considered how he would deploy his grandchildren as dynastic assets. To assist in reviving the international standing of the United Provinces and encourage the Dutch to resume the practice of electing a stadholder in each province, he was already suggesting in 1721 that the young Prince of Orange, only eleven at this point, should consider marrying one of his granddaughters. This was a marriage in British interests, which would continue the 'Old System' of alliances to protect the protestant succession between Britain and the Netherlands, in association with the emperor and other German princes. These plans eventually bore fruit with Princess Anne's marriage. In 1747 her husband was finally created Stadholder William IV.

In 1723, faced with rumours that Austria would cement her alliance with Spain by two marriages, George I decided to reinforce the alliance with Prussia by a fourth generation of Brunswick–Lüneburg–Hohenzollern marriages. The plan outlined in the Treaty of Charlottenburg, warmly favoured by Sophia Dorothea, was for George's grandson Frederick Prince of Wales to marry Princess Wilhelmina, and for his eldest granddaughter Anne to marry the Prussian crown prince, Frederick (the future Frederick II). This double alliance was entirely acceptable to the British ministers, who saw it as combining advantageously the naval power of Britain with the military strength of Prussia, but had not been favoured by the Hanoverian minister A. G. Bernstorff. George I's death in 1727, before the marriages could be solemnised in Hanover, halted proceedings. Sophia Dorothea's ambitions were thwarted by her brother and her husband.[32] For if George II wanted to show his independence from his father, by halting the marriage plans and hiding the will with its provision to end the dynastic union, Frederick William I wanted to assert his power over his wayward son, and was also under pressure from a pro-Imperial faction in Berlin, which believed the Anglo-Prussian marriages would undermine Prussia's relationship with the Imperial court. The Prussian king and his son were already in conflict over the latter's secular thinking. When the king dropped support for an English marriage (Princess Amelia was now

[32] *Ibid.*, pp. 280–1.

the candidate) though still retaining the idea of his daughter Wilhelmina marrying Frederick Prince of Wales, the Prussian crown prince, abetted by his mother, tried to keep alive the marriage project. In the end he was obliged to marry Elisabeth-Christine of Brunswick-Bevern instead; as the niece of the Empress Elisabeth-Christine she was the imperial candidate, though British diplomacy was hard at work up to the bitter end to press the candidacy of Princess Amelia.[33]

Sophia Dorothea's 'Guelph' policy of repeating the Hanoverian-Hohenzollern marriage alliances had been forced to yield to a Hohenzollern match with the elder branch of the Brunswick dynasty instead. Rivalry between Hohenzollern and Hanoverian policy, and the division of the Brunswick line, would also complicate George III's dynastic strategy, but in the meantime there was no Hanover–Brandenburg union in the fourth generation. Frederick Prince of Wales, after the failure of the double marriage project, was married instead to a Princess of Saxe-Gotha – a second cousin of his mother, Caroline. This was an appealing marriage from the point of view of the protestant succession, as the Ernestine line from which she came had been the patrons of Luther. It inaugurated a pattern of the British heir marrying a candidate from a minor German dynasty, in the hope, it must be inferred, she would prove biddable, and avoid the complication of powerful relatives with comparable diplomatic ranking pushing for their interests. But this strategy underestimated the adroitness and ambition of some of these lesser dynasties, especially the House of Saxe-Coburg-Gotha (as they became in 1817), which supplied consorts to Charlotte Princess of Wales and then Queen Victoria.[34] The only other sibling of Frederick to marry was his sister Mary, whose husband was Frederick II of Hesse-Cassel. This must be seen in the context both of protecting Hanover after Frederick II revealed his expansionist intent in 1740, and in the light of the protestant succession when, after her husband turned catholic, Mary became the guardian of the dynasty's Protestantism.[35] The descendants of this

---

[33] Baker-Smith, 'Daughters'; Thomas Biskup, 'The hidden queen: Elisabeth-Christine of Prussia and Hohenzollern queenship in the eighteenth century', in *Queenship in Europe*, pp. 193–206; Theodor Schieder, *Frederick the Great*, ed. and trans. Sabina Berkeley and Hamish Scott (London, 2000), pp. 17–32.

[34] David Cannadine has argued the Coburgs effectively took over the Hanoverian dynasty: 'The last Hanoverian sovereign? The Victorian monarchy in historical perspective, 1688–1988', in: A. L. Beier, David Cannadine and James M. Rosenheim, eds., *The first modern society, essays in English history in honour of Lawrence Stone* (Cambridge, 1989), pp. 127–65.

[35] See chapter by Andrew Thompson and Hannah Smith, 'Idea'; Baker-Smith, 'Daughters'; Mediger, 'Great Britain, Hanover and ... Prussia'.

marriage in unison with their Danish cousins were to provide a very important strand of Hanoverian family policy.

IV

The first two rulers of the dynastic union, George I and George II, made marriages which benefited both the kingdom and the Electorate, even if the marriages of George II's children did not all fulfil their diplomatic potential.[36] In the case of George III, it can be argued that although he was a good family man – to the advantage of the monarchy's public image in an age of evangelical revival and conflict with revolutionary, republican and Napoleonic France – he was an ineffective dynast. He had fifteen legitimate children; seven sons and six daughters survived infancy. Yet, when he became incapable of rule in 1811, the British succession rested on the shoulders of only one legitimate grandchild, Princess Charlotte of Wales, who would be ineligible to inherit the Electorate given the number of male uncles who would take precedence – even though none of them at this juncture had any legitimate heirs. Frederick's official marriage was childless; William and Edward had long-term liaisons, with the former producing ten children, and Augustus had two by his unofficial but dissolved marriage to Lady Augusta Murray. Ernest and Adolphus were unmarried and unpartnered.

Charlotte's death in childbirth, in 1817, having produced a stillborn son, precipitated a spate of marriages among these uncles. William, duke of Clarence, Edward, duke of Kent, and Adolphus, duke of Cambridge, all competed to produce an heir; Ernest of Cumberland's wife Frederica had a son at the same time. Victoria of Kent preceded her cousins George of Cambridge and George of Cumberland by only weeks, and as William's new bride Adelaide of Saxe-Meiningen had no surviving children – or indeed any sons – the prospect throughout the reign of George IV and William IV was that the Personal Union would come to an end with the accession of Victoria to the British crown.

In viewing George III's place in the Hanoverian dynastic system, the first point to make was that his mother was not a Hohenzollern, as she might have been, given the connections already traced in three generations, before Brandenburg-Prussia became a great power. Frederick William I and Frederick II were adroit dynasts, spreading Hohenzollern influence across the different branches of the family, reinforcing the

---

[36] Baker-Smith, 'Daughters', pp. 203–5.

Brunswick-Wolfenbüttel link, and creating a union with each of the Hesse-Cassel and Swedish dynasties, who were in turn closely linked (See Table 10.1).[37] Therefore many candidates theoretically available for Frederick Prince of Wales's children would have Hohenzollern connections. It is likely that he would have preferred continuing the link with his wife's family or with another of the Saxon duchies, or alternatively have looked to the Hesse-Cassels and their cadet branches. His death in 1751 left his son's marriage far more susceptible to George II's influence. His widow Augusta, Princess of Wales, was unable to create a positive alternative to his wishes; she could only frustrate them. From the Saxe-Gotha point of view, marriage to the future king of Great Britain had been a huge dynastic prize for a small principality comparable in size to Brunswick-Wolfenbüttel, but lack of dynastic standing meant Augusta's ambitions to repeat the Saxe-Gotha alliance were unsuccessful.

In 1755 George II attempted to arrange a Brunswick marriage for his grandson. The candidate was Sophie Caroline of Brunswick-Wolfenbüttel, a niece of Frederick II, but together George and his mother succeeded in overruling the ageing king. Significantly, James, 2nd Earl Waldegrave, the prince's former governor, commented 'the Prince of Wales was taught to believe that he was to be made a sacrifice, merely to gratify the King's private interests in the Electorate of Hanover'.[38] Part of George III's acculturation as a British-born Hanoverian was to be persuadable that the dynastic interests of the future king of Great Britain were *not* the same as the dynastic interests of Hanover. His youth – he was only seventeen – helped make his refusal successful. In fact had George II been twenty years younger he might have married Sophie Caroline himself.[39] The attraction of the Brunswick alliance was the protection it might afford Hanover, the need for which was supported at this point by British ministers, who were also courting Frederick. The commander-in-chief of the British Army of Observation during the Seven Years War begun the

---

[37] Louisa Ulrica's marriage to Adolphus Frederick of Sweden failed to draw Sweden into an effective Prussian alliance; during the Seven Years War brother and sister were on opposite sides. For the unmarried Amelia there was the useful imperial role of abbess of Quedlinburg, one of three protestant abbeys to keep its voting rights in the *Reichstag*, a second being Gandersheim (see note 48), thus extending the Hohenzollern presence in the empire. Frederick I of Hesse-Cassel had become king of Sweden in 1720, after his wife, Ulrika Eleonora, sister and heir of Charles XII, abdicated in his favour. Kingdom and landgraviate were ruled by separate branches.

[38] John Brooke, *George III* (London, 1974), p. 98.

[39] She married her uncle by marriage, Frederick of Bayreuth, after the death of his first wife, Wilhelmina, Frederick II's favourite sister.

following year was Duke Ferdinand of Brunswick, Sophie Caroline's uncle and Frederick of Prussia's brother-in-law three times over.[40]

Once he had become king, George III modified the dynastic pattern as a natural consequence of the transformation of foreign policy created by the 1762 break with Prussia. He wanted a return to the 'old system' of alliance with Austria, the Netherlands and other German protestant principalities against France – an unrealistic aim given the continuation of the Franco-Austrian alliance after 1763, and the weakness of the House of Orange. His marriage to Charlotte of Mecklenburg-Strelitz was, like his father's marriage, an alliance with a minor dynasty new to Hanoverian marriage patterns (though the long descent of the Mecklenburg dukes from the tenth century made Charlotte feel more than equal to the Brunswicks, however small her father's principality). For a second generation the British–Hanoverian heir married into a new, small, protestant German dynasty and not into the interlinked Brunswick–Hohenzollern system. In choosing a consort for George III, his advisers – mainly the earl of Bute – were thinking as much of her being protestant, in good health, docile and free of political ambition, and young enough to be biddable, as they were concerned with rank and dynastic background, although two candidates were ruled out because of mésalliances in their families. It is not as though the Hohenzollern or Brunswick dynasties were rejected outright. The rival candidates to Charlotte included Sophie Caroline of Brunswick-Wolfenbüttel's sister Elizabeth,[41] and their cousin Philippina of Brandenburg-Schwedt. Not only were they both nieces of Frederick II, they were also thought too young or too opinionated. A Hesse-Darmstadt princess was excluded because (ironically) there was thought to be a taint of madness in her father. Knowing how astute and ambitious his mother had been despite docile appearances, George was also determined not to marry another Saxe-Gotha – especially when he learnt that his cousin Frederica was addicted to 'philosophy', i.e. to enlightened secularism, as well as being thought unlikely to bear children easily.[42] So the outsider candidate, Charlotte of Mecklenburg-Strelitz, won through.

Her marriage was popular because of the myth that she had written to Frederick the Great to deplore his recruiting soldiers in her native Strelitz; though this was not literally true, Charlotte retained a lifelong distrust of

---

[40] Mediger, 'Great Britain, Hanover . . . and Prussia', p. 212.
[41] Who married as his first wife Frederick William II of Prussia and became the mother of Frederica, later duchess of York.
[42] However there were culturally important exchanges between the two courts in George III's reign: David Watkin, *The architect king; George III and the culture of the Enlightenment* (London 2004), pp. 191–2.

the Prussian monarch.[43] The House of Hohenzollern would inherit Mecklenburg territories if the various ducal lines ever failed; this made Frederick both patron and predator. His *Rêveries politiques* (1752) show that he believed this dynastic inheritance as well as the claims on Bayreuth and Ansbach were legally indisputable, and required none of the Machiavellian cunning he advocated for gaining Saxon, Polish or Swedish lands. Proprietary dynasticism was a useful and moral tool for him, as for any other dynasty. At the same time, Hanover was a rival patron of the Mecklenburgs, and had already absorbed some minor territories.[44] Both Guelph duchies had been commissioned by the Emperor Charles VI in 1717 to settle the dispute between Mecklenburg-Schwerin's estates and the ruling Duke Carl Leopold, though it was Frederick of Prussia who had finally imposed a settlement in 1755. George III's marriage to a Mecklenburg princess was thus also a way of needling the dynastic expectations of the House of Brandenburg and its recent influence in the main duchy.[45]

Charlotte and George had a successful marriage – at least until his recurrent porphyria after 1788 – and produced fifteen children, thirteen of whom survived. What went wrong – apart from biological mishap – with George's III's dynastic policy, that the succession in Britain should be relatively fragile? A key factor was the difficulty and expense, in a parliamentary monarchy, of settling the ruler's siblings and children. Just as a British parliamentary monarch did not exercise a completely free hand in forming foreign policy, so he was limited in using marriages in the pursuit of dynastic aggrandisement or useful foreign alliances. Parliamentary and public opinion would have to be considered if any money for princely establishments was to be voted.[46] George III's dynastic policy towards his sisters was relatively successful (though this was not reflected in his sisters' *personal* unhappiness); it was his brothers whom he failed to provide for and who had no sense of dynastic responsibility or family solidarity. His arrangements for his children were either unsuccessful or non-existent. George undoubtedly had good intentions, but both his own ill health and the changing circumstances brought about by

---

[43] Olwen Hedley, *Queen Charlotte* (London 1975), pp. 1–12, and *Letters from George III to Lord Bute 1756–1766*, ed. Romney Sedgwick (London 1939), for the bridal options. Hannah Smith, 'Idea', has pointed out though that in the early stages of the Seven Years War, Frederick II was seen popularly as a protestant hero.

[44] Erika Bosbach, ed., *Die 'Rêveries Politiques': In Friedrichs des Grossen Politischen Testament von 1752* (Köln and Graz, 1960).

[45] Wilson, *German armies*, pp. 142–8, 221–3.

[46] Hamish Scott, *British foreign policy in the age of the American Revolution* (Oxford, 1990), ch. 2.

Dynastic perspectives

the prolonged wars from 1793–1815 often frustrated or interrupted these. Nor was Queen Charlotte a powerful enough dynast in her own right to override these obstacles.

George's arrangements for his eldest sister Augusta illustrate both his attempts to retain useful links to Brunswick, which would protect Hanover, and to strengthen the Orange alliance, in pursuit of the 'Old System' (see Table 10.1). At the same time the Brunswick-Wolfenbüttel dukes had the dilemma of either perpetuating their links to Frederick the Great, despite Britain's rupture with Prussia, or continuing their alignment to Britain and Hanover. These tensions and dilemmas are apparent in George III's letters from his brother-in-law and in his private correspondence to the British minister in the Hague, Sir Joseph Yorke. In 1764 Augusta married Prince Charles of Brunswick, son of Frederick the Great's sister Charlotte Philippina, heir to the Wolfenbüttel line and a distinguished general who had fought for Britain in the Seven Years War. The marriage was a reward for this, and surely an attempt to cement the elder Brunswick line to the Hanoverian rather than the Hohenzollern cause. Despite their incompatibility, Augusta was ambitious for her husband: she suggested that he should assist the military regent for the young William V of the Netherlands.[47] This was her husband's maternal uncle Louis; his aunt had been Empress Elisabeth-Christine; and his sister, Elisabeth-Christine, Frederick II's unfortunate spouse. The advantage, George explained to Yorke, was

The acquiring so able an officer would be of great utility to the Prince of Orange ... besides ... it would be the most evident mark ... of that Good understanding between myself and the Stadtholder that every lover of the only stable Alliance (that of England & Holland) must rejoice at.[48]

Yorke's reply was that while Louis might have favoured this two years earlier, he was now sponsoring a marriage between the young Prince and his Prussian niece, Wilhelmina.[49] The reigning duke of Brunswick, Frederick the Great's brother-in-law, was not in a strong position to resist the Prussian candidate, even though there was no particular Dutch interest in a Prussian match, and the departure of Louis's brother, Field-Marshal Duke Ferdinand, from Prussian service also made it

---

[47] Sir John Fortescue, ed., *The correspondence of king George III from 1760–December 1783* (6 vols., London, 1927–8), vol. I, no. 336, George III to Yorke, 10 June 1766, referring to Augusta's suggestion.
[48] *Ibid.*
[49] This match ruled out an alternative Orange–Brunswick alliance to Augusta of Brunswick, the daughter of the reigning duke; she became the last princess-abbess of the Brunswick abbey of Gandersheim, before its secularisation in 1803.

awkward.[50] The prince did indeed marry Wilhelmina, but George III attempted to forestall the match, arguing that

> his own personal weight in the republic would be strengthened by his marrying my sister Louisa, as all the real friends to his family have ever been bred up in the system of close Union with my Crown, that is the real interest of both countrys [sic].

If the Dutch prince married a Prussian, the king of Prussia would look on him as a vassal. Marrying the duke of Brunswick's daughter would be less objectionable, because it would avoid slighting one royal match (the British) for another (the Prussian), and 'whether Prussia be ally'd or not with Great Britain I wish to see all Powers that are in [unity?] with my Crown being connected with its allys'.[51]

George and his envoy hoped the marriage would be delayed. But in June 1767 William told Yorke he would have to obey Prussian wishes, though he argued that this would not make him unfriendly to Britain. He added wistfully and somewhat perversely that he would have liked to marry another sister of George III's, Caroline Matilda. She had not been on offer, but he had entertained her on her journey to Denmark. Perhaps he liked the *idea* of a British marriage, but conveniently for a weak character he could safely pine for what was impossible, and still do what Louis of Brunswick wanted.[52]

Even if William had been able to postpone the marriage, George III was running out of dynastic players, as his sister Louisa died the following year. He continued to worry that Prussian influence in Holland was detrimental to Hanoverian interests: in December 1769 he asked Yorke to sound out whether the Dutch would assist Hanover in the event of any war. The disappointing answer was that they would incline to Prussia's plan of an armed neutrality. In 1771 George III again regretted this Prussian–Dutch marriage, this time from the British point of view, since he believed the system of William III, uniting the Houses of Orange, Austria and Great Britain, protected Britain best from the Bourbon family compact. The Prussian king, he argued, was no friend

---

[50] Fortescue, vol. I, nos. 31, 336, 339, 340, 345. [51] *Ibid.*, no. 339, draft to Yorke.
[52] Herbert H. Rowen, *The princes of Orange* (Cambridge, 1988), p. 199. Rowen does not query whether Caroline Matilda had been a realistic option; I would suggest she was not. Prince William had seen Caroline, but not Louisa, who *was* on offer. Fortescue, vol. I, no. 409, Journal of Caroline Matilda's arrival at Harwich to her arrival at Rotterdam, 2–9 October 1766, details her reception by Prince William and his sister. See also *Archives, ou correspondance inédite de la Maison Orange-Nassau*, eds. G. Groen van Prinsterer *et al.*, (5e série, 25 vols., Leiden and Utrecht 1835–1915), vol. I, pp. 39–82.

to Britain or the United Provinces – and painted an unfavourable picture of the Prince of Orange to the duke of Brunswick and his son.[53] The latter continued to express his support to his brother-in-law, and angled for command in Hanover.[54]

It is doubtful whether a dynastic marriage perpetuating the maritime powers' historical links would have had the desired outcome. The Netherlands was not a dynastic state; the stadholderate was an elective office, and its relationship with each of the seven provinces was often a delicate one, based on historical precedent but also requiring highly developed political skills which the Dutch prince and Louis of Brunswick both lacked. When the Americans rebelled against George III, the Dutch mercantile oligarchy favoured the Americans because of the opportunities for commercial expansion. Conflicting opinion over America helped to precipitate a 'Patriot' opposition against the Prince of Orange and his party, in which Prussian help, fostered by his characterful wife, helped to stabilise the prince's waning authority. A British wife might have made him even more unpopular when war was declared in 1780 by George III – who hoped that this crisis would somehow strengthen the stadholder's position again.[55] In 1784, the new British envoy to The Hague did finally help restore Orange authority, and four years later it would be joint intervention by the new king of Prussia, Wilhelmina's brother, supported by George III's diplomacy, which would again restore his cousin to the stadholderate and repair the maritime alliance.[56] As France had supported the anti-Orange patriots, Anglo-Prussian assistance to the House of Orange would give George III as elector of Hanover a helpful ally as well.[57] The dual Hanoverian and British character of George's strategy shows clearly in a letter to Wilhelmina of Orange in June 1788,

I consider the alliance I have made with your brother, the king, in my capacity as Elector, as a guarantee of the maintenance of the German Constitution; and I would consider a similar alliance between our two crowns, as a means of obliging the Court of Vienna and Versailles to wish to maintain the peace of Europe.[58]

---

[53] *Ibid.*, vol. II, nos. 736, 15 December 1769; 738, 22 December 1769 for Yorke's reply.
[54] *Ibid.*, nos. 728, 733.   [55] Scott, *British foreign policy*, pp. 307–8.
[56] Rowen, *Princes*, ch. 11.
[57] Throughout these political vicissitudes personal ties persisted between the two courts: cf. Campbell Orr, 'La Fite, Marie Elisabeth de (1737–1794)', *Oxford Dictionary of National Biography*, online edn, June 2005, accessed 9 June 2005; Campbell Orr, 'Queen Charlotte', in *Queenship in Europe*.
[58] A. Aspinall, ed., *The Later Correspondence of George III* (5 vols., Cambridge, 1962–70), vol. I, no. 453, 6 June 1788, George III to Wilhelmina Princess of Orange: 'je regarde l'alliance que j'ai fait avec le roi votre frère en ma qualité d'Electeur, comme un garant du

In January 1795 the House of Orange took refuge in England after the French revolutionary army overran the country and its Dutch sympathisers proclaimed a Batavian republic. British and Hanoverian troops commanded by the duke of York, with his brothers Ernest and Adolphus in Hanoverian regiments, had engaged with the Dutch in unsuccessful efforts to maintain the Dutch barrier and thereby protect Britain or Hanover. By this time the Orange heir was also linked in marriage to Frederick. In 1791 the latter married Frederica of Prussia, daughter of Frederick William II of Prussia, in a double ceremony which included the marriage of the bride's half-sister Frederica Wilhelmina to the Dutch hereditary prince, the future King William I of the Netherlands.[59] As in the early days of the Personal Union, there was a satisfactory triangular dynastic link again between Hanover, Orange and Hohenzollern. Both Houses of Brunswick joined in this three-way link when the Dutch prince's sister, Louisa, married the hereditary Prince of Brunswick, Charles George, son of Augusta and Charles of Brunswick.

Following his grandfather's precedent of an Anglo-Danish marriage, in 1766 George III married his sister Caroline Matilda, Louisa's niece, to Christian VII. The diplomatic context for this was the need for British rapprochement with Russia and its allies in order to guard Hanoverian and British interests against Prussia. The Danish foreign minister Bernstorff had detached Denmark from reliance on France, while Russia was aiming to create a Northern System to isolate Prussia, which would include Britain as well as Denmark. The dynastic link, which was popular in Anglophile Denmark, was an element in a less formal entente.[60] It was also complemented by cultural and intellectual ties between Britain, Denmark, Hanover and electoral Saxony – which remained determinedly protestant in culture despite the Catholicism of its elector.[61] However, from the personal point of view, the marriage went spectacularly wrong; married at only fifteen after a very secluded

maintien de la constitution Germanique; et que je considerois une alliance semblable entre nos deux couronnes, comme un moyen d'obliger les cours de Vienne et de Versailles à désirer la continuation de la paix de l'Europe'.

[59] Aspinall, vol. I, nos. 688, 694 and 714 show the progress of Frederick's courtship and describe the wedding. Frederica's father had hoped to marry her to the Prince of Wales in 1786 in order to consolidate George's membership, as elector, of the *Fürstenbund*: *ibid.*, vol. II, p. xvi. Letters from Frederick, Ernest and Adolphus in vol. II, show their frustration with the Prince of Orange and his sons over their military timidity. Parliamentary mistrust of the inexperienced Frederick of York prompted his recall to Britain in October 1794, with the duke of Brunswick designated to replace him: *ibid.*, pp. xxxiii–xxxvii, and nos. 1139, 1212.

[60] Hamish Scott, *Emergence*, p. 129; Michael Roberts, 'Great Britain, Denmark and Russia, 1763–70', in Hatton and Anderson, *Studies*.

[61] Campbell Orr, 'Queen Charlotte', in *Queenship in Europe*.

Dynastic perspectives

upbringing at Kew away from court intrigues, the young queen was ill-prepared for the factions in the Danish court, and had the double misfortune of being married to a schizophrenic. After her love affair with the royal physician and favourite Struensee, the queen was disgraced.[62] Her brother had to intervene to prevent her being imprisoned or even executed, but she was so morally compromised that George and Charlotte insisted she be kept at Celle in the Electorate, and denied royal status. As Hamish Scott has emphasised, the reputation of a dynasty was an asset, damaged by misconduct, but while Anglo-Danish *relations* were damaged, Anglo-Danish *interests* were not.[63]

V

George's deployment of his sisters in dynastic marriages was only partially successful, but at least he was alert to their usefulness for dynastic purposes. He was less adroit with his brothers. Frederick died in 1765, and Edward duke of York in 1767, but why were not appropriate marriages made for Gloucester and Cumberland? Why not look for a bride among the various members of the Holstein-Gottorp family, for instance, as Charlotte's brother Ernest Charles attempted to do, with little to recommend him except his sister's grandeur? A link here would have reinforced the Anglo-Russian entente, especially as Catherine the Great of Russia, and her murdered husband Tsar Peter III, were both of Holstein-Gottorp descent.[64] Queen Charlotte's brother, Charles, successfully married into the cadet branch of the Hesse-Darmstadts, where daughters abounded.[65] Did George's search for a suitable bride for himself persuade him there was a dearth of suitable princesses – that they would all be too awkward and obstinate and meddling? Or was it a deeper failure of dynastic imagination, connected to the insularity

---

[62] M. Bregnsbo, 'Danish Absolutism and queenship', in *Queenship in Europe*.
[63] Scott, *British foreign policy*, pp. 171–7. See also Bregnsbo, 'Danish absolutism and queenship'. Caroline Matilda's daughter by Struensee was acknowledged as royal, and married into the House of Schleswig-Holstein-Augustenburg; their grandson Christian married Queen Victoria's daughter Princess Helena. Between them, Queen Victoria and Christian IX of Denmark, father of Queen Alexandra, would become the grandmother and grandfather of Europe in the nineteenth and twentieth century. Friction between Alexandra and Princess Beatrice occurred however since the latter's husband, Christian of Schleswig-Holstein-Augustenburg, supported the German annexation of Schleswig-Holstein and Alexandra's family, the Schleswig-Holstein Sonderburg-Glucksburg line, vehemently did not. Theo Aronson, *A family of kings: the descendants of Christian IX of Denmark* (London, 1926), and Aronson, *The Grandmama of Europe: the crowned descendants of Queen Victoria* (London, 1973).
[64] See family tree in Hamish Scott, *Emergence*, p. 126 and discussion pp. 125–9.
[65] Campbell Orr, 'Queen Charlotte', in *Queenship in Europe*, pp. 368–402.

and incoherence of British foreign policy in the 1760s discerned by Hamish Scott?[66]

There may also have been a lack of sibling sympathy at work. George had enjoyed the seclusion of his Kew upbringing and would reproduce it in his own family life. Augusta wanted her son to be a morally upright, Christian king, and his probity would certainly turn out to be an asset in the age of evangelical revival and the replacement of aristocratic laxity with middle-class respectability. The younger brothers received much less attention in their upbringing: York, Gloucester and Cumberland soon showed their enjoyment of the relaxed morals of the mid-eighteenth-century aristocracy.[67] It was short sighted of Augusta to concentrate so hard on her eldest son, since had the duke of York been more conventionally respectable his brother might have considered nominating him as Prince-Bishop of Osnabrück, where, uniquely, catholic bishops elected by the cathedral chapter alternated with Guelph-nominated protestant ones. George I had appointed his brother as prince-bishop in 1715, a useful electoral Hanoverian dynastic strategy to strengthen their position in the Holy Roman Empire and provide financially for a member of the family. Instead George waited for a second son to be born and nominated Frederick when he was still a child.

George's accession when he was still only twenty two admittedly meant there had been relatively little time to find suitable alternative partners for George III to marry after his determination against a Brunswick match, let alone consider suitable brides for his younger brothers. Two other factors might help to explain these dynastic failures. On the one hand George had succeeded in finding a wife who would not be too meddling, and Charlotte fulfilled her side of the bargain. But naturally enough she was much more integrated into the Holy Roman Empire and *au fait* with its hatches, matches and dispatches than was her husband.[68] She could have advised on who was available and suitable for her brothers-in-law; but having chosen a non-meddling wife George forewent the kind of help wives often gave. Secondly, in a parliamentary monarchy there was the problem of voting household expenses to maintain extra members of the royal family. Dynastic issues were also issues of parliamentary

---

[66] Roberts, pp. 265–7; Scott, *Emergence*, ch. 3.
[67] John Bullion, '"George, be a king!" The relationship between Princess Augusta and George III', in S. Taylor, R. Connors, and C. Jones, eds., *Hanoverian Britain and empire* (Woodbridge, 1998).
[68] E.g. Campbell Orr, 'Queen Charlotte', pp. 375–6 for her advice when her brothers Charles and Ernest were wife-hunting, and p. 373 on Mecklenburg-Schwerin marriages. Her letters to her brother also discuss the matrimonial prospects of Prince Peter of Holstein who became co-adjutor of Lübeck and needed to marry.

management and fiscal prudence. After the expenses of the Seven Years War George was probably unwilling to ask for extra money to support yet more royal households, and he had not yet mastered the knack of creating stable ministries. He may have hoped that time was on his side, that his brothers were still young, and that they would be as dutiful as he was. But the dual status of George as elector and king actually made it even more important to arrange his dynastic affairs suitably. Had he merely been the elector, his brothers could have taken service in the imperial or Russian armies, as so many younger brothers of German princes did.[69] They could also have married morganatically, if they had chosen a woman of inferior rank. Failure to manage his siblings well meant costs of another kind: family discord, scandal and disrepute. It was not convenient to have royal dukes sitting in the Lords and opposing their royal brother; it was expensive to have parliament provide £13,000 from the civil list to foot the bill for the duke of Cumberland's crim. con. case; and the widow he did marry had four brothers and a father in the Commons. The king also paid a political price in getting the Royal Marriages Act passed in 1772 to shut the stable door after the horse had bolted, thereby stirring up Whig opposition. It might have been more economical in every way to make some dynastic outlay in getting his brothers properly married, despite the likely difficulty in persuading parliament that this was the right thing to do.

VI

George was a busy executive king who had to play many roles: how far he saw himself as prince of the Holy Roman Empire as well is addressed in chapter 4. In the 1760s and 1770s, his electoral bonnet was probably the most marginal and abstract of his roles. Nevertheless, he planned for all his sons to learn German when he arranged their households in 1780–1, simultaneously with his arrangements for Frederick of York to go to Hanover and Prussia to learn military science, and prepare for his role as Prince-Bishop of Osnabrück. Queen Charlotte wrote also to her brother Charles asking him to watch over his social and moral welfare.[70]

---

[69] After his private marriage to the widowed countess of Waldegrave, who descended illegitimately from Robert Walpole, the duke of Gloucester considered Russian service when desperate for money, before realising his position as a British prince precluded this. Fortescue, vol. III, nos. 1452, 1457, 1574, 2086/7; see also Christopher Hibbert, *George III, a personal history* (London, 1998), ch. 20.

[70] Mecklenburg-Strelitz Archives, Schwerin: Hausarchiv des Mecklenburg-Strelitzschen Fürstenhauses/Briefsammlung. All letters cited are from Charlotte to her brother Charles, Duke of Mecklenburg-Strelitz (MSA), 4. 3–2, No. 873, 3 October 1780; see also Campbell Orr, 'Queen Charlotte', p. 377.

In August 1783 the king was plainly disappointed that Frederick's need to be in Osnabrück to enter formally into his position as Prince-Bishop would preclude his attending military manoeuvres under Joseph in Austria and Bohemia – a useful training for a sovereign prince within the empire.[71] But although George was always eager for information about his electoral dominions, the fact that he had never physically been in Hanover must surely have impeded his grasp of its location in relation to other states – and their ruling dynasties. To put it in modern terms, Charlotte's knowledge of the German empire was real, whereas her husband's was 'virtual'. It is impossible to evaluate definitively how important her influence was in helping to educate their children to feel 'German' and to understand the dynastic links, imperial etiquette, and culture of their inherited German patrimony, but it cannot have been negligible. She was always aware of being both a princess of the Holy Roman Empire as well as the consort of the British king, as her letters to her favourite brother, Charles, amply illustrate.

By 1776 Charles was made military as well as civil governor of Hanover, at the time that the king was preoccupied with the rebellion in America. Some of the German issues mentioned in the letters from this period illustrate Charlotte's patriotism for her native duchy and her assumption of her electoral role, combined with a queenly interest in Britain's colonial problems. For instance, her sympathies were engaged when the Hanoverian troops hired to garrison Minorca in order to free British troops for America were wrecked off the island of Rhé, and she praised French generosity in assisting them. She supplied a list of those lost – presumably so that her brother could inform and help their families. She took a maternal interest in their electoral subjects in complement to George's paternalism. When some Mecklenburg troops were hired she hoped that knowledge she was watching over their welfare would hearten them. News that 3,000 troops would be sent from Hanover to Minorca was squeezed into a letter mainly about the broken betrothal of Charles's sister-in-law, Charlotte of Hesse-Darmstadt, to a Holstein Prince.[72] Charlotte had an inside knowledge of personalities, dynastic strategies and styles of rule among German principalities that alerted her to the small manoeuvres and opportunities that a less powerful dynasty such as hers could seize as a means of aggrandisement.

---

[71] Fortescue, vol. VI, nos. 4440–1, 6 August 1783, Charles James Fox to George III and reply.
[72] MSA, 4. 3–2, No. 870, Letters 18 July, 25 July, 13 October, 8 November, 1 December, 29 December, 1775; MSA, 4. 3–2, No. 871, 26 January 1776.

Dynastic perspectives 239

Table 10.2. *Saxon claims to Bavaria*

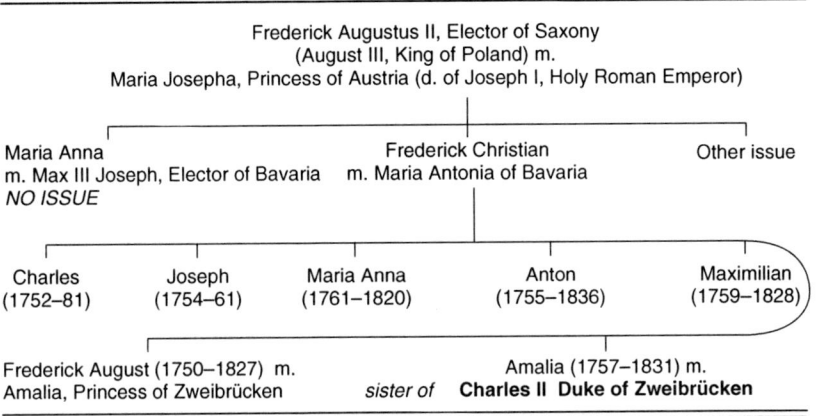

This is illustrated well in her comments on the build-up to the Bavarian War of Succession of 1777–8. The War was about the succession rights of Charles Theodore, Elector Palatine, to the undivided electoral lands in Bavaria, and in turn the rights of the duke of Zweibrücken to both inheritances. The Emperor Joseph's occupation of Upper Bavaria pending resolution of the succession was not solely in his imperial capacity, but mainly in protection of his claims on Bavaria-Straubing, through his late second wife, Josepha of Bavaria, who was also his second cousin. Some Bavarian lands were fiefs of the crown of Bohemia, and some freeholds could be inherited through the female line. The territorial cessions agreed by Charles Theodore in defiance of the late Bavarian elector's family agreement gave Frederick of Prussia the opportunity to rally the lesser principalities against Habsburg pretension, in support of the duke of Zweibrücken's undivided inheritance, and in defence of the balance of power within the empire. Hanover was officially an ally of Prussia, while officially Britain took no interest (see Tables 10.2–10.5).[73]

In January 1778 Frederick was dallying with the French and the Americans, and George III was preoccupied with the impending alliance

---

[73] For the Bavarian War I have consulted T. C. W Blanning, *Joseph II* (London, 1994); Derek Beales, *Joseph II*, vol. I: *In the Shadow of Maria Theresa 1741–1780* (Cambridge, 1987); Paul P. Bernard, *Joseph II and Bavaria: two eighteenth century attempts at German unification* (The Hague, 1965); Isabel de Madariaga, *Britain, Prussia and the armed neutrality of 1780* (London, 1962); Scott, *British foreign policy*. Frederick the Great told his brother Henry on 28 January 1778 he approved a Hanoverian memo disputing Habsburg claims: *Politische Correspondenz Friedrich's des Grossen* (46 vols., Berlin and Leipzig, 1879–1939), (PC), vol. XL, ed. G. B. Volz (Leipzig, 1928), p. 67.

Table 10.3. *Zweibrücken claims to Bavaria*

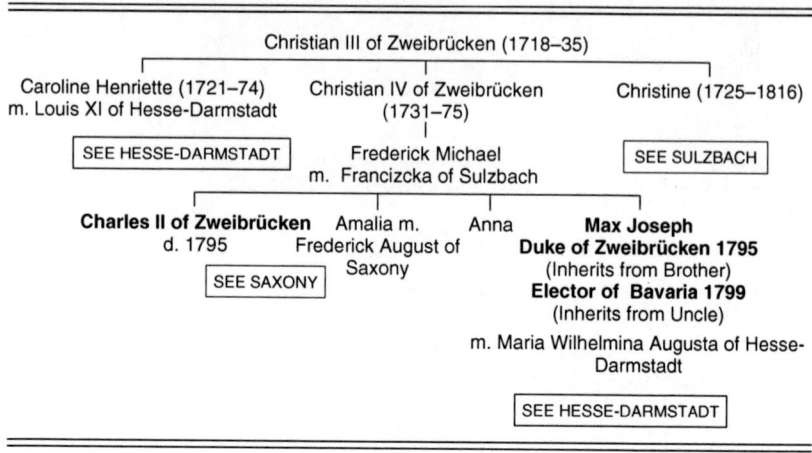

Table 10.4. *Sulzbach and Palatinate links to Zweibrücken, and claims to Bavaria*

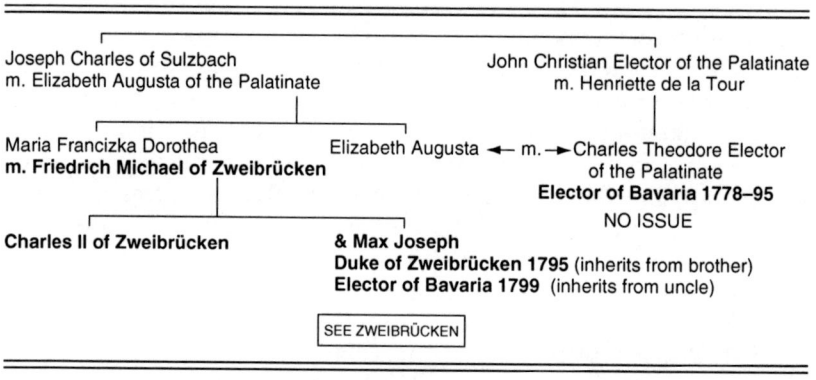

between the former and the latter, which would complicate British strategy in fighting the American rebels, and make a continental ally desirable. By April he had decided to align British and Hanoverian policy together in defence of imperial law, and to respond to Prussian overtures for an alliance, which would simultaneously protect Hanover. What brought about this Anglo-Prussian rapprochement? A fresh look at the dynastic perspectives suggests that pressure was being exerted both by Charlotte, and her brother-in-law the duke of Brunswick.

Table 10.5. *Hesse-Darmstadt links to Hohnzollern (Prussia), Zweibrücken and Mecklenburg-Strelitz*

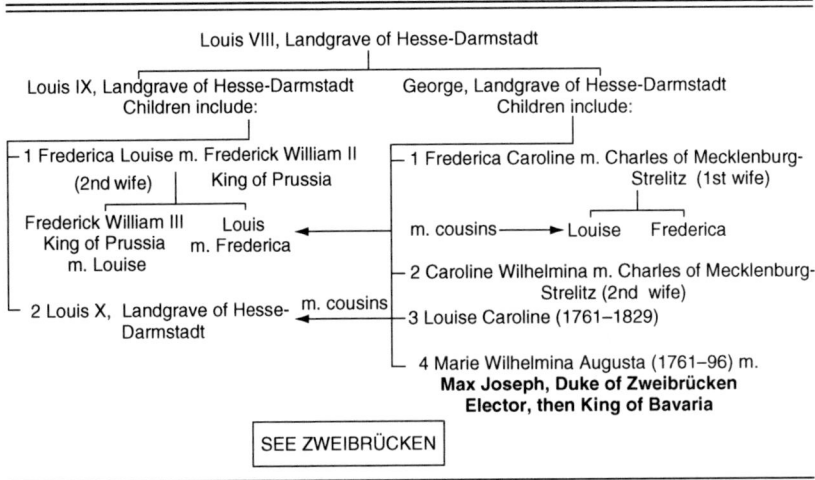

Although Frederick's actions are usually seen as part of Prussian state aggrandisement under the guise of legal, imperial concerns, the fact is that Frederick also had a dynastic interest in preserving the inheritance undivided to benefit the Zweibrücken claim: his heir's second wife, Frederica Louise of Hesse-Darmstadt, was the daughter of a Zweibrücken princess. Her mother was the talented and forceful Landgravine Henriette, daughter of Christian III duke of Zweibrücken, and great-aunt of the Zweibrücken claimant.[74] The Mecklenburg dynasty also had territorial claims on the landgraviate of Leuchtenberg, lost to Bavaria in 1646. Since February 1776, Charlotte had been both alert to, and suspicious of, the way the senior branch of her house was handling these claims, and doubted both that the duke of Mecklenburg-Schwerin had Strelitz interests at heart, and that Frederick of Prussia would really assist them.[75] Her

---

[74] Campbell Orr, 'Queen Charlotte', in *Queenship in Europe* summarises her patronage circle and links to Charles of Mecklenburg-Strelitz. Landgravine Henriette's nephew, Frederick Michael, converted to Catholicism in 1767, which made his line more eligible for inheriting the electoral lands in Bavaria. See also Rowen, *The king's state*, p. 130, on Frederick's 'proprietary dynasticism'.

[75] Mention of the Mecklenburg interest in the Bavarian succession probably occurs first in MSA 4. 3–2 No. 871, Letter 11 February 1776, where Charlotte fears the duke of Mecklenburg-Schwerin may have a secret understanding with the king of Prussia, presumably on this issue. Explicit discussion of the landgraviate of Leuchtenberg occurs in *ibid.*, No. 873, Letters 3 and 16 March 1778.

brother Adolphus, ruling duke of Mecklenburg-Strelitz, had been prompt in presenting a memo about his dynastic claims on 6 February 1778, and the Prussian king had instructed his foreign ministry to back up these claims, which he welcomed as additional piece of dynastic competition against Habsburg pretensions: 'Il est bien bon que cette maison joigne ses cris à ceux des autres compétiteurs de la succession Bavière.'[76] On 16 March 1778 the Prussian representative at the Imperial Diet in Ratisbon made a formal protest against Austrian claims to Bavarian lands, and included the Mecklenburg claims on the landgraviate of Leuchtenberg in his statement. According to Morton Eden, the British envoy at Munich as well as Ratisbon, the Zweibrücken representative acted under the direction of the Prussian one in making *his* formal protest.[77]

Charlotte was a determined critic of Frederick, based both on his aggressive militarism and his free-thinking views. She was contemptuous of his *Eulogy of Voltaire* when she read it in 1779, writing that the talents of princes, like those of plebeians, were limited.[78] During the early months of 1778 Charlotte had a shrewd grasp of how war with America in combination with the Bourbon powers prevented her husband from taking a great deal of interest in the imminent conflict over the Bavarian succession. In a letter dated 27 March she explained to Charles that George was at work from 6 a.m. to midnight and snatching at quick meals at his desk, so she couldn't get his attention over any Strelitz matters. She reminded him to route Strelitz concerns via Lord Suffolk, the secretary of state; but she was optimistic the Leuchtenberg claim would work out well.[79] It is possible to suggest from the sequence of comments to her brother that Mecklenburg-Strelitz concerns over the Bavarian question could have been a factor behind George III's willingness, by 7 April 1778, to abandon his anti-Prussian attitude and try to enlist Frederick II as a protector of Hanover and a check on Austrian ambitions.[80] Although as consort Charlotte was careful to keep out of British political affairs, the interests of her own dynasty coupled with those of Hanover may have emboldened her to argue her case directly with her husband, notwithstanding his absorption in his papers, and to direct her brother's

---

[76] PC, vol. XL, pp. 91–2, 100–1, 109–10, quote at p. 10.
[77] NA, SP 81/113/25, copy of Frederick the Great's protestations to Imperial Diet 16 March 1778, forwarded 18 March 1778; Hardwicke Papers, BL Add. Mss. 35573, f 148, latter from Morton Eden to Sir Robert Keith, 26 April 1778.
[78] MSA, 4. 3–2, No. 874, Letter 8 January 1779.
[79] MSA, 4. 3–2 873, Letter no. 2 from 1778 group, undated, between 9 January and February 5; 16 and 27 March 1778.
[80] Scott, *British foreign policy*, pp. 269–71, especially p. 270.

Dynastic perspectives

lobbying.[81] He may also have taken an additional interest in the Bavarian issue because of his marital links to the Hesse-Darmstadt family.[82]

But if Charlotte and Charles in their respective ways did 'lobby' George, his Brunswick brother-in-law was also intervening, he claimed, to direct Frederick II away from France and America, and towards imperial matters. As early as 20 February the British representative in Berlin, Hugh Elliott, was given an audience with the duke of Brunswick, in full knowledge of the Prussian king. He assured Elliott that Prussian–American overtures would now subside, and that he personally would remain neutral should there be any Franco-Prussian action in the empire over Bavaria. Elliott stressed to Suffolk how useful the duke could be both then and in the future, and argued that his professions of service were to be trusted: the duke, he claimed, was ambitious and wanted to be, or appear to be, the link between Prussia and Great Britain.[83] Elliott wrote to Suffolk:

> In general there is no doubt the intervention of His Highness may nearly remove the inconveniences to which His Majesty's service is exposed by the temper of the King of Prussia... and when your Lordship recollects the unguarded position of his Majesty's dominions in Germany, & the possible contingencies of the impending war, I imagine it will not be judged improper to make use of every laudable means to secure a degree of weight with those whose force will enable them to dispose despotically of the Northern part of the Empire.[84]

Elliott suggested that a private letter from George to the duke of Brunswick assuring him of his satisfaction would help 'destroy prejudices' in Prussia against Britain.[85] The four despatches Suffolk sent, on 7 April 1778, duly included one which conveyed to the duke of Brunswick George III's pleasure in finding that his talents combined with his friendly disposition toward Britain, as well as one offering a Prussian subsidy.[86]

It is difficult to know what were the decisive factors persuading George III in April 1778 to respond positively to Prussian overtures. Hamish Scott has suggested that the letter of instruction sent to Morton Eden on 7 April, to act in concert with the Hanoverian minister in Munich and to insist on upholding the imperial constitution against Austrian *force*

---

[81] I have not been able to trace in NA any correspondence to Suffolk from Charles of Mecklenburg-Strelitz, nor the memoranda on the Leuchtenberg claims from the Mecklenburg-Schwerin branch of the dynasty Charlotte said the king had received: MS Archives, 4 3-2 873, letter dated 27 March 1778.

[82] Campbell Orr, 'Queen Charlotte', in *Queenship in Europe* for Charles's rapport with his Hesse-Darmstadt connections. His first and second wives were nieces of the Landgravine Henriette, and their younger sister married into the Palatinate family.

[83] NA, SP 90/102/5.   [84] *Ibid.*   [85] NA SP 90/102/8.

[86] NA SP 90/102, 7 April 1778: see also discussion in Scott, *British foreign policy*, pp. 269–71.

majeure, reads as though drafted by an electoral minister. But Charlotte felt the Hanoverian minister in London was still lukewarm about Prussian usefulness: in a letter of 24 April to her brother, she reported what can only be described as an argument – or at any rate a strong statement of her views – with Alvensleben, that although she detested Frederick of Prussia's principles, it had to be recognised that he was very good at rallying and supporting the interests of lesser German principalities, and others might do well to follow his strategy.[87] This suggests Alvensleben was sceptical about Prussia's overtures and not over eager to align either Britain or Hanover with Prussia at the Imperial Diet. Perhaps then it was the combined persuasions of his wife and brother-in-law, in addition to Ellliot's diplomacy in Berlin, or even representations from the duke of Mecklenburg-Schwerin, that was behind George III's positive turn to Prussia.

George spent the rest of 1778 preoccupied with strengthening the fleet, and Charlotte too was involved in the naval review at Portsmouth and the review of the militia camp at Warley.[88] She was proud of the soldiers' and sailors' loyalty to her husband, all the while impatient to hear news of her 'chère patrie' as the 'sedate [military] manoeuvring' between Berlin and Vienna began.[89] In July, Charlotte learned from her brother of a fresh twist to the Bavarian succession issue. The duke of Mecklenburg-Schwerin would be offered an exchange of his territory with the margraviate of Ansbach, which Prussia was due to inherit. As his mother-in-law was a princess of Brandenberg-Schwedt Charlotte was afraid he would be susceptible to the plan. She urged her brother to object; but meanwhile Alvensleben told Charlotte that there would be opposition within the empire to this idea. Charlotte would display in later letters to her brother a respect for prescriptive rights and her doubts that people can feel loyalty to a new ruler.[90] During the rest of the year Charlotte's concerns abated – presumably because no real fighting took place even when Frederick put troops into Bohemia, and the issue was resolved by negotiation. When an armistice was established the following March she even hoped that

---

[87] MSA, 4, 3–2 873, letter 24 April 1778.
[88] For the naval review, see Celina Fox, 'George III and the Navy', in Jonathan Marsden, *The wisdom of George III* (London 2005). MSA, 4, 3–2, No. 873, letters 18 May 1778, for Portsmouth review, 23 October 1778.
[89] MS Archives 4, 3–2 873, letter June 8 1778; T. C. W. Blanning, *Joseph II*, p. 133.
[90] MS Archives 4, 3–2 873, letter 10 August 1778. For Charlotte's conversations on prescriptive right with the historian Mallet (who had formerly tutored Christian VII of Denmark), see Campbell Orr, 'Rousseau's disciples at the court of George III and Queen Charlotte', in S. Bahar and V. Cossy, eds., *Genève, Lieu d'Angleterre* (Geneva, 2004).

Frederick's life would be prolonged, as he would effectively be the guarantor of this peace, and that the German peace would be paralleled in America.[91] In short, Charlotte knew what it was like to actually live next door to the ever more powerful Prussia; to come from a small dynasty that could enlarge its power though marriage and by urging every inheritance claim, however minor, be pursued; and that in the growing duel between the courts of Berlin and Vienna, even Frederick the Great should receive some grudging admiration for his skill at manoeuvre.

As Tim Blanning has written, the Holy Roman Empire was 'a delicate web of prescriptive right and treaty obligations which kept the weaker states of Europe in being'.[92] If George III knew this with his head, perhaps it can be said that Queen Charlotte knew this with her heart – and her knowledge of German princely genealogy. Nor should we see any dynastic lobbying she may have done on behalf of the Mecklenburg dynasty as unusual. Morton Eden carefully watched the behaviour of the Bavarian claimants after the death of the last Bavarian elector in December 1777. He commented that when the duke of Zweibrücken arrived in Munich, he stiffened the Elector Palatine's resistance to the Habsburgs. Eden attributed this new resolve to 'the spiritedness of the Dutchess who as well as the reigning Electress is extremely anxious to aggrandise the Palatine house'.[93] The 'reigning Electress' was Charles Theodore's wife, Elizabeth Augusta, his cousin from the Sulzbach branch of the Palatinate family; the 'Dutchess' was her sister, Maria Franziska, Dowager Duchess of the Zweibrücken branch, and mother of the reigning duke, Charles II. Naturally enough the two Pfalz-Sulzbach sisters wanted to advance their family's dynastic claims over rivals in the Habsburg and electoral Saxony dynasties. Similarly, Frederick the Great instructed his envoy to the Elector Palatine at Ratisbon, Count Eustachius de Goertz, that the best way to reach him was via the dowager electress of Bavaria, his wife's aunt.[94]

---

[91] MSA, 4 3-2 No. 874, Letters 9 March 1779, 13 May 1779.
[92] Blanning, *Joseph II*, p. 134.
[93] NA SP/105/43, ff. 117-118, 5 February 1778; also Hardwicke Papers, vol. XI, BL Add. Mss. 35513, fol. 82.
[94] PC, pp. 69, 90-1. The dowager electress of Bavaria was a Saxon Princess, Maria Anna; her mother was Empress Maria Theresa's cousin, Maria Josepha. Charles Theodore's heir was married to dowager electress Maria Anna's niece, Amelia, daughter of the elector Frederick Christian of Saxony. Frederick the Great was supporting the Saxon claims as well as the devolved Zweibrücken claims. See also Kaiser, 'Who's afraid?' for the lobbying Marie Antoinette was supposed to do at Versailles on behalf of Habsburg claims.

VII

The 1780s are seen as a decade when George became more and more sympathetic to his 'patrie Germanique', and aided by the Hanoverian lobby, including his son Frederick and possibly also his wife, he joined Frederick's *Fürstenbund*, formed to protect once more the Bavarian succession.[95] The death of Elector Charles Theodore's son in 1784 now meant that his brother Maximilian Joseph was heir to the Zweibrücken and Bavarian territories; by marriage to Maria Wilhelmina of Hesse-Darmstadt, he was the brother-in-law of Charles of Mecklenburg-Strelitz, George III's brother-in-law. In 1786 he told the visiting novelist Sophie von la Roche he was proud of his German blood and that all his children spoke German.[96] Why then did he not start to plan German dynastic alliances for his children?

Poignantly for his elder daughters, he told them just when his serious illness began in 1788 that he would hold court in Hanover for them when he was better, to help find them some suitable German princely husbands.[97] This surely might have happened had not France become increasingly unstable after he recovered in 1789, rendering an absence from Britain untimely – although given George's habits of routine and devotion to 'business', it is questionable if he could have really found time to 'clear his desk' and leave the country.[98] But it is significant that George thought in Hanoverian terms when considering his daughter's marriages. Princess Mary later referred to Hanover as the 'old family estate', a sentiment surely inculcated early in her childhood.[99]

Queen Charlotte would have little influence over her children's marriages, accepting that the final decisions would always rest with her husband, although when her brother Charles became ruler of Mecklenburg-Strelitz, the dynasty became firmly in the ascendant, since two Prussian princely brothers married two of Charlotte's nieces, daughters of Charles. These were Princesses Louisa and Frederica, whose husbands, Crown Prince Frederick William and Louis, were the brothers of the new duchess of York. The 1790s thus saw dynastic links

---

[95] T. C. W. Blanning, ' "That horrid Electorate" or "Ma patrie Germanique"? George III, Hanover, and the Fürstenbund of 1785', *Historical Journal* 20, 2 (1977), 311–34; Campbell Orr, 'Queen Charlotte'.
[96] *Sophie in London 1786: the diary of Sophie von la Roche*, trans. Clare Williams (London, 1933), p. 200.
[97] Aspinall, vol. II, p. xxx; Fraser, *Princesses. The daughters of George III* (London, 2004), p. 108.
[98] Thanks to Veronica Baker-Smith for her insights on this.
[99] Fraser, *Princesses*, p. 393.

re-established with Prussia, to the benefit of Britain's ally the Dutch stadholder, and the Mecklenburg-Strelitzes. The marriage links with Prussia were reluctantly exploited by George III in 1797 when Louisa's husband succeeded in 1797, and it was hoped her birth in the Electorate would prompt her to encourage her husband to abandon his neutrality and assist Hanover.[100] The duke of York was George's favourite son, and, given the reluctance of the Prince of Wales to make an official marriage, the likely heir to the Personal Union – raising the prospect of the king of Great Britain combining the roles of elector with that of prince-bishop of Osnabrück. A better strategy would have been to create a dynastic 'spread' in case a union was childless – as was the duke and duchess of York's marriage.

When the Prince of Wales did marry in 1795 in order to get his debts paid, George thought in traditional terms of a Brunswick bride – the last time a Brunswick alliance was made. The pattern of allying with minor dynasties was resumed with William IV's marriage to a Saxe-Meiningen and Queen Victoria's with a Saxe-Coburg. King George III's brother-in-law was now the ruling duke and an important military ally in the coalition against France. So George chose his niece Caroline, but this time made the mistake of not enquiring fully into her character – and Charlotte, who disliked her Brunswick sister-in law, deplored the duke's morals, and had heard unsatisfactory things about their daughter, was powerless to remonstrate. It is well known what a disaster the marriage was from the start, but a fortnight of uneasy cohabitation was sufficient for Charlotte of Wales to be conceived, thus ensuring that Britain at least had an heiress presumptive.[101] The later project for her to marry the crown prince of the new kingdom of the Netherlands can thus be seen in the context of a long history of Orange–Brunswick connections, to support the Netherlands as a barrier against France for both British and electoral benefit. Her refusal was due partly to the complications of a dynastic marriage between two rulers which would not be a dynastic union; she did not want to reside in The Hague. Her choice fell on Leopold of Saxe-Coburg instead.[102] But when the barrier in the Netherlands was reconstituted in 1830 by creating two separate kingdoms, following Flemish revolt against Dutch rule, Charlotte's widower Leopold was selected as a 'British' candidate to be the new king of the Belgians.

---

[100] Campbell Orr, 'Queen Charlotte' in *Queenship in Europe*.
[101] Saul David, *Prince of pleasure: the Prince of Wales and the making of the Regency* (London, 1998), is the most recent account of the marriage.
[102] Thea Holme, *Prinny's daughter*, London, 1976.

With only two sons married, and the York marriage proving childless, it might have been a good idea to arrange something suitable for some of the others, as a further insurance policy, but by the late 1790s the times were out of joint for younger sons to marry. Adolphus of Cambridge hoped to marry his widowed Strelitz cousin Frederica, but was told to wait until his military duties were over. Again Charlotte was too deferential a consort to push for closer Strelitz dynastic links, although it was her cherished wish. She felt she had to leave these matters in her husband's hands. In 1805 she was overjoyed when he gave permission for his Strelitz nephew George, the heir, to come to Britain with courtship in mind: but he was required first in Paris, then in military action against Napoleon when Prussian neutrality was crushed at the battle of Jena. Sadly, when Ernest married his cousin Frederica, widowed while divorcing her second husband, Charlotte felt constrained to refuse them access to the court, in case Frederica's matrimonial past set a precedent for admitting the troublesome Caroline, Princess of Wales.[103]

The only daughter of George to marry before the Regency was Charlotte, Princess Royal, whose groom was Frederick William, hereditary prince of Württemberg. This followed an initiative from the ambitious Württemberg family, eager to move up in dynastic status. Hanover gained a potential ally to the south west against French encroachment, but France occupied the duchy. Württemberg became an Electorate briefly and then a kingdom – but with the patronage of the wrong dynasty, the Bonapartes. Worse still, Princess Charlotte became mother-in-law to Napoleon's brother Jerome, the new king of Westphalia, when he married her step-daughter Catherine. George's affection for his other daughters made them hostages to family sentiment; the wars interrupted the might-have-been of a Hanoverian court to find them partners; they were too grand, as the king of Britain's daughters, to marry just anyone, and certainly not the various equerries they fell for; and they soon became too old – though Mary and Elizabeth did finally marry in 1818.[104]

Meanwhile their unwed brothers only contributed to the moral contrast between their generation and that of their parents, thereby reducing the dynasty's moral capital.[105] It was hardly the king's fault that the duke of York's marriage – which had been his own choice – was childless, and became an amicable separation; but his subsequent affair with Mary Ann

---

[103] Campbell Orr, 'Queen Charlotte' in *Queenship in Europe*.
[104] Fraser, *Princesses*, details the Princesses' marital histories.
[105] Claire Tomalin, *Mrs Jordan's profession* (London 1995), and Mollie Gillen, *The prince's lady: the love story of the duke of Kent and Mme de St Laurent* (London, 1970), for Clarence's and Kent's mistresses, respectively. Apart from the Francophile Prince of Wales, Kent was the most 'French' of the dukes. He was educated in Geneva after being

Clarke precipitated a major scandal over royal and aristocratic patronage in the army, church and East India Company.[106]

Regardless of the Göttingen education of the three youngest sons, the Hanoverian commissions of Ernest and Adolphus, the latter's long residence as governor in Hanover after 1815, and the German brides of William, Edward, Adolphus and Ernest, they would always have a public life in Britain by virtue of their status as British dukes. The duke of Kent, who was living in Hanover when his wife was pregnant with the future Queen Victoria, made a point of returning to Britain in time for the birth, so that the heir presumptive of the British crown could seem indubitably British. Similarly Adolphus ensured his son's later education was in Britain.[107] The Hanoverian dimension to their lives could not be separated from the British identities of George III's sons. But as with his failure to marry his brothers, so the failure to marry all his sons had its political costs in the post-revolutionary era, when the institution of monarchy was no longer unquestioningly accepted. To the radical critics, cartoonists and satirists of the Regency, the late marriages of Kent and Clarence after terminating their long unofficial liaisons seemed odd, almost unnatural. Princess Elizabeth's marriage to the duke of Hesse-Homburg, was easily ridiculed in terms of minor German princelings of large girth looking for rich English dowries. Combined with the efforts of Princess Caroline of Brunswick to claim her rights to be queen in 1820, they contributed to a new sense in the 1820s that female rights specifically, as well as popular rights in general, were being trampled on, with the royal family in the lead, typifying the loose morals of a self-indulgent aristocracy. The relationship between parliament as the guardian of the constitution, and popular intervention to secure reform, became an urgent issue. The monarchy began to seem out of step both with some shades of political opinion, and evangelical morality.[108] George III and Charlotte had bequeathed a legacy of family respectability, resumed by

---

sent from Göttingen on getting a girl pregnant. His mistress Mme St Laurent was always known as Julie – surely after Rousseau's heroine in *La Nouvelle Eloïse* – though her baptismal name was Thérèse.

[106] Anna Clark, *Scandal*, ch. 7.
[107] Dulcie M. Ashdown, *Queen Victoria's mother* (London, 1974); Giles St Aubyn, *The royal George: the life of HRH Prince George Duke of Cambridge, 1819–1904* (London, 1964).
[108] Tamara Hunt ' "The prince of whales": caricature, charivari and the politics of morality', in M. Shirley and To. Larson, eds., *Splendidly Victorian, essays ... in honour of Walter L. Arnstein* (Aldershot, 2001); Anna Clark, *Scandal*, especially ch. 8; Frank Prochaska, *The republic of Britain, 1760–2000* (London, 2000); Marilyn Morris, *The British monarchy and the French Revolution* (New Haven, 1998); Linda Colley, 'The apotheosis of George III: loyalty, royalty and the British nation', *Past and Present* 102 (1994), 94–129.

Victoria and Albert to the benefit of the monarchy, but they were not successful dynasts.

VIII

Although George IV was as responsible as any of George III's sons for bringing the royal family into disrepute, he was also a prince with a strong sense of dynastic history,which was reflected in the fête in August 1814 at three royal London parks, celebrating the centenary of the Hanoverian succession. Hanoverian arms were also prominent in the costumes for his visit to Scotland in 1822. He was fascinated by the House of Brunswick's genealogy, and founded the Guelphic order to reward the German legion officers at Waterloo and civilian contributions to Hanover, as well as to commemorate the medieval ancestry of the family – another way of underlining ancient prescriptive rights in an era when Napoleon had occupied Hanover, swept away the old Holy Roman Empire, and redrawn the political and dynastic map. He visited Hanover in 1821, marking its restoration to his family as well as its elevation to a kingdom. The visits to Ireland and Scotland also suggest the aim of representing monarchy, of performing acts of kingship, throughout all the component kingdoms of a typically composite, ancien régime type of monarchy.[109]

Hanover was successfully governed by Adolphus of Cambridge, a duke who never brought any disrepute on the family. His bride was Augusta of Hesse-Cassel; her sister married Duke George of Mecklenberg-Strelitz, Charlotte's eldest nephew; and her brother William married his Danish cousin Louise-Charlotte, becoming the grandparents of Queen Alexandra, Edward VII's consort. After Victoria's accession and her Saxe-Coburg marriage, the Cambridges were seen as the 'old royal family'. Victoria's cousin Augusta, born in Hanover while her father was governor there, married Adolphus Frederick V of Mecklenburg-Strelitz, but remained, as she asserted on her deathbed in 1916, English at heart.[110] The other Cambridge cousin Mary Adelaide was the mother of Queen Mary, consort to George V. Her strong sense of dynastic duty and family history prompted her marriage to George after the death of her first fiancé, his brother Albert Edward, duke of Clarence. She acted in constructive partnership with the king to adapt the monarchy to the world after 1918, as well as reorganising and adding to the Royal Collections

---

[109] Steven Parissien, *George IV: the grand entertainment* (London, 2001); E.A. Smith, *George IV* (New Haven & London, 1999).
[110] James Pope-Hennessey, *Queen Mary* (London 1956), pp. 97–101.

Dynastic perspectives

and overseeing the restoration and opening of Kensington, Osborne and Brighton Pavilion to the public.[111]

Finally, through the Cumberland family who inherited Hanover, glimmers of the old dynastic union persisted. Two sons of Queen Victoria, Arthur and Leopold, seriously entertained hopes of marrying their Hanoverian cousins Mary and Frederica respectively, now exiles living in Paris after their father George V of Hanover lost his throne in 1866. Both marriage plans foundered from lack of interest from the prospective brides. Frederica lived at court after her morganatic marriage to her father's secretary, Count Pawel-Remmingen.[112] When their brother Ernest, who only reluctantly reconciled himself to the loss of the Hanoverian throne, attended George V's coronation he did so styled Duke Ernest of Brunswick-Lüneburg.[113] His marriage to Queen Alexandra's sister Thyra recreated the links between Britain, Denmark and Hanover which had been established during the Personal Union, but at a level where family sentiment was no longer able to cement the foundations or provide connections between dynastic states. Dynastic marriages could only join together the ruling families, not the states and empires, of nineteenth-century nation-states and empires.

---

[111] *Oxford DNB* 'Queen Mary'; Frank Prochaska; personal communication from Anna Keay of English Heritage, 21 June 2005.

[112] See Noble Frankland, *Witness of a century: the life and times of Prince Arthur, duke of Connaught 1850–1942* (London 1993). Mary's sister Thyra would gladly have married him but was not asked! He married Princess Louisa of Prussia instead, daughter of Emperor William II's second cousin. Frederica's morganatic marriage was supported by Victoria but opposed by her brother. *Leopold, the untold story of Queen Victoria's youngest son*, 1998, pp. 139–40; communication from Torsten Riotte, 1 September 2005.

[113] Pope-Hennessey, *Queen Mary*, p. 438.

11 British maritime strategy and Hanover 1714–1763

Richard Harding

In the thirty years before 1714 the Royal Navy had become the most powerful naval force in the world. It was practically unchallenged in the Atlantic and a force to be reckoned with in other waters. It had proved the shield of the state in defending the home islands and Britain's expanding trade, as well as its most potent sword. Superficially at least, the gains with which Britain emerged from the War of the Spanish Succession in 1713 – Gibraltar, Minorca and Newfoundland – were the fruits of her naval power. Queen Anne summed up this confidence in her last address to parliament in March 1714: 'Our situation points out to us our true interest, for this country can flourish only by trade and will be most formidable by the right application of our Naval force.'[1] The navy was by then a defining element in British political identity.[2]

In recent years, the factors underlying British foreign policy under the first two Hanoverian monarchs have been investigated in some detail.[3] We now have a much richer picture of the period between 1714 and 1760.[4] On the whole, there remains a broad consensus among historians that Hanover exercised an initial but declining influence on foreign policy as an overtly maritime or 'blue-water' strategy, exemplified by the vision of William Pitt, was consolidated during the middle decades of the eighteenth century.[5] This contrast of a 'Hanoverian' or continental strategy

---

[1] Quoted in J. Hattendorf, *England and the War of Spanish Succession: a study of the English view and conduct of grand strategy* (New York, 1987), p. 263.

[2] K. Wilson, *The sense of the people: politics, culture and imperialism in England, 1715–1785* (Cambridge, 1995), pp. 140–65; L. Colley, *Britons: forging the nation, 1707–1837* (New Haven, 1992), pp. 65–71.

[3] J. Black, *British foreign policy in the age of Walpole* (Edinburgh, 1985); Black, *America or Europe? British foreign policy, 1739–1763* (London, 1998); P. Woodfine, *Britannia's glories: the Walpole ministry and the 1739 war with Spain* (Woodbridge, 1998).

[4] K. Wilson, *The sense of the people*; Wilson, 'Empire of virtue: the Imperial Project and Hanoverian culture, 1720–1785', in: L. Stone, ed., *An Imperial state at war: Britain from 1689 to 1815* (London, 1991), pp. 128–64.

[5] R. Pares, 'American versus continental warfare, 1739–64', *English Historical Review* 51 (1936), 429–65; D. Baugh, 'Great Britain's blue water policy, 1689–1815', *International*

with a 'British' or maritime strategy has its roots in heated contemporary debates, but it has led to a neglect of the connections between Hanover and the exercise of maritime power. While it seems clear that the ideology of maritime war strengthened its grip on the British political nation during the first half of the century, it did so against the background of critical changes in Europe. Neither the monarch nor the ministry could ignore the fate of Hanover. The responses of the ministries to crises, their understanding of how maritime power worked and what its impact would be on other European powers evolved with Hanover as a central concern. An examination of the two major crises for relations between Britain and Hanover in this period, 1741 and 1757–8, sheds important light on this link between Hanover and the evolution of maritime strategy.

The first difficulty in exploring this issue is that the word strategy in the eighteenth century did not mean what it does now.[6] Modern notions of planning, proposing options, testing and reviewing were largely absent. The closest that the early eighteenth century got to the modern meaning of strategy is 'policy'. It carries the implication of a conscious decision to employ resources in a manner which furthered the ends of the state. Such decisions were made by monarchs with advice from ministers, military and naval men. The relative influence of each of these differed markedly depending on the particular circumstances of the decision. Some things were, however, fairly constant. Very seldom did the decision-makers have reliable or extensive intelligence of the enemy. Before commencing operations they often could not be sure of their own military capability, let alone that of the enemy.[7] These vacuums were natural and accepted. They were built into the administrative processes from the framing of instructions to commanders through to organisation of reinforcement and resupply.[8]

Another consistent feature was that whereas foreign policy decisions were undoubtedly the prerogative of the monarch, they had to be defended in parliament, in so far as they demanded expenditure from the public purse. This required ministers to explain decisions in a manner that lay within the boundaries of contemporary rationality. Early

---

History Review 10 (1988), 33–58; J. Black, *America or Europe? British foreign policy, 1739–1763*, pp. 146–9; Black, 'Hanover and British foreign policy 1714–60', *English Historical Review* 220 (2005), 303–39.

[6] N. A. M. Rodger, 'The continental commitment in the eighteenth century', in: L. Freedman, P. Hayes and R. O'Neile, eds., *War, strategy and international politics: essays in honour of Sir Michael Howard* (Oxford University Press, Oxford, 1992), pp. 39–55.

[7] R. Harding, 'The use of intelligence in Royal Navy amphibious operations, 1739–1783', in: R. C. Balano and C. L. Symonds, eds., *New interpretations in naval history* (Annapolis, 2001), pp. 1–20.

[8] R. Harding, *Amphibious warfare in the eighteenth century: the British expedition to the West Indies, 1740–1742* (Woodbridge, 1990), pp. 150–85.

eighteenth-century debates seldom took place against a background of rich or varied information. Speakers often consciously prefaced their remarks with a caution that they had neither detail on policy nor costs.[9] Arguments therefore tended towards the use of precedent, historical example and ideology. 'Rational' decisions which were clearly for the good of the country, could be justified by such factors as the safety, liberties and wealth of the kingdom, the honour of the monarch, the frugal use of the public purse, the balance of power, the protestant cause at home and abroad and the apparent practicality of proposals. Such debates, based on general principles rather than specific proposal and counter-argument, had an air of ritual about them. The annual debates on the mutiny bill, which provided the legal foundation for applying public funds to support the army, brought forth the same arguments year after year. Likewise, the debates to augment the army or to receive diplomatic correspondence. Arguments did evolve, but unless something unusual happened, either in the form of a crisis, combined with the intervention of an exceptional speaker, the result of a vote was seldom in question. Constitutionally, in a well-managed parliament, MPs and peers could give their advice with varying degrees of force and make some demands for details or clarification, before voting the supply needed for the policy to be carried out. The above description is, however, misleading. It ignores a critical feature of parliamentary debate. The debates provided a forum within which assumptions about policy were defined and refined – it was the prime environment in which the idea of a rational and reasonable policy was created.[10]

George I's initial enthusiasm for employing British naval power in Hanoverian interests is well known. He used the navy in the Sound and the Baltic between 1715 and 1717 in support of Hanoverian ambitions to take Bremen and Verden from Sweden. These ambitions happily coincided with the worries of British trading interests in the former Swedish provinces of Estonia and Livonia. Swedish interference with trade, particularly with the vital trade in naval stores, and their negotiations with Jacobites, made the employment of the navy in those waters entirely legitimate in British eyes.[11] However, the use of British resources to support Hanoverian objectives without parliamentary approval was

---

[9] See for example, W. Cobbett, *Parliamentary History*, ix (1733–1735), 561–690, Commons Debates on Augmentation, 28 March 1734. Other debates on diplomatic and naval issues show similar recognition of debate taking place in ambiguous circumstances.

[10] For a broad discussion of the relationship between parliament and foreign policy see J. Black, *Parliament and foreign policy in the eighteenth century* (Cambridge, 2004).

[11] D. Aldridge, 'Sir John Norris and the British naval expeditions in the Baltic Sea, 1715–1727' (Unpublished PhD thesis, University of London, 1972).

directly contrary to the Act of Settlement (1701), and whatever advantage George I derived from a coincidence of interest in the first years of his reign, he had, by 1718, come to accept that it was politically impossible for the Royal Navy to become an overt arm of Hanoverian policy.[12] Nonetheless, parliament remained extremely sensitive to suspicions that Hanoverian ambitions were driving British policy. The debates over the hiring of Hessian troops in 1730 was an occasion for questions to be asked about use of British funds. In 1734 the failure of George II to distinguish what he meant by his 'dominions' during his Speech from the Throne aroused similar concerns.[13] In all cases it had to be shown that policies were essential to British interests.

With the end of the Great Northern War in 1721, Hanoverian foreign policy became more defensive. Maintaining the status quo within the empire became the primary objective of this policy. The Russian threat to Mecklenburg and Holstein remained a problem for Hanover, and it was useful, from a Hanoverian perspective, that this threat to stability within the empire, coupled with additional worries about Baltic trade, also concerned the British. A British squadron was sent to Reval under Admiral Sir Charles Wager in 1726 to protect trade there, which turned out to be a significant factor in the general thawing of Anglo-Russian relations, eventually leading to the Anglo-Russian commercial treaty of 1734.[14]

However, during these years, Hanover was preserved from danger in the west by the Anglo-French alliance (1716–31) far more than by the Royal Navy. With the crumbling of this alliance from the late 1720s and its

---

[12] Hanoverian–British relations in this period have been explored by a number of writers. See particularly, G. C. Gibbs, 'English attitudes towards Hanover and the Hanoverian succession in the first half of the eighteenth century', in: A. M. Birke and K. Kluxen, eds., *England und Hannover* (Munich, 1986), pp. 33–51; J. Chance, *George I and the Northern War: a study of British-Hanoverian policy in the north of Europe in the Years 1709–1721* (London, 1909); W. Michael, *England under George I: the beginnings of the Hanoverian dynasty* (London, 1936); J. J. Murray, *George I, the Baltic and the Whig split of 1717* (London, 1969); D. McKay, 'The struggle for control of George I's northern policy, 1718–19', *Journal of Modern History* 44 (1973), 367–86 ; J. Black, *British foreign policy in the age of Walpole* (Edinburgh, 1985), pp. 27–45; U. Dann, *Hanover and Great Britain, 1740–1760* (Leicester, 1991).

[13] W. Cobbett, *Parliamentary History*, ix (1733–1735), cols. 182–8, Debate in the Commons on the Speech from the Throne, 17 January 1734/5. An outline of the political rhetoric and themes employed in the debates about Hanover during this period can be found in N. Harding, 'Sir Robert Walpole and Hanover', *Historical Research* 74 (2003), 163–88. For the way in which the link between Hanover and policy was seen in the press during the 1740s, see R. Harris, *A patriot press: national politics and the London press in the 1740s* (Oxford, 1993), particularly pp. 87–177.

[14] D. K. Reading, *The Anglo-Russian commercial treaty of 1734* (New Haven, 1938), pp. 93–100; D. Baugh, 'Sir Charles Wager', in: P. Lefevre and R. Harding, *Precursors of Nelson: British admirals of the eighteenth century* (London, 2001), pp. 113–14.

collapse in 1731, British subsidy money for Hessian troops, ostensibly to defend the common liberties of Europe, was a useful, indeed possibly vital, resource for Hanover. But even this could not last.[15] When war within the empire broke out in 1733 over the succession to the Polish crown Britain remained neutral. The war posed a potential threat to both Hanover and Britain, but without direct conflict, the precise relationship between British military preparations and the benefits expected by Britain and Hanover from them remained ambiguous. Even limited naval preparations proved controversial. In 1733 7,000 additional seamen were raised when the French mobilised a squadron at Brest and an additional 3,000 were proposed for 1734. The purpose of these precautionary measures stimulated intense debate in parliament as to their role and value.[16] Thus, by 1740 British political sensitivity to using British resources, including the Royal Navy, in defence of Hanover was well understood by ministers.

In December 1740 Europe was thrown into a violent clash over the Austrian succession that posed a grave threat to Hanover. The Emperor Charles VI, who died in October, left as his heir a daughter, Maria Theresa. This succession was open to challenge by, among others, the electors of Bavaria and Saxony, who also could claim the right to succession through the female line of Charles's predecessor, Joseph I. Charles had striven for years to ensure that a guarantee of Maria Theresa's undivided succession, the Pragmatic Sanction, would be respected by the powers of Europe, but the weakness of the Austrian state was too great a temptation for the new king Frederick II of Prussia. The Prussian invasion of Silesia in December 1740 initiated a war in which Bavaria, France and Spain also attacked Austrian possessions to advance dynastic or territorial claims. George II was obliged as elector and king to support the Pragmatic Sanction and give aid to Austria, but such action would open Hanover to attack by Prussia and France.[17]

British support for Hanover was potentially vital. During 1741 and into 1742 there was a major military and political crisis regarding what should be done. Eventually, a 'Pragmatic Army' assembled in Flanders consisting of British, Dutch, Danish and Hanoverian troops to defend Flanders, the empire (including Hanover) and Habsburg lands against France. Whether this was the best way of preserving British interests against France was a

---

[15] J. Black, 'Parliament and foreign policy in the age of Walpole: the case of the Hessians', in: Black, ed., *Knights errant and true Englishmen: British foreign policy, 1660–1800* (Edinburgh, 1989), pp. 41–54.

[16] W. Cobbett, ed., *Parliamentary History* (36 vols., London, 1806–20), ix (1733–1735), cols. 691–865, Debate on the number of seamen for 1735, 7 February 1734/5.

[17] For recent overviews of the war, see R. Browning, *The War of Austrian Succession* (Sutton, 1994); M. S. Anderson, *The War of Austrian Succession, 1740–1748* (London, 1995).

matter of heated political debate between 1742 and 1744 and the question of whether the war was being fought for Hanover was a central issue which remained unresolved by 1748. The heat was taken out of the debate in so far as the campaigns from 1744 were clearly fought to defend Austrian Flanders and the United Provinces rather than Hanover, but the general lack of success in this theatre and the residual suspicion of Hanoverian objectives served to maintain the mental link between a 'continental' war and a 'Hanover' war in people's minds.[18] On the other hand, the role of the Royal Navy as the obvious weapon in a 'British' or maritime war was reinforced. Louisbourg, on Cape Breton Island, was captured in June 1745, French support to the Jacobite rebels in 1745–6 was interdicted, the French West Indian colonies were successfully blockaded and two major naval victories in May and October 1747 were won. These successes were not translated into material gains at the peace in 1748. Louisbourg had to be given up in exchange for a French withdrawal from their conquests in Flanders, but by 1748 the vision that success at sea for 'British' ends could be contrasted directly with failure in Europe for 'British and Hanoverian' ends had been strengthened.

Britain's maritime confidence coincided with growing concerns about French expansion in North America after 1748 and it was not long before Britain and France were at war on that continent. In British politics, these hostilities from 1754 were understood as a naval and colonial war, but Hanover again assumed a central role in the evolution of policy. The invasion of Hanover by the French under Marshal d'Estrées and the battle of Hastenbeck on 26 July 1757 precipitated the collapse of the Hanoverian Army of Observation. By mid-1758 the French had been largely driven out of the Electorate, but hopes that naval power would deliver crushing blows to France in America had also begun to fade and the prospect of a renewed French invasion of Hanover was looming. As in 1741–2, a crisis in Hanover was to clarify the scope and effectiveness of maritime power.

I

Long before the accession of George I the Royal Navy had become entrenched in the collective mind of the British political nation. The standing army had been excoriated since the 1650s and the navy was

---

[18] For a useful example of how policy appeared to be evolving to contemporaries during the middle years of the war, see. R. Lodge, ed., *The private correspondence of Chesterfield and Newcastle, 1744–46* (Royal Historical Society, London, 1930). For Chesterfield's appreciation of the position of Hanover at the opening of the 1746 campaign, see p. 102, Chesterfield to Newcastle, 11 January 1745/6.

the political counterbalance. The navy represented a force that defended British liberties from foreign threats, while posing no danger to those liberties by overawing subjects ashore. The debates on policy in the Nine Years War (1688–97) and the War of the Spanish Succession (1701–13) had highlighted an ideological divide between a land war fought by a standing army in the interests of Britain's continental allies and a maritime war from which Britain was the prime beneficiary.[19] The debates produced contrasts in espoused policy that were never fully applied in practice by governments. Nonetheless, they provided what John Brewer described as 'the lingua franca for discussing war, foreign policy and the state'.[20] Unlike the army, the purpose and value of the navy was largely deemed self-evident. It defended the home islands. Since 1692, the British fleet had dominated the Channel. Invasion attempts such as that of 1708 had been deflected or were too small to be a serious threat, such as the Spanish invasion of 1719. On the other hand, parliamentary resistance to the army remained powerful. In 1734, whilst Europe was at war, the annual debate on the land forces centred on expanding the army by 1,800 men to 17,704. Opposition speakers rejected even this modest increase, doubting an enemy could muster a force to invade without warning and the navy would prevent its landing.[21] In 1738 the argument was extended by Lord Carteret, to urge that the army be reduced in a war with Spain so that the navy could be more easily expanded.[22]

The navy was also the defender of prosperity. The rhetoric of trade as the basis for prosperity and credit was not unchallenged, but was very powerful and capable of upsetting the direction of policy, as the events of 1737–9 were to prove. The strength of the arguments leading up to the Spanish war of 1739 lay partly in their long-term repetition since the late 1720s and their apparent intrinsic plausibility. They were based on historical example, current trends and a belief in the Royal Navy. For example, comparison was made with the policies of Queen Elizabeth and Cromwell. Legal justification was based on the Anglo-Spanish treaty of 1670. Attention was drawn to comparison with the growing trade of France. Last, but by no means least, there was the presumption that the

---

[19] J.A. Johnson, 'Parliament and the Navy, 1688–1714' (unpublished PhD thesis, University of Sheffield, 1968); T.J. Denman, 'The political debate over Strategy, 1689–1712' (unpublished PhD thesis, University of Cambridge, 1985).
[20] J. Brewer, *The sinews of power: war, money and the English state, 1688–1783* (London, 1989), p. 157.
[21] W. Cobbett, *Parliamentary History*, ix (1733–1737), cols. 262–321, Commons debate on the Number of Land Forces, 6 February 1734/5.
[22] Id., *Parliamentary History*, x (1737–1739), col. 488, Lords debate on the Reduction of the Army, 9 March 1737/8.

Royal Navy was an effective military tool, which properly applied, could force Spain to heel. Thus, part of the political pressure that periodically pushed the Spanish problem up the political agenda from 1721 was based on a parliamentary perception that the Royal Navy provided a successful solution to a long-term and unnecessary problem.

Ministers knew that some of the claims relating to the effectiveness of the navy were unrealistic. Opposition leaders also recognised this, but it was a convenient rhetorical device – ministers could hardly concede the point without conceding the weakness of the navy under their care. The disaster that befell Hosier's squadron blockading Porto Bello in 1726 was met with shock in parliament, but the debate focused around the expense rather than the fact that the plan exceeded the capability of the squadron. No such concerns were expressed about the successful operations of Jennings and Wager off Cadiz and in defence of Gibraltar.[23]

MPs realised that there were limitations on Britain's military and naval power. It was also recognised that naval power had not decisively undermined France, Russia or other European powers. It was recognised that there were limits to the Royal Navy's ability to protect Britain's interests. The home islands, the Atlantic and Mediterranean trades could be defended by the navy, but the vital Baltic trade could not. Keeping France out of the Low Countries was essential to British security, but could not be ensured by naval force alone. The solution to these problems lay in other means – particularly treaties, coalitions and subsidies. Nevertheless, the rhetoric of naval power sustained expectations and was a major influence on foreign policy. To a degree it shaped what it was thought could be done and it informed ideas of what it was safe to do. Ministers' lives could be made easier or more difficult depending on their ability to present policy in a manner that was consistent with these assumptions.

The expectations surrounding naval power led to it being developed to carry out the roles expected of it. Although the period between 1714 and 1739 was not one of high-intensity conflict, there were many wars and confrontations. Home waters were generally secure, despite a Spanish landing in Scotland in 1719. The British position in the Mediterranean proved to be strong enough for the operations demanded of it in 1718–20, 1726–7 and 1730–1, so little was done to develop the facilities at Gibraltar or Minorca. In the West Indies this was not the case. Conflict with Spain periodically demanded cruising forces in the Windward Passage and the assembling of relatively large squadrons at Jamaica.

---

[23] Id., *Parliamentary History*, viii (1722–1733), cols. 701–2, Lords motion that Admiral Hosier's expedition was an unreasonable burden, 17 April 1729.

Facilities at Port Antonio and Port Royal were developed to meet these needs in 1728 and 1735 respectively.[24] At home, the fleet was largely kept 'in ordinary', stripped down and water tight, in peacetime. It was anticipated that warning of impending action would be long enough for Britain to mobilise her large fleet. As the tensions with Spain and France rose and fell ships were commissioned as the occasion demanded. Most important, the dockyard facilities at Portsmouth and Plymouth were modestly developed. Thus, during this period the belief that the fleet could and should be used against potential enemies in the Atlantic and the Americas led to investment that increased its capability for oceanic operations.

II

In the spring of 1741 the British ministry was absorbed by a number of issues. Domestically, there was a general election. Parliament had been dissolved on 25 April and elections were in progress from early May. George II had departed from Greenwich for Hanover on 6 May. Affairs in London were from then on to be conducted by the Lords Justices of the Regency, in communication with the king at Herrenhausen. The war with Spain, which had been going on since October 1739, was beginning to show signs of long anticipated success. News that Vice Admiral Vernon had captured Porto Bello on 6 November 1739 had cheered the public and raised expectations of further significant conquests by the large expedition of over 8,000 troops that had left Spithead in October 1740 under convoy of 26 line-of-battle ships. The expedition arrived safely at Jamaica and on 17 May 1741 Captain Laws arrived in London with a letter from Vernon announcing the fall of the forts defending the outer harbour of Cartagena de las Indias. The news was met with 'universal joy' and the duke of Newcastle hoped that it would add great weight to George II's position against Spain and in the growing European crisis.[25] The immediate need was to determine what further help should be sent to Vernon. It was agreed that 2,000 additional troops should be sent out to Cartagena.[26] Other aspects of the war were less encouraging. In the Mediterranean, Vice Admiral Nicholas Haddock's squadron was stretched, watching the Spanish ports and the French Toulon squadron.

---

[24] D. A. Baugh, *British naval administration in the age of Walpole* (Princeton, 1965), pp. 343–54. The overall context of naval development in this period can be found in N. A. M. Rodger, *Command of the ocean: a naval history of Britain, 1649–1815* (London, 2004).

[25] The National Archives (TNA), Public Record Office (PRO), SP 43/100 (Regency Papers), Newcastle to Harrington, 19 May 1741; Newcastle to Trevor, 22 May 1741.

[26] BL, Add. Mss., 28133 (Norris Journal), fols. 82–3, 27 May 1741.

The Toulon squadron had given him the slip in September 1740 and Haddock was gradually succumbing to a nervous breakdown, as his squadron suffered from diminishing stores and manpower.[27]

Since the summer of 1739 the attitude of France to the Anglo-Spanish war had been continuously in the mind of ministers. Cardinal Fleury's ambiguous attitude and the movements of the French squadrons had shifted the ministers' mood between hope and fear. In September 1740 the departure of the Brest and Toulon squadrons for the West Indies seemed to promise war in the near future, but by March 1741 news from France indicated that these ships were on their way home, sickly, short of victuals and having achieved nothing.[28] For a short while the French threat diminished. Fleury seemed to be turning his attention to events in Germany, but the signals from France remained confusing. The Brest squadron was refitting, but Andrew Thompson, the British representative at Paris, could not determine whether Fleury intended it for the Baltic, the Mediterranean or the West Indies.[29]

By early May 1741, work on the French squadrons continued to progress and it was becoming clear that Fleury intended to intervene in the election of a new emperor in favour of the elector of Bavaria.[30] In mid-May news arrived that fifteen Spanish line-of-battle ships had left Cadiz. These different reports spurred the Lords Justices to demand an exact list of the dispositions of French and Spanish ships.[31] The news from Cartagena de las Indias in May confused matters further. If Cartagena fell, Fleury stated that France would almost certainly have to take a part in the war on the side of Spain, while other news suggested he still intended the fleet to go to the Baltic or even to the coast of Barbary.[32]

It was at this time that the navy was reaching a major logistical problem. The machinery for storing, victualling, manning and preparing the fleet had swung into action towards the end of 1739, and gradually built up to have the fleet at sea and operational by midsummer of 1740. The stretching of resources, both geographically and in total numbers, can be seen in

---

[27] *Ibid.*, fol. 77, 15 April 1741.
[28] TNA, PRO, SP 78/225 (State Papers – France), fol. 129, Thompson to Coraud, 22 March 1741 (n.s.).
[29] *Ibid.*, fol. 131, Thompson to Newcastle, 24 March 1741 (n.s.); fol. 184, same to same, 12 April 1741 (n.s.); fol. 189, same to same, 15 April 1741 (n.s.); SP 43/100 (State Papers – Regencies), Harrington to Newcastle, 24 May 1741 (n.s.).
[30] *Ibid.*, fol. 239, Thompson to Newcastle, 11 May 1741 (n.s.). Received in London 4 May (o.s.).
[31] TNA, PRO, SP 43/100 (State Papers – Regencies), unfoliated, 14 May 1741.
[32] *Ibid.*, fol. 297, Thompson to Newcastle, 7 June 1741 (n.s.); fol. 289, same to same, 31 May 1741 (n.s.); TNA, PRO, SP 42/28 (State Papers – Naval), 29 May 1741.

Table 11.1. *Dispositions of ships, 1739–1741*

	West Indies	Mediterranean	Home
1739			
Ships	7	25	25
Seamen	2,230	9,380	10,231
1740			
Ships	37	14	22
Seamen	15,155	4,780	15,560
1741			
Ships	33	43	41
Seamen	12,935	13,060	15,780

this simple table relating to the disposition of first to sixth rates on the three main stations at the end of each year 1739–41.[33]

During 1740 the widely dispersed fleet and the expeditionary army in the West Indies had to be victualled and stored, which demanded a rapid expansion of the transport provision. Generally, this had been successful, but as mid-1741 approached the strain was beginning to tell in all quarters. Reports from Vernon and Haddock in the early months of 1741 highlighted the growing problem.[34] Early in the year the Admiralty reassured Newcastle that there was no need to panic. The victuals in hand could last at short allowance until 27 March 1742.[35] Nevertheless, the system was creaking. There were bottlenecks on the despatch of victuals, convoys could not be found and manning was a serious problem on all stations.[36] By mid-March the ships at home still needed 8,000 more seamen – 45% of the entire complements. The ministers agreed that bounties must be offered, protections broken, and that George II be requested to release additional troops for use on the ships.[37] Haddock requested the use of troops from the Minorca garrison.[38]

---

[33] These figures have been abstracted from TNA PRO, SP 42/24, SP42/86, SP42/87, Adm 8/22; Library of Congress, Vernon–Wager Papers, 92.

[34] TNA, PRO, SP 42/28 (State Papers – Naval), 3 February 1740/1; SP 45/3 (State Papers – Various), unfoliated, 15 April 1741.

[35] TNA, PRO, SP 42/24 (State Papers – Naval), fol. 69, Admiralty to Newcastle, 12 February 1740/1.

[36] BL, Add. Mss. 28133 (Norris Journal), fol. 70, 10 January, 1740/1; TNA, PRO, SP 45/3 (State Papers – Various), unfoliated, 13 January, 1740/1. The orders were sent to the Victualling Board on 20 January, See TNA, PRO, SP 42/24 (State Papers – Naval), fol. 69, Admiralty to Newcastle, 12 February, 1740/1; same to same 24 February, 1740/1.

[37] TNA, PRO, SP45/3 (State Papers – Various), unfoliated, 18 March 1740/1.

[38] TNA, PRO, SP45/3 (State Papers – Various), unfoliated 15 April 1741.

It was into this mixed environment of strain, anxiety and optimism, that the Hanoverian crisis erupted in June 1741. The initial reaction to the growing crisis in early May had been to prepare an army of 12,000 British troops to support the Habsburgs, as was demanded by the provisions of the Pragmatic Sanction. By 25 May the army was assembling.[39] The pressure it placed upon manpower raised questions about whether more troops could be sent to Cartagena to exploit the initial success, and how the French would react. On 7 June news arrived that the French had postponed their Baltic expedition until more information had been received from the West Indies. With the Spanish Cadiz squadron already out at sea, this was an urgent signal to the British ministry that they would need a large squadron in home waters.[40] While dangers were growing at home and in Europe there were still important prospects of success in the West Indies, but it was becoming increasingly apparent that there were simply too few resources to reinforce all points.[41]

This tense situation was dramatically intensified after 19 June. On that day Captain Watson brought news of the retreat of the expeditionary army from Cartagena. Newcastle was devastated. He wrote to Hardwicke,

> I most sincerely condole with you My Dear Lord, upon it, who know and feel the extent of the ill consequences that must arise from it; the loss of so many brave men; the disappointment that has happened, after we had published our hopes and indeed almost certain dependence upon success and all over Europe, must touch everybody.[42]

Newcastle knew that this would have a direct impact on events in Europe. The precise impact it had on Fleury is unclear, but on 24 June news arrived that France had decided on war and 40,000 troops were to join the Bavarians in their attack upon Austria.[43] It would be at least six weeks before the British troops would be ready to embark for Germany. Under this new assault, Newcastle believed that Austria had to make peace with Prussia in order to preserve her territories elsewhere and limit French influence in Germany, but Britain had no power to coerce Maria Theresa.[44]

---

[39] BL, Add. Mss. 35407 (Hardwicke Papers), fol. 17, Newcastle to Hardwicke, 1 May 1741; TNA, PRO, SP 41/13 (Sec. at War Papers), unfoliated, 25 May 1741.
[40] BL, Add. Mss. 28133 (Norris Journal), fol. 84, 11 June 1741; TNA, PRO, SP43/100 (State Papers Regencies), unfoliated, 12 June 1741.
[41] TNA, PRO, SP 43/100 (State Papers – Regencies), unfoliated, 11 June 1741.
[42] BL, Add. Mss. 32697 (Newcastle Papers), fol. 213, Newcastle to Hardwicke, 20 June 1741.
[43] TNA, PRO, SP 78/225 (State Papers – France), fol. 330, Thompson to Newcastle, 1 July 1741 (n.s.).
[44] TNA, PRO, SP 43/101 (State Papers – Regencies), unfoliated, Newcastle to Harrington, 26 June 1741.

By mid-July the small group of ministers entrusted with secret correspondence were being overwhelmed by the quantity and variety of problems.[45] For some months a defensive treaty with Russia had been edging to completion, which could defend Hanover from Prussian attention. The Russian minister, Sherbatov, wanted a British naval force sent to the Baltic to deter the French, but Newcastle believed that the French would easily see this was impossible given the state of British resources.[46] For Newcastle the balance could only be redressed by renewed effort in the Caribbean, 'or we shall be disgraced in the Eyes of both Friends and Foes; and we shall submit our commercial interests in that part of the world to the arrogance and resentment of a merciless, provoked enemy'.[47] However, by the 18th, Walpole was wavering. Newcastle suspected that George II was putting private pressure on Walpole to divert resources to defend Hanover.[48] A difficult meeting on 19 June ensured the ministry stayed united on the priority of reinforcements being sent to the West Indies.[49] For the next month the deteriorating news from Germany was weighted finely with the progress of the reinforcements being prepared for the Caribbean.

By the end of July, Harrington in Hanover openly asked what support Hanover could expect from Britain if the French attacked. The ministry held firm on promising only the 12,000 troops required by treaty. By 8 August news from France indicated that Marshall Maillebois's army of 40–50,000 was moving on Hanover, while the Brest and Toulon squadrons were rumoured to be ready to come out. Still this did not deter the ministry, which, despite Walpole's anxiety, pushed for the immediate despatch of the reinforcements for the West Indies.[50] Throughout August the ministry worked on the final details for the despatch of the reinforcements. Further requests for precision in the type and extent of support Hanover could expect from Britain were resisted. This was despite threats that if Britain did not fund an army to oppose the French George II, in his capacity as elector, might be forced to negotiate a neutrality for his Electorate.[51] Under this pressure, Hardwicke recognised that the balance of power was changing, away from the Caribbean

---

[45] *Ibid.*, Newcastle to Harrington, 10 July 1741.
[46] *Ibid.*, same to same, 14 July 1741.
[47] BL, Add. Mss. 32607 (Newcastle Papers), fol. 310, Newcastle to Hardwicke, 14 July 1741.
[48] BL, Add. Mss. 35407 (Hardwicke Papers), fol. 43, Newcastle to Hardwicke, 18 July 1741.
[49] *Ibid.*, same to same, 20 July 1741.
[50] TNA, PRO, SP 43/101 (State Papers – Regencies), unfoliated, Newcastle to Harrington, 7 August 1741.
[51] BL, Add. Mss. 35407 (Hardwick Papers), fol. Newcastle to Hardwicke, 15 August 1741.

policy: 'It looked last year, as if the old world was to be fought for in the new, but the tables are turned and I fear that now America must be fought for in Europe.'[52] However, parliament expected that British assistance would only be given to Hanover if, as a result of her own or Britain's actions in defence of Austria, she was herself attacked.

The situation in the first week of September looked bleak. Newcastle warned that if the subsidy funds granted by parliament for the defence of Austria were applied to Hanover it could lead to a political crisis.[53] As Hanover had, as yet, sent no troops to assist Austria there was no case for assisting her.[54] On the other hand, the situation in Hanover was critical and orders were sent to evacuate the electoral archive from Bremen. Rumours circulated that France was planning an invasion of Scotland or Ireland. Although Newcastle gave this little credence and was comforted by the return of ten line-of-battle ships from the West Indies, he saw that events were moving out of the ministry's control and that political opinion in Britain would believe that Austria was being abandoned to protect Hanover.[55] On 26 September Newcastle informed Hardwicke that Hanover was negotiating with France for neutrality. The only hope now was that Prussia defected from the anti-Habsburg alliance.[56] That did not happen and after some final manoeuvring to try to get Danish assistance for Hanover failed,[57] Hanoverian ministers signed an agreement of neutrality at Neustadt on 28 October (new style).[58]

Meanwhile, on 9 October, 3,000 troops finally sailed from Spithead for the Caribbean. They arrived at Port Royal on 15 January 1741. By that time the original expeditionary force had largely spent itself and although another attack was launched on Porto Bello, intended to take Panama, it ended in complete failure.[59] In many respects it was the worst of all possible worlds. So much had been expected of the Caribbean

---

[52] BL, Add. Mss. 32697 (Newcastle Papers), fol. 434, Hardwicke to Newcastle, 17 August 1741.
[53] BL, Add. Mss. 35407 (Hardwicke Papers), Newcastle to Hardwicke, 19 August 1741.
[54] BL, Add. Mss. 32697 (Newcastle Papers), fol. 452, undated, Considerations on Lord Harrington's Letters of 12 and 19 August 1741.
[55] BL, Add. Mss. 32698 (Newcastle Papers), fol. 16, Newcastle to Hardwicke, 9 September 1741.
[56] BL, Add. Mss. 35407 (Hardwicke Papers), Newcastle to Hardwicke, 26 September 1741; Hardwicke to Newcastle, 28 September 1741.
[57] TNA, PRO, SP 43/101 (State Papers-Regencies), unfoliated, Newcastle to Harrington, 13 October 1741.
[58] U. Dann, *Hanover and Great Britain, 1740–1760*, p. 37.
[59] After Vernon had taken Porto Bello in November 1739, he had destroyed the fortifications and left it. The Spaniards reoccupied the town, but it was open to British naval attack at any time.

expedition. Newcastle feared that failure in the West Indies would weaken Britain abroad and the ministry at home. Thus, over the summer, despite the devastating news of failure at Cartagena and the mounting crisis in Germany, the ministry was not deflected from the plan to reinforce the Caribbean offensive. Support should have been given to Austria, in line with treaty obligations as parliament expected. In the event, the West Indian operation failed and it seemed Austria had been abandoned. It left British politicians confused both in terms of the effectiveness of policy and the integrity of the ministers. On 4 December 1741, the earl of Chesterfield expressed the exasperation of the opposition at the turn of events. He suggested during the debate on the King's Speech in the House of Lords that Haddock had let the Spaniards transport their army to attack Austrian possessions in Italy for the sake of Hanover: 'To the rest of Europe the conduct of Haddock's squadron, if astonishment were left, would be the greatest in the world. With a fleet superior he hath served as an escort to what the enemy had a mind to do. He hath let them embark and go for Italy about the time of the neutrality.' He concluded that this was in response to French demands that they would accept a Hanoverian neutrality only if it did not assist Austria: 'I apprehend that this was the consequence of the neutrality and an equivalent given for it.'[60]

These specific claims of the sinister consequences of Hanover on British policy were unjustified, but they illustrate the anxiety that the crisis of 1741 engendered and tell us something about the relationship between Hanover and maritime policy at this time. The Royal Navy was an important factor in determining the British response to diplomatic problems. Walpole's ministry saw naval power and the amphibious option as the most practicable way of restoring a deteriorating military balance and altering a deteriorating diplomatic balance. This was entirely consistent with deeply held assumptions about the power of the navy. What had not been fully appreciated was how pressure on Hanover would influence events. Despite this pressure, the ministry remained true to its belief in naval power and the deeply held assumption that Hanover should only be assisted as a direct result of her engagement with Britain in defence of the Pragmatic Sanction. French pressure at this point forced Hanoverian neutrality and undermined Britain's ability to mobilise resources in Europe to assist in the defence of the Austrian Netherlands. By the end of 1741 the ministry was faced with failure in the Americas and failure in Europe.

---

[60] W. Cobbett, *Parliamentary History*, xii (1741–1743), col. 225.

If the debates and some events of the war up to 1748 reinforced the traditional views of a distinction between British maritime and Hanoverian or continentalist policies, other events and particularly the prospect of peace negotiations highlighted the close relationship between them. The Dutch and the Austrians had to be kept fighting, which they may not have done without money and troops from Britain or auxiliaries paid by her. Colonial conquests could not be retained easily if the Low Countries or Hanover were in French hands.[61] Despite a powerful rhetoric to the contrary, ministers had to support the war in Europe. Naval power could secure great conquests, but something had to be done to prevent France counterbalancing that by conquest in Europe. Flanders and Hanover could not be divorced from a maritime policy. They were parts of the same policy.

III

This close relationship between the fate of Hanover and maritime policy was largely masked by the almost complete disconnection between the Royal Navy and Hanover in operational terms. The growing strength of the Royal Navy relative to the naval power of France and Spain confirmed its place as the first line of security at home and the means of projecting military resources into America.[62] In 1748 the conquests in America had been lost because of French victories in Europe, but in future, similar American conquests might completely neutralise French conquests in Germany or the Low Countries. British numerical naval superiority over the Bourbons by the end of the war had begun to slide by 1755 so it was by not means obvious that this neutralisation of French power in Europe would be achieved without great and focused effort.

As part of this effort Hanover could not be ignored. To many, it remained axiomatic that British resources would only be used to succour Hanover if she suffered as a result of her connection with Britain, but the ministry recognised that something had to be put in place to prevent French occupation in the first place or all maritime conquests would be put at risk. This was best done by treaties with other regional powers to act as a deterrent to French or Prussian aggression. Subsidy treaties with Bavaria (1750) and Saxony (1751) were part of a wider policy of holding together the old alliance of Britain, Austria and the United

---

[61] R. Lodge, ed., *The private correspondence of Chesterfield and Newcastle, 1744–46*, pp. 76–8, Chesterfield to Newcastle, 24 October 1745.
[62] J. Glete, *Navies and Nations: Warships, Navies and State Building in Europe and America, 1500–1860* (2 vols., Stockholm, 1993), I, pp. 268–9.

Table 11.2. *Comparative fleet sizes, 1745, 1750, 1755*

	Great Britain	France	Spain	Ratio of British numerical superiority
1745				
Battleships	104	45	31	1.4 : 1
Cruisers	67	23	6	2.3 : 1
1750				
Battleships	115	45	15	1.9 : 1
Cruisers	79	21	5	3 : 1
1755				
Battleships	117	57	39	1.2 : 1
Cruisers	74	31	22	1.4 : 1

Provinces.[63] As the 'Diplomatic Revolution' unfolded, the Anglo-Russian treaty (1755) and Anglo-Prussian treaty (1756) were designed in part to protect Hanover. Anglo-French hostilities in North America gradually increased from 1754, but while the peace in Europe held the treaties were apparently doing the job intended and British military and naval resources were channelled into operations in North America. Indeed, during 1756 Hanoverian troops were brought over to Britain to guard against a possible French invasion.[64] This made sense in so far as the Hanoverians provided additional defensive resources whilst the Royal Navy carried out its offensive and defensive roles, but it reignited within parliament the deep ideological conflict on the separateness of the king's British and German dominions, which lay at the heart of William Pitt's political position.

The simmering Austro-Prussian hostility finally shattered the fragile European peace in August 1756. Almost immediately, the new diplomatic alliances dragged France and Britain into this conflict merging the separate Anglo-French and Austro-Prussian conflicts into the global Seven Years War. British resources were stretched as ministers struggled to provide the necessary means for defeating France in America while defending the home islands. In 1757 France turned on Hanover and the Hanoverian Army of Observation collapsed in the face of the French invasion that summer. There was little Britain could do. Hanover was now largely occupied and the British response sheds light on how the relationship between Hanover and British maritime policy had developed.

[63] C. W. Eldon, *England's subsidy policy towards the continent during the Seven Years War* (Philadelphia, 1938), pp. 2–3.
[64] B. Williams, *The life of William Pitt, Earl of Chatham* (2 vols., London, 1913) II, p. 278.

The precise role of individuals in the formulation of policy is a matter of debate. The conduct of the war can be viewed as the achievement of William Pitt, who, in spite of his less clear-sighted cabinet colleagues, was the prescient war minister whose vision from 1756 of a reciprocal relationship between active defence in Germany associated with concentrated offensive action in the Americas, led inexorably to the decisive defeat of France.[65] Alternatively, it is possible to see the policy emerging over four years from the political tensions within the cabinet, allied to an understanding of what the Royal Navy could do in the face of the existing military situation in Europe. Pitt's power relied on his popular support within the Commons, which in turn was based upon a traditional anti-Hanoverian position, which ignored the close relationship between maritime policy and Hanover. Once in office he had to tailor this political stance with the realities of the war.

By mid-July 1758 the war was not going well. The planned invasion of Canada in 1757 had stalled and no news had arrived of the campaign that year. The coastal expeditions which Pitt had confidently expected would divert troops from Germany showed no sign of having a decisive impact. Britain's ally, Prussia, was forced to raise the siege of Olmütz and withdraw in the face of an Austrian advance, while the Russians were advancing into Pomerania. In April, Pitt had to accept the limited commitment of one regiment to garrison Emden.

In June, the French armies under Prince Soubise were on the move east of the Rhine towards Hesse and Hanover. Pitt was compelled to agree that 6,000 British infantry and some cavalry regiments would join Prince Ferdinand of Brunswick's field army on the Rhine. The duke of Newcastle wrote to Hardwicke, 'if Prince Soubise should once get into the King's electoral dominions, nobody can forsee [sic] all the ill consequences it will have. There is but one adequate remedy to all this; if Prince Ferdinand could be strong enough to have nothing to fear from the French Army – Prince Soubise must be called back.'[66] If Soubise entered Hanover again, George II would recall Ferdinand from the Rhine and pressure on the French would collapse: 'Pitt will certainly grumble at it, if not openly oppose it. The English troops will be recalled and we shall have all the disagreeable altercations about Hanover and the Hanover measures that we have formerly seen.'[67] Newcastle was fully supportive of

---

[65] The best and most extended presentation of the war as the fulfilment of Pitt's strategy is J. S. Corbett, *England and the Seven Years War* (2 vols., London, 1907).
[66] BL, Add. Mss., 32882 (Newcastle Papers) fols. 37–8, Newcastle to Hardwicke, 22 July 1758.
[67] BL, Add. Mss., 32882 (Newcastle Papers), fol. 45, Newcastle to Hardwicke, 23 July 1758.

the offensive policy in North America and even of extending it to the West and East Indies, but more than Pitt, who was constrained by his political supporters, he could envisage action that was consistent with the central role of preserving Hanover in British policy. There were costs and he summed up the strategic implications of his position in a letter to the MP for Retford, John White:

> For except that we can divert the power and forces of France, by measures upon the Continent all our other expeditions on their coasts and most expensive operations in both indies, and in North America, will turn upon us and signify nothing and prove a most useless expense. But if we can support the almost intolerable load of expense which we are now, it may do something. But to think of supporting it long is visionary and impracticable and therefore it highly imports us, even this winter if possible to seize the first opportunity of making a reasonable peace.[68]

As First Lord of the Treasury, Newcastle highlighted his departmental concern – financial strain would limit the time for extensive global operations and all would be lost again if Hanover fell in the meantime. The political pressure not to repeat the peace of 1748 and return colonial conquests was tremendous and the only way to avoid this was to secure both Hanover and the colonial conquests. Conquests in North America were still uncertain. On 18 August news arrived that Louisbourg had fallen, which raised spirits, but two days later disappointing news of the defeat at Ticonderoga arrived, quashing the hope of a rapid advance up the Hudson towards Montreal.

While Newcastle's concern was Britain's medium-term financial resilience in the face of this extended attack, Pitt's, as secretary of state for the Southern Department, was more immediate – where were the troops to come from to support Hanover and extend the conquests to the West Indies? Pitt had been assured by the wealthy Jamaican planter, William Beckford, that the French West Indian islands would fall with ease to a British force, and his initial plan anticipated only using 4,000 troops to attack Martinique – a figure which Hardwicke considered far too small.

Pitt's position became more difficult over the late summer. While the funds to mount another campaign in 1759 were obtained more easily than anticipated, the only source of revenue to guarantee the new loans was the Sinking Fund. This was not unusual, but part of the rhetoric of the maritime war was that it was more economical than a continental policy. By recognising an essential link between the defence of Hanover and aggressive action in the Americas, the cost of a campaign was far higher

---

[68] BL, Add. Mss. 32882 (Newcastle Papers), fol. 95, Newcastle to White, 29 July 1758.

than anticipated. Pitt denied that the work of the Treasury was any of his concern, but he was alarmed. Furthermore, the drive up the Hudson had failed and his preferred commander, General Abercrombie, could no longer by sustained in his role. On 17 September, news arrived that an amphibious attack on St Malo had failed with the loss of over 600 men. Neither Field Marshall Lord Ligonier, nor the first lord of the Admiralty, Lord Anson, were convinced of the practicality of the West Indies plan. Newcastle contemplated a peace that winter, but this was unacceptable to both George II and Pitt. For the king, there was nothing to compensate him for the years of despoliation Hanover had suffered. For Pitt there was no prize to ensure that Louisbourg would not have to be bargained away again in exchange for Minorca, which had been lost in 1756. His political position was in danger of crumbling.

Over three days, from Sunday 17 September to Wednesday 20 September Pitt and his cabinet colleagues had to re-evaluate their positions. Newcastle agreed to convince Anson of the practicality of the West Indian expedition and have it increased to a force of 6,000 troops. It would be a single blow at Martinique to provide a quick conquest, after which the force would be sent to reinforce the main effort in North America. Pitt agreed to drop the idea of any other coastal or distant expeditions and would support action in Hanover and a renewed treaty with Hesse. This compromise and the events of the preceding weeks did a great deal to undermine Pitt's reputation as a 'British' minister and over the next few weeks his behaviour was irritable and unpredictable. As the meeting of parliament drew closer in November, so Pitt's anxiety rose. On the day before the new session he heard of a plan for further subsidies to Hanover, which sent him into a rage. He accused Newcastle of duplicity and made an open threat: 'I find the object so changed upon me at the very eve of the opening of the session, that without things can be immediately and properly ascertained I am totally disarm'd of every means of being of the least use.'[69]

In the event, Pitt's popularity in parliament proved unshaken by events over the summer. During the first half of 1759 the situation remained in the balance. The Royal Navy maintained its grip on most contested waters. The West Indian expeditionary force eventually captured Guadeloupe. Reinforcements were sent out to mount an expedition to Quebec. Prince Ferdinand kept the French at bay in Westphalia. The great victories in the second half of the year – the battle of Minden (1 August 1759), the capture of Quebec (14 September 1759), Pocock's

---

[69] BL, Add. Mss. 32885 (Newcastle Papers), fols. 486–7, Pitt to Newcastle, 22 November 1758.

defence of the bay of Bengal, Coote's victories in India and Hawke's victory at Quiberon Bay (22 November 1759) – at last had a decisive impact on the war. From this point onward, France could not muster adequate naval or land forces to reverse the strategic balance in any part of the world. In the welter of colonial conquests that followed between 1760 and 1763, the rhetoric of the maritime war became further entrenched in the British political mind. The accession of George III in October 1760, with less concern for the Electorate than his grandfather, reflected a public mood of war weariness and fear that the German war would only drag on without the possibility of decisive victory that was being experienced elsewhere. That mood was captured so well in Israel Mauduit's famous pamphlet, *Considerations on the present German war* (1760).

Like the War of the Austrian Succession, the Seven Years War had shown that Britain did not have the military or naval resources to defend Hanover herself. The views that had taken shape during 1739–48, relating to what the Royal Navy could do and what should be done regarding Hanover, were powerfully reinforced. The promise of naval power that was discernible in 1748 delivered remarkable fruits by 1763. The belief that this was the result of conducting a British and maritime, as opposed to a continentalist and Hanoverian, war was sustained and deepened by the rhetoric that underpinned William Pitt's political position – so much so that when, during 1761–2, Pitt wished to maintain support for Prussia he found he was out of step with broad political opinion.[70]

However, British maritime policy always had two parts – containing the enemy in Europe and defeating him completely overseas. For naval power to be effective it had to have the capacity to deliver crushing blows at long range from the metropolitan centre. It also had to have a real impact on the interests of Britain's enemies. Furthermore, Britain had to be capable of preventing her enemy, in this case France, from countering those gains by territorial conquests in Europe. During the War of the Austrian Succession none of these conditions were fully met. In the Seven Years War they were all met. It was not a case of Europe/Hanover or the Americas/Asia, but a balance between the two. No policy is a simple formula. Policy works within unique temporal and geographical conditions and its meaning is conditioned by a vast range of contemporary perceptions. While the principles were largely unchanged since the 1690s, the diplomatic and military balance at any time changed views of the approach. Just as in the war of 1740–8, the defence of Flanders and Hanover played a vital role in the policy of the Seven Years War. The first

---

[70] B. Williams, *The life of William Pitt*, ii, pp. 67–73.

was secured by the diplomatic revolution, the second by force of arms, paid for by British money. Over the course of the war over £10 million was paid out in subsidies, approximately 11% of the entire wartime expenditure.[71] The successful defence of Hanover ensured that colonial conquests would not be returned at a peace. Yet the scale of the conquests was so spectacular, the defence of Hanover so mundane, and the political debates over a Hanoverian War so entrenched that the link between them was easily overlooked.

The critical period for Hanover and British maritime policy lay in the years 1740 to 1760. An ideology based upon maritime power to defend and expand explicitly British interests was clearly established as early as the 1690s. The Hanoverian succession complicated this by seeming to divert resources towards futile European wars for the benefit of the king. From 1714 the Royal Navy experienced gradual and unspectacular development which reinforced its global capability relative to its potential Bourbon enemies, but neither the ideology nor the capability were tested before 1739. In the crises of 1741 and 1758 the British cabinet was not diverted from main thrust of maritime conquest by Hanoverian interests. Yet the two crises made it clear that ministries were not prepared to abandon Britain's essential European interests, including Hanover. By 1758 the Royal Navy was indisputably the paramount global sea power and the British colonies could mobilise substantial land resources. Together they dwarfed the extra-European power of other states. Maritime power had come of age and what was easily overlooked in the early 1760s was that the defence of Hanover had also played a vital role in the eventual peace settlement.

The importance of Hanover changed significantly after 1763. With the apparent success of the blue-water ideology, George III's ostentatious distinction between British and Hanoverian interests, and the relative quietness of north-west German diplomacy, the centrality of Hanover declined in British policymaking. The apogee of British naval power during the eighteenth century, the decade 1760–70, coincided with the shift of European crises from western and southern Europe to central and eastern Europe.[72] France recognised the danger of entanglement in Germany and was not to be trapped again in the 1770s. Hanover was

---

[71] C. W. Eldon, *England's subsidy policy towards the continent during the Seven Years War*, appendix, table 2; B. R. Mitchell, *Abstracts of British historical statistics* (Cambridge, 1962), p. 390.

[72] N. Tracy, *Navies, deterrence and American Independence: Britain and seapower in the 1760s and 1770s* (Vancouver, 1988), *passim*; H. M. Scott, *British foreign policy in the age of the American Revolution* (Oxford, 1990); J. Black, *A system of ambition? British foreign policy, 1660–1793* (2nd edn, Stroud, 2000), pp. 234–82.

useful in the American War of Independence but not significant. Likewise Hanover played a part in the 1793–4 campaign, but the Low Countries were the focus of British concern. The neutralisation of Hanover was a factor in the collapse of Britain's ability to act in Europe between 1795–7. It played a small role in the negotiations for the second coalition, but it is possible Hanoverian interests would have been sacrificed in a final peace settlement to ensure Prussian adherence to the alliance. Hanover could not be defended militarily as the occupation by Prussia in 1801 and France in 1803 demonstrated. Nevertheless, it remained an integral part of British policy at least until early 1806. Despite the Peninsular War, the restoration of British interests in Northern Europe would depend directly on the containment of French power in that region. Without that restoration, the financial and commercial fruits of naval power might not have been sustainable at a peace.

Over the period 1714 to 1815 the relationship between Hanover and British maritime policy shifted. It was never as close as the anti-Hanoverian MPs in the Commons feared nor as disconnected as they demanded. British policy was firmly anchored in the exploitation of naval power, but Hanover's defence played a critical part in the ensuring the effectiveness of that power.

12 Hanover in mid-eighteenth-century Franco-British geopolitics

H. M. Scott

I

In the late summer of 1741 Britain's Northern secretary, the pliant earl of Harrington, was making his fourth trip to Hanover, accompanying George II on one of his frequent and extended visits to his German homeland. The international situation which confronted them was serious and would shortly become critical. In the previous December Prussia's new, youthful and ambitious ruler Frederick the Great (1740–86) – seizing the opportunity presented by the sudden death of the Emperor Charles VI (1711–40) without a male heir two months earlier – had invaded the Habsburg province of Silesia, occupying it easily. In the following spring the Prussian forces had won a fortuitous but significant victory at Mollwitz over an Austrian relieving army (April 1741). These two events launched the War of the Austrian Succession (1740–48), as a European coalition took shape with the intention of challenging Maria Theresa's succession and dividing her inheritance.[1] This was a clear threat to the German and, by extension, the European balance of power, and it was viewed as such by British ministers.

The central role was played not by Prussia but by France, who under the decisive leadership of the comte de Belle-Isle spearheaded a dramatic and large-scale intervention in central Europe, with the twin aim of defeating Austria militarily and electing the Bavarian claimant, Charles Albert, Holy Roman Emperor. Though Maria Theresa's succession to the Habsburg

---

I am grateful to the editors of this volume, Dr Torsten Riotte and Dr Brendan P. Simms, and particularly Professor Daniel A. Baugh, for their generous help, and to Professor Jeremy Black for sending me a copy of his suggestive article, 'Hanover and British foreign policy 1714–60', *English Historical Review* 120 (2005), 303–39, which appeared after this chapter had been written.

[1] For the wider international context see the early chapters of M. S. Anderson, *The war of the Austrian succession 1740–1748* (London, 1995) and Reed Browning, *The war of the Austrian succession* (Stroud, 1994).

territories was supposedly guaranteed by the Pragmatic Sanction, which most continental states had accepted, it was evident that as a woman she could not be elected to the imperial dignity, which effectively had been hereditary in the Habsburg family since the fifteenth century.

One dimension of Belle-Isle's plans was a French army which, at the end of August, began to advance towards Westphalia. Its progress north caught George II's Electorate in a pincer movement, with its traditional rival Prussia – now formally allied to France – directly to the east and a formidable French force advancing towards it. In this critical situation, Harrington reflected in a letter to his brother secretary, the duke of Newcastle (who was at the Southern Department), on the strategic predicament of Hanover. 'There is no manner of doubt [he wrote] but that the measures His Majesty shall pursue, as King, will be revenged upon him, as Elector, unless timely care be taken to prevent it.'[2] George II was even more forthright, declaring a few weeks later that the Hanoverian elector ought not to pay for the king of England.[3]

The King-Elector's comment was deeply ironical since, as will be seen, his problems were a consequence of his own private diplomacy, conducted without the full knowledge of either group of ministers, and highlighted the ever-present dangers of a *secret du roi* inherent in any system of personal monarchy. Though both remarks were prompted by the immediate threat, the point George II and Harrington were making has a much wider valency and was frequently repeated in the course of the next hundred years. Two years later the great lawyer, Lord Hardwicke, declared in the House of Lords that the Electorate was 'evidently hazarded by her Union with Great Britain'.[4] His point was to be echoed by Britain's foreign secretary, Viscount Castlereagh over seventy years later. Speaking in a parliamentary debate in March 1815, he declared that 'he was rather inclined to think that Hanover had, generally speaking, suffered more than she had gained from the connection'.[5]

In strict constitutional theory, as in administrative practice, Hanover and the British state were quite separate, two distinct polities which

---

[2] Quoted by Jeremy Black, *America or Europe?: British foreign policy, 1739–63* (London, 1998), p. 86. His letter was written on 2 August 1741.

[3] Bussy to Amelot, 6 September 1741, cited in J. B. G. de R. de Flassan, *Histoire générale et raisonnée de la diplomatie française* (2nd edn, 7 vols., Paris, 1811), V, p. 135.

[4] *The parliamentary history of England from the earliest period to the year 1803* (36 vols.; London, 1806–20), XII, col. 1179. Hardwicke was speaking in the debate on taking Hanoverian troops into British pay.

[5] Quoted by Torsten Riotte, 'Hanover in British policy, 1792–1815' (unpublished PhD thesis, University of Cambridge, 2003), p. 212.

happened to be ruled by the same person in a way which was not uncommon in early modern Europe. Dynastically united from 1714 to 1837, they were distinct in almost every other way: in language and law, society and economy, political structure and governing system. Yet diplomatically these divisions were bridged by one simple reality: king and elector were the same person.[6] Though they could and, periodically, did pursue different policies, contemporaries were surprised when this happened. Still accustomed to view international relations primarily in terms of the personalities and ambitions of their rulers, they assumed that Hanover and Britain would usually act as one entity, not two. They believed, in other words, that the two states marched politically in step: or rather, that Hanover fell in one step – at least – behind its British partner.

The consequences for the vulnerable and relatively weak Electorate were always potentially serious. It lacked defensible frontiers and, in the mid-eighteenth century, could field an army little more than 20,000 strong, and so was a tempting target for Britain's enemies. Unable to strike directly against the British Isles because of her naval supremacy, they could and did deploy their armies against the king's north German salient throughout the Personal Union. Hanover was threatened repeatedly in order to put pressure on London: by Russia in the later 1710s and early 1720s, then by an alliance headed by Austria in 1726–7, and subsequently by either Prussia or France – and occasionally both – in 1729, the mid-1730s, 1738, 1741, 1753, 1757 and 1772. While few of these threatened attacks actually materialised, the Electorate's strategic predicament was clear, and it worsened at the very end of the eighteenth century. During the later 1790s the armies of Revolutionary France and of Prussia once again posed a permanent challenge, while in the following decade the Electorate was occupied by Prussian and French soldiers, the prelude to formal incorporation into Napoleon's satellite Confederation of the Rhine. There was therefore ample evidence to support the central proposition articulated by George II, Harrington, Hardwicke and Castlereagh: that Hanover was frequently placed in the front line by the actions of its elector as British king.

The foundation stone of eighteenth-century Britain's political system, the Act of Settlement (1701), however, not merely did not provide for the eventuality of an attack by Britain's enemies upon the Electorate. It actually appeared to preclude defence against such aggression, though

---

[6] As French ministers always recognised: below, pp. 283–4, n. 25, and p. 291, n. 60.

this might well result from the circumstance that both states were governed by the same person.[7] The relevant clause was unambiguous:[8]

> That in case the crown and imperial dignity of this realm shall hereafter come to any person, not being a native of this kingdom of England, this nation be not obliged to engage in any war for the defence of any dominions or territories which do not belong to the crown of England, without the consent of Parliament.

The key phrase in this passage was of course 'without the consent of Parliament'. In view of the periodic and at times intense hostility to the Hanoverian connection, securing such approval was bound to prove difficult and might well be impossible. The constitutional barrier in the way of any such action was a familiar trope of opposition politicians.[9]

Though Hanover's neighbour and established rival to the east, Hohenzollern Prussia, periodically threatened the Electorate and certainly alarmed its ministers and, at times, observers in London, British statesmen with their usual myopia came to believe that the principal threat was posed by the established and major enemy, France. They feared a French army could occupy the Electorate almost at will, and it could then be used in peace negotiations to force the return of prized colonial conquests. Throughout the Seven Years War (1756–63) Newcastle believed it could be conquered by the French, confronting the government with an obvious dilemma, while at the end of the conflict he reacted to a breakdown in relations with Prussia by suggesting that Frederick the Great might seize the Electorate.[10] His anxieties underlined Hanover's apparent vulnerability, which was of course increased when France and Prussia were allies, which they were not at this period.

Newcastle's concern was exactly mirrored by the comment of the French foreign minister, the Cardinal de Bernis, in spring 1758 about how its capture would enable France to come to the conference table with her 'hands full'.[11] A year before he had declared that it was only

---

[7] As Richard Pares pointed out: 'American versus continental warfare, 1739–63', in Pares, *The historian's business and other essays* (Oxford, 1961), pp. 130–72, at p. 151 (this essay was first published in *English Historical Review* 51 (1936), 429–65).

[8] It is quoted, e.g., in E. N. Williams, ed., *The eighteenth century constitution, 1688–1815: documents and commentary* (Cambridge, 1965), p. 59. For a discriminating discussion of the Act of Settlement, see Graham C. Gibbs, 'English attitudes towards Hanover and the Hanoverian succession in the first half of the eighteenth century', in: Adolf M. Birke and Kurt Kluxen, eds., *England und Hannover/England and Hanover* (Munich, 1986), pp. 33–51, at pp. 44–6.

[9] E.g. Pulteney in 1741: Black, *America or Europe?*, p. 88; *Parliamentary history*, XII, col. 941.

[10] Pares, 'American versus continental warfare, 1739–63', pp. 130–72, especially pp. 137, 153, n. 12.

[11] Quoted by Lee Kennett, *The French armies in the Seven Years' War* (Durham, NC, 1967), p. 39.

'en faisant éprouver à l'Electeur tout le poids de notre juste ressentiment que nous forcerons le Roi à une paix honorable et utile pour nous. L'Electorat doit être entre nos mains un moyen de représailles et un gage de conciliation.'[12] The obvious corollary, as Bernis himself noted, was that the need to defend the Electorate would weaken the effort which Britain could make in the war overseas and in this way benefit France indirectly.[13] Always present from the moment of the Hanoverian accession to the British thrones in 1714, this anxiety increased notably from the 1740s with France's military resurgence and the conclusion of the first neutrality convention for Hanover, highlighting its extreme vulnerability to attack.

It did so because of the notable revival of Anglo-French rivalry during that decade, after a generation when relations had been relatively peaceful, if not harmonious. The long period of Anglo-French *détente* between 1716 and 1731, the product of mutual exhaustion after the final two wars of Louis XIV (1688/9–1713/14) and of dynastic uncertainty on both sides of the Channel, had effectively seen Hanover's defence devolved to France. It was especially so at the end of the 1720s when, ironically, established eighteenth-century roles were reversed, with France declining to intervene in the *Reich*, to protect her own position among the smaller German states, and Britain urging such intervention whatever the damage to the imperial constitution. The following decade had seen a change in Hanover's geopolitical situation, the result of the final breakdown of the *entente* in 1731, and a renewed threat from a resurgent France and her allies.

Though this was a foretaste of subsequent developments, the real sea change for the Electorate came about in the early 1740s. This was specifically because the late summer of 1741 was the first occasion on which French troops directly threatened to occupy the Electorate. Thereafter the fear was a central component in British strategic thinking. This concern was particularly potent during the reign of a ruler who cared as much for Hanover as did George II: in spring 1746 Harrington – with the events of 1741 clearly in his mind – would employ the spectre of a French attack in an unsuccessful attempt to influence the king.[14] The anxiety contributed above all to Britain's pursuit of continental alliances, particularly during the generation after the Peace of Aix-la-Chapelle

---

[12] Bernis to Stainville [the future duc de Choiseul], 12 September 1757, Archives du Ministère des Affaires Etrangères, Paris, Correspondance Politique [hereafter cited as AAE CP] (Autriche) 259, fol. 164.
[13] Black, *America or Europe?*, p. 151.
[14] Philip C. Yorke, *The life and correspondence of Philip Yorke, Earl of Hardwicke* (3 vols.; Cambridge, 1913; reprinted, New York, 1977), I, p. 636.

(1748), which concluded the War of the Austrian Succession. It was a central concern of those ministers, headed by Newcastle, who urged treaties with major continental powers partly intended to protect Hanover. Though the accession of George III, the first Hanoverian King to have been born in Britain, in 1760 weakened its impact, it did not remove it completely, and it was subsequently to revive notably. Down to the end of the revolutionary and Napoleonic Wars (1792–1815), the threat faced by Hanover was a central British concern, viewed in London as an inevitable consequence of the dynastic connection.

All this has been fully recognised by historians both of British foreign policy and of London's strategy in the wars with France, as other essays in this volume make clear.[15] Yet the perspective which such scholars have brought to the subject understandably has been firmly and even exclusively Anglocentric. The aim of this present article is rather different. It examines the strategic consequences of the Personal Union not from the perspectives of Whitehall or Westminister or even the Electorate itself, but from those of the government bureaus in Paris and the Bourbon court at Versailles. It aims, in other words, to explore how the Anglo-Hanoverian connection was viewed by France's foreign ministry and military high command. A French perspective and, more important, a knowledge of French sources modifies familiar assumptions about Hanover's role in British policy and strategy, though it does not overturn them completely. In particular it reveals that the direct military threat which France posed was consistently exaggerated by British statesmen. This immediately becomes clear when the formative episode for British thinking is examined: the French military thrust against the Electorate in 1741 – the immediate context of Harrington and the king's laments – and the hasty conclusion of the neutrality convention to which it led.

II

On 12 October 1741 George II in his capacity as elector and the French King Louis XV concluded the so-called 'Neustadt Protocol', by which Hanover's ruler abandoned his energetic efforts to aid the beleagured Maria Theresa, in progress since the previous spring. It was a humiliating end to that campaign: two years later Newcastle would describe the convention as 'the capitulation of the Electorate'.[16] It was certainly an

---

[15] See also the fundamental discussions by Pares, 'American versus continental warfare, 1739–63', especially pp. 149–53, and by Daniel A. Baugh, 'Great Britain's "blue-water" policy, 1689–1815', *International History Review* 10 (1988), 33–58.

[16] Quoted by Uriel Dann, *Hanover and Great Britain 1740–1760* (Leicester, 1991), p. 39; cf. Yorke, *Hardwicke*, I, p. 318.

agreement which – though never formally ratified – would exert a considerable and enduring impact upon British thinking, consolidating as it did the notion of the Electorate's extreme vulnerability to direct attack and the parallel assumption that France was the enemy most to be feared, particularly when allied to Prussia.

George II's nemesis had been brought about by the dramatic political and military successes orchestrated by Belle-Isle, who had seized control of French policy from the ageing first minister, Cardinal Fleury (1726–43), and launched a war intended to destroy Austrian Habsburg power for ever. France's response to the Emperor Charles VI's unexpected death (October) and Prussia's invasion of Silesia (December 1740) had initially been shaped by the powerful leading minister.[17] Fleury had confirmed France's established policy of peace with Austria and support for the Pragmatic Sanction, though the Cardinal also wished to see Charles Albert of Bavaria (an established French ally) elected emperor. He feared that if Maria Theresa's husband, Francis Stephen of Lorraine, were to secure the imperial dignity France's recent gain of Lorraine – the crowning achievement of his ministry – would be imperilled. Fleury's policy in central Europe was also influenced by his wish to send naval support to France's ally Spain, who had been at war with Britain in the New World since 1739.

In January 1741 Belle-Isle had begun to champion an alternative approach, set out fully in two memoranda.[18] Central to this was to be direct French diplomatic and military intervention in Germany, undertaken with the aim of destroying Habsburg power for ever. Its proponent the comte de Belle-Isle was fifty-six years old and, as Voltaire remarked, 'without having done great things had a great reputation', as a living monument to the age of French military power under Louis XIV.[19] A relative by marriage of the Bavarian elector, Belle-Isle was a powerful figure at court with important links into France's foreign policy establishment.[20] He was an old friend of the leading French expert on the *Reich*,

---

[17] The standard authority remains the vintage study by Arthur McCandless Wilson, *French foreign policy during the administration of Cardinal Fleury 1726–1743: a study in diplomacy and commercial development* (Cambridge, MA, 1936): see especially chapter xii. See also Paul Vaucher, *Robert Walpole et la politique de Fleury (1731–42)* (Paris, 1924), pp. 394–408.

[18] The most detailed narrative remains Maurice Sautai, *Les préliminaires de la Guerre de la Succession d'Autriche* (Paris, 1907); pp. 501–21, prints the two memoirs of 22 and 27 January 1741. Rohan Butler, *Choiseul, vol. I: Father and Son, 1719–1754* (Oxford, 1980), part 2, provides a lively and more recent account.

[19] Quoted by Butler, *Choiseul*, p. 260.

[20] Peter R. Campbell, *Power and politics in old regime France, 1720–1745* (London, 1996), pp. 166–71 and *passim*, is illuminating on his rise.

Anne-Théodore Chavignard de Chavigny, comte de Toulonjon, and became an acquaintance of the French minister to the Palatinate, Louis-Augustin Blondel, who was in turn a cousin of the influential *premier commis* in the French foreign ministry, Jean-Gabriel de La Porte du Theil.[21] This extensive network of correspondents and contacts gave him unusually detailed knowledge of the *Reich*, an expertise which was to be important during the first half of 1741.

Belle-Isle's bold scheme appealed to a wide constituency at Louis XV's court, and this secured its adoption. The king was tiring of the cautious and moderate policies of Fleury and of the restraining influence of the man who had been his own tutor. Younger courtiers, accustomed to view warfare as the nobility's true *métier*, were attracted by the prospect of winning reputation and renown in the army, while the plan was also supported by the military establishment and the influential maréchal-duc de Noailles. Fleury's hold on power was already slipping, and his dominant influence over policy came to be undermined during the first half of 1741. Initially the cardinal believed he could control and direct his rival: in late February Belle-Isle was appointed ambassador to the Imperial Diet at Frankfurt-am-Main and entrusted with proconsular powers, which placed him in charge of French diplomacy and military strategy in the *Reich* with the rank of Marshal of France.[22] The comte's independence became clear during the next few months, when the cardinal could do little more than delay the military preparations which were intended to support Belle-Isle.

By the summer, his triumphant progress through Germany and the accompanying diplomacy, had assembled a coalition of five electors to vote for Charles Albert: the three Rhineland ecclesiastical territories of Mainz, Trier and Cologne, Prussia's king in his capacity as ruler of Brandenburg, and Bavaria herself. In mid-September Saxony would join their ranks. Simultaneously an anti-Austrian coalition had taken shape, containing France and Prussia (formal allies after June 1741), Spain, Sardinia and Bavaria, and loosely united under the umbrella of the League of Nymphenburg; in the autumn Saxony would join this grouping too. The slow progress of French military preparations gave way to rapid mobilisation after Belle-Isle's triumphant return to France and to court in July, which brought about the eclipse of Fleury's

---

[21] Butler, *Choiseul*, p. 260. For du Theil, see Jean-Pierre Samoyault, *Les bureaux du secrétariat d'état des affaires etrangères sous Louis XV* (Paris, 1971), p. 293 and *passim*.

[22] The extensive 'Instructions' given to him and dated 26 February 1741, can be found in AAE CP (Allemagne) 428, fols. 1–62.

moderating influence. By the end of that month, the decision to send a French army to Westphalia had been taken.

With the obvious exception of Maria Theresa herself, George II was the only major ruler likely to oppose Belle-Isle's schemes.[23] The British ministry, headed by the cautious and now politically vulnerable Sir Robert Walpole and with a major war with Spain under way in the American hemisphere since 1739, was predictably reluctant to mount an active military defence of its ally Austria. French diplomacy, while acknowledging the separation in strict constitutional theory between the British king and Hanoverian elector, also recognised the political reality that the two rulers were the same man,[24] and certainly appreciated that the Electorate was a means of putting pressure on their rival. The defensive alliance enshrined in the Second Treaty of Vienna (1731) committed Britain to defend the Habsburgs and, after Prussia's invasion of Silesia, parliament duly voted a subsidy of £300,000, strengthening French anxieties about possible intervention by Britain. For much of 1741, however, George II was pursuing a much more active and aggressive policy than either his British or his electoral ministers wished. His journey to Hanover aimed to free himself from the influence of his British ministers and so pursue a more active diplomacy in a way which had become familiar.[25] The period of some six months which he spent in the Electorate during 1741 was two months longer than any other visit to Germany during his entire reign and naturally heightened British anxieties about electoral influence upon the ruler.[26] In fact for much of 1741 George II was pursuing his own private policy.[27]

Hanover was traditionally a rival of its Prussian neighbour, and that enmity had been intensifed by the military build-up during Frederick William I's reign (1713–40). Fear now reinforced dynastic and religious rivalry as the driving force behind electoral policy. In 1738 a Prussian official had warned that Hanover 'would only be a breakfast', and such

---

[23] French anxieties are apparent from the 'Instructions' for Belle-Isle: AAE CP (Allemagne) 428, fol. 39.
[24] E.g. AAE CP (Allemagne) 428, fol. 39.
[25] Andrew C. Thompson, 'The Protestant interest and foreign policy in Britain and Hanover, 1719–1736' (unpublished PhD thesis, University of Cambridge, 2003), p. 1 and *passim*; Mitchell D. Allen, 'The Anglo-Hanoverian connection: 1727–1760' (unpublished PhD thesis, Boston University, 2000), pp. 95–132, provides a useful account of the period 1740-2 based upon careful research on archival material from Hanover. I am grateful to Dr Thompson for permission to cite his own important thesis and for drawing my attention to Dr Allen's dissertation.
[26] Allen, 'The Anglo-Hanoverian Connection', p. 130. For the earlier period, there is much of interest in Uta Richter-Uhlig, *Hof und Politik unter den Bedingungen der Personalunion zwischen Hannover und England* (Hanover, 1992).
[27] This is plausibly suggested by Allen, 'The Anglo-Hanoverian Connection', p. 131.

anxieties were widely influential among George II's electoral ministers.[28] They were fuelled by Frederick's invasion of Silesia and by the conclusion of a Franco-Prussian alliance in early summer 1741. Support for the Pragmatic Sanction and for Austria mingled with opposition towards Prussia and France in George II's outlook at this time. Though always aware of his homeland's vulnerability, he pursued a particularly active diplomacy during the spring and early summer of 1741, committing British and Hanoverian resources to Maria Theresa's support. He envisaged – grandiloquently and almost certainly unrealistically – cooperation between his own territories, Russia, Denmark and Hesse-Cassel (as a source of mercenary soldiers) to frustrate Belle-Isle's grand design, with London cast principally as paymaster: the subsidy granted by parliament would pay for 12,000 Danish and Hessian mercenaries, and further, vaguer support would (it was hoped) be furnished by Britain and by Russia too. Only the obsequious Harrington, among his British ministers, had any inkling of the King-Elector's ambitious plans during these months, due entirely to his presence in Hanover with the ruler, and even that seems to have been incomplete. Sweden's attack on Russia in August 1741, prompted by France at Prussia's instigation, was a severe blow to George II's hopes. It diverted the strongest military power in this protean coalition which had been expected to attack Prussia and could also exert leverage at Dresden: the Saxon elector was king of Poland, and as such a Russian client. The Russo-Swedish War further compromised his aims by involving two potential members of the alliance in hostilities against each other, since the ruler of Hesse-Cassel was also king of Sweden. In fact, the Hanoverian knight-errant's plans were soon revealed to be founded in sand.

A subsidiary dimension of Belle-Isle's plans had always been to counter any threat from Hanover and its ruler, which would, indirectly, further reduce the likelihood of any opposition from Britain, which was in any case expected to be preoccupied with the naval war with Spain.[29] It would be accomplished by Maillebois's army, which finally crossed the Rhine at the end of August and advanced north. The impact upon the King-Elector proved decisive, exactly as Belle-Isle had calculated. Accompanied by Harrington, George II had been in northern Germany since June. Faced by what he believed would be an imminent French attack and now directly subject to the moderating influence of his

---

[28] Quoted by Browning, *War of the Austrian Succession*, p. 24. The remark was made to a British diplomat in Berlin.

[29] See his 'Mémoire' of 27 January 1741, printed in Sautai, *Préliminaires*, pp. 512–21, at p. 519.

Hanoverian ministers (the principal of these, G. A. von Münchhausen, who particularly feared Prussia's military threat, formally warned him in mid-July that war must be avoided), he now abandoned any thought of active opposition and sought a negotiated settlement with France.[30] Since the spring the King-Elector had been increasingly aware of the dangers inherent in his actions, and in the summer he panicked completely – in July he apparently suffered a nervous collapse and for a time took to his bed[31] – and effectively surrendered as Maillebois's army advanced. The first approach, made by Hanover in the second half of August, revealed that French terms would be stiff.[32] These were headed by demands that George II abandon any idea of military action against Louis XV's ally, the Prussian king, and also agree not to oppose Charles Albert in the forthcoming imperial election. The pressure which Fleury, who now recovered significant influence over French diplomacy, was able to exert during the negotiations was very real. Hanover's elector had little choice but to accept these conditions, which were incorporated into the Neustadt Protocol of 12 October.[33] This amounted to a neutrality convention and marked Hanover's withdrawal of support from Austria, the Electorate's political collapse and its ruler's complete defeat.

Though the military threat from Maillebois's army had forced George II to capitulate, it was less real than Hanoverian – and British – ministers believed, both at the time and subsequently. The Army of Westphalia, as the French force was styled, was a political demonstration and not a military operation, and was under orders to fight only as the last resort. It had several overlapping aims: to intimidate Hanover, to prevent any Hanoverian initiative against the French army sent to assist Bavaria, to encourage France's other German allies, the Rhineland electors and

---

[30] See Münchhausen's opinion of 15 July: W. Mediger, *Moskaus Weg nach Europa: Der Aufstieg Russlands zum europäischen Machtstaat im Zeitalter Friedrichs des Grossen* (Brunswick, 1952), pp. 386–8.

[31] Browning, *War of the Austrian Succession*, p. 64; Vaucher, *Robert Walpole et la politique de Fleury*, pp. 397–8, for the king's breakdown.

[32] For the negotiations, see the detailed account based on French sources in Maurice Sautai, *Les débuts de la guerre de la succession d'Autriche*, vol. I (Paris, 1909), pp. 285–306; Dann, *Hanover and Great Britain*, pp. 35–7 and Allen, 'The Anglo-Hanoverian connection', pp. 120–5, sketch the view from the Electorate; cf. Amelot to Belle-Isle, 6 September 1741, AAE CP (Allemagne) 428, fols. 316–19.

[33] This is not included in Clive Parry, ed., *The consolidated treaty series* (231 vols.; Dobbs Ferry, NY, 1969–86), XXXVI, but is printed in Sautai, *Débuts*, pp. 303–4. It is noteworthy that in this agreement George II is described as 'King', though he is clearly concluding it in his capacity as Hanoverian elector. This was presumably a matter of diplomatic protocol: the King-Elector was unwilling to use his inferior title in an agreement with the King of France. In the Convention of Kloster-Zeven in 1757 he was similarly referred to as 'S. M. Britannique': Parry, (ed.), *Consolidated treaty series*, XLI, p. 87.

Prussia's king. Actual military operations were not to be undertaken, however, unless absolutely necessary.[34] Any attack on the Electorate would in any case amount to a declaration of war upon Britain, which France was anxious to avoid.[35] Belle-Isle's remarkable energy and powers of organisation had given momentum to the military preparations, but these were hindered by the shortage of supplies and especially grain, after the disastrous harvest of 1740 when there had been near-incessant rain.[36]

The logistical difficulties involved in sending an army to attack Hanover – which would loom so large during the Seven Years War[37] – were clearly apparent to the French ministry in late summer 1741, but the principal reasons why Maillebois's orders prescribed only a military demonstration were political in nature, and were both general and specific. Now, as throughout the eighteenth century, France's policy and especially her freedom of action within the *Reich* were circumscribed by her prized status as joint guarantor – along with Sweden – of the political and territorial settlement embodied in the Peace of Westphalia. This position was taken very seriously indeed by the French foreign office.[38] Within a diplomatic culture which was strongly legalistic in nature and rooted in political precedent, the commitment was central to France's policy.[39] Official correspondence is full both of exhortations to remember the obligation and to uphold it, and of lamentations concerning the problems its existence posed for Versailles' policy.

The guarantee of the constitution of the *Reich*, however, was also politically useful. During the century after the Westphalian settlement French opposition to the Austrian Habsburgs was axiomatic. This rivalry had led France to build up a 'third party' among the medium-sized and smaller states of the *Reich*. French diplomacy had effectively exploited the role of defender of the imperial constitution against Vienna's ambitious schemes and growing power. These efforts to build up an anti-Habsburg party ostensibly to defend the status quo would be totally compromised

---

[34] A recurring theme in French ministerial despatches: see, e.g., Amelot to Belle-Isle, 22 August 1741, AAE CP (Allemagne) 428, fol. 290.
[35] As Amelot clearly recognised: to Belle-Isle, 31 August 1741, AAE CP (Allemagne) 428, fol. 306.
[36] Butler, *Choiseul*, pp. 248–9; for the continuing concern with the army's food supplies, see AAE CP (Allemagne) 428, fols. 346–7.
[37] See below, pp. 290–6.
[38] See, e.g., the 'Instructions' for Durfort, 21 September 1766, *Recueil des Instructions données aux ambassadeurs et ministres de France ... Autriche*, ed. Albert Sorel (Paris, 1884), pp. 421–2; cf. the 'Instructions' for Châtelet-Lomont, 29 June 1761, *ibid.*, p. 406.
[39] It was being strongly reaffirmed as late as the first year of Louis XVI's reign: 'Instructions' for the Baron de Breteuil, 28 December 1774, *Recueil des Instructions ... Autriche*, ed. Sorel, pp. 480–1.

by a French attack on any German ruler, particularly an elector. Though France's special status within the *Reich* could be circumscribed or finessed, it was significant and had to be taken into account. These consideration always made military action within Germany difficult, though Louis XIV had effectively ignored them and waged destructive operations there. Memories of these campaigns and especially their political repercussions inhibited France until the very different circumstances of the 1790s.[40] Specifically, in 1741 an attack on an elector was particularly to be avoided when the aim of French policy was to elect Charles Albert emperor, and this was why Maillebois was ordered to intimidate but not to attack Hanover.[41] He was completely successful in this aim: on hearing of the neutrality agreement, Belle-Isle triumphantly pronounced that the Electorate was 'out flat' (*ventre à terre*).[42] A potential source of opposition had been neutralised, exactly as the plans drawn up in January had envisaged, and early in 1742 the Bavarian elector was duly elected Emperor Charles VII, receiving the Hanoverian vote as George II had effectively promised.

The neutrality agreement was viewed in a very different light in Britain. Though Walpole had been informed in a private letter from George II received in late July 1741, the king's actions and apparent willingness to vote for Charles Albert provoked a political storm and, predictably, strengthened established anxieties about Hanoverian control of British policy.[43] This was intensified by widespread though ill-founded rumours that George II had also agreed to French mediation in Britain's war with Spain, which in turn appeared to be confirmed later in the year by the

---

[40] This was explicitly recognised in the 'Instructions' for François de Bussy, a *premier commis* in the French foreign office and former diplomat, who was sent to Hanover to represent the French king while George II was visiting the Electorate: 14 August 1741, AAE CP (Brunswick–Hanover), 49, fols. 58–9. For Bussy's career, see Samoyault, *Les bureaux du secrétariat d'état*, p. 278 and *passim*. Ironically, the French diplomat was at this time also in *British* pay: Samoyault, *Les bureaux du secrétariat d'état*, p. 50; Allen, 'The Anglo-Hanoverian connection', pp. 123–4.

[41] A particularly explicit statement of this consideration is Amelot to Belle-Isle, 18 September 1741, AAE CP (Allemagne) 428, fol. 344. These concerns also surface in the 'Instructions' for Bussy: 14 August 1741, AAE CP (Brunswick–Hanovre) 49, fols. 53–61.

[42] Quoted by Butler, *Choiseul*, p. 284. The slow progress of the negotiations which produced the Neustadt Protocol, and perhaps George II's stubbornness in these discussions, aroused some French anxieties, underlining the fragility of France's exposed military position in north Germany: Amelot to Belle-Isle, 3 October 1741 and Fleury to Belle-Isle, 4 October 1741, AAE CP (Allemagne) 429, fols. 21–3.

[43] Yorke, *Hardwicke*, i, pp. 260–1, 266, 269, for Newcastle's initial resentment; cf. Vaucher, *Robert Walpole et la politique de Fleury*, pp. 402–8, for the British ministers' reaction as they slowly came to realise what had been arranged.

failure of the Mediterranean squadron under Admiral Haddock to prevent a Spanish expedition landing in the Italian peninsula.[44]

Two further circumstances intensifed the neutrality convention's impact. In the first place, it was clear that the Anglo-Spanish war was going less well for Britain: in July 1741 news had arrived that Admiral Vernon had failed to capture Cartagena, and this dampened British spirits and encouraged her opponents. Within Europe, Austria's collapse in the second half of 1741 in the face of Belle-Isle's overpowering coalition removed Britain's traditional ally and so undermined her continental policy. Yet the immediate military and diplomatic impact of the neutrality agreement was surprisingly limited. Walpole's fall in February 1742 and his replacement by John, Lord Carteret immediately led Britain to adopt a more active continental policy. The Neustadt Protocol was observed but not extended. Negotiations between Hanover and France to make it permanent took place, but proved unsuccessful and instead Britain's new leader incorporated the Electorate into the war effort on the side of Austria.[45] Hanoverian troops were taken into British pay and its ruler abandoned any attempt to secure his territory's neutrality. Though Carteret fell from power little more than two years later, there was to be no return to the policy adopted in 1741.[46]

The longer-term repercussions of these events were far greater. The episode had starkly highlighted the Electorate's vulnerability to a French attack and Newcastle, who directed British foreign policy after Carteret's fall, recognised the need to protect Hanover. In 1749 the duke spoke openly of France's capacity to encircle the Electorate, underlining the strategic menace of the French alliance with Prussia at this period.[47] During the next decade this anxiety was central to British policy under his direction. He set out to counter the threat by concluding defensive alliances with leading continental states, principally Austria and Russia, and by his well-known efforts to sponsor the election of a king of the Romans and thereby stabilise the imperial succession and with it *Reich* politics, which would contribute to the wider European balance of power.

---

[44] Robert Harris, *A patriot press: national politics and the London press in the 1740s* (Oxford, 1993), pp. 103–4.

[45] This in itself produced considerable political controversy and press agitation in 1742–4: see the admirable account in Harris, *A patriot press*, pp. 122–77.

[46] Dann, *Hanover and Great Britain*, ch. 2, and Allen, 'The Anglo-Hanoverian Connection', pp. 133–65, provide accounts of this phase.

[47] Jonathan R. Dull, *The French navy and the Seven Years' War* (Lincoln, Nebraska, and London, 2005), p. 9. A good account of Newcastle's foreign policy at this time can be found in Reed Browning, *The duke of Newcastle* (New Haven, 1973), chs. 4 and 5.

These initiatives were the target of Horace Walpole's sally in 1749 that the duke 'Hanoverizes more and more each day'.[48]

Newcastle's initiatives were encouraged and may even have been fostered from the Electorate: the decade after the Peace of Aix-la-Chapelle saw his partnership with Münchhausen at its most cordial and significant, while Hanoverian anxieties were reinforced by the threat of a Prussian invasion in 1753, at a point when Berlin and Versailles were still allies.[49] The notion of the 'Old System', which assumed its final form at this period, had Hanoverian as well as British and Dutch roots.[50] Security seemed to be achieved by the Russian and Austrian guarantees of the Electorate's territory which resulted from George II's accession in 1750 to the anodyne public clauses – though not the secret provisions with their strongly anti-Prussian import – of the Russo-Austrian treaty of 1746.[51] In the event formal alliances were not to be signed with either state before the Seven Years War, as Newcastle's continental policy foundered.[52]

III

The Anglo-French confrontation in the colonies and particularly North America during the 1750s, together with the storm clouds which were gathering in Europe, once more emphasised Hanover's vulnerability and France's willingness to exploit this. Concern for the Electorate remained central to Newcastle's foreign policy at this time: it contributed to the agreement with Russia in autumn 1755 which was never ratified (convention of St Petersburg) and even more directly to the attempt in the following January to neutralise Germany through the convention of Westminister with Prussia. That it failed to do so during the Seven Years War was due to France's decision to attack the Electorate when fighting began in Europe.

French strategy had been considered during an extended debate in the late summer and early autumn of 1755, against the background of an

---

[48] Quoted by Black, 'Hanover and British Foreign Policy', p. 323.
[49] Dann, *Hanover and Great Britain*, ch. 4, provides a brief account, while there is much relevant detail scattered throughout Mediger, *Moskaus Weg nach Europa*; see also the same author's shorter account: Walther Mediger, 'Great Britain, Hanover and the rise of Prussia', in: R. Hatton and M. S. Anderson, eds, *Studies in diplomatic history: essays in memory of David Bayne Horn* (London, 1970), pp. 199–213.
[50] H. M. Scott, ' "The true principles of the revolution": the duke of Newcastle and the idea of the old system", in: Jeremy Black, ed., *Knights Errant and true Englishmen: British foreign policy, 1660–1800* (Edinburgh, 1989), pp. 55–91.
[51] 30 October 1750, Parry, ed., *Consolidated treaty series*, XXXIX, pp. 87–91.
[52] Black, *America or Europe?*, p. 66.

undeclared war with Britain, and it was further refined and clarified in the course of the next eighteen months.[53] These discussions assumed that French naval inferiority would lead to defeat overseas, and an evident and corresponding hope that a wider conflict in Europe could be avoided. This precluded any attack upon the Austrian Netherlands, since Austria – still assumed to be Britain's likely ally – would intervene against France, and led to the conclusion that the French objective when hostilities formally began should be Hanover. Though France's aims were not made clear when fighting began in earnest in Europe in 1757, her strategic priorities had been decided. The intention was to trade Minorca, seized by a French expedition in the previous year, and Hanover, the target of her military operations in Westphalia, for the anticipated losses overseas: exactly as Bernis had said would be done.[54] Twelve months later, however, the obstacles to this approach were becoming clear.

While the decisions made in 1755–7 appeared to confirm the pattern evident in the early 1740s, the situation was in some respects quite different and anticipated the very different dispensations which would prevail during the second half of the eighteenth century. The Seven Years War, which had begun formally with a British declaration of war upon France (May 1756) and a Prussian invasion of Saxony (late August), was in one respect a very novel struggle for France. The traditional antagonism towards Austria had been replaced by an alliance with Vienna (First Treaty of Versailles, 1 May 1756, the centrepiece of the celebrated 'Diplomatic Revolution'), and this transformed France's policy in Germany.[55] Though the guarantee of the *Reich* constitution remained important and indeed had been the basis of the First Treaty of Versailles,[56] for the next generation it ceased to be a means of opposing Austria. Instead France's foe became her traditional ally Prussia, who was supported – at least informally – by Britain. This meant that the military thrust directed against the Electorate in 1757, the first full campaign of

---

[53] Dull, *The French navy and the Seven Years' War*, pp. 36–8.
[54] *Ibid.*, pp. 73–4; cf. above, p. 278.
[55] There is now a major study by Eckhard Buddruss, *Die französische Deutschlandpolitik 1756–1789* (Mainz, 1995): see especially pp. 72–5 on the implications for Hanover and, more generally, chs. 1–3.
[56] See the 'Instructions' for the Baron de Mackau, [winter 1756–57], *Recueil des Instructions données aux ambassadeurs et ministres de France ... Diète Germanique*, ed. Bertrand Auerbach (Paris, 1912), pp. 249–50. The 'Instructions' for d'Estrées, who in spring 1757 was sent to command the French army on the lower Rhine, opened by underlining this commitment in a very formal and legalistic way: 20 April 1757, Service Historique de l'Armée de Terre, Vincennes [hereafter cited as SHAT], A1 3430, No. 147.

the continental war, was quite different from Maillebois's advance sixteen years earlier and, indeed, it came to be viewed at Versailles as a setback for French strategy.

The events of summer and autumn 1757 are well known and can be briefly outlined.[57] William, duke of Cumberland, George II's second and favourite son, was sent to Westphalia to command a composite but entirely German army, as a Hanoverian general, and entrusted with the Electorate's defence. But he was both outnumbered and outmanoeuvred by a French force commanded by maréchal d'Estrées, forced to retreat and then defeated in a small-scale engagement at Hastenbeck (26 July). Obliged to pull back towards Hanover, Cumberland sought terms. The duc de Richelieu, who had assumed command in the aftermath of the battle, pushed forward and overran the exposed Electorate. But he and his forces faced logistical problems of their own, and Richelieu agreed to a neutrality agreement for the Electorate, concluded in September under Danish mediation: the convention of Kloster-Zeven.[58]

Anglophone scholarship on these events has largely concentrated on Cumberland's culpability or otherwise for what has been viewed simply as a surrender, and on the question of whether his actions were sanctioned and even directed by his father George II. From France's perspective, however, the agreement at Kloster-Zeven was a political and military reverse, rather than a triumph as might have been assumed. In the first place it was an axiom of French policy that Hanover should not be allowed to make a unilateral settlement and that George II should be forced to make peace as British king as well as Hanoverian elector: which, of course, had not been done.[59] France's commander was acting both without instructions and against the whole tenor of the orders he had received, as Bernis did not fail to make clear.[60] Richelieu's motive in granting Cumberland terms was to free his own left flank for a planned advance against Prussia. France's wider policy aimed at the rapid defeat of Frederick the Great and a swift end to the continental war, and the

---

[57] Richard Waddington, *La Guerre de Sept Ans* (5 vols.; Paris, 1899–1914), I, chs. 8–9, and Sir Reginald Savory, *His Britannic Majesty's army in Germany during the Seven Years War* (Oxford, 1966), pp. 14–46, provide judicious narratives.
[58] Printed in Parry, ed., *Consolidated treaty series*, XLI, pp. 85–90.
[59] Bernis to Ogier, 20 September 1757, AAE CP (Danemark) 136, fol. 85.
[60] Waddington, *Guerre de Sept Ans*, I, p. 474; Bernis to Richelieu, 12 September 1757, AAE CP (Allemagne) 595, fol. 144. The foreign minister clearly feared that Richelieu was assuming proconsular powers, of the kind Belle-Isle had enjoyed sixteen years before: AAE CP (Allemagne) 596, fol. 4. France's representative in Copenhagen was even more roundly rebuked for his part in negotiating the agreement, since – unlike the general, who was a *duc* and notably well-connected at court – his social and political status did not offer any protection from Bernis's wrath: AAE CP (Denmark) 135, fols. 248–51.

continued presence of a hostile force in Hanover could compromise this plan. The second problem from an operational point of view was that the terms of Kloster-Zeven appeared to neutralise areas to the west and north west of Brandenburg which subsequently became crucial. Richelieu initially moved south east planning to assist Soubise in attacking Frederick's territory, but was greatly weakened in the process and sought to pull back towards Hanover. The terms of Kloster-Zeven now became important, as they prevented French troops from exploiting this region as a base for an attack upon Brandenburg and so impeded the rapid end to the fighting in Europe at which France aimed.[61] Hanover had already been occupied by French troops, but by autumn 1757 the Electorate had once again become subordinate to a more important French aim: Prussia's swift defeat.

Before the resulting problems for France's continental war could become clear, circumstances changed with the great French defeat at Rossbach. On 5 November a Franco-Imperialist army was routed in little more than two hours by a Prussian force half its size and occupying an inferior strategic position. In the battle's aftermath the French army came close to disintegration, as the confidence of the high-command evaporated and the army's administrative and logistical shortcomings became fully apparent.[62] It was a blow to French martial spirit which was not fully repaired until the very different circumstances of the 1790s.[63] By early 1758 the breakdown of the French supply system was evident: neither provisions nor troops were being sent to Westphalia.[64] The occupation of Hanover was effectively over by March: French troops remained only in a tiny enclave in the south. For the rest of the Seven Years War the Electorate was defended by a British-financed 'Army of Observation' in north Germany, now commanded by Ferdinand duke of Brunswick, which also protected Prussia's western flank.[65] Brunswick was to demonstrate considerable strategic flair and tactical skill in this defensive role, and his success increased the problems facing France in acting against Hanover. He was able to do so because of the support which was now provided by London. The convention of Kloster-Zeven, exactly like its

---

[61] Bernis to Richelieu, 12 September 1757, AAE CP (Allemagne) 595, fols. 143–6, provides the foreign minister's immediate and detailed response; cf. *Mémoires du Cardinal de Bernis*, eds. Jean-Marie Rouart and Philippe Bonnet (Paris, 1980), pp. 241–3, for his considered verdict.
[62] There is abundant detail on this in SHAT A1 3444, 3445, 3446, 3472 and 3473, *passim*.
[63] See especially Bernis to Stainville, 7 April 1758, SHAT A1 3474, No. 59.
[64] Waddington, *Guerre de Sept Ans*, II, ch. 1.
[65] Its operations are narrated by Savory, *His Britannic Majesty's army in Germany*.

predecessor sixteen years earlier, was never to be ratified. Instead William Pitt accepted the need to incorporate the defence of the Electorate into British strategy for the war against France and provided funds for the 'Army of Observation'. The Seven Years War saw the defence of Hanover hidden inside Pitt's rhetoric of support for protestant Prussia's survival.[66]

The events of 1757–8, like those of 1741, highlighted a more fundamental problem which is central to the argument of this article. Given the logistical constraints of eighteenth-century warfare and the difficulties of moving and supplying armies, there were real operational problems in the way of a successful and enduring French military occupation of Hanover. As the crow flies, the territories which comprised the Electorate are between 300 and 400 miles from military bases in northern France. This was an immense distance across which to move and supply an army in the eighteenth century, especially a force of any size, given the prevailing doctrines about secure lines of communication. A relatively small, fast-moving army could threaten Hanover: exactly as Maillebois did very successfully in 1741. In the summer campaign of 1757 d'Estrées's force advanced at an average of 5 miles a day, and that too was unusually fast.[67] To remain in northern Westphalia and to be supplied and financed there for an extended period was much more difficult. Even d'Estrées's advance had been slowed by the difficulties of feeding and moving an army nominally over 100,000 strong, and these increased in the months that followed: the French forces were running into serious logistical problems even before Rossbach, and these became acute during the following winter, when transportation was a particular problem.[68] When the French evacuated Hanover in late February 1758, the serious shortage of horses forced them to leave several thousand casualties behind in order to transport essential food on the retreat.[69] There seems to have been a limited improvement in French commissariat arrangements during the middle years of the war. Yet without a forward base in Germany from which to launch an attack, it was always difficult to conquer Hanover in the way in which British observers assumed was possible.

Here there is an important distinction between British fears for Hanover and French perceptions of the Electorate's vulnerability. It

---

[66] This is a central thesis of the important monograph by P. F. Doran, *Andrew Mitchell and Anglo-Prussian diplomatic relations during the Seven Years War* (New York, 1986); cf. Pares, 'American versus continental warfare', p. 151.
[67] Savory, *His Britannic Majesty's army in Germany*, p. 24.
[68] See especially Clermont to Paulmy, Hanover, 18 February 1758, SHAT A1 3472, No. 100; cf. Dull, *The French navy and the Seven Years' War*, p. 95.
[69] Waddington, *Guerre de Sept Ans*, II, pp. 47–49; Kennett, *French armies in the Seven Years' War*, p. 124.

was not that France believed that her forces were unable to threaten and even attack George II's territories: on the contrary they could and did, both in 1741 and 1757. But the French military and political elite recognised that it would be difficult to occupy and hold Hanover *in the way* in which British observers always feared: a crucial distinction. Pressure could be applied and would be effective, but it was always likely to be temporary because of the problems of operating for any period of time in Westphalia, which could not support a large army. France's difficulties were underlined by a far-fetched and ill-fated attempt to threaten Hanover by proxy in spring 1758.[70] Denmark, an established French client and an important regional power in north-west Germany, was offered a loan – significantly, not a subsidy – to enable her to create and equip an army of 24,000 men to threaten the Electorate. Nothing came of this scheme: the French government was unable to raise the six million *livres* it had promised, while the Danish government would have had problems fielding an army of that size – it was a naval power, not a military state – and in any case it had always intended to use the money for defence and not aggression. But the very fact that the initiative was pursued at all underlines the growing difficulties of the French war effort by this period.

The problem of logistics was clearly evident in the campaigns of 1760–1. By that point Louis XV's state had clearly lost the Seven Years War: resources were overstretched and the monarchy's financial plight was serious, defeats had piled up both in Europe and overseas, especially during Britain's *annus mirabilis* of 1759, while the failure of a Jacobite attempt to invade the British Isles in the same year left only Hanover as a potential target for a French initiative. Though the ageing maréchal de Belle-Isle was by now war minister, it was the foreign minister after December 1758, the duc de Choiseul, who exercised most influence over strategy and his authority became complete with Belle-Isle's death in late January 1761. Choiseul's aim in the extended though unsuccessful negotiations at this time was to secure peace with dignity, by limiting French losses when a final settlement was concluded.[71] The means he adopted provide one of the clearest illustrations both of what British ministers always feared and, at the same time, of the real problems facing France in threatening the Electorate for an extended period of time.

---

[70] Dull, *The French Navy and the Seven Years' War*, p. 127.
[71] A full account is provided by Waddington, *Guerre de Sept Ans*, IV, ch. 8–10, and Zenab E. Rashed, *The Peace of Paris 1763* (Liverpool, 1951), chs. 2–3; cf. Kennett, *French armies in the Seven Years War*, pp. 40–2.

Choiseul had initially disdained securing a better peace by occupying Hanover, and instead had backed the attempted invasion. Its failure, and the scale of French reverses, left him with no realistic alternative, and naval expenditure was reduced and instead funds were concentrated on Germany.[72] The military occupation of the Electorate, to serve as a lever in peace negotiations, became central to the duc's thinking at this time.[73] It was initially intended to capture the Electorate in one campaign, but this proved impossible: exactly because of the considerable logistical challenge it posed.[74] Though in 1760 military operations were initially successful, the successes were not sustained as France had hoped. Hesse-Cassel was captured and Göttingen reoccupied, but the maréchal-duc de Broglie – now commanding in Germany – was forced to halt at the southern frontier of Hanover due to the familiar logistical problems and had to retreat. In the next year Broglie raided Hanoverian territory on several occasions, but was always forced back because of a threat to his supply lines, underlining that the Electorate effectively remained beyond the radius of French operations.[75] It was hoped in ministerial circles that with the occupation of Hesse France had secured a forward base from which an attack could be mounted on Hanover in the following year. In the event, however, the anticipated invasion never came, as Choiseul adopted a different path to peace.[76] The whole episode underlined the obstacles to seizing Hanover, particularly with the decline in the French army revealed by the Seven Years War, and France's recognition of these.[77]

That conflict, moreover, brought about an enduring change in France's international position and outlook, and this had significant implications for the Electorate.[78] When the fighting began in 1756,

---

[72] Dull, *The French Navy and the Seven Years' War*, pp. 132, 169–70.
[73] In March 1761 Choiseul, having enhanced his own control over the ministry after Belle-Isle's death, set out his thinking in two memoirs which can be found in SHAT A1 3584, nos. 68 and 76, and these reveal his approach and how it had changed under the pressure of events.
[74] The Westphalian campaigns of 1760 and 1761 can be followed in Waddington, *Guerre de Sept Ans*, IV, chs. 4–5, and V, chs. 3–6.
[75] Dull, *The French navy and the Seven Years' War*, p. 189.
[76] 'Instructions' for Châtelet-Lomont, 29 June 1761, *Recueil des Instructions ... Autriche*, ed. Sorel, pp. 400–2, outlines his hopes.
[77] See the duc's subsequent account: 'Instructions' for Durfort, 21 September 1766, *Recueil des Instructions ... Autriche*, ed. Sorel, p. 416.
[78] Two contrasting though overlapping views of this are provided by D. A. Baugh, 'Withdrawing from Europe: Anglo-French maritime geopolitics, 1750–1800', *International History Review* 20 (1998), 1–32, and H. M. Scott, 'The decline of France and the transformation of the European states system, 1756–92', in: P. Krüger, P. W. Schröder and K. Wüstenbecker, eds., *"The transformation of European politics, 1763–1848": Episode or model in modern history?* (Münster, 2003), pp. 105–28.

France had widely been viewed as Europe's leading military monarchy, as it had been since the later seventeenth century. By the time it ended it had declined both relatively and absolutely. Louis XV's state was ranked below Britain, Russia and even Prussia. Military failure and defeat, mounting financial problems and domestic political upheavals all contributed to this decline, which would not be reversed for a generation. The Seven Years War had made clear that even a state with France's abundant demographic and economic resources could not fight simultaneously on the continent and overseas with any real prospect of success.

IV

Under Choiseul, who consolidated his own power in 1761 and remained leading minister until the very end of 1770, French strategy came to concentrate on fighting Britain overseas. This and not the established continental role based upon opposition to the Habsburgs was now seen as pre-eminent, as ministerial and public attitudes changed fundamentally.[79] For a generation after the Seven Years War, first under Choiseul and then his political executor the comte de Vergennes, foreign minister from 1774 to 1787, France's aim was to neutralise the continent, as French strategists sought to learn the lesson of the Seven Years War and avoid involvement in two simultaneous struggles in the future. It was why, when the long-planned war of revenge was launched in 1778, with French intervention to support the rebellious British colonies in North America, Vergennes kept out of the simultaneous War of the Bavarian Succession (1778–9). France's changed objectives enhanced Hanover's security. The second military threat, that from the north east, was also much reduced during the 1760s and 1770s. The cautious and fundamentally pacific policies pursued by Prussia's Frederick the Great during the second half of his long reign, when the ageing monarch sought peace to rebuild his devastated state, was welcomed in Hanover. The Franco-Prussian alliance, which had broken down on the eve of the Seven Years War, remained in abeyance for the next four decades, and that provided a further source of security during a period when the Electorate's ministers accepted the fact of Prussia's hegemony in north Germany and, indeed, became a junior partner in this.[80]

---

[79] See the fascinating study by E. Dziembowski, *Un nouveau Patriotisme français: La France face à la puissance anglaise à l'époque de la guerre de Sept Ans* (Oxford, 1998).
[80] Volker Press, 'Kurhannover im System des alten Reiches 1692–1803', in: Birke and Kluxen, eds., *England und Hannover/England and Hanover*, pp. 53–78, at pp. 69–71.

The shift in France's strategy was not fully apparent to British observers, who long exaggerated the nature and even the extent of the threat they faced. Their miscalculation became evident during the War of American Independence (1775–83). In 1778 ministers reacted to war with France – as they had always done – by scouring Europe for alliances intended to protect Hanover: failing to realise that the last thing France wanted was the War of American Independence to spread to Europe and that the Electorate was not at risk.[81] They were encouraged by the growing Austro-Prussian confrontation over Bavaria, which threatened a continental war in which electoral issues might become entangled and which Britain could exploit. Their search led to rebuffs from all three eastern powers, Austria, Prussia and Russia, and was in any case unnecessary: there was no longer any intention at Versailles to use Hanover as a lever against George III. In fact, the accession in 1760 of this King-Elector had been a watershed.[82] It had brought to the two thrones the first ruler during the Personal Union to have been born on the British side of the North Sea, and – while he was an active and conscientious ruler of the Electorate – there was little apparent concern with the security of Hanover and, specifically, with a French or Prussian threat during the 1760s and for much of the 1770s. It would be a different story during the mid-1780s and thereafter, when a more active electoral policy became evident in response to a changing political environment.[83]

That was particularly so after 1792, when the long struggle between Revolutionary France and the established European powers began.[84] This fighting not merely revived but actually increased the military threat to the Electorate, for two separate reasons. The rebirth of French military power during the French Revolution, and the military changes upon which it rested, notably enhanced the mobility and operational range of France's armies, which began once again to live off the land in the manner of European armies during the Thirty Years War (1618–48). The dependence

---

[81] For this search see H. M. Scott, *British foreign policy in the age of the American Revolution* (Oxford, 1990), pp. 263–71.

[82] See Jeremy Black, 'The crown, Hanover and the shift in British foreign policy in the 1760s', in Black, ed., *Knights errant and true Englishmen*, pp. 113–34, and more recently the same author's *America or Europe?*, pp. 81–103.

[83] See the seminal article by T. C. W. Blanning, ' "That horrid Electorate" or "Ma patrie Germanique"?: George III and the *Fürstenbund* of 1785', *Historical Journal* 20 (1977), 311–44, and the chapter by Torsten Riotte in this volume, chapter 4, above.

[84] See especially Riotte, 'Hanover in British Policy', now revised and published as *Hannover in der britischen Politik (1792–1815): Dynastische Verbindung als Element außenpolitischer Entscheidungsprozesse* (Münster, 2005). I am indebted to Dr Riotte for sending me a copy of his informative book.

upon military depots and supply lines, and the resulting limits upon the potential radius of operations, which had afforded a measure of security to Hanover in the mid-eighteenth-century wars, now gave way to much more rapid, wide-ranging campaigning, particularly after the advent of Napoleon Bonaparte to supreme power in France after 1799.

Even more immediately, after 1795 there was a notable revival of the threat represented by Prussia which once again moved into the French orbit, first as would-be client, then as ally and finally as satellite.[85] In that year the Hohenzollern state ended its unsuccessful participation in the first coalition and instead completed the final partition of Poland–Lithuania. The ambitious regime of Frederick William II (1786–97) had demonstrated a healthy territorial appetite, as did that of his successor Frederick William III (1797–1840), and sweeping gains in the east now gave way to potential expansion westwards, where Hanover was an established and enticing target. Prussia initially protected her own interests and the security of north Germany by establishing a neutral zone within which the Electorate clearly lay, arousing anxieties both there and in London. These fears were strengthened by the reappearance of the Prusso-French axis, albeit in a novel form, as the Hohenzollern monarchy, financially exhausted by Frederick William II's wide-ranging policies, pursued its own security through alignment with the new republican regime in Paris. Under the clear threat of a Prussian military occupation if it did not join, the Electorate became part of the neutrality system and even provided troops for the army which protected the region.[86]

The more ambitious French policies which were apparent by the later 1790s and especially Bonaparte's vast and increasing territorial appetite and political aims, brought the fighting into northern Germany and to Hanover's borders by the early 1800s when – in sharp contrast to most of the eighteenth century – France's armies penetrated the region with some ease. By 1801 a temporary Prussian occupation had to be endured; two years later French troops occupied the Electorate, which was first subjected to a temporary Prussian occupation (1805–6) and then largely

---

[85] For Prussian foreign policy in this period see: Brendan Simms, *The impact of Napoleon: Prussian high politics, foreign policy and the crisis of the executive, 1797–1806* (Cambridge, 1997), a notably penetrating study; a series of well-researched articles by Philip G. Dwyer: 'Prussia and the armed neutrality: the invasion of Hanover in 1801', *International History Review* 15 (1993), 661–87; 'The politics of Prussian neutrality, 1795–1806', *German History* 12 (1994), 351–74; and 'Two definitions of neutrality: Prussia, the European states-system, and the French invasion of Hanover in 1803', *International History Review* 19 (1997), 522–40; and, most recently, the large-scale Lothar Kittstein, *Politik im Zeitalter der Revolution: Untersuchungen zur preussischen Staatlichkeit 1792–1807* (Stuttgart, 2003).

[86] Riotte, 'Hanover in British Policy', pp. 77–8.

incorporated into two successive Napoleonic creations: the kingdom of Westphalia and the Confederation of the Rhine. Its independence was only recovered in 1815, as part of the final settlement at the end of the Napoleonic Wars, when it became the kingdom of Hanover.

By the winter of 1805–6, British ministers had recognised that George III's Electorate had to be protected against the French threat and, for the first time in almost half a century, decided to intervene militarily in northern Germany: in the event unsuccessfully.[87] An expedition was prepared with the intention of evicting the French occupiers, troops were found, ships and supplies gathered together. There was only one problem: though the War Office hunted high and low, it could not find a single map of the Electorate to guide the expedition's commanders, and had to borrow one from the king's extensive collection.[88] The *lacuna* is suggestive, particularly in an era when the quality of maps and their role in decision-making were both increasing. If British ministers really feared a French invasion of Hanover and believed – as they sometimes professed – that Britain's own forces might have to defend or reconquer it, might it not have been prudent (to say no more) to have secured a map of the Electorate?

The circumstances of the later 1790s and 1800s were in fact very different from those which had prevailed during the eighteenth century. France's revived military power, Prussia's territorial ambitions and the restored axis between Paris and Berlin combined to produce a far greater and more immediate threat to the Electorate. In a very general sense Hanover was always vulnerable to an attack and therefore a potential hostage, as British ministers recognised. Yet France's capacity to exploit the Electorate's vulnerability before the later 1790s was usually rather less than they assumed. Military operations in north Germany posed considerable problems before the revolution in logistics during that decade, while France's cherished status as guarantor of the political and territorial status quo of the *Reich* was could be an obstacle.

Throughout much of the eighteenth century, however, British ministers and their political opponents spoke repeatedly and at times forcefully about the danger of a French military coup against the Electorate. Their enduring concern was, very obviously, a reaction to the effective military pressure applied in 1741 and the temporary occupation sixteen years later. Both episodes stimulated and, simultaneously, reinforced

---

[87] See Brendan Simms, '"An odd question enough": Charles James Fox, the crown and British policy during the Hanoverian crisis of 1806', *Historical Journal* 38 (1995), 567–96, for an important re-examination of British policy at this time.

[88] C. D. Hall, *British Strategy in the Napoleonic Wars, 1803–15* (Manchester, 1992), p. 49.

anti-Hanoverianism which was a potent force in domestic political debate. But there was also a realistic appreciation that means had to be found to defend the Electorate against France. If they were not, and Hanover were to be forced to pay for the King of England, then Britain in turn might well have to pay for the Elector when peace was made. Such, at least, was the widespread assumption of British observers and, at times, the hope of French statesmen. The strategic reality was rather different: France's military and political elite appreciated the logistical and, at times, diplomatic obstacles to be surmounted if Hanover were to be directly attacked, rather than simply threatened. Only Napoleonic armies, with their new mobility and equally novel capacity to win decisive victories, could consistently enforce the direct threat which had long been feared in the Electorate, as in London.

13 Hanover and British republicanism

Nicholas B. Harding

During recent decades, the notion of natural-law theory's pre-eminence in eighteenth-century political thought has come under sustained challenge.[1] One significant exception to this rule can be found in the history of Britain's connection with its king's German Electorate of Hanover. Specialists have considered Britain and Hanover to have formed a 'Personal Union',[2] a category of natural law in which states sharing the same ruler remained legally independent of one another. The concept itself is eighteenth century; in fact, it was first coined and applied to the electoral relationship with Britain by the Hanoverian jurist Johann

---

This paper benefited from suggestions it received at a Peterhouse colloquium, 'The Hanoverian dimension in British foreign policy and domestic politics 1714–1837'. I would like to thank its organisers, Brendan Simms and Torsten Riotte, for their hospitality and advice. I am also grateful for the comments of attendees at the 2004 North American Conference on British Studies (NACBS) in Philadelphia, Pennsylvania. Finally I want to thank my fellow panelists Margaret Jacob, Marc Lerner, Jonathan Scott, and Stefania Tutino, for their input and assistance.

[1] See, for example, John Dunn, *The political thought of John Locke* (Cambridge, 1969); John Dunn, 'The politics of Locke in England and America in the eighteenth century', in: John W. Yolton, ed., *John Locke: problems and perspectives* (Cambridge, 1969), pp. 45–80.

[2] Ernst von Meier, *Hannoversche Verfassungs- und Verwaltungsgeschichte 1680–1866* (2 vols., Leipzig, 1898), I, pp. 122–3; Adolphus William Ward, *Great Britain and Hanover: some aspects of the personal union* (Oxford, 1899), pp. 1–2; Karl Bingmann, *Das rechtliche Verhältnis zwischen Großbritannien und Hannover von 1714 bis 1837* (Celle, 1925), pp. 51–2; Kenneth L. Ellis, 'The administrative connections between Britain and Hanover', *Journal of the Society of Archivists* 3 (October 1969), 548; Georg Schnath, 'Die Personalunion zwischen Großbritannien und Hannover 1714–1837', *Lüneburger Blätter* 20 (1969), 7–8; Waldemar Röhrbein and Alheidis von Rohr, *Hannover im Glanz und Schatten des britischen Weltreiches: die Auswirkungen der Personalunion auf Hannover von 1714–1837* (Hannover, 1977), p. 20; Ragnhild Hatton, 'The Anglo-Hanoverian connection 1714–1760' (The Creighton Trust Lecture, London, 1982), pp. 2–3; Sabine Haselau, 'Die Organisation der Personalunion – ihr verfassungsmäßiger Charakter und das rechtliche Verhältnis zwischen Großbritannien und Hannover', in: Heide N. Rohloff, ed., *Großbritannien und Hannover: Die Zeit der Personalunion 1714–1837* (Frankfurt am Main, 1989), p. 236; Uriel Dann, *Hanover and Great Britain 1740–1760: diplomacy and survival* (Leicester, 1991), p. 137; Philip Konigs, *The Hanoverian kings and their homeland: a study of the personal union 1714–1837* (Sussex, 1993), p. 172; Jeremy Black, *The Hanoverians: the history of a dynasty* (London, 2004), pp. 21–2.

Stephan Pütter.[3] While Pütter's terminology was new, it clearly drew upon the classics of natural law.[4] Personal Union tended to legitimate the status quo, but cannot explain opposition to Britain's relationship with Hanover. This derived instead from ancient and Renaissance republicanism.

Republicanism and natural law were not always as incompatible as they were in the case of Hanover; indeed, writers often used them interchangeably in other contexts.[5] But in order to correct the traditional focus on natural law, historians have had to examine republicanism separately.[6] Of course, the nomenclature of republicanism more often refers to its historical origins in Rome and Florence than to the objectives of its later British exponents. As J. G. A. Pocock put it, 'republicanism in England was a language, not a programme'.[7] Some republicans compassed the overthrow of the monarchy. But others merely sought to restrain it within a mixed or balanced constitution, such as that first described by the Greek historian Polybius.[8] Republicanism also promoted self-restraint, most often through the exercise of martial patriotism. As the military ideal of the age was firmly male, republicanism was often capable of pronounced misogyny.[9] And their selflessness made republicans tireless foes of personal venality, as evidenced in corrupt assemblies and professional armies.[10] Their antidote to corruption was the volunteer militia, which was to be underwritten by landed property.[11] On the world stage, local patriotism (known as reason of state) opposed the universalism which characterised natural law theory.[12]

---

[3] For Pütter's invention of 'Personal Union', see his *Elementa iuris publici germanici* (Göttingen, 1760), p. 106. For its application to Britain and Hanover, see his *Beyträge zum teutschen Staats- und Fürsten-Rechte* (Göttingen, 1777), p. 22.

[4] Hugo Grotius, *De jure belli ac pacis libri tres*, trans. Francis W. Kelsey (2 vols., Oxford, 1925), II, p. 103; Samuel Pufendorf, *De jure naturae et gentium libri octo*, trans. C. H. and W. A. Oldfather (2 vols., Oxford, 1934), II, p. 1044.

[5] Knud Haakonssen, 'Republicanism', in Robert E. Goodin and Philip Pettit, eds., *A companion to contemporary political philosophy* (Oxford, 1993), pp. 568–74; Jonathan Scott, *Commonwealth principles: republican writing of the English revolution* (Cambridge, 2004).

[6] Bernard Bailyn, *The ideological origins of the American Revolution* (Cambridge, MA, 1967).

[7] J. G. A. Pocock, ed., *The political works of James Harrington* (Cambridge, 1977), p. 15.

[8] Zera S. Fink, *The classical republicans* (Evanston, 1945); Corinne Comstock Weston, 'The theory of mixed monarchy under Charles I and after', *The English Historical Review* 75 (1960), 426–43; Arihiro Fukuda, *Sovereignty and the sword: Harrington, Hobbes, and mixed government in the English civil wars* (Oxford, 1997).

[9] See, for example, Kathleen Wilson, *The sense of the people: politics, culture and imperialism in England 1715–1785* (Cambridge, 1995), pp. 185–205.

[10] Lois G. Schwoerer, *No standing armies!* (Baltimore, 1974).

[11] J. G. A. Pocock, *The Machiavellian moment: Florentine political thought and the Atlantic republican tradition* (Princeton, 1975).

[12] Friedrich Meinecke, *Machiavellism*, trans. by Douglas Scott (London, 1957).

Given republicanism's local priorities, it is perhaps not surprising that its English adherents were skeptical when parliament considered the Hanoverian succession while preparing the Act of Settlement in 1701. Indeed the first author to address Hanover was the Irish-born republican John Toland.[13] Toland anonymously published a pamphlet entitled *Limitations for the next foreign successor, or new Saxon race*, which endorsed his patron Robert Harley's effort to impose conditions upon an eventual Hanoverian successor. Toland even proposed that the candidates should renounce their German possessions upon inheriting the English crown.[14] He supported this argument with reference to a medieval statute (14 Edward III c. 3), which he inaccurately implied had prohibited dynastic union with France. Nevertheless criticism of England's medieval empire on the continent was to become a staple of 'blue-water' grand strategy,[15] which dovetailed with republicanism in so far as it preferred the navy to a standing army.

Toland feared Hanover's standing army even more than England's. He wrote that the Hanoverian successors

will lie under a mighty temptation to enlarge their dominions beyond sea, in order to make the communication betwixt their old and new dominions more speedy and easy. This the family of *Hanover* may attempt by falling down upon the *Elbe* and the *Weser*, and swallowing up *Hamburg, Bremen, Emden,* etc . . . [so] that if at any time we come to struggle with those princes for our privileges they will have an opportunity of landing men upon us from their foreign dominions, which may prove as fatal to our liberty, as the *German* invasion did formerly to our ancestors.[16]

Although Toland explicitly referred to the ancient Saxon conquest of his subtitle, an obvious subtext was the more recent Dutch invasion under William III. Indeed Toland had cut his republican teeth during the 'Standing Army controversy' of 1697–9, in which the opposition had forced the last Dutch troops to depart and pared back the British army.

If Hanoverian expansion towards the North Sea would endanger English freedom, it would also imperil European liberty more generally. Toland predicted 'it will occasion a jealousy in the *Dutch* and the

---

[13] Justin Champion, *Republican learning: John Toland and the crisis of Christian culture, 1696–1722* (Manchester, 2003).
[14] [John Toland], *Limitations for the next foreign successor, or new Saxon race* (London, 1701), p. 9.
[15] Daniel Baugh, 'Great Britain's "blue-water" policy, 1689–1815', *The International History Review* 10 (1988), 33–58; N. A. M. Rodger, 'The continental commitment in the eighteenth century', in: Lawrence Freedman, Paul Hayes and Robert O'Neill, eds., *War, strategy, and international politics: essays in honour of Sir Michael Howard* (Oxford, 1992), pp. 39–55.
[16] [Toland], *Limitations*, pp. 9–10.

Northern princes ... [in which] case they will be sure to join with *Scotland* to keep the balance equal'.[17] Toland referred to a regional balance of power, a microcosm of Europe's continental equilibrium. In so doing, he paid homage to the republican tradition. For the idea of an international balance originated with Machiavelli,[18] even if it was later appropriated by natural law theorists. It might be seen as the international extension of the Polybian ideal of the balanced constitution for, as Jonathan Swift wrote, 'there is a balance of power to be carefully held by every state within it self, as well as among several states with each other'.[19]

Toland was typical of early modern republicanism in that he was religiously heterodox,[20] seeing clerical hierarchies as the spiritual equivalent of a standing army. Toland defined Hanoverian absolutism in religious terms, predicting that if

> a politic and ambitious *Lutheran* prince succeeds to our throne, and ... he has a mind to make himself as arbitrary in *England* as most of the princes are in *Germany* ... he may readily fall upon a method to effect it. He has no more to do but to fall in with our bigoted ceremonialists, as all our kings of the *Scots* race ever did; and provided he give them leave to persecute others, they will advance his prerogative as high as he pleases ... The Lutherans ... are rather for augmenting than diminishing ceremonies in worship.[21]

Toland knew little about Hanover, other than that its established church was Lutheran. But this fact ruined the Electorate for Toland, as his fellow Irishman, republican, and freethinker Robert Molesworth had already described Lutheranism as even better suited for absolutism than Catholicism.[22]

Toland's propaganda helped to procure a number of conditions upon the Hanoverian succession, of which the most important were the exclusion of foreigners from English patronage and the requirement that parliament approve any war for foreign dominions. Although the Act of Settlement did not require the Hanoverian dynasty to renounce the Electorate upon its succession to the English throne, Harley and Toland hastened to promote it. Toland did this in a book entitled

---

[17] [Toland], *Limitations*, p. 25. [18] Meinecke, *Machiavellism*, trans. Scott, p. 29.
[19] [Jonathan Swift], *A discourse of the contests and dissensions in Athens and Rome* (London, 1701), p. 5.
[20] J. C. D. Clark, *English society 1688–1832* (Cambridge, 1985); J. A. I. Champion, *The pillars of priestcraft shaken* (Cambridge, 1992); Mark Goldie, 'Priestcraft and the birth of Whiggism', in: Nicholas Phillipson and Quentin Skinner, eds., *Political discourse in early-modern Britain* (Cambridge, 1993), pp. 209–31; Scott, *Commonwealth principles*.
[21] [Toland], *Limitations*, pp. 7–8.
[22] [Robert Molesworth], *An account of Denmark as it was in the year 1692* (London, 1694), pp. 260–1.

Anglia libera, which he proudly published under his own name. Having disavowed any involvement with the *Limitations*,[23] Toland had no reason to maintain argumentative consistency between the two works. For example he scoffed at the possibility of a Hanoverian invasion, which he had mooted in the *Limitations*. Among the factors protecting English liberty from a Hanoverian king, Toland wrote in *Anglia libera*, was 'the distance of his other dominions if he shou'd attempt anything against these kingdoms by their assistance: a thing in itself absolutely impossible, considering the several countries lying betwixt us, especially our good friends of *Holland*'.[24] In less than a year, Toland had moved from concern to complacency respecting the North Sea littoral between Hanover and England.

The retraction of his assertion that dynastic union would endanger the independent cities and principalities of the North Sea coast implied that Toland no longer perceived a threat to the balance of power from the dynastic union. Indeed, Toland now believed Anglo-Hanoverian dynastic union would positively support the European balance of power. 'Settling the succession in the house of Hanover', he wrote, 'is the most likely way in the world of restoring and preserving to *England* her ancient privileg'd greatness of holding the balance of *Europe*'.[25] The idea that England played a pivotal role in the European balance had been introduced by Geffray Fenton in the dedication to Queen Elizabeth of his 1579 translation of Guicciardini,[26] who had taken up Machiavelli's notion of an Italian equilibrium. Explaining how dynastic union with Hanover might assist England's maintenance of the balance of power, Toland wrote that the

> finishing stroke in making us the arbiters of *Europe* as well as a particular balance against *France* was the present *Act of Succession*, whereby the crown of *England* descends to one of the powerfullest families in the *Empire* for their territory and more diffusive than all the rest in their kindred and alliances.[27]

The Hanoverian successors would be able to harness their Electorate and their dynastic connections to England's defence of the European balance. Although Toland's conclusions differed radically from those of his

---

[23] T. Burnet to Sophia, 13/23 June 1701, London, in Klopp, ed., *Die Werke von Leibniz*, VIII, p. 265.
[24] John Toland, *Anglia libera, or the limitation and succession of the crown of England explain'd and asserted* (London, 1701), p. 147.
[25] Toland, *Anglia libera*, p. 144.
[26] Martin Wight, 'The balance of power', in Herbert Butterfield and Martin Wight, eds., *Diplomatic investigations* (London, 1966), p. 164.
[27] Toland, *Anglia libera*, p. 142.

Limitations, his postulates remained impeccably republican; he had fashioned republican arguments for and against dynastic union with Hanover.

The latter position was the more influential. Jacobites salvaged the republican critique of union after Toland abandoned it. It is well known that Jacobites dabbled it republicanism,[28] but the extent to which they borrowed Toland's religious opposition to dynastic union with Hanover is nonetheless surprising. Like Toland, they compared Lutheranism to Catholicism. But Jacobite leaders, who were often ordained Anglican clergymen, cared little for Toland's fulminations against priestcraft. Rather, they conflated Lutheran doctrine concerning the eucharist with its catholic counterpart. If Jacobites substantially adapted the religious case against Hanover, they took up the secular fear of electoral invasion without significant cavil.

Jacobites first explored the republican case against union in response to James Drake, a Tory physician who had elaborated upon Toland's 'bluewater' skepticism about dynastic union with Hanover in 1702.[29] But by 1705, he had followed Toland's trajectory from opposition to support. Drake looked increasingly to the Hanoverian successors to restore Toryism, which found itself out of power despite Queen Anne's early support. Tories began to consider inviting the Hanoverian successors to England. Were the ministers to reject it, they risked alienating the heirs presumptive. But should they accept it, they would certainly offend Queen Anne, whose influence could only be reduced by such a move. For their part, the Tories had nothing to lose. Drake advanced the republican case for Hanover in his journal, which took its name from Marchamont Nedham's *Mercurius politicus*. Drake wanted a Hanoverian in England, to keep an eye on its standing army[30] and political corruption.[31] Unfortunately for Drake, he made a stray reference to the Saxon conquest of late antiquity.[32]

'How this serves his *purpose* I know not' was the immediate response of the Jacobite polemicist Charles Leslie.[33] Leslie was an Irish-born nonjuror who had resided in England since forfeiting his church offices in the wake of the Revolution. He had already adapted Toland's implicit comparison of Lutheranism and Catholicism in 1704, when he wrote that

---

[28] Paul Chapman, 'Jacobite political argument in England, 1714–1766' (unpublished PhD dissertation, Cambridge, 1983); Paul Monod, 'Jacobitism and country principles in the reign of William III', *The Historical Journal* 30 (1987), 289–310.
[29] [James Drake], *The history of the last parliament* (London, 1702), p. ix.
[30] *Mercurius politicus* 1 no. 33 (29 September–2 October 1705), p. 131.
[31] *Mercurius politicus* 1 no. 35 (6–9 October 1705), p. 139.
[32] *Mercurius politicus* 1 no. 34 (2–6 October 1705), p. 135.
[33] *The rehearsal* 1 no. 67 (17–24 October 1705), p. 2.

'*German princes* are *Presbyterian Lutherans*. And ... their *consubstantiation* is in a manner as adverse to us as *transubstantiation*'.³⁴ Leslie located Lutheranism's overlap with Catholicism in doctrine, rather than church government. But now, Leslie's cryptic response to Drake echoed Toland's allusions to the Saxon invasion.

Drake might have overlooked Leslie's comment, but decided to take a position on the possibility of Hanoverian invasion. It was irrelevant to the invitation scheme, Drake argued. He wrote that 'if they were able to come in an hostile manner, so attended as to enter the land against our will, they might do it whether we invited 'em or no, and might rather be supposed to attempt such a thing upon our denial of an invitation'.³⁵ But the threat of Hanoverian invasion was only useful to Drake in so far as it promoted the invitation project. He felt obliged to doubt its possibility. Hanover, he wrote was 'an inland country ... in no capacity of invading us, who are not to be approached but by sea'.³⁶ Drake echoed Toland's retraction from *Anglia libera* as much as Leslie had taken up the original allegation from the *Limitations*.

Abandoning all allusions to the ancient Saxon invaders in favor of the more recent precedent set by William III, Leslie sarcastically replied that an electoral visitor might

> think the *English* a sort of *inconstant* people, and desire some *guards* of his own *countrymen* for the *security* of his *person* as well as *succession*. Who cou'd deny so reasonable a request? Wou'd it be fitting to show any greater *suspicion* of him than of our late *glorious deliverer*?³⁷

This was the final volley in Leslie's debate with Drake. For the first time, a Jacobite had deployed republican language against the union with Hanover. Leslie adopted it in order to dispute Drake's own ideological consistency and to stall the Tory momentum for invitation. In the latter, he failed somewhat. Lord Haversham still proposed an invitation in the House of Lords that November, which was defeated by Whig rather than Jacobite compunctions.

Whatever the sincerity of his republican utterances in 1705, Leslie himself effected their transmission to the Stuart court in exile. Shortly after an arrest warrant necessitated his flight to the continent in 1711, Leslie recapitulated the invasion thesis in a memorial to the pretender himself. He warned that the 1709 act for naturalising foreign protestants

---

³⁴ [Charles Leslie], *The wolf stript of his shepherd's cloathing* (London, 1704), p. 44.
³⁵ *Mercurius politicus* 1 no. 38 (16–20 October 1705), p. 151.   ³⁶ *Ibid.*, p. 152.
³⁷ *The Rehearsal* 1 no. 69 (24–31 October 1705), p. 2.

might provide cover for a Hanoverian invasion, writing that 'if the prince of Hanover is once in possession he will bring along with him his German troops, who in virtue of the last act of Parliament will be naturalized the moment they arrive'.[38] The pretender rapidly absorbed this idea, and wrote to his half-sister, Queen Anne, a month later that the elector 'by the general naturalization may bring over crowds of his countrymen to supply the defect of his right and enslave the nation'.[39] Leslie's activities marked a sea change in Jacobite ideology. The first Stuart experiment with republicanism, in April 1693, had foundered on the opposition of nonjurors.[40] By contrast, later Jacobite republicanism was partially influenced and orchestrated by the nonjuring Leslie.

While the Stuart court focused increasingly on the elector's army, British Jacobites remained fixated upon his Lutheranism. When he arrived in Britain, George I was greeted by a chorus of Anglican criticism.[41] This reprised Charles Leslie's case against Lutheranism, which supposedly combined presbyterian church government with catholic doctrine on the eucharist. But it did not include Leslie's republican argument against Hanover's standing army. This only filtered into British Jacobitism following an intervention by the pretender himself.

This was his protest against the succession of George I. James Stuart criticised the nascent dynastic union on two levels, addressing Britain and Europe in turn. He first labelled George I 'a foreigner, a powerful prince, and absolute in his own country, where he has never met with the least contradiction from his subjects. He is ignorant of our laws, manners, customs, and language, and supported by a good army of his own people.'[42] The implication was clear: the electoral army supported absolute rule in Hanover, and might eventually serve the same purpose in Britain. Broadening the Hanoverian threat from Britain to the European balance of power, he added that

We likewise hope that all Christian princes and potentates ... will reflect upon ... the formidable effects they are threaten'd with from such an united force as that of

---

[38] [Charles Leslie], 'The memorial of the Sieur Lamb', in James Macpherson, ed., *Original papers containing the secret history of Great Britain from the Restoration to the Accession of the House of Hanover* (2 vols., London, 1775), II, p. 217.

[39] James Francis Edward Stuart to Queen Anne, May 1711, published in Macpherson, *Original papers*, II, p. 224.

[40] For this, see Monod, 'Jacobitism and country principles', p. 299.

[41] See especially Thomas Brett, *A review of the Lutheran principles* (London, 1714); [Thomas Brett], *A letter to the author of the history of the Lutheran Church from a country school-boy* (London, 1714).

[42] James Francis Edward Stuart, *James R. James the Third, by the Grace of God King of Great Britain, France & Ireland, Defender of the Faith, &c.: to all kings, princes, & potentates and our loving subjects greeting* (n. p., 1714), p. 1.

England and Hanover, and that they'll seriously consider whether the exorbitant power that now accrues to the house of Brunswick be consistent with the balance of power they have been fighting for all this last war.[43]

Conspicuously absent was any attack upon Hanoverian religion. The pretender could hardly raise the question of George I's Lutheranism, knowing that he was vulnerable because of his own exotic Catholicism. Jacobites knew that catholics were as open to the charge of supporting absolute rule as Lutherans.[44] Furthermore, James Stuart's Catholicism made him less sympathetic towards polemic which elevated Anglican doctrine or church government above those of other denominations. Mindful of his party's religious divisions, the pretender hoped to maintain cohesion by hewing to secular language.

The pretender's case was elaborated in two anonymously authored tracts of 1715. *The Church of England's advice to her children* was the work of Leslie, who continued to write from exile. The other, *English advice to the freeholders of England*, was by Bishop Atterbury of Rochester. Both dutifully attacked the king's religion,[45] but focused upon secular grievances. Leslie warned his readers against the threat of Hanoverian invasion, writing of George I that '*Dutch* bottoms can bring in 'more ... *Hanoverians* ... than succeeding generations may be able to weed out again. The army being obtain'd, he may ... make himself as absolute in *England* as he was in *Hanover*'.[46] And just as the pretender had juxtaposed Hanover's threats to domestic and international liberty, Leslie worried about dynastic union's baleful consequences for the European balance of power.[47]

While repeating the familiar invasion scenario, Atterbury fleshed it out with corollary. Targeting a political corruption, Atterbury alleged that the Whigs 'will desire an inlet may be made for foreigners into employments ... to establish their present power'.[48] This was because

> nothing is more natural than for the king's old subjects to have the advantage, in point of his affection, over his new. By speaking the same language, their conversation is most agreeable to him; and by having been partners with him in his pleasures, which open the heart, they may know ... how to win upon his nature

---

[43] James Francis Edward Stuart, *James R. James the Third*, p. 2.
[44] See, for example, Anthony Aufrere, ed., *The Lockhart papers, containing memoirs and commentaries upon the affairs of Scotland from 1702 to 1715 by George Lockhart, Esq., of Carnwath* (2 vols., London, 1817), I, pp. 474–5.
[45] [Francis Atterbury], *English advice to the freeholders of England* (1714), p. 20; Charles Leslie, *Mr Lesley to the Lord Bishop of Sarum* (1715), pp. 1–2.
[46] [Charles Leslie], *The Church of England's advice to her children, and to all kings, princes, and potentates* (London, 1721), p. 44.
[47] Ibid., p. 46.   [48] [Atterbury], *English Advice*, p. 24.

and to render themselves more acceptable than the *English*. There is likewise on their side a natural inclination most people have for their countrymen.[49]

British republicans might admire this Hanoverian patriotism *per se*, but feared that it might exacerbate Britain's political corruption.

Atterbury alleged that the Act of Settlement had been broken, reporting that the Hanoverian diplomat 'Baron Bothmer is trusted with the privy purse, that the king may dispose his money here or send it to *Hanover* without the privity of the *English*'.[50] But why would George I transfer British money to Hanover? Leslie advanced two theories. Informing his readers that 'you will be impoverish'd by all the means in your pretended king's power to continue your subjection to him',[51] Leslie followed the old republican dictum that wealth was a precondition for esistance to a standing army. He nonetheless recognised that fiscal-military oppression might not secure Hanoverian empire over Britain, and wrote that

in case a standing army should not answer all the ends proposed ... it may be expected that he should make use of your *blood* and *treasure* before his *harvest* be over, to enlarge his dominions in the *Empire* and to fill his *foreign* coffers, that if the princes abroad or the people at home should oblige him to retire, he may have the larger country and the better purse to retire to.[52]

Electoral expansion fulfilled two purposes. As Toland had put it in the *Limitations*, it facilitated invasion of Britain. But Leslie added that it was also an insurance policy against the possibility of Stuart restoration in Britain.

Of course, the Stuarts might try to govern Britain absolutely also. Leslie felt obliged to defend his master from the same charge of autocratic ambition, to which he was also vulnerable. The nonjuror considered it absurd that

he who never knew the least *restriction*, but always a power without any *limitation*, must be placed in the gap to keep out a power which it is only supposed might prove *absolute*, which is as if the taking one into your house with the *plague* upon him were the best remedy against that distemper.[53]

The evolution of the republican case against dynastic union was complete. But it remained in the realm of speculation.

Events soon conspired to validate republican theory. Hanover bought the coastal duchies of Bremen and Verden from Denmark in 1715,

---

[49] *Ibid.*, p. 25. [50] *Ibid.*, p. 25. [51] [Leslie], *The Church of England's Advice*, p. 48.
[52] *Ibid.*, p. 47. [53] *Ibid.*, p. 41.

apparently fulfilling Toland's precondition for a Hanoverian invasion of Britain. 'By taking possession of the duchy of Bremen in violation of the public faith', the pretender warned in a second manifesto, 'a door is opened by the usurper to let in an inundation of foreigners from abroad and reduce these nations to the state of a province to one of the most inconsiderable provinces of the Empire.'[54] How an 'inconsiderable' state would overwhelm Britain, the pretender did not specify. In fact, the wording was actually that of his secretary of state Lord Bolingbroke.[55] Bolingbroke's predilection for republican argument was to last longer than his employment with the pretender.

Nevertheless, Hanover receded from republicanism during Bolingbroke's *Craftsman* years. It only reappeared in 1742, when the government employed Hanoverian auxiliaries during the War of the Austrian Succession. Republicans naturally opposed mercenaries, but particularly so when they were foreign subjects of George II. As Britain had not hired Hanoverian forces since before the inception of dynastic union in 1714, the subsidy treaty temporarily unified the opposition, both Whig and Tory, against the Electorate.

It was possible to argue, as the Tory courtier Lord Bathurst did, that Hanoverian auxiliaries would be more reliable than other mercenaries. 'They were', he told the House of Lords, 'subjects of the same prince and ... therefore we could have no reason to fear their defection or to suspect their fidelity'.[56] But their loyalty to George II also made them suspect. The earl of Marchmont, an opposition Whig, contrasted the Hanoverian mercenaries with those from other countries, whose

natural masters will not agree to their acting but in consequence of the design and upon the principles for which they were hir'd ... How very different is this from the case where both principals and auxiliaries own the same prince as their natural head? For then, in case of any arbitrary views he may entertain upon the rights and the liberty of that part of his dominions which is free, he is sure of being assisted with the forces of the other part where he is absolute, and who are paid by the very people whom he may design to suppress.[57]

---

[54] James Francis Edward Stuart, *His Majesty's Most Gracious Declaration* (n. p., 1715).
[55] See Philip Henry Stanhope, Viscount Mahon, *History of England from the Peace of Utrecht* (7 vols., London, 1836), I, appendix, pp. xxvii–xxxi, *passim*; HMC, *Calendar of the Stuart Papers*, I, pp. 432–51, *passim*.
[56] William Cobbett, ed., *The parliamentary history of England* (36 vols., London, 1806–20), XII, col. 1099.
[57] [Hugh Hume Campbell, 3rd earl of Marchmont], *The present interest of the people of Great Britain at home and abroad, considered in a letter to a member of parliament* (London, [1742]), pp. 21–2. For the attribution, see Allen T. Hazen, *A catalogue of Horace Walpole's library* (3 vols., New Haven, 1969), I, p. 449.

Mercenaries were notoriously unreliable, but ones from Hanover might be loyal to a fault where others were fickle.

Marchmont had raised the spectre of invasion, which seemed less remote when the allied army moved into Belgium. The anonymous author of *Seventeen hundred forty-two* did 'not like the vicinity of Hanoverian troops... Tis true, Flanders is sever'd from us by the sea, but that country is much nearer than Hanover.'[58] That notwithstanding, republicans still watched the electoral coastline. When Horatio Walpole celebrated Hanover's possession of the approaches to Bremen and Hamburg as advantageous to British commerce,[59] the Whig earl of Chesterfield responded that

> he cannot look upon His Majesty's having *German ports* which open into the *British* seas any additional security to his *freedom* ... Suppose any [future king] should take a whim of being as absolute here as at *Hanover*, and should think ... to become so when he should see us reduced by *poverty* ... could anything facilitate the execution ... of *slavery* so much as the having ports of his own, where he might order ... foreign troops to be embark'd ... for fitting us with manacles by means of these ports, these outlets from *Germany*?[60]

This was, of course, the invasion scenario first posited by Toland in the *Limitations*. Nevertheless, critics of Hanover struggled to square their alarmism about invasion against their tendency to belittle the Electorate. Marchmont attempted to reconcile these seemingly incompatible positions, writing that 'the forces of *H –* in themselves are too weak' to invade Britain, but wondered what they might be capable of 'when join'd on the continent by a body of mercenaries in our own pay'.[61] British republicans had always feared their own army, but worried that its repressive potential would be exacerbated by prolonged exposure to the values of its Hanoverian auxiliaries. The Jacobite member of parliament Sir John St Aubyn informed the Commons that

> the Elector of Hanover, as Elector of Hanover, is an arbitrary prince; his electoral army is the instrument of that power. As King of Great Britain, he is a restrained monarch ... The hearts of the British soldiery are as yet free and untainted, yet I fear that too long an intercourse may beget a dangerous familiarity, and they may hereafter become a joint instrument ... to invade our liberties.[62]

---

[58] *Seventeen hundred forty-two, being a review of the conduct of the new ministry the last year with regard to foreign affairs* (London, 1743), p. 60.
[59] [Horatio Walpole], *The interest of Great Britain steadily pursued* (London, 1743), pp. 12–13.
[60] [Philip Dormer Stanhope, 4th earl of Chesterfield], *The interest of Hanover steadily pursued since the a – n* (London, 1743), pp. 38–9.
[61] [Marchmont], *The present interest of the people of Great Britain*, p. 22.
[62] Cobbett, ed., *The parliamentary history of England*, XII, col. 952.

The electoral army continued to define Hanoverian despotism during the early 1740s.

Opposition figures also denounced payments to Hanover as corrupt. St Aubyn alleged that the secretary of state, John Lord Carteret, 'had flattered his master's passions to secure his own power and had taken advantage of a virtuous quality in his prince, a love for his native country, to persuade him to a thing which might be a prejudice both to that country and this'.[63] St Aubyn blamed Carteret for the corruption, but other opposition figures were less generous. Marchmont alleged that 'the King of *Great Britain*, as possess'd of absolute power in *Hanover*, must look upon all the advantages of a good bargain to that Electorate as accruing to his own pocket'.[64] Marchmont probably felt vindicated when he later heard that George II had justified his visits to the Electorate by likening it to a British country seat.[65] If the king was enriching what amounted to a private estate, he was just as venal as his ministers.

Whether financed through debt or taxation, corruption weakened the material basis of resistance to tyranny. The Jacobite member of parliament John Philipps worried that the Hanoverian auxiliaries 'must suck the blood and vitals of this kingdom. And as they drain us they must necessarily tend to enslave us, and to deprive us of that power of resistance which every Englishman is entitled to whenever his property shall happen to be invaded.'[66]

Republican worries might have abated after the British army and its Hanoverian auxiliaries moved away from Flanders, and thereby the English Channel, in spring 1743. But the ensuing battle at Dettingen am Main served only to inflame them. Republicans were bound to be uncomfortable when George II led his multinational army to victory, still more so when allegations of royal favouritism towards Hanoverian troops surfaced. Dettingen may have been the last battle personally directed by a British king, but the king identified more as the elector of Hanover by wearing a yellow rather than red sash.

---

[63] Stephen Taylor and Clyve Jones, eds., *Tory and Whig: the parliamentary papers of Edward Harley, 3rd Earl of Oxford, and William Hay, M. P. for Seaford 1716–1753* (Woodbridge, 1998), p. 187.
[64] [Marchmont], *The present interest of the people of Great Britain*, p. 22.
[65] George II 'said ... that the people here were angry at his going to Hanover when they went all out of town to their country seats, but it was unjust, for Hanover was his country seat and he had no other'. Sir George Henry Rose, ed., *A selection from the papers of the Earls of Marchmont* (3 vols., London, 1831), I, p. 54.
[66] Cobbett, ed., *The parliamentary history*, XII, col. 1017.

The colour yellow signified not just Hanover, but its defining characteristic. British critics accused the king of having connived at the cowardice of his Hanoverian forces at Dettingen. The efforts of one Hanoverian officer, Thomas Eberhard von Ilten, to preserve his forces earned him the droll epithet of 'confectioner general'. Yet attacks on Hanoverian bravery could undercut the invasion panic which republicans had been inciting months earlier. Ilten himself observed that 'the E——h are above dreading to be enslaved by a people whom they themselves represent as the most cowardly nation in *Europe*'.[67] Anticipating the objection, *Old England* observed that 'it is one thing to be a dexterous *collector* and another to be a good *soldier*'.[68] But republicans suspected that Hanoverian inactivity at Dettingen bespoke more than just cowardice.

The opposition argued that auxiliaries had no interest in prosecuting the allied advantage. *The Westminster Journal* observed that 'this was the reasoning of the *Ha – ns* when they communed together: do we not receive *E – sh* pay? Wherefore then should we at once put an end to the war?'[69] This perspective explained the king's tolerance for his Hanoverian subjects' hesitancy. *Old England* echoed Marchmont, observing that

> sovereigns are not less govern'd by their interests than private men. Now though the whole *executive power* of this kingdom is vested in the k———, the gains which may arise from a wise and honest use of it belong to the *people*. But with regard to *H* ———, 'tis far otherwise. All acquisitions there are the *sole property* of the e ———. Whence it is easy to imagine into what channel a *selfish* prince would turn the whole current of his favors, and how very effectually this *executive power* of the k ——— m might be apply'd to enrich the e ——— e.[70]

By transferring wealth from Britain to Hanover, George II weakened his kingdom's ability to resist tyranny.

His favouritism to Hanoverian troops did this another way, as well. *Old England* considered the king hoped 'to break the spirit of a nation by breaking the spirit of their *national troops*'.[71] The newspaper examined the king's motives, speculating that

> He that govern'd by *will* and *pleasure* in one country would be apt to think himself extremely unlucky that he could not do the same in another, and other than continue thus unhappy he would endeavour to introduce and establish, if not exactly his own arbitrary system, something that might answer his ends almost as

---

[67] [Thomas Eberhard von Ilten], *Popular prejudice concerning partiality to the interests of Hanover, to the subjects of that electorate, and particularly to the Hanoverian troops in British pay, freely examined and discussed* (London, 1743), p. 55.
[68] *Old England, or the Constitutional Journal* no. 36 (8 October 1743), 1.
[69] *The Westminster Journal, or New Weekly Miscellany* no. 100 (22 October 1743), 1.
[70] *Old England, or the Constitutional Journal* no. 44 (3 December 1743), 1.
[71] *Old England, or the Constitutional Journal* no. 39 (29 October 1743), 1.

well. And this might be easily and safely done by his dodging between the two capacities of k —— and e ——.⁷²

Republicans still doubted that Britain might preserve its liberties in dynastic union with absolutist Hanover.

Of course, the king was not the only link between domestic corruption and the Hanoverian threat. Some observers considered that Carteret exploited George II's Hanoverian patriotism to stay in office. Speaking before the Lords in December 1743, Chesterfield observed that

> other nations generally suffer by ministers parasitically indulging the vices and private passions of their sovereign, but we may suffer by ministers parasitically indulging the virtues and public affections of our king. The love of one's native country is one of the most virtuous and useful affections of the human mind, and as His Majesty is endowed with that as well as every other laudable affection, it is the duty and ought to be the business of his ministers to take care that his natural partiality towards the people of his electorate shall extend no farther than is consistent with the interest and happiness of the people that freely and generously made him a king.⁷³

Perspectives like these suggested that the uproar over Hanoverian troops would only subside alongside Carteret's political career. Indeed, the Hanoverians were only dismissed after a ministerial majority managed to eject Carteret from office in November 1744. Although the subsidy continued, the Hanoverians moved under Austrian command.⁷⁴ One of Carteret's supporters, Lord Doneraile, rightly complained that Britain retained the Hanoverians' cost but not their services.⁷⁵ But the cosmetic change was enough to reduce public outrage.

Republican vigilance revived again in 1756, when the duke of Newcastle's government brought 8,000 Hanoverian auxiliaries to Britain. That they were there to defend against an expected French invasion only partially neutralised opposition. After Bremen and Verden, after the Hanoverians' deployment in Flanders during the 1740s, Toland's nightmare seemed even closer to fruition. For the first time since 1714, a Hanoverian force was on British soil.

Given such circumstances, a republican outcry was inevitable. A Tory newspaper, *The Monitor*, conceded that

---

⁷² *Old England, or the Constitutional Journal* no. 44 (3 December 1743), 1–2.
⁷³ William Cobbett, ed., *The parliamentary history of England* (36 vols., London, 1806–20), XIII, cols. 339–40.
⁷⁴ Gert Brauer, *Die hannoversch-englischen Subsidienverträge 1702–1748* (Aalen, 1962), pp. 168–70.
⁷⁵ Cobbett, ed., *Cobbett's Parliamentary History*, XIII, col. 1176 (note).

His Majesty's native subjects the *Hanoverians* ... are ready to die in the defence of our sovereign. But ... is not that very disposition to sacrifice everything to the will of their elector a caution against their admission into Britain? Is it not straining our constitution and giving too great a power to one part thereof? Is not the wisdom of the nation as discernible in the preserving an equal balance of power in the legislature as in providing means of defence against an enemy? Would not our loss be as great to be reduced under a military power of Hanoverians as of any other nation?[76]

The Monitor combined republican skepticism about mercenaries with a Polybian defence of Britain's constitutional balance. As it had in 1742, the employment of Hanoverian mercenaries – this time in Britain itself – revived and legitimated the republican case against union, recognisable by its reverence for Britain's mixed constitution, hatred of mercenaries, and anxiety about invasion.

Republicans saw the British government and its Hanoverian counterpart as benefiting symbiotically from the establishment of absolute rule in Britain. *The Monitor* claimed that British ministers 'have formed a design to render their m――― y absolute and to change the government into an oligarchy by the aid of a powerful standing army of natives ... and Hanoverians'.[77] Absolute power had an attraction for British politicians, but also for Hanoverians (including the king). A published letter purporting to be that of a Hanoverian soldier explained that 'we ... shall always tarry here unless H ――― be attacked, to prevent any insurrection that may arise on the account of so much of their money being spent in our defence'.[78] Although the author could not decide whether Hanoverian security suffered or gained from the auxiliaries' presence in Britain, the Electorate was damned either way.

Republicans feared Hanoverians might take more than British freedoms. After a long treatment of the Saxon precedent, when a previous government had given up hostages to fortune by inviting German mercenaries into Britain, the anonymous author of *German Mercy* warned his readers that Hanoverians might 'ravish your wives [and] deflower your daughters'.[79] The earl of Bath's chaplain, John Douglas, joked in *A serious defence of some late measures of the administration* that the government intended to breed the Hanoverian soldiers with British women. He wrote,

---

[76] *The Monitor, or British Freeholder, from August 9 1755 to July 31 1756, both inclusive*, p. 346.
[77] *The Monitor, or British Freeholder* no. 52 (31 July 1756), p. 309.
[78] *England's warning, or the copy of a letter from a H – n officer in England to his brother in H – r found near Canterbury and faithfully translated from the German, together with a letter to the author of the citizen* (n. p., [1756]), p. 4.
[79] *German mercy: a fair warning to the people of Great Britain* (London, 1756), p. 21.

German solidity, which some have maliciously termed stupidity, being once brought into our constitutions, will in time extinguish a troublesome race of mere *Englishmen*, some of whom at present, though happily their number is small, by the vivacity of their genius clog the wheels of government and distress the administration by unseasonable oratory and obstinate opposition in both houses of Parliament. Blessed days when the influence of *Germanic* phlegm shall extend itself o'er our public councils, when the pertness of *English* eloquence shall be checked![80]

Instead of the rough-and-ready martial virtues inherited from the Saxons, Douglas expected these modern Germans to inculcate the vices of obedience and political quietism.

Republicans also raised the question of the Hanoverian auxiliaries' legal status while in Britain. *The Monitor* inquired

are they within the limitations and conditions under the restrictions, penalties, and punishments of the mutiny bill? If they are not, what dependence can there be on their service in case of national danger? May they not refuse to act under the command of our sovereign? Can they be punished for desertion? Yet this is not the worst reflection that arises from this measure. May it not be a cause of great disgust in the soldiery of this realm to be supplanted by a foreign army, to be sent abroad like felons to America to make room for ... Hanoverians to eat the bread of idleness in old England?[81]

The Monitor clearly worried more about the latter scenario, in which the departure of British regulars for America rendered their homeland vulnerable to Hanoverian conquest. But it was the former question of the legal extraterritoriality of Hanoverian troops which was to prove most prescient.

Republican anxieties seemed justified when, in September 1756, a Maidstone shopowner named Christopher Harris accused a Hanoverian soldier of stealing two silk handkerchiefs worth eight shillings.[82] Apparently the soldier, one Wilhelm Schröder, had mistaken a packet of six handkerchiefs for one containing four.[83] Nevertheless, the mayor and another justice of the peace jailed Schröder in advance of trial. The Hanoverian commander, Count Kielmansegge petitioned for Schröder's release, claiming that 'it was expressly stipulated by treaty that no Hanoverian soldier was to be tried by the laws of England during their

---

[80] [John Douglas], *A serious defence of some late measures of the administration, particularly with regard to the introduction and establishment of foreign troops* (London, 1756), pp. 17–18.
[81] *The Monitor, or British Freeholder, from August 9 1755 to July 31 1756, both inclusive*, p. 424.
[82] *The London Evening Post* no. 4507 (25–8 September 1756), p. 1.
[83] Horace Walpole, *Memoirs of King George II*, ed. John Brooke (3 vols., New Haven, 1985), II, p. 175.

stay here'. When rebuffed, Kielmansegge aggravated the situation when he 'talked of making use of force' to spring Schröder from prison.[84] But he later simply applied to George II for Schröder's discharge.

Newcastle reported that 'His Majesty was very angry, and said he must send away his troops if they were to be subject to our laws . . . to be tried by *themselves*'.[85] Already worried that the Hanoverians' presence in Britain left his Electorate unguarded,[86] George II may have seen in the Maidstone incident a convenient excuse to repatriate his troops. But the king's agenda ran up against that of Newcastle, who wanted to keep the Hanoverians in Britain. The attorney general, William Murray, drafted a warrant for Schröder's release. This was in turn signed by Lord Holdernesse, the secretary of state for the Northern Department. Schröder's transfer from British to Hanoverian jurisdiction simply enabled an electoral court martial to proceed. Although fear of prosecution for *praemunire* deterred Harris from testifying,[87] Schröder received three hundred lashes.[88] But Schröder's punishment, excessive at it was, did not appease British republicans, who were distressed that Hanoverian extraterritoriality seemed to have prevailed.[89]

Publicists on either side of the case appealed to international law. The author of *Some particular remarks upon the affair of the Hanoverian soldier* wrote that 'auxiliaries, and indeed all troops, have their own particular laws, laws ever independent of any country they are in',[90] and concluded that the Hanoverians should be accorded the same immunity from prosecution as diplomats.[91] Opposition voices refuted this defence outright. A contributor to *The London Evening Post* claimed that

all hireling soldiers who come into any country and receive the pay of it are by the *lex gentium* subject to the laws of such country for any crimes they commit on the natives of that country. Nor does indeed the Hanoverian general himself pretend that his soldiers have any right to be exempted from the laws of this land by the *jus gentium* as auxiliaries, to which he well knows and indeed

---

[84] *The London Evening Post* no. 4505 (21–23 September 1756), 4.
[85] Newcastle to Hardwicke, 18 September 1756, London, British Library (BL), Add. Mss. 32867, fol. 328.
[86] See Newcastle to Hardwicke, 28 August 1756, Claremont, BL, Add. Mss. 32867, fols. 115–16.
[87] *The Gazetteer and London Daily Advertiser* no. 4704 (9 October 1756), 1.
[88] Walpole, *Memoirs of King George II*, ed. Brooke, II, p. 176.
[89] For a recent treatment of the Maidstone incident, see Eliga H. Gould, *The persistence of empire: British political culture in the age of the American Revolution* (Chapel Hill, 2000), pp. 35–8.
[90] Edward Lancer, *Some particular remarks upon the affair of the Hanoverian soldier* (London, 1757), pp. 5–6.
[91] Ibid., p. 11.

acknowledges they have no manner of title by his declaring and insisting upon such exemption only *by treaty*.[92]

The London Evening Post shifted the argument from general principles of international law, about which there was no consensus, to the particular treaty provision cited by Kielmansegge when seeking Schröder's release. But because the treaty provision's existence was doubtful, there was little more agreement on its function. *The London Evening Post* essayist initially questioned it,[93] but later recanted:

There is too much reason to fear that some such cruel and unconstitutional treaty is really subsisting, a treaty ... that, by presupposing their committing the crimes of murder, robbery, etc. on the subjects of Great Britain and providing that they should not be imprison'd or punish'd for the same by the laws of England, seems to me to bespeak an intention of allowing these mercenaries to commit such atrocious crimes here.[94]

This account seemed particularly justified by Kielmansegge's reported threat to free Schröder's by force.[95] Pro-government authors naturally offered a countervailing interpretation. *The Gazetteer* returned to first principles to absolve the treaty of evil intention, asking

are not such crimes [as Schröder's] punishable by the laws of Germany and the laws of every civilized nation? They certainly are so; consequently the treaty in question (if such a treaty exists) does not mean to tolerate them, but could only be intended as a kind of security for the Hanoverian soldiery against the informations of envious and evil-minded people.[96]

The writer deemed any such contractual condition to be fair, given the urgency with which Britain had required the electoral troops earlier in 1756.

The argument surrounding Schröder had been conducted in the language of natural law, but there was no mistaking the republican subtext. Extraterritoriality opened up a Pandora's box of crime and subversion; its confirmation made republicans doubly eager to be rid of the Hanoverian auxiliaries. Their ultimate departure coincided with the fall of Newcastle, who dismissed them days before resigning in November 1756. But his successor, William Pitt the Elder, took credit for the Hanoverians' embarkartion, which he had made a condition of service in government. And he continued to posture against them from office, threatening to

---

[92] *The London Evening Post* no. 4513 (9–12 October 1756), p. 1.
[93] *The London Evening Post* no. 4507 (25–18 September 1756), p. 1.
[94] *The London Evening Post* no. 4513 (9–12 October 1756), p. 1.
[95] *England's warning*, p. 7.
[96] *The Gazetteer and London Daily Advertiser* no. 4704 (9 October 1756), 1.

resign if the Commons joined the Lords in thanking George II for having furnished the auxiliaries.[97] The change of government, and the Hanoverians' redeployment, allayed republican fears for the time being.

The last time Hanoverian troops offended British republicanism was during the Napoleonic Wars, when the British army accepted volunteers from the French-occupied Electorate for incorporation into the 'King's German Legion'. The legion distinguished itself in British expeditions to the continent (including the Peninsular war, Walcheren, and Waterloo), but based itself in Britain. Most histories of the Hanoverian legion have been nostalgic,[98] downplaying British opposition to their presence. Because Hanover was occupied during the existence of the King's German Legion, it featured in the republican imagination more as a Praetorian guard than as the vanguard of a larger Hanoverian invasion.[99]

The leader of opposition to the King's German Legion was the radical journalist William Cobbett. A constitutional radical, Cobbett nevertheless drew upon humanist republicanism, particularly its aversion to professional armies. He was initially sympathetic to Hanover; in 1802, he reassured his readers that Prussia's impending expansion in the *Reichshauptdeputationsschluß* had freed them 'from the dread of seeing the Hanoverian troops in garrison at the Tower, which is doubtless a comforting reflection ... we have no longer to fear that the House of Hanover will enslave England by means of soldiers from the continent'.[100] But as Cobbett radicalised, so did his views on Hanover. One irritant was Britain's 1806 declaration of war against Prussia, in retaliation for that kingdom's annexation of Hanover. That war, which was the policy of Charles James Fox, now foreign secretary but previously a stalwart opponent of George III, seemed to prove the impossibility of official probity so long as the royal claim on Hanover persisted.[101]

---

[97] Horace Walpole to Mann, 8 December 1756, published in W. S. Lewis, ed., *The Yale edition of Horace Walpole's correspondence* (48 vols., New Haven, 1960), XXI, pp. 30–1.

[98] See N. Ludlow Beamish, *History of the king's German legion* (2 vols., London, 1832–7); Bernhard Schwertfeger, *Geschichte der königlichen deutschen Legion* (2 vols., Hanover and Leipzig, 1907); Adolf Pfannkuche, *Die königlich deutsche Legion 1803–1816* (Hanover, 1926); Andreas Einsel, Dieter Kutschenreiter and Wolfgang Seth, 'The King's German Legion: Hannoversche Soldaten unter britischer Flagge', in: Heide N. Rohloff, ed., *Großbritannien und Hannover: Die Zeit der Personalunion 1714–1837* (Frankfurt, 1989), pp. 299–323.

[99] I thank Christopher Thompson for this insight.

[100] *Cobbett's Annual Register* 2 (1802), col. 176.

[101] See Brendan Simms, '"An odd question enough": Charles James Fox, the crown, and British policy during the Hanoverian crisis of 1806', *The Historical Journal* 38 (1995), 567–96.

Hanover and British republicanism

Cobbett began to criticise the new war and the King's German Legion, even though the latter had already been in Britain for three years.

One of Cobbett's correspondents excused the king, whose 'fond attachment to the dominions of his ancestors is naturally to be expected'. Here was the old republican admiration for patriotism, even that of another country. He added that

> true British interests must ever be the primary object of a British sovereign, and it were almost treason to suppose it possible that His Majesty could wish, his cabinet advise, or his people acquiesce in the protraction of a hopeless contest or the sacrifice of any great national object for the redemption of continental dominions.[102]

So George III was corrupt if he did not put aside his Hanoverian resentments as king of Britain. Also corrupt were any politicians who indulged the king's nostalgia for his ancestral homeland.

Another of Cobbett's correspondents complained that the government had not consulted parliament about Prussian policy, in contravention of the Act of Settlement and the republican preference for balanced government.[103] He even wished that parliament had stipulated to George I

> that unless you consent to part with dominions where political liberty is unknown and the people are in a condition . . . of political servitude, we cannot think you qualified to rule over us, the people of England. How could we contemplate him as the guardian of our freedom, who we should behold elsewhere swaying an arbitrary scepter?[104]

Of course, George III no longer ruled Hanover. But the King's German Legion opened the possibility that he might govern Britain in an electoral manner at some point in the future.[105]

Cobbett himself believed the presence of the King's German Legion was illegal, writing in 1807 that

> the Act of Settlement provides that no foreigner shall hold in this kingdom any place of *trust*, civil or military. And to suppose that this meant to exclude foreign officers from our army while it left room for the introducing of both foreign officers and foreign troops into the nation . . . to remain established is an absurdity not for one moment to be tolerated.[106]

Although Cobbett complained that the Hanoverians were more expensive to maintain than an equivalent number of British regulars,[107] he

---

[102] *Cobbett's Political Register* 9 (1806), col. 668.   [103] *Ibid.*, col. 276.   [104] *Ibid.*, col. 277.
[105] *Ibid.*, col. 278 (note).   [106] *Cobbett's Political Register* 11 (1807), col. 428.
[107] *Ibid.*, cols. 429–30.

reiterated that he would be less troubled 'if these Hanoverians were ... hired by us to be sent to the *West* or the *East Indies* or to *Gibraltar* in order to spare the lives of our native troops'. He playfully argued that the King's German Legion exacerbated the overpopulation recently diagnosed by Thomas Malthus,[108] but Cobbett's real concern – left unstated – was that it could subvert Britain's liberties from within.

The timing of Cobbett's remarks was revealing; Fox was dead, France had repossessed Hanover in autumn 1806, and its war ensuing with Prussia had enabled Britain to conclude peace with that country at the beginning of the new year. But while Hanover's influence upon British diplomacy ebbed, Cobbett remained anxious about the King's German Legion. He felt vindicated in 1809, when the King's German Legion helped to suppress and flog militiamen protesting about the price of knapsacks in the Cambridgeshire town of Ely.[109] Unaware of the deadly clash between Hanoverian legionnaires and Irish militiamen in Tullamore three years earlier,[110] Cobbett sensationalised the scarcely less violent incident in East Anglia. It would have been bad enough had Hanoverians flogged British enlisted men,[111] but it was far worse to discipline the citizen soldiers who had always represented the republican alternative to standing armies. For his breathless account of the events at Ely, Cobbett was arraigned for seditious libel at King's Court Bench. After the attorney general successfully claimed that Cobbett was impeding the government's ability to hire foreign auxiliaries,[112] the chief justice Lord Ellenborough consigned the defendant to Newgate prison for two years. Cobbett's example seems to have given pause to other critics of the King's German Legion, which remained in Britain until war's end.

By Cobbett's time, humanist republicanism was losing ground to the natural law-based variant epitomised by Tom Paine. Dynastic union's days were numbered in any case, as Hanover discouraged female succession; its 123-year union with Britain ended when Queen Victoria ascended the British throne and her uncle the duke of Cumberland inherited Hanover. The relationship's peaceful, anti-climactic dissolution reinforced the argument that it had always been a Personal Union. Moreover, Personal Union allowed historians to project the nineteenth-century nation-state onto the past. But in the process, republican critics

---

[108] *Ibid.*, cols. 430–1.   [109] *Cobbett's Political Register* 15 (1809), cols. 993–4.
[110] Beamish, *History of the king's German legion*, I, pp. 95–100.
[111] For opposition to the practice of flogging, see J. R. Dinwiddy, 'The early nineteenth-century campaign against flogging in the army', *The English Historical Review* 97 (1982), 308–31; Linda Colley, *Captives* (New York, 2002), pp. 328–41.
[112] *Cobbett's Political Register* 18 (1810), cols. 5–6.

of dynastic union were forgotten or dismissed as conspiracy theorists. As they produced a large proportion of commentary on Hanover, historians' perspective on dynastic union was incomplete. Perhaps current events are aligning so as to allow present-day historians to appreciate the republican critics of Hanover. Republicans, with their sensitivity to Hanoverian encroachments on British sovereignty, seem more relevant to an age of European political integration.

Index

Abercrombie, General James 271
Aberdeen, George Hamilton Gordon, 4th earl of 96
absolutism, German (German 'despotism') 71, 188, 189
Académie des Sciences (Paris) 153
Act of Settlement (1701) 12, 15, 94, 162, 167, 189, 203, 204, 218, 255, 277, 303, 304, 305, 310, 321
Act of Union
  Scotland (1707) 15
Adair, Robert 140, 142
Addington, Henry, 1st Viscount Sidmouth 75
Adelaide of Saxe-Meiningen, Queen Adelaide 227, 247
Adolphus, duke of Mecklenburg-Strelitz 242
Adolphus Frederic (or Adolf Friedrich), duke of Cambridge 8, 88, 89, 92, 116, 117, 119, 123, 141, 159, 227, 234, 248, 249, 250
Adolphus Frederick V, duke of Mecklenburg-Strelitz 250
African Society 149
Albert von Saxe-Coburg-Gotha, Prince Consort 109, 247, 250
Albert Edward, duke of Clarence 250
Alexander I, Tsar of Russia 79
Alexandra, queen of Great Britain 250, 251
Alps 115
Alvensleben, Johann Friedrich Carl von 67, 244, 245
Amelia, Princess 225, 226
Anderson, Fred 2
Andrié, Prussian envoy 196
Anglo-French alliance (1716–31) 255
Anglo-Hanoverian connection 1, 4, 11, 13, 15–16, 17, 18, 22, 23–4, 28–57, 87, 90, 92, 95, 96, 101, 103, 104, 108, 110, 132, 143, 155–7, 158, 161, 170, 171, 178, 183, 202, 204, 205, 212, 213, 224, 227, 234, 276, 278, 280
Anne I, queen of Great Britain 12, 17, 167, 168, 218, 220, 252, 306, 308
Anne, Princess Royal 172, 173
Anne, daughter of George II 220, 225
Ansbach 230, 244
Anson, Admiral George 1st Baron 271
Anton Ulrich of Brunswick-Wolfenbüttel 219
Archduke Charles of Austria 224
Arnall, William 193
Aretin, Karl Otmar von 59, 65, 179
Armitage, David 2, 207
Arthur, duke of Connaught 251
Asiatic Society 147, 148, 149
  Asiatic researches 148, 156
Aspinall, Arthur 83
Atterbury, Bishop Francis 309–10
  English advice to the freeholders of England (1714) 189
Auerstedt, battle of 83
August the Strong, Elector of Saxony and king of Poland 165, 218, 224
Augusta, duchess of Brunswick 68, 141, 231, 234, 247
Augusta, duchess of Cambridge (daughter to Adolphus Frederick, duke of Cambridge) 250
Augusta of Hesse-Cassel (wife of Adolphus Frederick, duke of Cambridge) 250
Augusta, Princess of Wales (wife of Frederick, Prince of Wales) 227, 228, 229, 236
Augusta Sophia, Princess 113
Augustus, duke of Sussex 88
Austrasia 113
Austria (Habsburg Monarchy) 7, 11, 12, 18, 22, 23, 24, 26, 33, 66, 69, 70, 105, 108, 115, 169, 177, 179, 180, 195, 197, 207, 208, 214, 216, 218, 220,

Index

225, 229, 232, 233, 239, 267, 286, 288, 297
Austrian Netherlands 32, 69, 256, 257, 266, 290, 312, 313, 315
Habsburg dynasty 31–2, 33, 34, 36, 165, 263, 276
Pragmatic Sanction 256, 263, 266, 281, 284
Seven Years War 45, 47, 65, 184, 268, 290
War of the Austrian Succession 20, 32, 177, 263, 265, 266, 267, 283, 288
War of the Bavarian Succession 69, 242, 243, 244–5, 296
War of the Polish Succession 31
French Revolutionary and Napoleonic Wars 72, 73, 74, 78
Ayscough, Dr Francis 196

Baack, Lawrence 217
balance of power 6, 69, 115, 136, 138, 169–70, 173, 180, 190, 201, 202, 207, 239, 252, 255, 264, 267, 272, 275, 288, 304, 305, 306, 308–9
Baltic policies 6 *see also* Russia and British-Hanoverian
ballads 185, 186
Bangorian controversy 191
Banks, Sir Joseph 130, 133, 140, 147, 148, 149, 150, 151, 152, 153, 154, 155, 158, 159
De Generis Humani Varietate Nativa 153
Barnard, John, MP 192
Batavian Republic (*see also* United Provinces, House of Orange) 234
Bath, William Pulteney, 1st earl of 192, 316
Bathurst, Allen Bathurst, 1st earl 311
Bavaria, Electorate/kingdom (1806) of (*see also* Wars and War of the Bavarian Succession) 32, 36, 69, 70, 125, 159, 165, 171, 197, 263, 282, 285, 297
Wittelsbach dynasty 179
Bayreuth 230
Beattie, J. M. 3
Beckford, William 270
The Monitor, or British Freeholder 200
Beddoes, Thomas 130, 143
Beddoes, Thomas Lovell (son) 143
Bedford, John Russell, 4th duke of 26, 29
Beeke, Henry 79
Behr, Burckhard Heinrich von 67, 68, 145
Belgium 79, 122
Belle-Isle, Charles Louis Auguste Fouquet, marshall comte (later duc) de 24, 275, 281–2, 284, 286, 287, 288, 294

Berlin 78, 80, 83, 224, 225
Berlin Academy 152
Berlin University 159
Bernadotte, Jean Baptiste, king of Sweden 155
Bernis, Cardinal François Joachim Pierre de 278, 290, 291
Bernstorff, A. G. 225
Bernstorff, Danish foreign minister 234
Bernstorff family 217
Bertram, Mijndert 8, 9
Best, Georg August (son) 156, 157, 158
Best, Wilhelm Philipp (father) 157, 158
Bill of Rights (1689) 167
Biskup, Thomas 4, 6, 217
Bismarck, Otto von 9
Black, Jeremy 2, 3, 5, 8, 59, 63, 111
Blanc, Abbé le 202
Bland, Henry 194
Blanning, Tim 3, 59, 61, 70, 71, 180, 244–5
'blue-water' policy (maritime strategy) 31, 162, 176, 201, 252, 267, 272, 273, 303
Blumenbach, Johann Friedrich 140, 143, 148, 149, 150, 151, 152, 153, 154, 155, 158, 159, 160
Bohemia 136, 238, 239, 244–5
Böhmer, Georg Ludwig 158
Bolingbroke, Henry St John, 1st Viscount 5, 193, 194, 311
Remarks on the history of England 193
Bonaparte, Catherine 248
Bonn University 159
Bosten, Lord 140
Bothmer, Hans Kaspar von 310
Brandenburg-Schwedt 244
Brandes, Ernst Friedrich 158
Bremen, duchy of 14, 134, 187, 189, 203, 221, 254, 265, 310, 315
Breslau University 159
Brewer, John 258
British empire 120, 128, 130–1, 138, 152, 158, 206
British empiricism 143
British identity 12, 17, 39, 90, 91, 162, 177, 188
British-Hanoverian Baltic policy 13–15, 16, 75, 183, 187, 188, 191, 193, 220
British (English) liberties 5, 6, 189, 197, 199, 202, 203, 205, 211
British Museum 131, 147, 150, 205
Broglie, Marshall François-Marie duc de 172, 295
Brooke, John 2
Brougham, Henry, 1st Baron Brougham 90

Bruce, James 156
Bruce, William 156, 157
Brunswick 122
  army 46, 47
  dynasty 89, 94, 95, 309
  clubs 94
Brunswick-Wolfenbüttel 64, 134, 215, 218, 219, 220, 224, 225, 227, 228, 231
Brussels 122
Buckingham, marquess of 78
Burckhardt, Johann Ludwig 149
Buffon, Georges 156
Bryant, Jacob 146, 147, 158
Bulwer, Henry Lytton, 1st Baron Dalling and Bulwer 86, 106
Bussy, Charles Castelnau, marquis de, French envoy 51–2
Bute, John Stuart, 3rd earl of 58, 60, 64, 69, 140, 180, 201, 229

Cambridge University 139, 140, 141, 150, 160
Campbell Orr, Clarissa 4, 7, 8, 9, 133, 180-1
Canning, George 8, 83, 84, 88, 95, 97, 98, 99, 100, 101, 102, 106, 110, 142, 160
Cape Breton (1748) 200
Cardwell, Stephen 43, 54
Carmarthen, Francis Osborne, marquess of 180
Caribbean, British trade in the 194
Carl Leopold, duke of Mecklenburg-Schwerin 230
Carlton House 82
Caroline of Brandenburg-Ansbach, Queen Caroline 215, 219, 221, 224, 226
Caroline of Brunswick, queen consort 89, 98
Caroline of Brunswick, Princess of Wales, wife of George IV 247, 248, 249
Caroline Matilda, Princess, sister of George III 232, 234
Carretta, Vincent 60
Carte, Thomas 205
Carteret, John, 2nd earl of Granville 12, 22, 24, 26, 32, 34, 46, 52, 57, 175, 196, 210, 258, 288, 313, 315
Cartoons/satire 185
Carysfort, John Joshua, 1st earl of 77
Castlereagh, Robert Stewart, Viscount 88, 95, 97, 99, 110, 115, 116, 121, 276, 277
Cathcart, William Shaw Cathcart, 1st earl of 96
Catherine II ('the Great'), Tsarina of Russia 235

Catholicism, catholics 23, 92, 165, 167, 169, 170, 171, 173, 177, 182, 218, 224, 234, 304, 306, 309
  catholic emancipation 80, 86, 91, 92–5, 122, 181
Celle 120, 235
  Agricultural Academy 65
Chalus, Elaine 216
Charles II, king of Great Britain 220
Charles II, duke of Zweibrücken 239, 244, 245
Charles V, Holy Roman Emperor 168
Charles VI, Holy Roman Emperor 219, 230, 256, 275, 281
Charles VII, Holy Roman Emperor 275
Charles X of France 122
Charles XII of Sweden 14
Charles Albert of Bavaria 20, 256, 261, 281, 282, 285, 287; see also Charles VII
Charles, duke of Brunswick 68, 91, 231, 232, 233, 234, 238, 240, 243, 247
Charles, duke of Mecklenburg-Strelitz 218, 231, 235, 237, 238, 242, 243, 246
Charles George, duke of Brunswick (son to Charles, duke of Brunswick) 234
Charles Theodore, Elector Palatine 239, 244–5, 246
Charlotte, Princess 108, 110
Charlotte, Princess Royal, duchess/queen of Württemberg 248
Charlotte of Hesse-Darmstadt 238
Charlotte, duchess of Mecklenburg-Strelitz, queen of Great Britain 8, 112, 133, 144, 150, 154, 180, 218, 229, 230, 231, 235, 236, 237, 238, 239, 240, 241, 242, 243, 244–5, 246, 247, 248, 249, 250
Charlotte, Princess of Wales (daughter of George IV) 226, 227, 247
Charlotte Felicitas of Brunswick 219
Charlotte Philippina of Brunswick-Wolfenbüttel 231
Chesterfield, Philip Dormer Stanhope, 4th earl of 26, 28, 29, 31, 49, 50, 194, 196, 201, 205, 266, 294, 312, 315
  A further vindication of the case of the Hanover troops (1742-3) 186–7
Chillingham 196
Choiseuil (d'Amboise), Etienne-François, duc de 294, 296
Christian III, duke of Zweibrücken 241
Christian VII, king of Denmark 234
Clark, Anna 216
Clark, J. C. D. 1, 6, 181, 217

Index

Clemens August von Wittelsbach, archbishop of Cologne 179
Cleve and Mark, Hohenzollern duchies 220
Cobbett, William 320–2
Coleridge, Samuel Taylor 142, 143
Colley, Linda 1, 82, 87, 89, 91, 184
Cologne, Electorate of 165, 282
colonies 25, 28, 31, 34, 35, 45, 50, 53, 55, 94, 155, 217, 252, 260, 266, 267, 269, 270, 271, 272
  East and West Indies 259, 261, 262, 263, 264, 265, 270, 271
  Gibraltar 190, 208, 252, 259
  Minorca 20, 200, 238, 252, 259, 262, 271, 290
  North America 3, 71, 131, 147, 198, 207
  war/rebellion in 69, 70, 200, 201, 233, 238, 239, 240, 242, 245
commerce 189
Confederation of the Rhine 277, 299
Conrady, Sigisbert 60, 64
'continental policy' 32–4, 35–6, 37, 41, 46–7, 48, 56, 97, 200, 206
conventions
  Kloster-Zeven (1757) 45, 46, 47, 55, 63, 199, 291–2
  Neustadt (1741) 265, 280, 285, 288
  St Petersburg (1755) 289
  Westminster (1756) 37, 268, 289
Cook, Harold J. 132
Cook, James 128, 129, 148, 149, 152
Coote, (Sir) Eyre 272
Copenhagen 209
Corpus Evangelicorum 179, 218, 219
corruption 189
Coxe, William 21
Croker, John Wilson 93, 94, 181
Cromwell, Oliver 258
Cust, Sir John 196

Dann, Uriel 3, 28, 38, 58–9, 184, 196
Darwin, Charles 151
Decken, Friedrich (Frederic) von der 76, 119
de Luc, Jean, André 146, 154
Denmark 13, 18, 75, 151, 175, 194, 209, 217, 218, 220, 221, 265, 284, 294, 310
  (Danish dynasty) 220, 221, 227, 232, 234
despotism, German *see* absolutism
Dettingen, battle of (1743) 34, 136, 187, 207, 210, 313–14
diplomatic immunity 188
Diplomatic Revolution (1756) 216, 268, 290

dissenters 190
Ditchfield, Grayson 59, 61, 178
Doneraile, Arthur Mohun St Leger, 3rd Viscount 315
Doran, Patrick 44
Dornford, Josiah 142
Douglas, John 316–17
Drake, James 188, 306–7
Draper, Theodore 2
du Bourgay, Charles 172
Dublin 185
Dundas, Henry 74, 79
Dunkirk 193

Earberry, Mathias 205
  An historical account of the advantages that have accrued to England, by the succession of the illustrious House of Hanover (1721–2) 189
East Friesland 19, 115
East India Company
  English East India Company 190, 249
  Imperial Ostend East India Company 190
  Danish East India company 209
Eden, Morton, British envoy to Bavaria and the Holy Roman Empire 242, 243, 244, 245
Edict of Nantes (1685) 168
Edinburgh 140, 185, 186
Edward III, king of England 193
Edward VII, king of Great Britain 250
  As Prince of Wales 126
Edward, duke of Kent 126, 227, 249
Edward, duke of York 141, 235, 236
Egmont, earl of
  Factions detected by the evidence of facts (1743) 186
Elbe, river 113, 125, 189
Eldon, John Scott, 1st earl of 91
Eleonore of Saxe-Eisenach 224
Elisabeth Christine, Empress 226, 231
Elisabeth-Christine of Brunswick-Bevern 226, 231
Elisabeth-Christine of Brunswick-Wolfenbüttel 219, 224, 229
Elizabeth I, queen of England 12, 194, 258, 305
Elizabeth Augusta, Electress Palatine 245
Elizabeth, Princess, daughter of George III 248, 249
Ellenborough, Edward Law, 1st Baron 322
Elliot, Hugh, British envoy in Berlin 243, 244
Ems, river 125

Enlightenment 128, 132, 137, 143, 144, 159, 180–1, 214, 229
Ernest Augustus, duke of Cumberland (king of Hanover 1837–51) 8, 88, 89, 94, 109, 116, 117, 126, 159, 160, 180, 213, 227, 234, 249, 322
Ernst August, duke of Cumberland (grandson of king of Hanover) 251
Ernest Augustus, duke of Cumberland (great grandson of king of Hanover) 126
Ernest Augustus of Hanover (born 1954) 127
Ernest Charles of Mecklenburg-Strelitz 235, 248
Ernst August, elector of Hanover 166, 167, 219
Esterhazy, Paul Prince 98
Estonia 254
Estrées, Louis le Tellier, Marshall duc d' 257, 291, 293
exclusion bills 204
Europe 1, 2, 4, 5, 8, 61, 62, 65, 69, 71, 72, 73, 74, 76, 78, 113, 115, 130, 131, 132, 134, 138, 140, 142, 148, 152, 153, 158, 160, 188, 189, 191, 195, 198, 199, 201, 206, 212, 213, 216, 233, 244, 245

Feder, Heinrich 143
Fenton, Geffray 305
Ferdinand, duke of Brunswick 30, 229, 231, 269, 271, 292
Finckenstein, count 216
Finke, H. J. 3
Flanders 6
Fleury, Cardinal André-Hercule de 261, 263, 281, 282, 285
Fontenoy, battle of (1745) 197
Forster, Georg 129, 147
Forster, Johann Reinhold 129, 146, 147
Fox, Charles James 96, 97, 142, 320, 322
  (Fox–North coalition) 69
  (as foreign secretary) 80
Fox, Henry 38, 42, 43, 46
France 18, 23, 24, 57, 96, 100, 101, 105, 113, 115, 117, 120, 136, 142, 168, 169, 172, 180, 192, 194, 199, 207, 208, 209, 218, 220, 229, 232, 233, 234, 239, 247, 256, 258, 259, 260, 267, 273, 278, 299
  American possessions 6, 34, 51, 54, 198, 242, 243, 257, 270, 271
  army of Westphalia 285
  French Revolution 246, 297
  French strategy towards Hanover 4, 7, 266, 277, 278–9, 280–3, 285–7, 289–99
  Guadeloupe 53, 257, 271
  French invasion scare 198, 199, 205
  Lorraine 281
  Martinique 53, 257, 270, 271
  occupation of Hanover (1741) 19, 32, 36, 256, 260, 277, 280, (1757) 62, (1803) 78, 158, 274, 298 (1806) 7, 63, 84, 154, 322
  Seven Years War 7, 19, 36, 41, 46, 47, 55, 64, 200, 257, 269, 272, 278, 295–6
  and War of the Austrian Succession 7, 19, 26, 32, 33, 35, 177, 178, 195, 260, 263, 264, 265, 266, 267, 275, 284, 285, 288
  French Revolutionary and Napoleonic Wars 72 (Basle) 72, 73, 74, 75, 78, 227, 233, 234, 248
Francis Stephen of Lorraine, 281
Frankfurt 125
Franklin, Benjamin 140, 145
Frederica, Princess of Hanover 251
Frederica of Mecklenburg-Strelitz, daughter of Charles, duke of Mecklenburg-Strelitz 246, 248
Frederica of Prussia 234
Frederica of Saxe-Gotha 229
Frederica, queen of Hanover (wife to Ernest August) 227
Frederica-Louise of Hesse-Darmstadt 241
Frederica Wilhelmina, half sister to Frederica of Prussia 234
Frederick, duke of York, Prince-Bishop of Osnabrück 4, 68, 88, 92, 112, 139 n. 41, 179, 227, 234, 236, 237, 238, 246, 247, 248
Frederick William, brother to George III 235
Frederick II, Landgrave of Hesse-Cassel 140, 173, 226
Frederick, Landgrave of Hesse-Homburg 249
Frederick, Prince of Wales, father of George III 117, 140, 196, 224, 225, 226, 228
Frederick I of Prussia 220, 224
Frederick II (the Great) of Prussia 14, 19, 136, 144, 180, 216, 217, 218, 220, 221, 227, 228, 229, 230, 231, 232, 234, 239–41, 242, 243, 244, 245, 296
  Eulogy of Voltaire 242
  Rêveries politiques (1752) 230
  War of the Austrian Succession 14, 136, 177, 221, 256, 275, 285
  Seven Years War 19, 25, 26, 43, 44, 45, 46, 47, 178, 200, 278, 291

Index

Frederick William I, king of Prussia 14, 19, 220, 225, 227, 283
Frederick William II, king of Prussia 234, 298
Frederick William III, king of Prussia 75, 79, 80, 220, 298
Frederick William (the Great Elector) of Brandenburg-Prussia 166, 220
Frederick William, Hereditary Prince/king of Württemberg 248
Frederik V, king of Denmark 221
Freiburg University 159
Freytag, Wilhelm von 68

game laws 205
Gascoigne, John 133
Gash, Norman 111
Gay, Peter 164
Geological Society 150
George I, king of Great Britain 2, 11, 12, 14, 16, 18, 19, 22, 66, 90, 108, 162, 163, 164 n.11, 167, 168, 172, 174, 187, 191, 205, 208, 210, 211, 214, 219, 254, 308, 309, 310, 321
  accession of (1714) 185, 187
  as champion of Protestantism 170, 172, 175, 177, 210
  and expansion of Hanover 6, 13–15, 16, 17, 18–20
  and Guelph dynasty 219, 220, 221, 224–5, 227, 236
  and Holy Roman Empire 175
  visits to Hanover 121, 203, 215
George II, king of Great Britain 6, 10, 16, 18, 19, 20, 25, 28, 40, 50, 52, 54, 56, 57, 61, 89, 90, 136, 138, 162, 163, 164 n.11, 172, 173, 174, 177, 178, 185, 192, 195, 196, 209, 210, 220, 260, 271, 275, 283, 287, 320
  and dynastic arrangements 8, 221, 224, 225, 226, 227, 228
  effects of Personal Union 7, 18, 23, 26, 43, 136, 210, 211, 255, 264, 276, 277, 279, 311, 313, 314, 315, 318, 320
  expansion of Hanover 17, 18–20, 51–2, 196
  favours Hanoverian interests 58, 60, 62–3, 64, 65, 187
  Holy Roman Empire 25, 134, 135, 136, 138, 264
  as Prince of Wales 172, 219, 224
  Seven Years War 43, 46, 51, 55, 62, 136, 199, 269, 291
  and War of the Austrian Succession 20, 32, 135, 256, 262, 280, 283, 284–5, 287, 289
  visits to Hanover 120, 121, 135, 136, 139, 203
George III, king of Great Britain 8, 10, 27, 54, 56, 92, 93, 96, 112, 114, 116, 120, 137, 138, 140, 147, 157, 164, 178, 180, 181, 182, 212, 217, 218, 233, 235, 243, 272, 273, 280, 297, 320, 321
  'glories in the name of Britain' 7, 56, 58, 178
  and Holy Roman Empire 7, 60, 61, 64, 65–6, 69, 88, 180, 244, 245, 246, 247 (War of Bavarian Succession) 243, 244, 246 (*Fürstenbund*) 70, 71, 76 (Regency Crisis) 71 (territorial indemnification) 72 (revolutionary menace) 2, 4, 7, 73, 74, 243
  physical crisis 3, 61, 71, 83, 84, 230, 246
  and dynastic arrangements 8, 225, 226, 227, 228, 229, 230–1, 232, 235, 236, 248, 249
  as Prince of Wales 27, 58, 185, 228
  relationship with the Electorate of Hanover 7, 58, 59, 60, 61, 62, 64, 65, 66, 67, 68, 69, 75–6, 77, 78, 81, 84, 85, 140, 141, 160
  and the Seven Years War 58, 62, 63–4, 65, 137, 201, 237
  and religion 144
  threat to abdicate 140
  and the French Revolutionary and Napoleonic Wars 72 (Basle) 73, 76, 83, 84, 231
  and the War in North America 71, 233, 239, 242, 243
George IV, king of Great Britain 8, 86, 91, 92, 93, 94, 97, 98, 99, 100, 101, 102, 111, 120, 121, 181, 227, 250
  and German politics 8, 114, 115, 120
  visit to Hanover 89–90, 111, 120, 159, 160, 250
  as Prince Regent 8, 84, 114, 115, 117, 119, 120
  as Prince of Wales 71, 82, 88, 112, 114, 247
George V, king of Great Britain 250, 251
George V, king of Hanover 251
George, king of Denmark 220
George, duke of Cambridge 227
George, duke of Cumberland 227, 235, 236, 237
George, duke of Mecklenburg-Strelitz 248, 250
Georg/George Wilhelm, duke of Celle 168, 219

German Confederation 92, 96, 97, 102, 106, 107, 116, 124, 125, 159
  Customs Union 110, 111, 125 (South German Customs Union) 125 (North German Customs Union) 125 (Mitteldeutscher Handelsverein) 125
  Karlsbad Decrees 97, 159
  Six Articles 103, 104–6, 124
German Chancery in London 66, 67, 68, 76, 80, 81, 112, 116, 118, 121, 122, 145, 155, 157, 158
German idealism 143
German romanticism 143
Geyken, Frauke, 184
Gierl, Martin 132
Giesecke, Carl Ludwig 150
Glorious Revolution 11, 12, 15, 163, 167, 205, 213, 215, 220, 306
Gibbs, G. C. 2, 183
Goertz, Baron, German nobleman in Swedish service 187, 190, 191
Goertz, Count Eustachius de, Prussian envoy 245
Goethe, Johann Wolfgang von 143, 154
Goslar 143
Göttingen, city of 122, 123, 128, 141 (Botanic Gardens) 149
Göttingen seven 109, 160
Göttingen, university of 6, 68, 128, 129, 130, 131, 132, 133, 134–5, 136, 138, 139–40, 142, 144, 149, 155, 156, 157, 158, 160, 249 (50th anniversary) 137 (university library) 141 (and French Revolution) 142, 144, 154, 155, 159 (Royal Society of Science) 140, 141, 145, 146, 159
grand alliance 180, 213
Grantham (Lincolnshire) 196
Granville, Granville Leveson-Gower, 1st Earl 99
Greengrass, Mark 215
Grenville, William Wyndham, 1st Baron 73, 74, 78, 79, 81
Greenough, George Bellas 150
Grey, Charles 2nd Earl 104, 106, 107
Gruber, Johann Daniel 134
Gruner, W. D. 96, 112
Guicciardini, Francesco 305
Gustavus (II) Adolfus of Sweden 175
Gyllenborg, Count Karl, Swedish minister in London 187, 188, 188 n.21, 190, 191

Haase, Carl 60
Habeas Corpus 50
Haddock, Vice-Admiral Nicholas 260, 262, 266, 288
Halle, university of 134, 153
Haller, Albrecht von 140, 145, 158
Hambach festival 102
Hanover
  assembly of estates 92, 103, 113, 117
  Army/Hanoverian troops/mercenaries 5, 32, 34, 35, 39, 41, 44, 47, 51, 57, 100–2, 166, 186, 187, 199, 205, 311–22 (King's German Legion) 91, 118, 119–20, 238, 250, 256, 320, 321–2
  constitution 89, 92, 104, 109, 116, 122, 123–4, 126
  general assembly (1814–66) 117–18, 119, 120, 121–2
  (Peace of Basle) 73, (dissolution of ministry) 80 (insurrection against the French, 1809) 84
  and subversion of British interest, 183, 185, 195, 197, 205
  State Archives 68
  University 158
Hanham, Andrew 221
Hanoverian Army of Observation 199, 257, 268, 292
Hardenberg, Carl August 72
Harding, Nicholas (Nick) 3, 4, 5
Harding, Richard 6
Hardwicke, Philip Yorke, 1st earl of 29, 41, 52, 53, 177, 263, 264, 265, 269, 270, 276, 277
Harley, Robert, 1st earl of 303, 304
Harrington, William Stanhope, 1st earl of 19, 264, 275, 276, 277, 279, 284
Harris, Bob 5
Harris, Christopher 317, 318
Harrowby, Lord 78
Harz mountains 143
Haslang, Joseph, Count, Bavarian minister in London 48 n. 122, 65, 195
Hastenbeck, Battle of (1757) 45, 199, 257, 291
Hatton, Ragnhild 2, 214, 224
Haversham, John Thompson, 1st baron 307
Hawke, Vice-Admiral Sir Edward 272
Heidelberg University 159
Helmstedt University 134
Henley, Sir Robert, 206
Henriette of Hesse-Darmstadt 241
Henry the Lion, duke of Brunswick 221
Herder, Johann Gottfried 152

Index

Herschel, William 141
Hesse-Cassel 218, 228, 295
　mercenaries 37, 39, 41, 47, 192, 199, 284
　British subsidies 15
　protestants in 173, 269
Hesse-Darmstadt 229, 235, 243
Hesse, Electoral 125
Hesse, Grand Duchy of 122, 125
Heyne, Christian Gottlob 138, 158
high politics 3, 4, 8, 20, 29, 181
Hildesheim, bishopric of 65, 72, 92, 113, 115
　use of Hanoverian issue in 50
Hildesheim, city of 157
Holbach, Paul-Henri Thiry, baron de 144
Holdernesse, Robert Darcy, 4th earl of 26, 30, 30 n.8, 39, 41, 318
Holstein 255
Holstein–Gottorp dynasty 218, 220, 235, 238
Holy Alliance 99, 103
Holy Roman Empire (*Reich*/Old *Reich*) 4, 7, 36, 37, 38, 56, 65, 69, 72, 89, 113, 115, 116, 134, 135, 136, 139, 162, 165, 166, 168, 169, 178, 180, 196, 207, 208, 209, 214, 215, 217, 218, 219, 221, 224, 225, 236, 237, 238, 239, 243, 244, 245, 250, 255, 256, 263–4, 266, 267, 269, 279, 286, 288, 290, 299, 304
　constitution 38, 89, 218, 240, 241, 243, 286
　Fürstenbund (1785) 3, 59, 61, 180
　Diet (*Reichstag*) in Regensburg 72, 165, 166, 170–2, 179, 242, 244, 282
　new territorial order 72
Hollmann, Samuel Christian 136
Homer
　Iliad 145
Hoppit, Julian 2
Hornemann, Friedrich 149, 155, 157
Hornsby, Thomas, 141
Hosier, Vice-Admiral Francis 259
Huguenots 168, 209
Humboldt, Alexander von 152
Humboldt, Wilhelm von 159
Hume, Joseph 106
Hungary 169
Hyndford, John Carmichael, 3rd earl of 177

Ilten, Thomas Eberhard von 314
India 131
international law 188

Irby, William 140
Ireland 2, 120, 139, 185, 197, 198, 250

Jablonski, Daniel Ernst 171
Jacobi-Kloest, Konstans Philipp Wilhelm von 76, 80, 82
Jacobitism 5, 14, 162 n.1, 176, 187, 188, 189, 190, 202, 204, 205, 211, 212, 221, 254, 257, 294, 308, 312, 313
　invasion plans 190
　Jacobite propaganda (*see also* newspaper) 190 n.33, 197, 204, 205, 211, 212, 213, 219
　Jacobite rebellion, the 'forty-five' (1745) 197, 198, 211 (Culloden) 136
　use of republican arguments 306, 307–8
　Stuart dynasty 10, 12, 13, 22, 174, 205, 206, 211, 213, 219, 220, 221, 307, 310
James I, king of Great Britain 167, 213
James II, king of Great Britain 167, 174, 205
　and Catholicism 205
James Edward Stuart ('Old Pretender') 187, 192, 308–9, 311
Jena, battle of 83, 248
Jennings, Admiral Sir John 259
Jérome Bonaparte, king of Westphalia 159, 248
John Frederick of Brandenburg-Ansbach 224
John Frederick of Brunswick 219
John George IV of Saxony 224
Jones, William 148
Joseph I, Holy Roman Emperor 219, 256
Joseph II, Holy Roman Emperor 66, 70, 71, 179, 180, 238, 239
Josepha of Bavaria, wife of Joseph II 239
journal *see* newspapers
July Revolution (1830) 102, 122

Kahle, Ludwig Martin 136
Kant, Immanuel 143
Karl, Landgrave of Hesse-Cassel 19, 140
Keith, George, 10th Earl Marischal 177
Kennicott Benjamin 140, 146
Kielmansegge, Ferdinand, count of 77, 317, 319
Kinnoull, Thomas Hay, 9th earl of 52
Knighton, Sir William 89
Knierim, Göttingen merchant 128
Koenig, Carl Dietrich Eberhard 150
Kotzebue, August von 97

La Croze, Mathurin Veyssière de 146
La Mettrie, Julien Offray de 144
La Roche, Sophie von 246

332 Index

Lange, G. 96
Langford, Paul 2
Lansdowne, Petty William, 2nd earl Shelburne, 1st marquess of 73
Laws, Captain 260
Leipzig 125
Lenthe, Ernst Ludwig von 67, 75, 77, 80, 83
Leopold of Saxe-Coburg, king of the Belgians 247
Leopold, duke of Albany 251
Leslie, Charles 306–8, 309–10
Leß, Gottfried 137, 138
Lessing, Gothold Ephraim 154
Leuchtenberg, landgraviate of 241, 242
Lewis, Judith S. 216
Liberal Movement 102
Library, the King's, Buckingham House 138
Lichtenberg, Georg Christoph 141
Lieven, Christoph Heinrich Prince 98
Lieven, Dorothea Princess 89, 98
Ligonier, Field Marshall Jean Louis 1st Earl 271
Linné, Carl von 151
Liverpool, Robert Banks Jenkinson, 2nd earl of 92, 97, 99
Livonia 254
London 5, 8, 66, 67, 79, 112, 113, 116, 121, 129, 131, 132, 133, 148, 149, 150, 151, 153, 155, 156, 157, 158, 160, 184, 185, 187, 191, 193, 195, 209, 244 (City of) 84, 200, 205 (Haymarket Theatre) 160 (University of) 62, 67, 160
Lodge, Sir Richard 165
Lombardy 115
Louis XIV, king of France 11, 55, 165, 168, 207, 224, 279, 281, 287
Louis XV, king of France 169, 172, 280, 282, 294, 296
Louis of Brunswick-Wolfenbüttel, Regent for William V of the Netherlands/Orange 231, 232, 233
Louis, prince of Prussia 246
Louisa, Princess (daughter of George II) 221, 232, 234
Louisa of Orange 234
Louisa of Mecklenburg-Strelitz, daughter of Charles, duke of Mecklenburg-Strelitz 246, 247
Louise-Charlotte of Denmark 250
Lowth, Robert, bishop of Oxford 140, 146, 147, 148
Luther, Martin 226
Lux, David S. 132
Lyttelton, George 194

Machiavelli, Niccolò 230, 304, 305
Maidstone, incident at (1756) 199, 317–18
Maillebois, Jean-Baptiste Desmarets, marshall marquis de 264, 284, 285, 286, 287, 291, 293
Mainz, Electorate of 165, 282
Malthus, Thomas 322
Marchmont, Alexander Hume-Campbell, 2nd earl of 311, 312, 313, 314
Marie Antoinette, queen of France 216
Maria Franziska, dowager duchess of Zweibrücken 245
Maria Theresa, Empress of Austria 19–20, 33, 34, 35, 46, 256, 263, 275, 280, 283, 284
Maria Wilhelmina of Hesse-Darmstadt 246
Marlborough, Charles Spencer, 3rd duke of 49
Marschner, Joanna 221
Marsh, Herbert 147
Martyn, Samuel 198
Mary, queen of Great Britain 220
Mary, wife of King George V of Great Britain 250
Mary, Princess 173
Mary, daughter of King George II 226
Mary, daughter of King George III 246, 248
Mary, sister to King Charles II 220
Mary, princess of Hanover 251
Mary Ann Clarke, mistress of Frederick, duke of York 248
Mary Adelaide, duchess of Cambridge 250
Matilda Plantagenet, Princess 221
Mauduit, Israel 52, 198, 201, 272
Considerations on the Present German War (1760) 201, 208
Maximilian III Joseph, elector of Bavaria 25, 246
Maximilian William of Brunswick-Lüneburg 219
Mecklenburg, duchies of 191, 218, 229, 230, 241, 242, 244, 245, 246, 247, 248
Troops in British service 238
Mediger, Walter 63
Meiners, Christoph 143
Metternich, Klemens Wenzel Prince 97, 99, 102, 105, 108, 121
Michaelis, Caroline 128, 158
Michaelis, Johann David 128, 138, 143, 144, 145, 146, 147, 148, 149, 151, 153, 154, 155, 156, 158, 160
Old Testament 144
Orientalische Bibliothek 147
Middleton, Richard 31, 39
militia issue
and Hanover 50, 205

Minden, territory of 115
Minden, battle of (1759) 271
Mist, Nathaniel 175, 176
Mitchell, Andrew 30, 44, 47, 49
Molanus, Gerard 171
Molesworth, Robert 304
Mollwitz, Battle of (1741) 275
monarchy 12, 15–16, 17, 86–99, 106, 163, 176, 302
  loyalism 162, 162 n.1
  Personal Union 86–110, 166, 182, 277, 280, 297, 301, 305, 306, 309, 322
  universal monarchy 6, 168–70
  transformation of 61–2, 74, 82–3, 249–50
Morphew, John 188 n.21, 191
Mortier, Edouard 155
Morris, Marylin 82
Mosheim, Lorenz Johnann 135
Münchhausen, Gerlach Adolf von 21, 26, 30, 62, 63, 134, 135, 178, 285, 289
Münchhausen, Philipp von 47, 49, 51, 62, 63, 66, 67
Münster, Ernst Friedrich Herbert 8, 59, 67, 68, 80, 81, 82, 83, 84, 94, 95, 96, 97, 101, 102, 112, 113, 114, 115, 116, 117, 118, 119, 120, 121, 122, 123, 124, 159
Münster, Wilhelmine von 112 n.13, 123 n.50
Mulgrave, Henry Phipps, baron 79
Munich University 159
Murray, J.J. 3
Murray, William 318

Napoleon I of France 7, 78, 79, 82, 84, 89, 96, 113, 115, 155, 159, 248, 250, 277, 298
Nedham, Marchmont 306
Netherlands 12, 26, 115, 122, 142, 168, 173, 190, 225, 229, 232, 233, 247, 257, 259, 266, 267, 274, 305
Neumann, Philip Baron 98
Newcastle, Thomas Pelham, 3rd duke of 1, 6, 10, 21, 25, 29, 30, 34, 36, 39, 40, 43, 46, 48, 50, 53, 135, 139 n.41, 172, 177, 178, 210, 271, 276
  foreign policy 22, 24, 25, 36, 37, 54, 55, 173, 177, 264, 270, 280
  issue of Hanoverian auxiliaries (1756) 315, 318, 319
  ministry with Pitt 185
  Seven Years War 26, 133, 136, 195, 269, 271, 278, 289
  War of the Austrian Succession 19, 195, 197, 260, 262, 263, 265, 280, 288–9
newspapers 159, 185, 187, 193, 209
  The Anti-Jacobin 160, 194

  Craftsman, or Country Journal, weekly opposition journal 192, 193, 194, 210
  Common Sense, or the Englishman's Journal 194
  Gentleman's Magazine 156
  The Morning Chronicle 82
  Old England or the Constitutional Journal, weekly opposition journal 204
  Post boy, Tory newspaper 187, 191
  Saint James's Chronicle 83
  The Times 81
  The True Briton 190 n.33
Newton, Sir Isaac 129, 130
Noailles, Marshall Adrien Maurice duc de 282
Norris, Sir John 175
North, Frederick Lord 39, 56, 146, 147
  (Fox–North coalition) 69

O'Connel, Daniel 94
Ompteda, Ludwig Conrad Georg von 103, 104, 106, 108, 123
Opposition 183
  parliamentary 183, 187
Orange, House of 220, 225, 231, 232, 233, 234
Order of the Bath 123
Order of the Guelph (Welfenorden) 124, 250
Osnabrück, bishopric of 68, 72, 92, 179, 236, 237, 238, 247
Ossorio, Giuseppe, Sardnian envoy 203
Oxford University 130, 139, 140, 141
  (Archives) 132 (Dons) 153, 160
  (Trinity College) 142

Paine, Thomas 322
Palatinate 22, 165, 175, 282
Palmerston, Henry Temple 3rd Viscount 88, 95, 102, 105, 106, 107, 108, 110, 124, 125
pamphlets 5, 142, 185, 186, 187, 188, 191, 192, 193, 196, 201, 204, 205
  The case of the Hanover forces in the pay of Great Britain (1742) 186, 187
  Defence of the people (1744) 186
  The confectioner general setting forth the H[anoveria]n desert (1743) 187
  Deliberate thoughts on the system of late treaties (1756) 198
  An English merchant's remarks (1716) 187
  A third letter to the people of England (1756) 205
  To Robert Walpole (1716) 189
Pares, Richard 204, 210
Paris 142, 248

Park, Mungo 149
parliament 13, 14, 24, 25, 33, 35, 41, 48, 49, 50, 60, 69, 71, 93, 99, 101, 102, 105, 106, 110, 117, 122, 163, 188, 192, 196, 203, 209, 210, 230, 236, 237, 249, 252, 253–4, 256, 259, 260, 265, 266, 271, 274, 276, 278, 283, 284, 304, 307, 317, 320, 321
   role of Hanover in debates 2, 18, 25, 38, 49, 56, 73–4, 81, 107, 198, 205, 255, 269, 308, 311, 312, 313, 315
Parry, Charles Henry 143
Pawel-Rammingen, Luitbert Alexander, baron of 251
Peerage Bill 191
Pelham, Henry 10, 25, 35, 36, 163, 177
Peter the Great, tsar of Russia 191
Peter III, tsar of Russia 235
Peterloo massacre (1819) 97
Peters, Marie 28, 31, 36, 44, 199
Pfaff, Mattheus 171
Philip II, king of Spain 168, 208
Philippina of Brandenburg-Schwedt 229
Philipps, Sir John 49, 313
philosophical transactions 156
Piedmont-Sardinia 115
Pitt, William, 1st earl of Chatham 4, 6, 20, 25, 26, 100, 163, 185, 198, 199, 201, 202, 207, 212, 252, 269, 270, 271, 272, 293
   issue of Hanoverian auxiliaries (1756) 319
   ministry with Newcastle 185
   on the Hanoverian connection 28–57
Pitt, William (the Younger) 69, 70, 74, 75, 79, 80, 93, 95, 142, 181
Planta, Joseph 150
Plumb, J. H. 2, 21
Pocock, Vice-Admiral Sir George 271
Pocock, J. G. A. 302
Poland 13, 22, 104, 166, 169, 230
   First Partition of (1772) 12
   Third Partition (1795) 298
Polignac, Auguste Jules Armand duc de 98
Pölnitz, Karl Ludwig von
   Histoire secrette de la duchesse d'Hanover, epouse de Georges Premier, roi de la Grande Bretagne 209
Polybius 302, 304, 316
Pomerania 118
Porter, Roy 131, 151
Portsmouth 244
Portugal 100–1, 118, 120
Potter, Thomas 39, 44, 198
Prado, convention of (1739) 196

press 40, 42, 44, 68, 94, 98, 124, 185, 191, 192, 193, 197, 200, 204
   and Hanover 18, 42, 49, 50, 51, 80, 81, 86, 90, 91, 94, 100, 102, 103, 104, 109, 183, 314, 315–17, 318, 320–2
Preysing, Count 48
primogeniture 218, 219
Pringle, John 140, 144, 145, 147, 148, 156, 157, 158
Protestantism 4, 5, 22, 161–2, 164, 166, 171, 173, 176, 179, 180, 189–90, 211, 224, 226, 229, 234, 307
   Anglicanism 12, 143, 161, 174, 176, 179, 190, 306, 308, 309
   Calvinism 92, 165, 171, 175, 176, 181, 220
   Lutheranism 5, 92, 143, 161, 165, 171, 174, 176, 181, 304, 306, 308, 309
   (*Neologie*) 144
   protestant succession 21, 93, 167–8, 170, 181, 190, 213, 219, 224, 225, 226
Prussia-Brandenburg (Hohenzollern Monarchy) 11, 12, 18, 22, 24, 66, 94, 96, 100, 105, 108, 113, 115, 119, 125, 127, 134, 159, 165, 171, 175, 177, 179, 192, 193, 206, 208, 214, 218, 220, 221, 225, 226, 227, 229, 230, 231, 232, 233, 234, 237, 247, 267, 277, 278, 282, 288, 297, 299, 321, 322
   Borussian myth 166
   Fürstenbund (1785) 70
   occupation of Hanover (1801) 75, 76, 77, 79, 274, 298, (1806), 80, 96, 320
   Seven Years War 27, 37, 41, 65, 185, 200, 201, 268, 269, 272, 290, 292, 293
   War of the Austrian Succession 20, 26, 32, 208, 256, 263, 265, 276, 281, 284
   War of the Bavarian Succession 69, 239–41, 243, 244–5
   French Revolutionary and Napoleonic Wars 72, 113, 115, First Coalition (1792–5) 298, (Basle) 73, (armed neutrality) (Third Coalition) 78, 79 (restoration of Hanover) 83
public opinion/ public sphere 5, 156, 183
Pütter, Johann Stephan 137, 301
   Historical Development of the Present Political Constitution of the Germanic Empire 142
Pyrmont, Waldeck principality 128

Quadruple Alliance (1718) 191
Quebec 201

Index

Ravensburg 115
rebellion
  (1715) 13, 187, 188, (1745) 197, 211, 212, 257
Reform Act (1832) 91, 103, 105
Reichenbach, Prussian envoy in London, 193
republic of letters 6, 129, 131, 151, 160
republicanism, republicans 302, 310, 322
  attack on Hanoverian connection 4, 5, 303, 310, 311, 312, 313, 315, 316–17, 320
  definition of 302
  support for Hanoverian connection 306
Rhé, island of 238
Rhine, River 72, 115
Richardson, Samuel
  Pamela 153
Richelieu, Louis François Armand de Vignerot du Plessis, duc de 291
Riotte, Torsten 4, 7
Rochefort (Bay of Biscay) 199
Rodney, Admiral George 128
Rome 142
Rossbach, battle of (1757) 292, 293
Rowen, Herbert 214
royal collections 250
Royal Dublin Society 150
Royal Marriages Act (1772) 237
Royal Navy 6, 33, 35, 44, 136, 254, 255, 256, 257–9, 260, 261–2, 265–7, 269, 271, 272, 273
Royal Society 129, 130, 133, 144, 148, 149, 150, 157, 160
Russia 7, 11, 12, 18, 24, 105, 113, 115, 175, 191, 192, 234, 255, 259, 264, 277, 284, 288, 297
  Baltic policy 14, 187
  revolutionary and Napoleonic Wars 72, 75, 78, 84

Sackville, George 1st Viscount 49
Savoy 115, 169
Saxon duchies 218, 228
Saxony (Electorate, from 1806 kingdom of) 13, 23, 26, 41, 122, 165, 171, 218, 230, 234, 245, 256, 282, 284, 290
Saxony-Gotha, from 1817 Saxe-Coburg-Gotha (*see also* Saxon duchies) 1, 226, 228, 229
  mercenaries from 47
Schelde, river 113
Schlegel, August 143
Schlenke, Manfred 178
Schleswig-Hostein 14, 218, 235 n.63

Schlözer, August Ludwig 159
Schlözer, Dorothea 137 n.35
Schröder, Wilhelm 317–18, 319
Schulenburg, Melusine von der 219
Schweizer, Karl 29
Scotland 2, 60, 139, 185, 198, 250
Scott, Hamish 3, 4, 7, 59, 61, 69, 235, 236, 243
Severn, river 189
Sewell, George 188
Shapin, Steven 132
Shackleton, Robert 128
Shebbeare, John 200, 205, 206, 207, 212
  A sixth letter to the people of England on the progress of national ruin (1757) 186, 205
  Letters to the people in England (1755–7) 200
Sherbatov, Prince M. 264
Sherrard, A. O. 28
Sherwig, John M. 79
Shippen, William 188, 189 n.26
Sicily 118
Simms, Brendan 4, 6, 59, 61
Sloane, Sir Hans 152
Smith, E. A. 98
Society of Dilettanti 147, 148
Sophia, electress of Hanover 162, 168, 213, 221
Sophia Charlotte, sister of King George I 220, 224
Sophia Dorothea, daughter of King George I 225, 226
Sophia Dorothea, wife of King George I 219, 225
Sophie Caroline of Brunswick-Wolfenbüttel 228, 229
Soubise, Charles de Rohan, Marshall Prince de 269
South Sea Bubble (1711–20) 13, 185
Spain 13, 22, 31, 42, 54, 100, 120, 191, 194, 195, 207, 225, 256, 258, 261, 263, 266, 267
Splitter, Ludwig Timotheus 128
Sporcken, General Baron von 49
St Andrews University Library 212
St Aubyn, Sir John 205, 312–13
St Helens, Alleyne Fitzherbert, Baron 77, 78
Stafford, Thomas Wentworth 1st earl of 39, 193
Stair, John Dalrymple 2nd earl of 26, 196
Stanhope, James, 1st Earl Stanhope 13, 16, 24, 190
Stein, Heinrich Friedrich Karl baron vom 97, 113

Stewart, Sir Charles 96, 97
Struensee, Johann Friedrich 235
Stüve, Carl Bertram 121–2
Suffolk, earl of 69, 70, 242, 243
Sunderland, Charles Spencer, 3rd earl of 13, 16
Sweden 13, 14, 15, 18, 75, 174, 176, 221, 254, 284, 286 (dynasty) 228, 230
Swift, Jonathan 304
Swiss Federation 168

Tadmor, Naomi 182
Tankerville, Earl of 196
Taylor, Herbert 84
Temperley, Harold 87, 98
Temple, Richard Grenville, 2nd Earl 52
Thames, river 189
Theil, Jean-Gabriel de La Porte du 282
Thomas, Peter D. G. 58
Thomasius, Christian 153
Ticonderoga, battle of (1758) 270
Thompson, Andrew C. 2, 3, 5, 6, 261
Thompson, Christopher D. 4, 8
Thyra of Denmark, duchess of Cumberland 251
Toland, John 303–6, 307, 310, 311, 312, 315
Tories/Toryism 2, 16, 17, 23–4, 44, 45, 50, 93, 94, 103, 109, 164, 167, 176, 181, 190 n.33, 207, 307
   attack on Hanover 21–2, 49, 306
   attack on use of Hanoverian auxiliaries 315
Toulonjon, Anne-Théodore Chavignard de Chavignard, comte de 281
Tower of London 188
Townshend, Charles 2nd Viscount 22, 26, 172, 191
Treaties
   Amiens (1802) 77
   Aix la Chapelle (1748) 37, 279, 289
   Anglo-Bavarian subsidy treaty (1750) 267
   Anglo-French alliance (1716) 13, 15, 22
   Anglo-Hessian treaty (1755) 36, 38, 39, 50, 198, 271
   Anglo-Prussian treaty (1756) 198
   Anglo-Russian commercial treaty (1734) 255
   Anglo-Russian agreement (1755) 37, 39, 198, 268; *see also* convention of St Petersburg
   Anglo-Saxon subsidy treaty (1751) 267
   Austro-Spanish alliance (1725) 14
   Charlottenburg treaty (1723) 225
   first treaty of Versailles/Diplomatic revolution (1756) 216, 229, 290
   Franco-Prussian alliance (1741) 284, 296
   Hanover (1725) 19, 31–2, 192 n.43
   Hubertusburg (1763) 65
   Memel (1807) 83
   Paris (1763) 138
   Peace of Basle (1795) 142 (neutrality zone) 76, 142
   Peace of Travendal (1700) 220
   Reichenbach (1813) 113
   Russo-Austrian treaty (1746) 289
   Ryswick (1697) 166
   second treaty of Vienna (1731) 208, 210, 283
   Seville (1729) 195
   Utrecht (1713) 17, 51, 169, 193
   Vienna (1815) 92, 96, 106, 112, 115, 116, 117
   Westphalia (1648) 164, 165, 175, 179, 286
Trier, Electorate of 165, 282
Turretini, Jean Alphonse 171

United Provinces 197, 200, 209, 225, 233, 247
United States of America 115
universities 130, 133, 134, 139, 142, 143, 155, 159 (*see also* Berlin, Breslau, Bonn, Cambridge, Freiburg, Göttingen, Halle, Hanover, Heidelberg, Helmstedt, London, Munich *and* Oxford)

Venice 115
Verden, duchy of 14, 134, 187, 189, 203, 221, 254, 310, 315
Vergennes, Charles Gravier, Comte de 296
Vernon, Vice-Admiral Edward 35, 260, 262, 288
Versailles 216
Victoria, duchess of Kent 227
Victoria, Queen 1, 8, 89, 91, 108, 109, 110, 126, 213, 226, 227, 247, 249, 250, 322
Voltaire, François-Marie Arouet de 144, 281

Wager, Sir Charles 255, 259
Wake, William 171
Waldegrave, James 2nd earl of 40, 42, 228
Waller, Edmund 205
   A further vindication of the case of the Hanover troops (1743–44) 187
Walpole, Horace, son of Robert 37, 40, 42, 43, 49, 200

Index

Walpole, Horatio, brother of Robert 29, 172, 312
Walpole, Robert, 1st earl of Orford 2, 4, 5, 10, 13, 14, 15, 16, 17, 18, 19, 20–1, 23, 24, 25, 26, 31, 56, 163, 184, 191, 192, 193, 194, 195, 196, 198, 209, 264, 266, 283, 287, 288
Ward, A. W. 28
Waring, Edward 141
Warley 244
Wars
  American War of Independence (1775–83) 56, 57, 140, 179, 217, 274, 297
  Anglo-Spanish War (War of Jenkins's Ear, 1739–48) 11, 13, 281, 284, 287, 288
  Austro-Prussian War (1866) 166
  First Silesian War (1740–42) 20; see also War of the Austrian Succession
  Great Northern War (1700–21) 134, 220
  Napoleonic Wars (1799–1815) 8, 61, 90, 92, 108, 113, 154, 160, 274, 280, 299, 320 (Armed Neutrality) 75, 76
  Nine Year War (1688–97) 258
  revolutionary and Napoleonic Wars (1792–1915) 4, 72, 142, 274, 298
  Russo-Swedish War (1741–43) 284
  Seven Years War (1756–63) 3, 6, 12, 27, 29, 44, 48, 55, 65, 66, 138, 139, 154, 155, 178, 180, 198, 228, 231, 268, 272, 278, 286, 289, 290, 292, 294
  Thirty Years War (1618–48) 165, 220, 297
  War of the Austrian Succession (1740–48) 3, 26, 29, 32, 177, 184, 215, 256, 272, 275, 281, 283 see also First Silesian War and Anglo-Spanish War
  War of the Bavarian Succession (1778–9) 8, 59, 69, 215, 217, 218, 239, 241, 242, 243, 244, 245, 246, 296
  War of the Polish Succession (1733–5) 139, 194, 256
  War of the Spanish Succession (1701–14) 13, 166, 213, 214, 215, 252, 258
Waterloo 250
Watson, Charles, Captain 263
Webster, Charles 87
Wellenreuther, Hermann 59, 138
Wellesley, Richard Colley, Viscount 84
Wellington, Arthur Wellesley, 1st duke of 93, 94, 100, 101, 103
Weser, River 189
Westphalia, kingdom of 155, 159, 299

Whigs/Whigism 2, 10, 12, 13, 15, 16, 17, 20, 23–4, 31, 33, 51, 57, 98, 130, 162 n.1, 163, 167, 174, 176, 181, 204, 205, 208, 211, 212, 237, 307, 309
  and Hanover 5, 21–2, 90, 109, 311
  Whig historiography 163, 165
  Whig Split 188
White, John 270
Wienfort, Monika 82
Wilhelmina Amelia of Brunswick-Calenburg 219
Wilhelmina of Orange 225, 226, 231, 232, 233
Wilkie, Sir David 91
William I, king of the Netherlands 234
William III, king of Great Britain 12, 17, 167, 168, 173, 206, 220, 232, 303, 307
William IV, king of Great Britain 86, 90, 102, 103, 104, 105, 106, 107, 109, 110, 111, 122, 123, 124, 126, 181, 216, 227, 247
  As duke of Clarence 88, 89, 93, 94, 122, 159, 227, 249
William IV of Orange 218, 220, 225
William V of Orange 231, 232, 233
William, duke of Cumberland 43, 45, 199, 224, 291
William, duke of Gloucester 139 n.41, 141, 167, 235, 236, 249
William of Hesse-Cassel 250
Wilson, Kathleen 1, 2
Wilson, Peter 214
Winckelmann, Johann Joachim 148
Windsor 67, 74, 80, 82, 112, 121
Woide, Charles Godfrey 146, 147,
Wood, Robert 146, 148, 151
  Essay on the original genius of Homer 148
Wordsworth, William 142
Wrisberg, Rudolf von 171
Württemberg, Grand Duchy/Kingdom (1806) of 125, 248

Yarmouth, Amalie Sophie Marianne von Wallmoden, countess of 40, 47, 48, 50, 203
Yorke, Joseph 173, 177, 231, 232

Zamboni, agent of Hesse-Darmstadt 195
Zeeland 118
Ziegenhagen, Franz Heinrich 153
Zweibrücken 241, 242, 246
Zweibrücken, Karl August von 239

Lightning Source UK Ltd.
Milton Keynes UK
29 October 2010

162113UK00001B/64/P